Books and Plays

BY

Stanley Richards

BOOKS

Modern Short Comedies from Broadway and London
Best Short Plays of the World Theatre: 1958–1967
Best Plays of the Sixties: A Dramatic Prologue to the Seventies
The Best Short Plays 1970
The Best Short Plays 1969
The Best Short Plays 1968
Canada on Stage

PLAYS

Through a Glass, Darkly
August Heat
Sun Deck
Tunnel of Love
Journey to Bahia
O Distant Land
Mood Piece
Mr. Bell's Creation
The Proud Age
Once to Every Boy
Half-Hour, Please
Know Your Neighbor
Gin and Bitterness
The Hills of Bataan
District of Columbia

MODERN
SHORT COMEDIES
FROM
BROADWAY
AND
LONDON

Modern Short Comedies from Broadway and London

Edited WITH AN Introduction AND

Prefaces TO THE Plays BY

STANLEY RICHARDS

Random House · *New York*

FOR

Warren Bayless

Contents

MODERN

SHORT COMEDIES

FROM

BROADWAY

AND

LONDON

Introduction

Although the history of stage comedy may be traced with comparative ease back to ancient times, it is generally conceded that modern comedy's most significant forebear is Molière. His comic spirit differed greatly from that of his esteemed predecessors—the romantic comedy of Shakespeare, the ecstatic abandonment of Aristophanes, the hilarious merriment of Plautus, the sophisticated sentimentalism of Terence and the crudities of medieval farce.

The ancestral giant of modern comedy was born Jean Baptiste Poquelin (1622–73); as Molière he was to become France's greatest actor and dramatist. In 1659, with the presentation of *Les Précieuses ridicules* he originated the "comedy of manners," and he himself defined the genre when he declared, "Correction of social absurdities must at all times be the matter of true comedy." Instead of waxing indignant over human faults and behavior, he was content to laugh at them, for he possessed the inestimable gift of gaiety—that cherished capacity that reshapes ugliness, makes it amusing and softens its colors when they are too sharp. For Molière the salient task was to shed comic laughter on inequities he deemed inimical within the social structure of his times; indeed, his plays would be dismal without laughter to temper their bitterness. He knew that the gift of laughter could conquer even in the most untoward and dire of situations, and he set a comedic torch aglow, a torch that has been carried in the theatre, brightly and joyously, for four centuries.

While I can hear murmurs of refutation emanating from assorted belfries, I like to believe that Molière's spirit hovers over the authors collected in this volume, for they, too, examine and dissect contemporary mankind and society with pertinent wit, style and authentic laughter.

In genre comedy, the author must both comment wittily and be humorously revealing, for comedy—at least good comedy—can and should be as illuminative as serious drama. It is axiomatic that no dramatic literature lasts that has not founded its arguments on the inner truths of life. Even the lightest wit, if it be true wit, is as durable as granite when it deals with the essentials of human nature. Beneath the surface, then, of an effective comedy there always must be that element of truth, that thread of credibility, no matter how unorthodox or bizarre the characters and situations.

Admittedly, a playwright is at liberty to interpret his theme, characters and plot in any way he chooses, provided he makes them artistically convincing and dramatically effective. But laughter is always more effective than anger. Dramatist S. N. Behrman once observed: "I feel that playwrights should approach all forms of drama with a sense of humor and that a line of humorous dialogue sometimes can be more revealing and penetrating than any dramatic explanation. The ability to laugh at its own pretensions and shortcomings is the true mark of the civilized nation, as it is of the civilized man."

Comedy, like all forms of drama, must originate with the characters, for valid and appreciable humor can only emerge from their reactions to a situation. As Neil Simon has written: "I seem to begin a play with two people of completely opposite nature and temperament, put them in an intolerable situation, and let the sparks fly. The extra ingredient, and very important, is that they must both emphatically *believe* that their way of life is the right one . . ."

If the characters themselves did not believe in what they were doing, there would be no pursuing a situation that will lead to more complex involvements and implications. Lines of dialogue in themselves do not necessarily have to be bristling with hilarity. Genuine humor emerges from a character's reaction to a situation, and it is often that element of unexpectedness which makes a line of dialogue comically effectual.

Paradoxical as it may sound, it is essential to the fulfillment of comedy that the author, director and company of players treat their work with a passionate earnestness; for it is their resolute seriousness, generally in the face of the play's absurdities or inordinate circumstances, that produces genuine humor.

Comedy, though deceptively simple on the surface, probably is the most precise and demanding of all theatrical forms, both for author and players. Two of the most luminous performers of this century, Alfred Lunt and Lynn Fontanne, know well that comedy is a tough disciplinarian. In Miss Fontanne's words, when playing comedy, "You really have to have that ear out and that eye on yourself. . . . You really do. You have to be very up and very brilliant and faster, much faster, than you are when you play tragedy." Mr. Lunt, too, admits that a performer in comedy never can slip up, "You must always keep working." When he and Miss Fontanne were performing in London in Noël Coward's *Quadrille*, he customarily received a warm laugh on a certain line, then one night lost it. Curious, he asked Miss Fontanne, "Why have I lost that laugh?" "Because," she said, "you are not asking for a cup of tea, you are asking for a laugh."

Comedy requires, or more suitably, *demands* enormous discipline from its creators, and perhaps that is why it is so compatible with the short play form. A short play must be concise, stringent, and have instantaneous impact upon the viewer. It must dismiss all superfluities and get to the core of the matter with the swiftness of an arrow. It is a taxing art and, as John Van Druten once observed, ". . . seems to me quite extraordinarily difficult of achievement, needing enormous compression, and a high degree of technical facility."

That very same statement may well be applied to comedy . . .

The plays included in this collection represent, to me, the finest examples of recent comedies in the short play form. As editor, I alone am responsible for the selections; but somehow, and instinctively, I feel (and do hope) that my readers will share with me the enormous pleasure, laughter and entertainment that permeated my study while working on this book.

Stanley Richards
New York, New York
April, 1969

Black Comedy

B Y

Peter Shaffer

Peter Shaffer

Peter Shaffer was born in Liverpool, England, in 1926. He attended St. Paul's School in London and spent three years at Trinity College, Cambridge. In 1951, he came to the United States, where he worked in a book shop and in the Acquisitions Department of the New York Public Library while pressing on toward a writing career. He then returned to England for productions of several of his plays on British television.

Mr. Shaffer's extraordinary range as a playwright has enabled him to write in many different forms with consistent success. This versatility and fine craftsmanship have produced such diverse works as *Five Finger Exercise*, a serious probing of a neurotic family; *The Private Ear* and *The Public Eye*, a tandem bill of sharply contrasting comedies; and *The Royal Hunt of the Sun*, an impressive epic drama dealing with the confrontation between Atahuallpa, the sixteenth-century Inca sovereign of Peru, and the Spanish conquistador leader Pizarro. *The Royal Hunt of the Sun* had an overwhelming reception on the occasion of its premiere at the Chichester Festival on July 7, 1964. This success was repeated when the drama joined the National Theatre repertory at the Old Vic in London and, again, when it was presented in New York (1965), where it ran for 247 performances.

Black Comedy originally was commissioned and produced by Sir Laurence Olivier for the National Theatre during its 1965–66 season. In 1967 the comedy opened in New York, where it was hailed by the critics and ran for 337 performances. Its companion piece, *White Lies*, was written expressly for the New York stage and later, in 1968, was taken to London in revised form as *The White Liars* when *Black Comedy* was revived at the Lyric Theatre on February 21, 1968.

Black Comedy was first presented on July 27, 1965, by the National Theatre in Chichester, England, and subsequently at The Old Vic Theatre, London, with the following cast:

(*In order of appearance*)

BRINDSLEY MILLER	Derek Jacobi
CAROL MELKETT	Louise Purnell
MISS FURNIVAL	Doris Hare
COLONEL MELKETT	Graham Crowden
HAROLD GORRINGE	Albert Finney
SCHUPPANZIGH	Paul Curran
CLEA	Maggie Smith
GEORG BAMBERGER	Michael Byrne

Black Comedy was first presented in New York City on February 12, 1967, by Alexander H. Cohen at the Ethel Barrymore Theatre with the following cast:

(*In order of appearance*)

BRINDSLEY MILLER	Michael Crawford
CAROL MELKETT	Lynn Redgrave
MISS FURNIVAL	Camila Ashland
COLONEL MELKETT	Peter Bull
HAROLD GORRINGE	Donald Madden
SCHUPPANZIGH	Pierre Epstein
CLEA	Geraldine Page
GEORG BAMBERGER	Michael Miller

Both productions were directed by JOHN DEXTER

BLACK COMEDY

Characters

BRINDSLEY MILLER: *A young sculptor (mid-twenties), intelligent and attractive, but nervous and uncertain of himself.*

CAROL MELKETT: *His fiancée. A young debutante; very pretty, very spoiled; very silly. Her sound is that unmistakable, terrifying deb quack.*

MISS FURNIVAL: *A middle-aged spinster. Prissy; and refined. Clad in the blouse and sack skirt of her gentility, her hair in a bun, her voice in a bun, she reveals only the repressed gestures of the middle-class spinster—until alcohol undoes her.*

COLONEL MELKETT: CAROL's *commanding father. Brisk, barky, yet given to sudden vocal calms which suggest a deep and alarming instability. It is not only the constant darkness which gives him his look of wide-eyed suspicion.*

HAROLD GORRINGE: *The camp owner of an antique-china shop, and* BRINDSLEY's *neighbor,* HAROLD *comes from the North of England. His friendship is highly conditional and possessive: sooner or later, payment for it will be asked. A specialist in emotional blackmail, he can become hysterical when slighted, or (as inevitably happens) rejected. He is older than* BRINDSLEY *by several years.*

SCHUPPANZIGH: *A middle-class German refugee, chubby, cultivated, and effervescent. He is an entirely happy man, delighted to be in England, even if this means being employed full time by the London Electricity Board.*

CLEA: BRINDSLEY's *ex-mistress. Mid-twenties; dazzling, emotional, bright and mischievous. The challenge to her to create a dramatic situation out of the darkness is ultimately irresistible.*

GEORG BAMBERGER: *An elderly millionaire art collector, easily identifiable as such.*

THE SCENE: *The action of the play takes place in* BRINDSLEY's *apartment in South Kensington, London. This forms the ground floor of a large house, now divided into flats.* HAROLD GORRINGE *lives opposite;* MISS FURNIVAL *lives above.*

There are four ways out of the room. A door at the left leads directly across the passage to HAROLD's *room. The door to this, with its mat laid tidily outside, can clearly be seen. A curtain screens* BRINDSLEY's *studio; when it is parted we glimpse samples of his work in metal. To the right of this an open stair shoots steeply up to his bedroom above, reached through a door at the top. To the left, a trap in the floor leads down to the cellar.*

It is a gay room, when we finally see it, full of color and space and new shapes. It is littered with marvelous objects—mobiles, mannikins, toys, and dotty bric-a-brac—the happy paraphernalia of a free and imaginative mind. The total effect is of chaos tidied in honor of an occasion, and of a temporary elegance created by the furniture borrowed from HAROLD GORRINGE *and arranged to its best advantage.*

This consists of three elegant Regency chairs in gold leaf; a Regency chaise-longue to match; a small Queen Anne table bearing a fine opaline lamp with a silk shade; a Wedgwood bowl in black basalt; a good Coalport vase containing summer flowers; and a fine porcelain Buddha.

The only things which actually belong to BRINDSLEY *are a cheap square table bearing the drinks; an equally cheap round table in the middle of the room, shrouded by a cloth and decorated with the Wedgwood bowl; a low stool, improved by the Buddha; a record player; and his own artistic creations. These are largely assumed to be in the studio awaiting inspection; but one of them is visible in this room. On the dais stands a bizarre iron sculpture dominated by two long detachable metal prongs, and hung with metal pieces which jangle loudly if touched. On the wall hang paintings, some of them presumably by* CLEA. *All are nonfigurative: colorful geometric designs, splashes, splotches and splats of color; whirls and whorls and wiggles—all testifying more to a delight in handling paint than to an ability to achieve very much with it.*

THE TIME: 9:30 *on a Sunday night.*

THE LIGHT: *The stage is in complete darkness. On the few occasions when a lighter is lit, matches are struck or a torch is put on, the light onstage merely gets dimmer. When these objects are extinguished, the stage immediately grows brighter.*

Two voices are heard, those of BRINDSLEY *and* CAROL. *They must give the impression of two people walking round a room with ab-solute confidence, as if in the light. We hear sounds as of furniture being moved. A chair is dumped down.*

BRINDSLEY   There! How do you think the room looks?

CAROL (*Quacking*)   Fabulous! I wish you could always have it like this. That lamp looks divine there. And those chairs are just the right color. I told you green would look well in here.

BRINDSLEY   Suppose Harold comes back?

CAROL   He is not coming back till tomorrow morning.

(BRINDSLEY *paces nervously*)

BRINDSLEY   I know. But suppose he comes tonight? He's mad about his antiques. What do you think he'll say if he goes into his room and finds out we've stolen them?

CAROL   Don't dramatize. We haven't stolen all his furniture. Just three chairs, the sofa, that table, the lamp, the bowl, and the vase of flowers, that's all.

BRINDSLEY   And the Buddha. That's more valuable than anything. Look at it.

CAROL   Oh, do stop worrying, darling.

BRINDSLEY   Well, you don't know Harold. He won't even let any-one touch his antiques.

CAROL   Look, we'll put everything back as soon as Mr. Bamberger leaves. Now stop being dreary.

BRINDSLEY   Well, frankly, I don't think we should have done it. I mean—*anyway,* Harold or no.

CAROL   Why not, for heaven's sake? The room looks divine now. Just look at it!

BRINDSLEY   Darling, Georg Bamberger's a multi-millionaire. He's lived all his life against this sort of furniture. Our few stolen bits aren't going to impress him. He's coming to see the work of an unknown sculptor. If you ask me, it would look much better to him if he found me exactly as I really am: a poor artist. It might touch his heart.

CAROL   It might—but it certainly won't impress Daddy. Remem-ber, he's coming too.

BRINDSLEY   As if I could forget! Why you had to invite your mon-ster father tonight, I can't think!

CAROL   Oh, not again!

BRINDSLEY   Well, it's too bloody much. If he's going to be persuaded I'm a fit husband for you just by watching a famous collector buy some of my work, he doesn't deserve to have me as a son-in-law!

CAROL   He just wants some proof you can earn your own living.

BRINDSLEY   And what if Bamberger *doesn't* like my work?

CAROL   He will, darling. Just stop worrying.

BRINDSLEY   I can't. Get me a whiskey. (*She does. We hear her steps, and a glass clinking against a bottle—then the sound of a soda syphon*) I've got a foreboding. It's all going to be a disaster. An A-one, copper-bottomed, twenty-four-carat disaster.

CAROL   Look, darling, you know what they say. Faint heart never won fair ladypegs!

BRINDSLEY   How true.

CAROL   The trouble with you is you're what Daddy calls a Determined Defeatist.

BRINDSLEY   The more I hear about your Daddy, the more I hate him. I loathe military men anyway . . . and in any case he's bound to hate me.

CAROL   Why?

BRINDSLEY   Because I'm a complete physical coward. He'll smell it on my breath.

CAROL   Look, darling, all you've got to do is stand up to him. Daddy's only a bully when he thinks people are afraid of him.

BRINDSLEY   Well, I am.

CAROL   You haven't even met him.

BRINDSLEY   That doesn't make any difference.

CAROL   Don't be ridiculous. (*Hands him a drink*) Here.

BRINDSLEY   Thanks.

CAROL   What can he do? To you?

BRINDSLEY   For one thing, he can refuse to let me marry you.

CAROL   Ah, that's sweetipegs.
     (*They embrace*)

BRINDSLEY   I like you in yellow. It brings out your hair.

CAROL   Straighten your tie. You look sloppy.

BRINDSLEY   Well, you look divine.

CAROL   Really?

BRINDSLEY   I mean it. I've never seen you look so lovely.

CAROL   Tell me, Brin, have there been many before me?

BRINDSLEY   Thousands.

CAROL   Seriously!

BRINDSLEY Seriously—none.

CAROL What about that girl in the photo?

BRINDSLEY She lasted about three months.

CAROL When?

BRINDSLEY Two years ago.

CAROL What was her name?

BRINDSLEY Clea.

CAROL What was she like?

BRINDSLEY She was a painter. Very honest. Very clever. And just about as cozy as a steel razor blade.

CAROL When was the last time you saw her?

BRINDSLEY (*Evasively*) I told you ... two years ago.

CAROL Well, why did you still have her photo in your bedroom drawer?

BRINDSLEY It was just there. That's all. Give me a kiss ... (*Pause*) No one in the world kisses like you.

CAROL (*Murmuring*) Tell me something ... did you like it better with her—or me?

BRINDSLEY Like what?

CAROL Sexipegs.

BRINDSLEY Look, people will be here in a minute. Put a record on. It had better be something for your father. What does he like?

CAROL (*Crossing to the record player*) He doesn't like anything except military marches.

BRINDSLEY I might have guessed ... Wait—I think I've got some! That last record on the shelf. The orange cover. It's called "Marching and Murdering with Sousa," or something.

CAROL This one?

BRINDSLEY That's it.

CAROL (*Getting it*) "The Band of the Coldstream Guards."

BRINDSLEY Ideal. Put it on.

CAROL How d'you switch on?

BRINDSLEY The last knob on the left. That's it ... Let us pray! Oh God, let this evening go all right! Let Mr. Bamberger like my sculpture and buy some! Let Carol's monster father like me! And let my neighbor Harold Gorringe never find out that we borrowed his precious furniture behind his back! Amen. (*A Sousa march; loud. Hardly has it begun, however, when it runs down— as if there is a failure of electricity. Brilliant light floods the stage. The rest of the play, save for the times when matches are struck, or for the scene with* SCHUPPANZIGH, *is acted in this light, but as if in pitch darkness. They freeze:* CAROL *by the end of the sofa;* BRINDSLEY *by the drinks table. The girl's dress is a silk flag of chic wrapped round her greyhound's body. The boy's look is equally cool: narrow, contained, and sexy. Throughout the evening, as things slide into disaster for him, his crisp, detached shape degenerates progressively into sweat and rumple—just as the elegance of his room gives way relentlessly to its usual near-slum appearance. For the place, as for its owner, the evening is a progress through disintegration*) God! We've blown a fuse!

CAROL   *Oh no!*

BRINDSLEY   It must be.

   (*He blunders to the light switch, feeling ahead of him, trying to part the darkness with his hands. Finding the switch, he flicks it on and off*)

CAROL   It is!

BRINDSLEY   Oh no!

CAROL   Or a power cut. Where's the box?

BRINDSLEY   In the hall.

CAROL   Have you any candles?

BRINDSLEY   No. Damn!

CAROL   Where are the matches?

BRINDSLEY   They should be on the drinks table. (*Feeling round the bottles*) No. Try on the record player. (*They both start groping about the room, feeling for matches*) Damn, damn, damn, damn, damn, damn!

   (CAROL *sets a maraca rattling off the record player*)

CAROL   There! (*Finding it*) No . . .

   (*The telephone rings*)

BRINDSLEY   Would you believe it?! (*He blunders his way toward the sound of the bell. Just in time he remembers the central table —and stops himself from colliding into it with a smile of self-congratulation*) All right: I'm coming! (*Instead he trips over the dais, and goes sprawling—knocking the phone onto the floor. He has to grope for it on his knees, hauling the receiver back to him by the wire. Into receiver*) Hallo? . . . (*In sudden horror*) Hallo! . . . No, no, no, no—I'm fine, just fine! . . . You? . . . (*His hand over the receiver; to* CAROL) Darling—look in the bedroom, will you?

CAROL   I haven't finished in here yet.

BRINDSLEY   Well, I've just remembered there's some fuse wire in the bedroom. In that drawer where you found the photograph. Go and get it, will you?

CAROL   I don't think there is. I didn't see any there.

BRINDSLEY (*Snapping*)   Don't argue. Just look!

CAROL   All right. Keep your hairpiece on.
> (*During the following she gropes her way cautiously up the stairs—head down, arms up the banisters, silken bottom thrust out with the effort*)

BRINDSLEY (*Controlling himself*)   I'm sorry. I just know it's there, that's all. You must have missed it.

CAROL   What about the matches?

BRINDSLEY   We'll have to mend it in the dark, that's all. Please hurry, dear.

CAROL (*Climbing*)   Oh God, how dreary!

BRINDSLEY (*Taking his hand off the receiver and listening to hear* CAROL *go*)   Hallo? . . . Well, well, well, well! How are you? Good. That's just fine. Fine, fine! . . . Stop saying what?
> (CAROL *reaches the top of the stairs—and from force of habit pulls down her skirt before groping her way into the bedroom*)

BRINDSLEY (*Hand over the receiver*)   Carol? . . . Darling? . . . (*Satisfied she has gone; in a rush into the telephone, his voice low*) Clea! What are you doing here? I thought you were in Finland . . . But you've hardly been gone six weeks . . . Where are you speaking from? . . . The Air Terminal? . . . Well, no, that's not a good idea tonight. I'm terribly busy, and I'm afraid I just can't get out of it. It's business.

CAROL (*Calling from the bedroom door, above*)   There's nothing there except your dreary socks. I told you.

BRINDSLEY (*Calling back*)   Well, try the other drawers . . . (*He rises as he speaks, turning so that the wire wraps itself around his legs.* CAROL *returns to her search. Low and rapid, into phone*) Look: I can't talk now. Can I call you tomorrow? Where will you be? . . . Look, I told you *no*, Clea. Not tonight. I know it's just around the corner, that's not the point. You can't come round . . . Look, the situation's changed. Something's happened this past month—

CAROL (*Offstage*)   I can't see anything. Brin, *please!*—

BRINDSLEY   Clea, I've got to go . . . Look, I can't discuss it over the phone . . . Has it got to do with what? Yes, of course it has. I mean you can't expect things to stay frozen, can you?

CAROL (*Emerging from the bedroom*)   There's nothing here. Haven't we any matches at all?

BRINDSLEY   Oh stop wailing! (*Into phone*) No, not you. I'll call you tomorrow. Good-bye.
> (*He hangs up sharply—but fails to find the rest of the tele-phone so that he bangs the receiver hard on the table first. Then he has to disentangle himself from the wire. Already* BRINDSLEY *is beginning to be fussed*)

CAROL (*Descending*)   Who was that?

BRINDSLEY   Just a chum. Did you find the wire?

CAROL   I can't find anything in this. We've *got* to get some matches!—

BRINDSLEY   I'll try the pub. Perhaps they'll have some candles as well.
> (*Little screams are heard approaching from above. It is* MISS FURNIVAL *groping her way down in a panic*)

MISS FURNIVAL (*Squealing*)   Help! Help! . . . Oh please someone help me!

BRINDSLEY (*Calling out*)   Is that you, Miss Furnival?

MISS FURNIVAL   Mr. Miller? . . .

BRINDSLEY   Yes?

MISS FURNIVAL   Mr. Miller!

BRINDSLEY   Yes!
> (*She gropes her way in.* BRINDSLEY *crosses to find her, but narrowly misses her*)

MISS FURNIVAL   Oh, thank God, you're there; I'm so frightened!

BRINDSLEY   Why? Have your lights gone too?

MISS FURNIVAL   Yes!

BRINDSLEY   It must be a power cut. (*He finds her hand and leads her to a chair*)

MISS FURNIVAL   I don't think so. The street lights are on in the front. I saw them from the landing.

BRINDSLEY   Then it must be the main switch of the house.

CAROL   Where is that?
> (MISS FURNIVAL *gasps at the strange voice*)

BRINDSLEY   It's in the cellar. It's all sealed up. No one's allowed to touch it but the electricity people.

CAROL   What are we going to do?

BRINDSLEY   Get them—quick!

CAROL   Will they come at this time of night?

BRINDSLEY   They've got to. (BRINDSLEY *accidentally touches* MISS FURNIVAL'*s breasts. She gives a little scream.* BRINDSLEY *gropes his way to the phone*) Have you by any chance got a match on you, Miss Furnival?

MISS FURNIVAL   I'm afraid I haven't. So improvident of me. And I'm absolutely terrified of the dark.

BRINDSLEY   Darling, this is Miss Furnival, from upstairs. Miss Furnival—Miss Melkett.

MISS FURNIVAL   How do you do?

CAROL (*Extending her hand into the darkness*)   How do you do?

MISS FURNIVAL   Isn't this frightful?

   (BRINDSLEY *picks up the phone and dials "O"*)

CAROL   Perhaps we can put Mr. Bamberger off.

BRINDSLEY   Impossible. He's dining out and coming on here after. He can't be reached.

CAROL   Oh, flip!

BRINDSLEY (*Sitting on the dais, and speaking into the phone*) Hallo, Operator, can you give me the London Electricity Board, please? Night Service . . . I'm sure it's in the book, Miss, but I'm afraid I can't see . . . There's no need to apologize. No, I'm not blind!—I just can't see: we've got a fuse . . . No we *haven't* got any matches! (*Desperate*) Miss, *please:* this is an emergency . . . Thank you! . . . (*To the room*) London is staffed with imbeciles!

MISS FURNIVAL   Oh, you're so right, Mr. Miller.

BRINDSLEY (*Rising, frantic; into the phone*)   Miss, I *don't want* the number: I can't dial it! . . . Well, have *you* ever tried to dial a number in the dark? . . . (*Trying to keep control*) I just want to be connected . . . Thank you. (*To* MISS FURNIVAL) Miss Furnival, do you by any remote chance have any candles?

MISS FURNIVAL   I'm afraid not, Mr. Miller.

BRINDSLEY (*Mouthing nastily at her*)   "I'm afraid not, Mr. Miller" . . . (*Briskly, into phone*) Hallo? Look, I'd like to report a main fuse at Eighteen Scarlatti Gardens. My name is Miller. (*Exasperated*) Yes, yes! All right! . . . (*Maddened; to the room*) Hold on! Hold bloody on!

MISS FURNIVAL   If I might suggest—Harold Gorringe opposite might have some candles. He's away for the weekend, but always leaves his key under the mat.

BRINDSLEY   What a good idea. That's just the sort of practical thing he would have (*To* CAROL) Here—take this . . . I'll go and see, love. (*He hands her the telephone in a fumble; then makes for the door—only to collide smartly with his sculpture*) Bugger!

MISS FURNIVAL   Are you all right, Mr. Miller?

BRINDSLEY   I knew it! I bloody knew it. This is going to be the worst night of my life! . . .

(*He collides with the door*)

CAROL Don't panic, darling. Just don't panic!

(*He stumbles out and is seen groping under* HAROLD's *mat for the key. He finds it and enters the room opposite*)

MISS FURNIVAL You're so right, Miss Melkett. We must none of us panic.

CAROL (*On the phone*) Hallo? Hallo? (*To* MISS FURNIVAL) This would have to happen tonight. It's just Brindsley's luck.

MISS FURNIVAL Is it something special tonight then, Miss Melkett?

CAROL It couldn't be more special if it tried.

MISS FURNIVAL Oh, dear. May I ask why?

CAROL Have you ever heard of a German called Georg Bamberger?

MISS FURNIVAL Indeed, yes. Isn't he the richest man in the world?

CAROL Yes. (*Into phone*) Hallo? . . . (*To* MISS FURNIVAL) Well, he's coming here tonight.

MISS FURNIVAL Tonight!

CAROL In about twenty minutes, to be exact. And to make matters worse, he's apparently stone deaf.

MISS FURNIVAL How extraordinary! May I ask why he's coming?

CAROL He saw some photos of Brindsley's work and apparently got madly excited about it. His secretary rang up last week and asked if he could come and see it. He's a great collector. Brin would be absolutely *made* if Bamberger bought a piece of his.

MISS FURNIVAL Oh, how exciting!

CAROL It's his big break. Or was—till a moment ago.

MISS FURNIVAL Oh my dear, you *must* get some help. Jiggle that thing.

CAROL (*Jiggling the phone*) Hallo? Hallo? . . . Perhaps the Bomb's fallen, and everyone's dead.

MISS FURNIVAL Oh, please don't say things like that—even in levity.

CAROL (*Someone answers her at last*) Hallo? Ah! This is Number Eighteen, Scarlatti Gardens. I'm afraid we've had the most dreary fuse. It's what's laughingly known as the Main Switch. We want a *little man* . . . Well, they can't all have flu . . . Oh, please try! It's screamingly urgent . . . Thank you. (*She hangs up*) Sometime this evening, they hope. That's a lot of help.

MISS FURNIVAL They're not here to help, my dear. In my young days you paid your rates and you got satisfaction. Nowadays you just get some foreigner swearing at you. And if they think you're of the middle class, that only makes it worse.

CAROL Would you like a drink?

MISS FURNIVAL I don't drink, thank you. My dear father, being a Baptist minister, strongly disapproved of alcohol.

(*A scuffle is heard amongst milk bottles offstage, followed by a stifled oath*)

COLONEL MELKETT (*Offstage*) Damn and blast! . . . (*Barking*) Is there anybody there?

CAROL (*Calling*) In here, daddypegs!

COLONEL Can't you put the light on, dammit? I've almost knocked meself out on a damn milk bottle.

CAROL We've got a fuse. Nothing's working.

(COLONEL MELKETT *appears, holding a lighter which evidently is working—we can see the flame, and of course the lights go down a little*)

MISS FURNIVAL Oh what a relief! A light!

CAROL This is my father, Colonel Melkett, Miss Furnival. She's from upstairs.

COLONEL Good evening.

MISS FURNIVAL I'm taking refuge for a moment with Mr. Miller. I'm not very good in the dark.

COLONEL When did this happen?

(MISS FURNIVAL, *glad for the light, follows it pathetically as the* COLONEL *crosses the room*)

CAROL Five minutes ago. The main just blew.

COLONEL And where's this young man of yours?

CAROL In the flat opposite. He's trying to find candles.

COLONEL You mean he hasn't got any?

CAROL No. We can't even find the matches.

COLONEL I see. No organization. Bad sign!

CAROL Daddy, please. It could happen to any of us.

COLONEL Not to me. (*He turns to find* MISS FURNIVAL *right behind him and glares at her balefully. The poor woman retreats to the sofa and sits down.* COLONEL MELKETT *gets his first sight of* BRINDSLEY's *sculpture*) What the hell's that?

CAROL Some of Brindsley's work.

COLONEL Is it, by Jove? And how much does that cost?

CAROL I think he's asking fifty pounds for it.

COLONEL My God!

CAROL (*Nervously*) Do you like the flat, Daddy? He's furnished it very well, hasn't he? I mean it's rich, but not gaudipegs.

COLONEL Very elegant—good: I can see he's got excellent taste.

(*Seeing the Buddha*) Now that's what I understand by a real work of art—you can see what it's meant to be.

MISS FURNIVAL   Good heavens!

CAROL   What is it?

MISS FURNIVAL   Nothing . . . It's that Buddha—it so closely resembles the one Harold Gorringe has.

> (CAROL *looks panic-stricken*)

COLONEL   It must have cost a pretty penny, what? He must be quite well off. . . . By Jove—it's got pretty colors.

> (*He bends to examine it*)

CAROL   (*Sotto voce, urgently, to* MISS FURNIVAL)   You know Mr. Gorringe?

MISS FURNIVAL   Oh, very well indeed. We're excellent friends. He has such lovely things . . . (*For the first time she notices the sofa on which she is sitting*) Oh . . .

CAROL   What?

MISS FURNIVAL   This furniture . . . (*Looking around her*) Surely—? My goodness!—

CAROL   (*Hastily*)   Daddy, why don't you look in there? Its Brin's studio. There's something I particularly want you to see before he comes back.

COLONEL   What?

CAROL   It—it—er—it's a surprise, go and see.

COLONEL   Very well, Dumpling. Anythin' to oblige. (*To* MISS FURNIVAL) Excuse me.

> (*He goes off into the studio, taking his lighter with him. The light instantly gets brighter onstage.* CAROL *sits beside the spinster on the sofa, crouching like a conspirator*)

CAROL   (*Low and urgent*)   Miss Furnival, you're a sport, aren't you?

MISS FURNIVAL   I don't know. What is this furniture doing in here? It belongs to Harold Gorringe.

CAROL   I know. We've done something absolutely frightful. We've stolen all his best pieces and put Brin's horrid old bits into *his* room.

MISS FURNIVAL   But why? It's disgraceful!

CAROL   (*Sentimentally*)   Because Brindsley's got nothing, Miss Furnival. Nothing at all. He's as poor as a church mouse. If Daddy had seen this place as it looks normally, he'd have forbidden our marriage on the spot. Mr. Gorringe wasn't there to ask —so we just took the chance.

MISS FURNIVAL   If Harold Gorringe knew that anyone had touched his furniture or his porcelain, he'd go out of his mind! And as for that Buddha—(*Pointing in the wrong direction*) it's the most precious piece he owns. It's worth hundreds of pounds.

CAROL   Oh, please, Miss Furnival—you won't give us away, will you? We're desperate! And it's only for an hour . . . Oh, please! *please!*

MISS FURNIVAL (*Giggling*)   Very well! I won't betray you!

CAROL   Oh, thank you!

MISS FURNIVAL   But it'll have to go back exactly as it was, just as soon as Mr. Bamberger and your father leave.

CAROL   I swear! Oh, Miss Furnival, you're an angel! Do have a drink. Oh no, you don't. Well, have a bitter lemon.

MISS FURNIVAL   Thank you. That I won't refuse.

> (*The* COLONEL *returns, still holding his lighter. The stage darkens a little*)

COLONEL   Well, they're certainly a surprise. And that's supposed to be sculpture?

CAROL   It's not supposed to be. It is.

COLONEL   They'd make good garden implements. I'd like 'em for turnin' the soil.

> (MISS FURNIVAL *giggles*)

CAROL   That's not very funny, Daddy.

> (MISS FURNIVAL *stops giggling*)

COLONEL   Sorry, Dumpling. Speak as you find.

CAROL   I wish you wouldn't call me Dumpling.

COLONEL   Well, there's no point wastin' this. We may need it!

> (*He snaps off his lighter.* MISS FURNIVAL *gives her little gasp as the stage brightens*)

CAROL   Don't be nervous, Miss Furnival. Brin will be here in a minute with the candles.

MISS FURNIVAL   Then I'll leave, of course. I don't want to be in your way.

CAROL   You're not at all. (*Hearing him*) Brin?—

> (BRINDSLEY *comes out of* HAROLD's *room; returns the key to under the mat*)

BRINDSLEY   Hallo?

CAROL   Did you find anything?

BRINDSLEY (*Coming in*)   You can't find anything in this. If there's candles there, *I* don't know where they are. Did you get the electric people?

CAROL   They said they might send someone around later.

BRINDSLEY   How much later?

CAROL   They don't know.

BRINDSLEY   That's a lot of help. What a lookout! Not a bloody candle in the house. A deaf millionaire to show sculpture to—and your monster father to keep happy. Lovely!

COLONEL   (*Grimly lighting his lighter*)   Good evenin'.
    (BRINDSLEY *jumps*)

CAROL   Brin, this *is* my father—Colonel Melkett.

BRINDSLEY   (*Wildly embarrassed*)   Well, well, well, well, well! . . . (*Panic*) Good evening sir. Fancy you being there all the time! I —I'm expecting some dreadful neighbors, some neighbor monsters, monster neighbors, you know . . . They rang up and said they might look round . . . Well, well, well . . .

COLONEL   (*Darkly*)   Well, well.

MISS FURNIVAL   (*Nervously*)   Well, well!

CAROL   (*Brightly*)   Well!
    (*The* COLONEL *rises and advances on* BRINDSLEY, *who retreats before him across the room*)

COLONEL   You seem to be in a spot of trouble.

BRINDSLEY   (*With mad nervousness*)   Oh, not really! Just a fuse— nothing really, we have them all the time . . . I mean, it won't be the first fuse I've survived, and I daresay it won't be the last!
    (*He gives a wild, braying laugh*)

COLONEL   (*Relentless*)   In the meantime, you've got no matches. Right?

BRINDSLEY   Right.

COLONEL   No candles. Right?

BRINDSLEY   Right.

COLONEL   No basic efficiency, right?

BRINDSLEY   I wouldn't say that, exactly . . .

COLONEL   By basic efficiency, young man, I mean the simple state of being At Attention in life, rather than At Ease. Understand?

BRINDSLEY   Well, I'm certainly not at ease.

COLONEL   What are you goin' to do about it?

BRINDSLEY   Do?

COLONEL   Don't echo me, sir. I don't like it.

BRINDSLEY   You don't like it. . . . I'm sorry.

COLONEL   Now look you here. This is an emergency. Anyone can see that.

BRINDSLEY   No one can see anything: that's the emergency.

(*He gives his braying laugh again*)

COLONEL   Spare me your humor, sir, if you don't mind. Let's look at the situation objectively. Right?

BRINDSLEY   Right.

COLONEL   Good. (*He snaps off the lighter*) Problem: Darkness. Solution: Light.

BRINDSLEY   Oh very good, sir.

COLONEL   Weapons: Matches—none! Candles—none! What remains?

BRINDSLEY   Search me.

COLONEL (*Triumphantly*)   Torches. Torches, sir! what?

BRINDSLEY   Or a set of early Christians.

COLONEL   What did you say?

BRINDSLEY   I'm sorry. I think I'm becoming unhinged. Very good. Torches—brilliant.

COLONEL   Routine. Well, where would you find one?

BRINDSLEY   The pub. What time is it?

(*The* COLONEL *lights his lighter, but now not at the first try. The stage light flickers up and down accordingly*)

COLONEL   Blasted thing. It's beginnin' to go. (*He consults his watch*) Quarter to ten. You can just make it, if you hurry.

BRINDSLEY   Thank you, sir. Your clarity of mind has saved the day.

COLONEL   Well, get on with it, man.

BRINDSLEY   Yes, sir! Back in a minute.

(*The* COLONEL *sits in the Regency chair*)

CAROL   Good luck, darling.

BRINDSLEY   Thank you, my sweet.

(*She blows him a kiss. He blows her one back*)

COLONEL (*Irritated*)   Stop that at once.

(BRINDSLEY *starts for the door—but as he reaches it,* HAROLD GORRINGE *is heard, offstage*)

HAROLD (*Broad Lancashire accent*)   Hallo? Hallo? Anyone there?

BRINDSLEY (*Freezing with horror*)   HAROLD!!

HAROLD   Brindsley?

BRINDSLEY (*Meant for* CAROL)   It's Harold. He's back!

CAROL   Oh no!

BRINDSLEY   THE FURNITURE!!

HAROLD   What's going on here?

(HAROLD *appears. He wears a smart raincoat and carries a weekend suitcase. His hair falls over his brow in a flossy attempt at elegance*)

BRINDSLEY Nothing, Harold. Don't go in there—come in here. We've had a fuse. It's dark—it's all over the house.

HAROLD Have you phoned the electric? (*Reaching out*)

BRINDSLEY (*Reaching out and grabbing him*) Yes. Come in here.

HAROLD (*Grabbed*) Ohh! ... (*He takes* BRINDSLEY's *hand and enters the room cozily on his arm*) It's rather cozy in the dark, isn't it?

BRINDSLEY (*Desperately*) Yes! I suppose so ... So you're back from your weekend then ...

HAROLD I certainly am, dear. Weekend! Some weekend! It rained the whole bloody time. I feel damp to my knickers.

BRINDSLEY (*Nervously*) Well, have a drink and tell us all about it.

HAROLD Us? (*Disengaging himself*) Who's here, then?

MISS FURNIVAL (*Archly*) I am, Mr. Gorringe.

HAROLD Ferny?

MISS FURNIVAL Taking refuge, I'm afraid. You know how I hate the dark.

COLONEL (*Attempting to light his lighter*) Blasted thing! ... (*He succeeds*) There we are! (*Raising it to* GORRINGE's *face, with distaste*) Who are you?

BRINDSLEY May I present my neighbor. This is Harold Gorringe —Colonel Melkett.

HAROLD How do?

COLONEL How d'ye do?

BRINDSLEY And this is Miss Carol Melkett, Harold Gorringe.

CAROL (*Giving him a chilly smile*) Hello! ...
    (HAROLD *nods coldly*)

BRINDSLEY Here, let me take your raincoat, Harold.
    (*He is wearing a tight, modish, gray suit and a brilliant strawberry shirt*)

HAROLD (*Taking it off and handing it to him*) Be careful, it's sopping wet.
    (*Adroitly,* BRINDSLEY *drops the coat over the Wedgwood bowl on the table*)

COLONEL You got no candles, I suppose?

HAROLD Would you believe it, Colonel, but I haven't? Silly me!
    (BRINDSLEY *crosses and blows out the* COLONEL's *lighter, just as* HAROLD *begins to look round the room. The stage brightens*)

COLONEL What the devil did you do that for?

BRINDSLEY I'm saving your wick, Colonel. You may need it later and it's failing fast.

(*The* COLONEL *gives him a suspicious look.* BRINDSLEY *moves quickly back, takes up the coat and drops it over the right end of the sofa, to conceal as much of it as possible*)

HAROLD   It's all right. I've got some matches.

CAROL (*Alarmed*)   Matches!

HAROLD   Here we are! I hope I've got the right end. (*He strikes one.* BRINDSLEY *immediately blows it out from behind, then moves swiftly to hide the Wedgwood bowl under the table and drop the tablecloth over the remaining end of the sofa.* MISS FURNIVAL *sits serenely unknowing between the two covers*) Hey, what was that?

BRINDSLEY (*Babbling*)   A draft. No match stays alight in this room. It's impossible. Cross currents, you know. Old houses are full of them. They're almost a permanent feature in this house . . .

HAROLD (*Bewildered*)   I don't know what you're on about.
   (*He strikes another match.* BRINDSLEY *again blows it out as he nips over to sit in a chair, but this time is seen*) What's up with you?

BRINDSLEY   Nothing!

HAROLD   Have you got a dead body in here or something?

BRINDSLEY   NO!
   (*He starts his maniacal laughter*)

HAROLD   Here, have you been drinking?

BRINDSLEY   No. Of course not.
   (HAROLD *strikes another match.* BRINDSLEY *dashes up. All these strikings and blowings are of course accompanied by swift and violent alterations of the light*)

HAROLD (*Exasperated*)   Now look here! What's up with you?

BRINDSLEY (*Inspired*)   Dangerous!

HAROLD   What?

BRINDSLEY (*Frantically improvising*)   Dangerous! It's dangerous! . . . We can all die! Naked flames! Hideous accidents can happen with naked flames!

HAROLD   I don't know what you're on about—what's up with you?
   (BRINDSLEY *clutches the bewildered* HAROLD *and backs him across to the center table*)

BRINDSLEY   I've just remembered! It's something they always warn you about. In old houses the fuse box and the gas meter are in the same cupboard. They are here!

COLONEL   So what about it?

BRINDSLEY   Well . . . electrical blowouts can damage the gas supply. They're famous for it. They do it all the time! And they say you've got to avoid naked flames till they're mended.

COLONEL   I've never heard of that.

HAROLD   Me neither.

BRINDSLEY   Well, take my word for it. It's fantastically dangerous to burn a naked flame in this room!

CAROL (*Catching on*)   Brin's absolutely right. In fact, they warned me about it on the phone this evening when I called them. They said, "Whatever you do, don't strike a match till the fuse is mended."

BRINDSLEY   There, you see!—it's terribly dangerous.

COLONEL (*Grimly*)   Then why didn't you warn me, Dumpling?

CAROL   I—I forgot.

COLONEL   Brilliant!

MISS FURNIVAL   Oh goodness, we must take care.

BRINDSLEY   We certainly must! . . . (*Pause*) Let's all have a drink. Cheer us up! . . .

CAROL   Good idea! Mr. Gorringe, would you like a drink?

HAROLD   Well, I must say, that wouldn't come amiss. Not after the journey I've had tonight. I swear to God there was thirty-five people in that compartment if there was one—babes in arms, toddlers, two nuns, three yapping poodles, and not a sausage to eat from Leamington to London. It's a bloody disgrace.

MISS FURNIVAL   You'd think they'd put on a restaurant car, Mr. Gorringe.

HAROLD   Not them, Ferny. They don't care if you perish once they've got your fare. Excuse me, I'll just go and clean up.

BRINDSLEY (*Panic*)   You can do that here.

HAROLD   Well, I must unpack anyway.

BRINDSLEY   Do it later.

HAROLD   No, I hate to keep clothes in a suitcase longer than I absolutely have to. If there's one thing I can't stand, it's a creased suit.

BRINDSLEY   Five more minutes won't hurt, surely?

HAROLD   Ooh, you aren't half bossy!

CAROL   What will you have? Winnie, Vera or Ginette?

HAROLD   Come again?

CAROL   Winnie Whiskey, Vera Vodka, or dear old standby Ginette.

HAROLD (*Yielding*)   I can see you're the camp one! . . . If it's all the same to you, I'll have a drop of Ginette, please, and a little lime juice.

COLONEL Young man, do I have to keep reminding you that you are in an emergency? You have a guest arrivin' any second.

BRINDSLEY Oh God, I'd forgotten!

COLONEL Try the pub. Try the neighbors. Try who you damn well please, sir—but *get a torch!*

BRINDSLEY Yes . . . Yes! . . . Carol, can I have a word with you, please?

CAROL I'm here.

(*She gropes toward him and* BRINDSLEY *leads her to the stairs*)

COLONEL What now?

BRINDSLEY Excuse us just a moment, please, Colonel.

(*He pulls her quickly after him, up the stairs*)

MISS FURNIVAL (*As they do this*) Oh, Mr. Gorringe, it's so exciting. You'll never guess who's coming here tonight.

HAROLD Who?

MISS FURNIVAL Guess.

HAROLD The Queen!

MISS FURNIVAL Oh, Mr. Gorringe, you are ridiculous!

(BRINDSLEY *arrives at the top of the stairs, then opens the bedroom door and closes it behind them*)

BRINDSLEY What are we going to do?

CAROL (*Behind the door*) I don't know!

BRINDSLEY (*Behind the door*) Think!

CAROL But—

BRINDSLEY *Think!*

COLONEL Is that boy touched or somethin'?

HAROLD Touched? He's an absolute poppet.

COLONEL A what?

HAROLD A duck. I've known him for years, ever since he came here. There's not many secrets we keep from each other, I can tell you.

COLONEL (*Frostily*) Really?

HAROLD Yes, really. He's a very sweet boy.

(BRINDSLEY *and* CAROL *emerge from behind the bedroom door*)

BRINDSLEY We'll have to put all Harold's furniture back in his room.

CAROL *Now?!*

BRINDSLEY We'll have to. I can't get a torch till we do.

CAROL We can't!

BRINDSLEY   We must. He'll go mad if he finds out what we've done.

HAROLD   Well come on, Ferny, don't be a tease. Who is it? Who's coming?

MISS FURNIVAL   I'll give you a clue. It's someone with money.

HAROLD   Money? . . . Let me think.

COLONEL (*Calling out*)   Carol!

CAROL   Look, can't you just tell him it was a joke?

BRINDSLEY   You don't know him. He can't bear anyone to touch his treasures. They're like children to him. He cleans everything twice a day with a special swansdown duster. He'd wreck everything. Would you like him to call me a thief in front of your father?

CAROL   Of course not!

BRINDSLEY   Well, he would. He gets absolutely hysterical. I've seen him.

COLONEL (*Mildly*)   Brindsley!

CAROL   Well, how the hell can we do it?

HAROLD   It's no good. You can't hear up there.

BRINDSLEY (*Stripping off his jacket*)   Look, you hold the fort. Serve them drinks. Just keep things going. Leave it all to me. I'll try and put everything back in the dark.

CAROL   It won't work.

BRINDSLEY   It's *got* to!

COLONEL (*Roaring*)   *Brindsley!!*

BRINDSLEY (*Dashing to the door*)   Coming, sir . . . (*With false calm*) I'm just getting some empties to take to the pub.

COLONEL   Say what you like. That boy's touched.

BRINDSLEY (*To* CAROL, *intimately*)   Trust me, darling.
     (*They kiss*)

COLONEL   At the double, Miller.

BRINDSLEY   Yes, sir! Yes, sir! (*He rushes out, and in his anxiety he misses his footing and falls neatly down the entire flight of stairs. Picking himself up*) I'm off now, Colonel! Help is definitely on the way.

COLONEL   Well, hurry it up, man.

BRINDSLEY   Carol will give you drinks. If Mr. Bamberger arrives, just explain the situation to him.

HAROLD (*Feeling for his hand*)   Would you like me to come with you?

BRINDSLEY   No, no, no—good heavens, stay and enjoy yourself. (HAROLD *kisses his hand.* BRINDSLEY *pulls it away*) I mean, you must be exhausted after all those poodles. A nice gin and lime will do wonders. I shan't be a minute.

(*He reaches the door, opens it, then slams it loudly, remaining on the inside. Stealthily he opens it again, stands dead still for a moment, silently indicating to himself the position of the chairs he has to move—then he finds his way to the first of the Regency chairs, which he lifts noiselessly*)

CAROL (*With bright desperation*) Well now, drinks! What's everyone going to have? It's Ginette for Mr. Gorringe and I suppose Winnie for Daddy.

COLONEL And how on earth are you going to do that in the dark?

CAROL I remember the exact way I put out the bottles.

(BRINDSLEY *bumps into her with the chair and falls back, gored by its leg*) It's very simple.

HAROLD Oh look, love, let me strike a match. I'm sure it's not that dangerous, just for a minute.

(*He strikes a match*)

CAROL Oh no! . . . (BRINDSLEY *ducks down, chair in hand, and blows out the match*) Do you want to blow us all up, Mr. Gorringe? . . . All poor Mr. Bamberger would find would be teensy weensy bits of us. Very messypegs.

(*She snatches the box of matches, feels for the ice bucket, and drops them into it.* BRINDSLEY *steals out, Felix-the-cat-like, with the chair as* CAROL *fumbling starts to mix drinks. He sets it down, opens* HAROLD's *door, and disappears inside it with the chair*)

HAROLD Bamberger? Is that who's coming? Georg Bamberger?

MISS FURNIVAL Yes. To see Mr. Miller's work. Isn't it exciting?

HAROLD Well, I never. I read an article about him last week in the Sunday Pic. He's known as the mystery millionaire. He's almost completely deaf—deaf as a post, and spends most of his time indoors alone with his collection. He hardly ever goes out, except to a gallery or a private studio. That's the life! If I had money that's what I'd do. Just collect all the china and porcelain I wanted.

(BRINDSLEY *returns with a poor, broken-down chair of his own and sets it down in the same position as the one he has taken out. The second chair presents a harder challenge. It sits right across the room. Delicately he moves toward it— but he has difficulty finding it. We watch him walk round it in desperately narrowing circles till he touches it and with relief picks it up*)

MISS FURNIVAL   I've never met a millionaire. I've always wondered if they feel different to us. I mean their actual skins.

COLONEL   Their skins?

MISS FURNIVAL   Yes. I've always imagined they must be softer than ours. Like the skins of ladies when I was a girl.

CAROL   What an interesting idea.

HAROLD   Oh she's very fanciful is Ferny. Real imagination, I always say.

MISS FURNIVAL   Very kind of you, Mr. Gorringe. You're always so generous with your compliments. (*As she speaks her next speech staring smugly into the darkness, hands clasped in maidenly gentility, the second Regency chair is being moved slowly across what should be her field of vision, two inches from her face. During the following,* BRINDSLEY *unfortunately misaims and carries the chair past the door, bumps into a wall, retreats from it, and inadvertently shuts the door softly with his back. Now he cannot get out of the room. He has to set down the chair, grope for the door handle, turn it, then open the door—then refind the chair which he has quite lost. This takes a long and frantic time. At last he triumphs, and staggers from the room, nearly exhausted*) But this is by no means fancy. In my day, softness of skin was quite the sign of refinement. Nowadays, of course, it's hard enough for us middle classes to keep ourselves decently clothed, let alone soft. My father used to say, even before the bombs came and burnt our dear little house at Wendover: "The game's up, my girl. We middle classes are as dead as the dodo." Poor father, how right he was.

　　(*If the counter-point of face action goes well,* MISS FURNIVAL *may have to ad-lib a fair bit during all this, and not mind too much if nobody hears her. The essential thing for all four actors during the furniture-moving is to preserve the look of ordinary conversation*)

COLONEL   Your father was a professional man?

MISS FURNIVAL   He was a man of God, Colonel.

COLONEL   Oh. (BRINDSLEY *returns with a broken-down rocking chair of his own. He crosses gingerly to where the* COLONEL *is sitting*) How are those drinks coming, Dumpling?

CAROL   Fine, Daddy. They'll be one minute.

COLONEL (*Speaking directly into* BRINDSLEY's *face*)   Let me help you.

(BRINDSLEY *staggers back, startled*)

CAROL   You can take this bitter lemon to Miss Furnival if you want.

(BRINDSLEY *sets down the rocker immediately next to the* COLONEL's *chair*)

COLONEL   Very well.

(*He rises just as* BRINDSLEY's *hand pulls the chair from beneath him. With his other hand* BRINDSLEY *pulls the rocker into the identical position. The* COLONEL *moves slowly across the room, arms outstretched for the bitter lemon. Unknowingly* BRINDSLEY *follows him, carrying the third chair. The* COLONEL *collides gently with the table. At the same moment* BRINDSLEY *reaches it, and searches for the Wedgwood bowl. Their hands narrowly miss. Then the young man remembers the bowl is under the table. Deftly he reaches down and retrieves it—and carrying it in one hand and the chair in the other, triumphantly leaves the room through the arch unconsciously provided by the outstretched arms of* CAROL *and the* COLONEL, *giving and receiving a glass of Scotch—which they think is bitter lemon*)

CAROL   Here you are, Daddy. Bitter lemon for Miss Furnival.

COLONEL   Right you are, Dumpling. (*To* MISS FURNIVAL) *So your* father was a minister then?

MISS FURNIVAL   He was a saint, Colonel. I'm only thankful he never lived to see the rudeness and vulgarity of life today.

(*The* COLONEL *sets off to find her, but goes much too far to the right*)

HAROLD (*He sits on the sofa beside her*)   Oooh, you're so right, Ferny. Rudeness and vulgarity—that's it to a T. The manners of some people today are beyond belief. Honestly. Did I tell you what happened in my shop last Friday? I don't think I did.

MISS FURNIVAL   No, Mr. Gorringe, I don't think so.

(*Her voice corrects the* COLONEL's *direction. During the following he moves slowly up toward her*)

HAROLD   Well, I'd just opened up—it was about quarter to ten and I was dusting off the teapots—you know, Rockingham collects the dust something shocking!—when who should walk in but that Mrs. Levitt, you know—the ginger-haired bit I told you about, the one who thinks she's God's gift to bachelors.

COLONEL (*Finding her head with his hand and presenting her with the Scotch*)   Here's your lemonade.

MISS FURNIVAL   Oh, thank you. Most kind.

(*Throughout* HAROLD's *story,* MISS FURNIVAL *nurses the glass, not drinking. The* COLONEL *finds his way slowly back to the chair he thinks he was sitting on before, but which is now a rocker.* BRINDSLEY *re-appears, triumphantly carrying one of the original Regency chairs he took out. He moves slowly across the room getting his bearings*)

HAROLD   Anyway, she's got in her hand a vase I'd sold her last week—it was a birthday present for an old geezer she's having a bit of a ding dong with somewhere in Earls Court, hoping to collect all his lolly when he dies, as I read the situation. I'm a pretty good judge of character, Ferny, as you know—and she's a real grasper if ever I saw one.

(*The* COLONEL *sits heavily in the rocking chair, which over-balances backward, spilling him onto the floor*)

COLONEL   Dammit to hell!

CAROL   What's the matter, Daddy?

(*A pause.* BRINDSLEY *sits down panic-stricken on the chair he has carried in. The* COLONEL *feels the chair and sets it on its feet*)

COLONEL (*Unbelieving*)   It's a blasted rockin' chair! I didn't see a blasted rockin' chair here before! ...

(*Astounded, the* COLONEL *remains on the floor.* BRINDSLEY *rises and moves the chair to the original position of the second chair he moved*)

HAROLD   Oh yes, you want to watch that. It's in a pretty ropey condition, I've told Brin about it several times. Anyway, this vase. It's a nice bit of Kang Tsi, blue and white with a good orange-peel glaze, absolutely authentic—I'd let her have it for twenty-five pounds, and she'd got infinitely the best of the bargain, no argument about that. (HAROLD *rises and leans against the center table to tell his story more effectively. The* COLONEL *seats himself again, gingerly*) Well, in she prances, her hair all done up in one of them bouffant hairdos, you know, tarty—French-like—it would have looked fancy on a girl half her age with twice her looks—

(BRINDSLEY *mistakenly lifts the end of the sofa.* MISS FURNI-VAL *gives a little scream at the jolt*)

HAROLD   Exactly. You know the sort. (BRINDSLEY *staggers in the opposite direction onto the dais*) And d'you know what she says to me? "Mr. Gorringe," she says, "I've been cheated."

MISS FURNIVAL   No!

HAROLD   Her very words. "Cheated." (BRINDSLEY *collides with the sculpture. It jangles violently. To it*) Hush up, I'm talking!

CAROL (*Covering up*)   I'm frightfully sorry.

(HAROLD *whirls round, surprised*)

HAROLD   Anyway—"Oh, I say, and how exactly has that occurred, Mrs. Levitt?" "Well," she says, "quite by chance I took this vase over to Bill Everett in the Portobello, and he says it's not what you called it at all, Chinese and very rare. He says it's a piece of nineteenth-century trash." (BRINDSLEY *finds the lamp on the table and picks it up. He walks with it round the rocking chair, on which the* COLONEL *is now sitting again*) "Does he?" I say. "Does he?" I keep calm. I always do when I'm riled. "Yes," she says. "He does. And I'd thank you to give me my money back."

(*The wire of the lamp has followed* BRINDSLEY *round the bottom of the rocking chair. It catches.* BRINDSLEY *tugs it gently. The chair moves. Surprised, the* COLONEL *jerks forward.* BRINDSLEY *tugs it again, much harder. The rocking chair is pulled forward, spilling the* COLONEL *out of it, again onto the floor, and then falling itself on top of him. The shade of the lamp comes off. During the ensuing dialogue* BRINDSLEY *gets on his knees and crawls right across the room following the wire of the lamp. He finds the plug, pulls it out, and—still on his knees—retraces his steps, winding up the wire around his arm, and becoming helplessly entangled in it. The* COLONEL *remains on the floor, now really alarmed*)

MISS FURNIVAL   How dreadful, Mr. Gorringe. What did you do?

HAROLD   I counted to ten, and then I let her have it. "In the first place," I said, "I don't expect my customers to go checking up on my honesty behind my back. In the second, Bill Everett is ignorant as Barnsley dirt, he doesn't know Tang from Ting. And in the third place, that applies to you, too, Mrs. Levitt."

MISS FURNIVAL   You didn't!

HAROLD   I certainly did—and worse than that. "You've got in your hand," I said, "a minor masterpiece of Chinese pottery. But in point of fact," I said, "you're not even fit to hold a 1953 Coronation mug. Don't you ever come in here again," I said, "—don't you cross my threshold. Because if you do, Mrs. Levitt, I won't make myself responsible for the consequences."

CAROL   (*With two drinks in her hands*)   My, Mr. Gorringe, how splendid of you. Here's your gin and lime. You deserve it.

(*She hands him the bitter lemon*)

HAROLD (*Accepting it*)   Ta. I was proper blazing, I didn't care.

CAROL   Where are you? Where are you, Daddy? Here's your Scotch.

COLONEL   Here, Dumpling!

(*He gets up dazedly and fumbles his way to the glass of gin and lime.* BRINDSLEY *meanwhile realizes he has lost the shade of the lamp. On his knees, he begins to look for it*)

HAROLD   Carrotty old bitch—telling *me* about pottery! *Oooh!!*

(*He shakes himself indignantly at the recollection of it*)

MISS FURNIVAL   Do you care for porcelain yourself, Colonel?

COLONEL   I'm afraid I don't know very much about it, Madam. I like some of that Chinese stuff—you get some lovely colors, like on that statue I saw when I came in here—very delicate.

HAROLD   What statue's that, Colonel?

COLONEL   The one on the packing case, sir. Very fine.

HAROLD   I didn't know Brin had any Chinese stuff. What's it of then, this statue?

(BRINDSLEY *freezes*)

CAROL (*Desperately*)   Well, we've all got drinks, I'd like to propose Daddy's regimental toast. Raise your glasses everyone! "To the dear old Twenty-Fifth Horse. Up the British, and Death to All Natives!"

MISS FURNIVAL   I'll drink to that!

HAROLD   Up the old Twenty-Fifth!!

(*Quickly* BRINDSLEY *finds the Buddha, moves it from the packing case to the table, then gets* HAROLD's *raincoat from the sofa, and wraps the statue up in it, leaving it on the table*)

COLONEL   Thank you, Dumpling. That was very touchin' of you. Very touchin' indeed. (*He swallows his drink*) Dammit, that's gin!

HAROLD   I've got lemonade!

MISS FURNIVAL   Oh! Horrible! . . . Quite horrible! That would be alcohol, I suppose! . . . Oh dear, how unpleasant! . . .

HAROLD (*To* MISS FURNIVAL)   Here, love, exchange with me. No —you get the lemonade—but I get the gin. Colonel—

COLONEL   Here, sir.

(*Seizing her chance,* MISS FURNIVAL *downs a huge draft of Scotch. They all exchange drinks.* BRINDSLEY *resumes his frantic search for the shade*)

HAROLD   Here, Ferny.

(*The* COLONEL *hands her the gin and lime. He gets instead the bitter lemon from* HAROLD. HAROLD *gets the Scotch*)

MISS FURNIVAL   Thank you.

HAROLD   Well, let's try again. Bottoms up!

COLONEL   Quite. (*They drink. Triumphantly,* BRINDSLEY *finds the shade. Unfortunately at the same moment the* COLONEL *spits out his lemonade in a fury all over him, as he marches toward the* COLONEL *on his knees*) Look here—I can't stand another minute of this!

(*He fishes his lighter out of his pocket and angrily tries to light it.*)

CAROL   Daddy, please!

COLONEL   I don't care, Dumpling. If I blow us up, then I'll blow us up! This is ridiculous ... (*His words die in the flame. He spies* BRINDSLEY *kneeling at his feet, wound about with lamp wire*) What the devil are you doin' there?

BRINDSLEY (*Blowing out his lighter*)   Now don't be rash, Colonel! Isn't the first rule of an officer "Don't involve your men in unnecessary danger"?

(*Quickly he steals, still on his knees, to the table*)

COLONEL   Don't be impertinent. Where's the torch?

BRINDSLEY   Er ... the pub was closed.

HAROLD   You didn't go to the pub in that time, surely? You couldn't have.

BRINDSLEY   Of course I did.

MISS FURNIVAL   But it's five streets away, Mr. Miller.

BRINDSLEY   Needs must when the devil drives, Miss Furnival. Whatever that means.

(*Quickly he lifts the table, and steals out of the room with it and the wrecked lamp*)

COLONEL (*Who thinks* BRINDSLEY *is still kneeling at his feet*)   Now look here: there's somethin' very peculiar goin' on in this room. I may not know about art, Miller, but I know men. I know a liar in the light, and I know one in the dark.

CAROL   Daddy!

COLONEL   I don't want to doubt your word, sir. All the same, I'd like your oath you went out to that public house. *Well?*

CAROL (*Realizing he isn't there, raising her voice*)   Brin, Daddy's talking to you!

COLONEL   What are you shoutin' for?

BRINDSLEY (*Rushing back from* HAROLD's *room, still entangled in the lamp*)   Of course. I know. He's absolutely right. I was—just thinking it over for a moment.

COLONEL   Well? What's your answer?

BRINDSLEY   I . . . I couldn't agree with you more, sir.

COLONEL   What?

BRINDSLEY   That was a very perceptive remark you made there. Not everyone would have thought of that. Individual. You know. Almost witty. Well, it *was* witty. Why be ungenerous? . . .

COLONEL   Look, young man, are you trying to be funny?

BRINDSLEY (*Ingratiatingly*)   Well, I'll try anything once . . .

HAROLD   I say, this is becoming a bit unpleasant, isn't it?

CAROL   It's becoming drearypegs.

COLONEL   Quiet, Dumpling. Let me handle this.

BRINDSLEY   What's there to handle, sir?

COLONEL   If you think I'm going to let my daughter marry a born liar, you're very much mistaken.

HAROLD   Marry!

CAROL   Well, that's the idea.

HAROLD   You and this young lady, Brin?

CAROL   Are what's laughingly known as engaged. Subject of course to Daddy's approval.

HAROLD   Well! (*Furious at the news, and at the fact that* BRINDSLEY *hasn't confided in him*) What a surprise! . . .

BRINDSLEY   We were keeping it a secret.

HAROLD   Evidently. How long's this been going on, then?

BRINDSLEY   A few months.

HAROLD   You old slyboots.

BRINDSLEY (*Nervous*)   I hope you approve, Harold.

HAROLD   Well, I must say, you know how to keep things to yourself.

BRINDSLEY (*Placatingly*)   I meant to tell you, Harold . . . I really did. You were the one person I was going to tell.

HAROLD   Well, why didn't you then?

BRINDSLEY   I don't know. I just never got around to it.

HAROLD   You saw me every day.

BRINDSLEY   I know.

HAROLD   You could have mentioned it at any time.

BRINDSLEY   I know.

HAROLD (*Huffy*)   Well, it's your business. There's no obligation to share confidences. I've only been your neighbor for three years. I've always assumed there was more than a geographical closeness between us, but I was obviously mistaken.

BRINDSLEY   Oh don't start getting huffy, Harold.

HAROLD   I'm not getting anything. I'm just saying it's surprising, that's all. Surprising and somewhat disappointing.

BRINDSLEY   Oh look, Harold, please understand—

HAROLD   (*Shrill*)   There's no need to say anything! It'll just teach me in future not to bank too much on friendship. It's silly me again! Silly, stupid, trusting me!

>   (MISS FURNIVAL *rises in agitation and gropes her way to the drinks table*)

COLONEL   Good God!

CAROL   (*Wheedling*)   Oh come, Mr. Gorringe. We haven't told anybody. Not one single soulipegs. Really.

COLONEL   At the moment, Dumpling, there's nothing to tell. And I'm not sure there's going to be!

BRINDSLEY   Look, sir, we seem to have got off on the wrong foot. If it's my fault, I apologize.

MISS FURNIVAL   (*Groping about on the drinks table*)   My father always used to say, "To err is human: to forgive divine."

CAROL   I thought that was somebody else.

MISS FURNIVAL   (*Blithely*)   So many people copied him.

>   (*She finds the open bottle of gin, lifts it and sniffs it eagerly*)

CAROL   May I help you, Miss Furnival?

MISS FURNIVAL   No, thank you, Miss Melkett. I'm just getting myself another bitter lemon. That is—if I may, Mr. Miller?

BRINDSLEY   Of course. Help yourself.

MISS FURNIVAL   Thank you, most kind!

>   (*She pours more gin into her glass and returns slowly to sit upstage on the edge of the dais*)

COLONEL   Well, sir, wherever you are—

BRINDSLEY   Here, Colonel.

COLONEL   I'll overlook your damn peculiar behavior this once, but understand this, Miller. My daughter's dear to me. You show me you can look after her, and I'll consider the whole thing most favorably. I can't say fairer than that, can I?

BRINDSLEY   No, sir. Most fair, sir. Most fair.

>   (*He pulls a hideous face one inch from the* COLONEL'S)

CAROL   Of course he can look after me, Daddy. His works are going to be world-famous. In five years I'll feel just like Mrs. Michelangelo.

HAROLD   (*Loftily*)   There wasn't a Mrs. Michelangelo, actually.

CAROL   (*Irritated*)   Wasn't there?

HAROLD   No. He had passionate feelings of a rather different nature.

CAROL   Really, Mr. Gorringe. I didn't know that.

(*She puts out her tongue at him*)

BRINDSLEY   Look, Harold, I'm sorry if I've hurt your feelings.

HAROLD (*Loftily*)   You haven't.

BRINDSLEY   I know I have. Please forgive me.

CAROL   Oh, do, Mr. Gorringe. Quarreling is so dreary. I hope we're all going to be great friends.

HAROLD   I'm not sure that I can contemplate a friendly relationship with a viper.

MISS FURNIVAL   Remember: to err is human, to forgive divine!

COLONEL (*Irritated*)   You just said that, madam.

(CLEA *enters, wearing dark glasses and carrying an air bag. She stands in the doorway, amazed by the dark. She takes off her glasses, but this doesn't improve matters*)

MISS FURNIVAL (*Downing her gin happily*)   Did I?

CAROL   Brin's not really a viper. He's just artistic, aren't you, darling?

BRINDSLEY   Yes, darling.

(CAROL *sends him an audible kiss across the astonished* CLEA. *He returns it, equally audibly*)

CAROL (*Winningly*)   Come on, Mr. Gorringe. It really is a case of forgive and forgettipegs.

HAROLD   Is it reallypegs?

CAROL   Have another Ginette and lime. I'll have one with you.

(*She rises and mixes the drink*)

HAROLD (*Rising*)   Oh, all right. I don't mind if I do.

CAROL   Let me mix it for you.

HAROLD   Ta. (*He crosses to her, narrowly missing* CLEA *who is now crossing the room to the sofa, and gets his drink*) I must say there's nothing nicer than having a booze up with a pretty girl.

CAROL (*Archly*)   You haven't seen me yet.

HAROLD   Oh, I just know it. Brindsley always had wonderful taste. I've often said to him, you've got the same taste in ladies as I have in porcelain. Ta.

(HAROLD *and* BRINDSLEY—*one from upstage, one from across the room—begin to converge on the sofa. On the word "modest" all three,* CLEA *in the middle, sit on it.* BRINDSLEY *of course imagines he is sitting next to* HAROLD)

BRINDSLEY   Harold!

CAROL   Oh don't be silly, Brin. Why be so modest? I found a photograph of one of his bits from two years ago, and I must say she was pretty stunning in a blowsy sort of way.

HAROLD   Which one was that, then? I suppose she means Clea.

CAROL   Did you know her, Mr. Gorringe?

HAROLD   Oh yes. She's been around a long time.

(BRINDSLEY *nudges* CLEA *warningly—imagining she is* HAR-OLD. CLEA *gently bumps* HAROLD)

CAROL (*Surprised*)   Has she?

HAROLD   Oh yes, dear. Or am I speaking out of turn?

BRINDSLEY   Not at all. I've told Carol all about Clea. (*He bangs* CLEA *again, a little harder—who correspondingly bumps against* HAROLD) Though I must say, Harold, I'm surprised you call three months "a long time."

(CLEA *shoots him a look of total outrage at this lie.* HAROLD *is also astonished*)

CAROL   What was she like?

BRINDSLEY (*Meaningfully, into* CLEA'*s ear*)   I suppose you can hardly remember her, Harold.

HAROLD (*Speaking across her*)   Why on earth shouldn't I?

BRINDSLEY   Well, since it was two years ago, you've probably forgotten.

HAROLD   Two years?!

BRINDSLEY   *Two years ago!*

(*He punches* CLEA *so hard that the rebound knocks* HAROLD *off the sofa, drink and all*)

HAROLD (*Picking himself up. Spitefully*)   Well, now since you mention it, I remember her perfectly. I mean, she's not one you can easily forget!

CAROL   Was she pretty?

HAROLD   No, not at all. In fact, I'd say the opposite. Actually she was rather plain.

BRINDSLEY   She wasn't!

HAROLD   I'm just giving my opinion.

BRINDSLEY   You've never given it before.

HAROLD (*Leaning over* CLEA)   I was never asked! But since it's come up, I always thought she was ugly. For one thing, she had teeth like a picket fence—yellow and spiky. And for an-other, she had bad skin.

BRINDSLEY   She had nothing of the kind!

HAROLD   She did. I remember it perfectly. It was like new pink wallpaper, with an old gray crumbly paper underneath.

MISS FURNIVAL   Quite right, Mr. Gorringe. I hardly ever saw her, but I do recall her skin. It was a strange color, as you say—and very coarse . . . Not soft, as the skins of young ladies should be, if they *are* young ladies.

    (CLEA *rises in outrage*)

HAROLD   Aye, that's right. Coarse.

MISS FURNIVAL   And rather lumpy.

HAROLD   Very lumpy.

BRINDSLEY   This is disgraceful.

HAROLD   You knew I never liked her, Brindsley. She was too clever by half.

MISS FURNIVAL   And so tiresomely Bohemian.

CAROL   You mean she was as pretentious as her name? (CLEA, *who has been reacting to this last exchange of comments about her like a spectator at a tennis match, now reacts to* CAROL, *openmouthed*) I bet she was. That photograph I found showed her in a dirndl and a sort of a sultry peasant blouse. She looked like "The Bartered Bride" done by Lloyds Bank.

    (*They laugh,* BRINDSLEY *hardest of all. Guided by the noise,* CLEA *aims her hand and slaps his face*)

BRINDSLEY   Ahh!

CAROL   What's wrong?

MISS FURNIVAL   What is it, Mr. Miller?

BRINDSLEY   (*Furious*)   That's not very funny, Harold. What the hell's the matter with you?

    (CLEA *makes her escape*)

HAROLD   (*Indignant*)   With me?

BRINDSLEY   Well, I'm sure it wasn't the Colonel.

COLONEL   What wasn't, sir?

    (BRINDSLEY, *groping about, catches* CLEA *by the bottom, and instantly recognizes it*)

BRINDSLEY   Clea! . . . (*In horror*) Clea!!

    (CLEA *breaks loose and moves away from him. During the following he tries to find her in the dark, and she narrowly avoids him*)

COLONEL   What?

BRINDSLEY   I was just remembering her, sir. You're all talking the most awful nonsense. She was beautiful . . . And anyway, Harold, you just said I was famous for my taste in women.

HAROLD   Aye, but it had its lapses.

BRINDSLEY   (*Frantically moving about*)   Rubbish! She was beautiful and tender and considerate and kind and loyal and witty and adorable in every way!

CAROL   You told me she was as cozy as a steel razor blade.

BRINDSLEY   Did I? Surely not! No. What I said was . . . something quite different . . . Utterly different . . entirely different . . . As different as chalk from cheese. Although when you come to think of it, cheese isn't all that different from chalk.

(He gives his braying laugh)

COLONEL   Are you sure you know what you're talking about?

(During this CLEA *has reached the table, picked up a bottle of Scotch, and rejected it in favor of vodka, which she takes with her)*

CAROL   You said to me in this room when I asked you what she was like, "She was a painter. Very honest. Very clever, and just about as cozy—"

BRINDSLEY *(Stopping, exasperated)*   As a steel razor blade! Well then, I said it! So bloody what? . . .

CAROL   So nothing!

(He throws out his hands in a gesture of desperate exhaustion and bumps straight into CLEA. *They instantly embrace,* CLEA *twining herself around him, her vodka bottle held aloft. A tiny pause)*

COLONEL   If that boy isn't touched, I don't know the meaning of the word!

CAROL   What's all this talk about her being kind and tender, all of a sudden?

BRINDSLEY *(Tenderly, holding* CLEA*)*   She could be. On occasion. *Very.*

CAROL   Very rare occasions, I imagine.

BRINDSLEY   Not so rare. *(He kisses* CLEA *again)* Not so rare at all. *(He leads her softly past the irritated* CAROL, *toward the stairs)*

CAROL   Meaning what, exactly? . . . *(Shouting) Brindsley, I'm talking to you!*

BRINDSLEY *(Sotto voce, into* CLEA's *ear as they stand just behind* HAROLD*)*   I can explain. Go up to the bedroom. Wait for me there.

HAROLD *(In amazement, thinking he is being addressed)*   Now? Do you think this is quite the moment?

BRINDSLEY   Oh God! . . . I wasn't talking to you.

CAROL   What did you say?

HAROLD (*To* CAROL) I think he wants *you* upstairs. (*Slyly*) For what purpose, I can't begin to imagine.

COLONEL They're going to do some more of that plotting, I daresay.

MISS FURNIVAL Lover's talk, Colonel.

COLONEL Very touching, I'm sure.

(BRINDSLEY *pushes* CLEA *ahead of him up the stairs*)

MISS FURNIVAL "Journeys end in lovers meeting," as my father always used to say.

COLONEL What a strikingly original father you seem to have had, madam.

(CAROL *joins the other two on the stairs. We see all three groping blindly up to the bedroom,* BRINDSLEY's *hands on* CLEA's *hips,* CAROL's *on* BRINDSLEY's)

CAROL (*With a conspirator's stage whisper*) What is it, darling? Has something gone wrong? What can't you move?

(*This next dialogue sotto voce*)

BRINDSLEY Nothing. It's all back—every bit of it—except the sofa, and I've covered that up.

CAROL You mean, we can have lights?

BRINDSLEY Yes . . . NO!!

CAROL Why not?

BRINDSLEY Never mind!

CAROL Why do you want me in the bedroom?

BRINDSLEY I don't. Go away!

CAROL Charming!

BRINDSLEY I didn't mean that.

COLONEL There you are. They *are* plotting again. What the hell is going on up there?

BRINDSLEY Nothing, Colonel. I've just remembered—there may be a torch under my bed. I keep it to blind the burglars with. Have another drink, Colonel!

(*He pushes* CLEA *into the bedroom and shuts the door*)

COLONEL What d'you mean another? I haven't had one yet.

MISS FURNIVAL Oh! Poor Colonel! Let me get you one.

COLONEL (*Rising*) I can get one for myself, thank you. Let me get you another lemonade.

MISS FURNIVAL (*Rising*) No thank you, Colonel, I'll manage myself. It's good practice!

(*They grope toward the drinks table. Above,* CLEA *and* BRINDSLEY *sit on the bed*)

CLEA   So this is what they mean by a blind date. What the hell is going on?

BRINDSLEY (*Sarcastic*)   Nothing! Georg Bamberger is only coming to see my work tonight, and we've got a main fuse.

CLEA   Is that the reason for all this furtive clutching?

BRINDSLEY   Look, I can't explain things at the moment.

CLEA   Who's that—(*Debutante accent*) "frightful gel"?

BRINDSLEY   Just a friend.

CLEA   She sounded more than that.

BRINDSLEY   Well, if you must know, it's Carol. I've told you about her.

CLEA   The Idiot Deb?

BRINDSLEY   She's a very sweet girl. As a matter of fact we've become very good friends in the last six weeks.

CLEA   How good?

BRINDSLEY   Just good.

CLEA   And have you become friends with her father too?

BRINDSLEY   If it's any of your business, they just dropped in to meet Mr. Bamberger.

CLEA   What was it you wanted to tell me on the phone tonight?

BRINDSLEY   Nothing.

CLEA   You're lying!

BRINDSLEY   Ah, here comes the inquisition! Look, Clea, if you ever loved me, just slip away quietly with no more questions, and I'll come round later and explain everything, I promise.

CLEA   I don't believe you.

BRINDSLEY   Please darling . . . Please . . . Please . . . Please!!

(*They kiss, passionately, stretched out on the bed*)

COLONEL (*Pouring*)   At last . . . a decent glass of Scotch. Are you getting your lemonade?

MISS FURNIVAL (*Cheerfully pouring herself an enormous gin*)   Oh yes, thank you, Colonel!

COLONEL   I'm just wonderin' if this Bamberger fellow is goin' to show up at all. He's half an hour late already.

HAROLD   Oh! That's nothing, Colonel. Millionaires are always late. It's their thing.

MISS FURNIVAL   I'm sure you're right, Mr. Gorringe. That's how *I* imagine them. Hands like silk, and always two hours late.

CAROL   Brin's been up there a long time. What can he be doing?

HAROLD   Maybe he's got that Clea hidden away in his bedroom, and they're having a tête-à-tête!!

CAROL   What a flagrant suggestion, Mr. Gorringe.

BRINDSLEY (*Disengaging himself*)   No one in the world kisses like you.

CLEA   I missed you so badly, Brin. I had to see you. I've thought about nothing else these past six weeks. Brin, I made the most awful mistake walking out.

BRINDSLEY   Clea—*please!*

CLEA   I mean we've known each other for four years. We can't just throw each other away like old newspapers.

BRINDSLEY   I don't see why not. You know my politics, you've heard my gossip, and you've certainly been through all my entertainment section.

CLEA   Well, how about a second edition?

BRINDSLEY   Darling, we simply can't talk about this now. Can't you trust me just for an hour?

CLEA   Of course I can, darling. You don't want me down there?

BRINDSLEY   No.

CLEA   Then I'll get undressed and go quietly to bed. When you've got rid of them all, I'll be waiting.

BRINDSLEY   That's a terrible idea!

CLEA (*Reaching for him*)   I think it's lovely. A little happy relaxation for us both.

BRINDSLEY (*Falling off the bed*)   I'm perfectly relaxed!

CAROL   Brindsley!

CLEA   "Too solemn for day, too sweet for night. Come not in darkness, come not in light." That's me, isn't it?

BRINDSLEY   Of course not. I just can't explain now, that's all.

CLEA   Oh, very well, you can explain later . . . in bed!

BRINDSLEY   Not tonight, Clea.

CLEA   Either that or I come down and discover your sordid secret.

BRINDSLEY   There *is* no sordid secret!

CLEA   Then you won't mind my coming down!

CAROL, COLONEL (*Roaring together*)   BRINDSLEY!!!

BRINDSLEY   Oh God!! . . . All right, stay. Only keep quiet . . . Blackmailing bitch! (*He emerges at the top of the stairs*) Yes, my sweet?

CAROL   What are you doing up there? You've been an eternity!

BRINDSLEY   I . . . I . . . I'm just looking in the bathroom, my darling. You never know what you might find in that clever little cabinet.

COLONEL (*Moving to the stairs*)   Are you trying to madden me, sir? Are you trying to put me in a fury?

BRINDSLEY   Certainly not, sir!!

COLONEL   I warn you, Miller, it's not difficult! In the old days in the regiment I was known for my furies. I was famous for my furies . . . Do you hear?

CLEA   I may sing!

(*She goes off into the bathroom*)

BRINDSLEY   I may knock your teeth in!

COLONEL   What did you say?

CAROL   Brin! How dare you talk to Daddy like that!

BRINDSLEY   Oh!! I . . . I . . . I wasn't talking to Daddy like that . . .

CAROL   Then who *were* you talking to?

BRINDSLEY   I was talking to no one! Myself I was talking to! I was saying . . . "If I keep groping about up here like this, I might knock my teeth in!"

COLONEL   Mad! . . . Mad! . . . Mad as the south wind! It's the only explanation—you've got yourself engaged to a lunatic.

CAROL   There's something going on up there, and I'm coming up to find out what it is. Do you hear me, Brin?

BRINDSLEY   Carol—no!

CAROL   (*Climbing the stairs*)   I'm not such a fool as you take me for. I know when you're hiding something. Your voice goes all deceitful—very, very foxipegs!

BRINDSLEY   Darling please. That's not very ladylike . . . I'm sure the Colonel won't approve of you entering a man's bedroom in the dark!

(*Enter* SCHUPPANZIGH. *He wears the overcoat and peaked cap of the London Electricity Board and carries a large tool bag, similarly labeled*)

CAROL   I'm comin' up, Brindsley, I'm comin' up!!!

BRINDSLEY   (*Scrambling down*)   I'm coming down . . . We'll all have a nice cozy drink . . .

SCHUPPANZIGH   'Allo please? Mr. Miller? Mr. Miller? I've come as was arranged.

BRINDSLEY   My God . . . it's Bamberger!

CAROL   Bamberger?

BRINDSLEY   Yes, Bamberger.

(BRINDSLEY *rushes down the remaining stairs, pulling* CAROL *with him*)

SCHUPPANZIGH   You must have thought I was never coming!

(*He takes off his overcoat and cap*)

BRINDSLEY   Not at all. I'm delighted you could spare the time.

I know how busy you are. I'm afraid we've had the most idiotic disaster. We've had a fuse.

HAROLD   You'll have to speak up, dear. He's stone deaf!

BRINDSLEY (*Yelling*)   We've had a fuse—not the best conditions for seeing sculpture.

SCHUPPANZIGH   Please not to worry. Here!

> (*He produces a torch from his pocket and "lights" it. The light on stage dims a little, as usual, to indicate this. All relax with audible sighs of pleasure.* SCHUPPANZIGH *at once places his tool bag on the Regency chair, and puts his coat and cap on top of it, concealing that it is one of* HAROLD's *chairs*)

CAROL   Oh what a relief!

BRINDSLEY (*Hastily dragging the sheet over the rest of the sofa*) Do you always travel with a torch?

SCHUPPANZIGH   Mostly, yes. It helps to see details   (*Seeing the others*) You are holding a private view?

MISS FURNIVAL   Oh no! I was just going. I'd hate to distract you.

SCHUPPANZIGH   Please not on my account, dear lady. I am not as easily distracted.

MISS FURNIVAL (*Charmed*)   Oh! . . .

BRINDSLEY (*Yelling in his ear*)   May I present Colonel Melkett?

COLONEL (*Yelling in his other ear*)   A great honor, sir!

SCHUPPANZIGH (*Banging his ear, to clear it*)   No, no, mine—mine!

BRINDSLEY   Miss Carol Melkett.

CAROL (*Screeching in his ear*)   I say: hello. So glad you got here! It's terribly kind of you to take such an interest!

SCHUPPANZIGH   Not at all. *Vous êtes très gentil.*

CAROL (*Yelling*)   What would you like to drink?

SCHUPPANZIGH (*Bewildered*)   A little vodka, would be beautiful!

CAROL   Of course!

BRINDSLEY   Harold Gorringe—a neighbor of mine!

HAROLD   How do? Very honored, I'm sure.

SCHUPPANZIGH   Enchanted.

HAROLD   I must say it's a real thrill, meeting you!

BRINDSLEY   And another neighbor, Miss Furnival.

SCHUPPANZIGH   Enchanted.

MISS FURNIVAL (*Hooting in his ear*)   I'm afraid we've all been taking refuge from the *storm*, as it were. (*Exclaiming as she holds* SCHUPPANZIGH's *hand*)   Oh! It *is* true! They *are* softer! Much, much softer!

SCHUPPANZIGH (*Utterly confused as she strokes his hand*) Softer? Please?

> (BRINDSLEY *and* HAROLD *pull her away, and she subsides onto the sofa*)

BRINDSLEY Miss Furnival, please!

CAROL (*At the drinks table*) Darling, where's the vodka?

BRINDSLEY It's on the table.

CAROL No, it isn't.

BRINDSLEY It must be!

> (*Above*, CLEA *reenters wearing the top half of* BRINDSLEY's *pajamas and nothing else. She gets into bed, still clutching the vodka bottle and carrying a plastic tooth-mug*)

CAROL Well, see for yourself. There's Winnie and Ginette, and Vera has quite vanished, the naughty girl.

BRINDSLEY She can't have done.

SCHUPPANZIGH Please don't concern yourselves. I am pressed for time. If I might just be shown where to go.

BRINDSLEY Of course. It's through the studio there. Darling, if you would just show our guest into the studio—*with his torch.*

CAROL What?? . . .

BRINDSLEY (*Sotto voce*) The sofa! . . . Get him out of here.

CAROL Oh yes!!

SCHUPPANZIGH (*Sighting the sculpture*) Oh! Good gracious! What an extraordinary object!

BRINDSLEY Oh, that's just a spare piece of my work I keep in here!

SCHUPPANZIGH Spare, maybe, but fascinating!

BRINDSLEY You really think so?

SCHUPPANZIGH (*Approaching it*) I do! Ja!

BRINDSLEY Well, in that case you should see my main collection. It's next door. My fiancée will show you!

> (MISS FURNIVAL *sits on the sofa. She is now quite drunk*)

SCHUPPANZIGH One amazement at a time, if you please! In this gluttonous age it is easy to get visual indigestion—hard to find visual Alka Seltzer . . . Permit me to digest this first!

BRINDSLEY Oh, by all means . . . Good, yes . . . There's no hurry —no hurry at all . . . Only . . . (*Inspired*) Why don't you digest it *in the dark?*

SCHUPPANZIGH I beg your pardon?

BRINDSLEY You'll never believe it, sir, but I actually made that piece to be appreciated in the dark. I was working on a very interesting theory. You know how the Victorians said, "Children should be seen and not heard"? Well, I say, "Art should be felt and not seen."

SCHUPPANZIGH   Amazing.

BRINDSLEY   Yes, isn't it. I call it my theory of Factual Tactility. If it doesn't stab you to the quick—it's not art. Look! Why don't you give me that torch, and try for yourself?

SCHUPPANZIGH   Very well, I will!! (*He hands* BRINDSLEY *the torch*)

BRINDSLEY   Thank you! (*He turns off the torch and hands it to* CAROL. *At the same moment* MISS FURNIVAL *quietly lies down, her full length on the sofa*) Now just stretch out your arms and feel it all over, sir. (*He steals toward the studio*) Have a good long feel! (SCHUPPANZIGH *embraces the metal sculpture with a fervent clash. He pulls at the two metal prongs*) Do you see what I mean?

(*Silently he opens the curtains*)

SCHUPPANZIGH   Amazing! . . . Absolutely incredible! . . . It's quite true . . . Like this, the piece becomes a masterpiece at once.

BRINDSLEY (*Astonished*)   It does??

SCHUPPANZIGH   But of course! I feel it here—and here—the two needles of man's unrest! . . . Self love and self hate, leading to the same point! That's the meaning of the work, isn't it?

BRINDSLEY   Of course. You've got it in one! You're obviously a great expert, sir!

(*Quietly he pulls the sofa into the studio, bearing on it the supine* MISS FURNIVAL, *who waves good-bye as she disappears*)

SCHUPPANZIGH   Not at all. *Vous êtes très gentil*—but it is evident . . . Standing here in the dark, one can feel the vital thrust of the argument! The essential anguish! The stress and the torment of our times! It is simple but not simpleminded! Ingenious, but not ingenuous! Above all, it has real moral force! Of how many modern works can one say that, good people?

CAROL   Oh, none, none at all really.

SCHUPPANZIGH   I hope I do not lecture. It can be a fault with me.

CAROL   Not at all! I could listen all night, it's so profound.

HAROLD   Me too. Really deep!

COLONEL   I don't know anything about this myself, sir, but it's an honor to listen to you.

(*He starts off upstage in search of the sofa, seating himself tentatively in the air, then moving himself along in a sitting position, trying to find it with his rear end. At the same mo-*

ment BRINDSLEY *emerges from the studio, closes the curtains behind him, and gropes his way to a corner where there stands a small packing-case. This he carries forward, hopefully to do duty for the missing sofa. Just as he places it on the ground the traveling* COLONEL *sits on it, trapping* BRINDSLEY's *hand beneath his weight. During the following,* BRINDSLEY *tries frantically to free himself*)

SCHUPPANZIGH   *Vous êtes très gentil!*

HAROLD   You mean to say you see all that in a bit of metal?

SCHUPPANZIGH   A *tiny* bit of metal, that's the point. A miracle of compression! You want my opinion, this boy is a genius. A master of the miniature. In the space of a matchbox he can realize anything he wants—the black virginity of Chartres! The white chorale of the Acropolis! *Wunderbar!*

CAROL   Oh how super!

SCHUPPANZIGH   You should charge immense sums for work like this, Mr. Miller. They should be very very expensive! This one, for example, how much is this?

BRINDSLEY   Fifty.

CAROL   Five hundred guineas.

SCHUPPANZIGH   Ah so! Very cheap.

HAROLD   Cheap!

CAROL   I think so, Mr. Gorringe. Well . . . so will you have it then?

SCHUPPANZIGH   Me?

BRINDSLEY   Darling . . . aren't you rushing things just a little? Perhaps you would like to see the rest of my work.

SCHUPPANZIGH   Alas, I have no more time. To linger would be pleasant, but alas, I must work . . . Also, as Moses discovered, it is sufficient to glimpse milk and honey. One does not have to wolf them down!

BRINDSLEY   Well.

COLONEL   Well . . .

HAROLD   Well . . .

CAROL   Well . . . Would you like it then?

SCHUPPANZIGH   Very much.

COLONEL   (*Rising.* BRINDSLEY *is freed at last*)   For five hundred guineas?

SCHUPPANZIGH   Certainly—if I had it!

HAROLD   According to the Sunday Pictorial, you must be worth at least seventeen million pounds.

SCHUPPANZIGH   The Sunday papers are notoriously ill-informed. According to my bank statement, I was worth one hundred pounds, eight shillings and fourpence.

HAROLD   You mean you've gone broke?

SCHUPPANZIGH   No. I mean I never had any more.

COLONEL   Now look, sir, I know millionaires are supposed to be eccentric, but this is gettin' tiresome.

CAROL   Daddy, ssh!—

SCHUPPANZIGH   Millionaires? Who do you think I am?

COLONEL   Dammit, man!—You must know who you are!

CAROL   Mr. Bamberger, is this some kind of joke you like to play?

SCHUPPANZIGH   Excuse me. That is not my name.

BRINDSLEY   It isn't?

SCHUPPANZIGH   No. My name is Schuppanzigh. Franz Schuppanzigh. Born in Weimar 1905. Student of Philosophy at Heidelberg 1934. Refugee to this country, 1938. Regular employment ever since with the London Electricity Board.

   (*All rise*)

CAROL   Electricity?

MISS FURNIVAL   Electricity!

BRINDSLEY   You mean you're not?—

HAROLD   Of course he's not!

SCHUPPANZIGH   But who did you imagine I was?

HAROLD (*Furious*)   How dare you?

   (*He snatches the electrician's torch*)

SCHUPPANZIGH (*Retreating before him*)   Please?—

HAROLD   Of all the nerve, coming in here, giving us a lecture about needles and virgins, and all the time you're simply here to mend the fuses!

COLONEL   I agree with you, sir. It's monstrous!

SCHUPPANZIGH (*Bewildered*)   It is?

   (*The* COLONEL *takes the torch and shines it pitilessly in the man's face*)

COLONEL   You come in here, a public servant, and proceed to harangue your employers, unasked and uninvited.

SCHUPPANZIGH (*Bewildered*)   Excuse me. But I *was* invited.

COLONEL   Don't answer back. In my day you would have been fired on the spot for impertinence.

CAROL   Daddy's absolutely right! Ever since the Beatles, the lower classes think they can behave exactly as they want.

COLONEL (*Handing the torch to* BRINDSLEY)   Miller, will you kindly show this feller his work?

BRINDSLEY   The mains are in the cellar. There's a trapdoor. (*Indicating*) Do you mind?

SCHUPPANZIGH (*Snatching the torch furiously*)   Why should I mind? It's why I came, after all! (*He takes his coat, cap, and bag off* HAROLD's *Regency chair . . . Seeing it*) Now there is a really beautiful chair!

(BRINDSLEY *stares at the chair aghast—and in a twinkling seats himself in it to conceal it*)

BRINDSLEY (*Exasperated*)   Why don't you just go into the cellar?

SCHUPPANZIGH   How? Where is it?

BRINDSLEY (*To* CAROL)   Darling, will you open the trap, please.

CAROL   Me? (*Understanding—as he indicates the chair*) Oh—yes!

(*She kneels and struggles to open the trap*)

COLONEL (*To* BRINDSLEY)   Well, I must say, that's very gallant of you, Miller.

BRINDSLEY   I've got a sudden touch of lumbago, sir. It often afflicts me after long spells in the dark.

CAROL (*Very sympathetic*)   Oh, darling! Has it come back?

BRINDSLEY   I'm afraid it has, my sweet.

HAROLD (*Opening the trap*)   Here, let me. I'm not as frail as our wilting friend (*To* SCHUPPANZIGH) Well, down you go, you!

SCHUPPANZIGH (*Shrugging*)   So. Farewell. I leave the light of Art for the dark of Science.

HAROLD   Let's have a little less of your lip, shall we?

SCHUPPANZIGH   Excuse me.

(SCHUPPANZIGH *descends through the trap, taking the torch with him.* HAROLD *slams the trap door down irritably after him, and of course the lights immediately come up full. There is a long pause. All stand about embarrassed. Suddenly they hear the noise of* MISS FURNIVAL *singing "Rock of Ages" in a high drunken voice from behind the curtain. Above, attracted by the noise of the slam,* CLEA *gets out of bed, still clutching the vodka and tooth-mug, opens the door, and stands at the top of the stairs listening*)

BRINDSLEY   None of this evening is happening.

CAROL   Cheer up, darling. In a few minutes everything will be all right. Mr. Bamberger will arrive in the light—he'll adore your work and give you twenty thousand pounds for your whole collection.

BRINDSI EY (*Sarcastic*)   Oh, yes!

CAROL   Then we can buy a super Georgian house and live what's laughingly known as happily ever after. I want to leave this place just as soon as we're married.

(CLEA *hears this. Her mouth opens wide*)

BRINDSLEY (*Nervously*) Sssh!

CAROL Why? I don't want to live in a slum for our first couple of years—like other newlyweds.

BRINDSLEY Sssh! Ssssh! . . .

CAROL What's the matter with you?

BRINDSLEY The gods listen, darling. They've given me a terrible night so far. They may do worse.

CAROL (*Cooing*) I know, darling. You've had a filthy evening. Poor babykins. But I'll fight them with you. I don't care a fig for those naughty old Goddipegs. (*Looking up*) Do you hear? Not a single little fig! (CLEA *aims at the voice and sends a jet of vodka splashing down over* CAROL) *Ahh!!!*

BRINDSLEY What is it?

CAROL It's raining!

BRINDSLEY Don't be ridiculous.

CAROL I'm all wet!

BRINDSLEY How can you be?

(CLEA *throws vodka over a wider area.* HAROLD *gets it*)

HAROLD Hey, what's going on?

BRINDSLEY What?

COLONEL What the devil's the matter with you all? What are you hollerin' for? (*He gets a slug of vodka in the face*) Ahh!!

BRINDSLEY (*Inspired*) It's a leak—the water mains must have gone now.

HAROLD Oh good God!

BRINDSLEY It must be!

(*Mischievously,* CLEA *raps her bottle on the top stair. There is a terrified silence. All look up*)

HAROLD Don't say there's someone else here.

BRINDSLEY Good Lord!

COLONEL Who's there? (*Silence from above*) Come on! I know you're there!

BRINDSLEY (*Improvising wildly*) I—I bet you it's Mrs. Punnet.

(CLEA *looks astonished*)

COLONEL Who?

BRINDSLEY (*For* CLEA'S *benefit*) Mrs. Punnet. My cleaning woman.

HAROLD Cleaning woman?

BRINDSLEY   She does for me on Mondays, Wednesdays, and Fridays.

CAROL   Well, what would she be doing here now?

BRINDSLEY   I've just remembered—she rang up and said she'd look in about six to tidy up the place.

COLONEL   Dammit, man, it's almost eleven.

HAROLD   She's not that conscientious. She couldn't be!

CAROL   Not these days!

COLONEL   Well, we'll soon see. (*Calling up*) Mrs. Punnet?

BRINDSLEY   (*Desperately*)   Don't interrupt her, sir. She doesn't like to be disturbed when she's working. Why don't we just leave her to potter around upstairs with her duster?

COLONEL   Let us first just see if it's her. Is that you, Mrs. Punnet? . . .

   (CLEA *keeps still*)

COLONEL   (*Roaring*)   MRS. PUNNET!

CLEA   (*Deciding on a cockney voice of great antiquity*)   Hello! Yes?

BRINDSLEY   (*Weakly*)   It is. Good heavens, Mrs. Punnet, what on earth are you doing up there?

CLEA   I'm just giving your bedroom a bit of a tidy, sir.

BRINDSLEY   At this time of night?

   (*The mischief in* CLEA *begins to take over*)

CLEA   Better late than never, sir, as they say. I know how you like your bedroom to be nice and inviting when you're giving one of your parties.

BRINDSLEY   Yes, yes, yes, of course . . .

COLONEL   When did you come, madam?

CLEA   Just a few minutes ago, sir. I didn't like to disturb you, so I come on up 'ere.

HAROLD   Was it you pouring all that water on us, then?

CLEA   Water? Good 'eavens, I must have upset something. It's as black as Newgate's Knocker up 'ere. Are you playing one of your saucy games, Mr. Miller?

BRINDSLEY   No, Mrs. Punnet. We've had a fuse. It's all over the house.

CLEA   Oh! A *fuse!* I thought it might be one of them saucy games in the dark, sir: Sardines or Piccadilly. The kind that end in a general squeeze-up. I know you're rather partial to kinky games, Mr. Miller, so I just wondered.

   (*She starts to come down the stairs*)

BRINDSLEY (*Distinctly*) It is a fuse, Mrs. Punnet. The man's mending it now. The lights will be on *any minute!*

CLEA Well, that'll be a relief for you, won't it?
(*She dashes the vodka accurately in his face, passes him by and comes into the room*)

BRINDSLEY Yes, of course. Now why don't you just go on home?

CLEA I'm sorry I couldn't come before, sir. I was delayed, you see. My Rosie's been taken queer again.

BRINDSLEY I quite understand!
(*He gropes around trying to hide her, but she continuously evades him*)

CLEA (*Relentlessly*) It's her tummy. There's a lump under her belly button the size of a grapefruit.

HAROLD Oh how nasty!

CLEA Horrid. Poor little Rosie. I said to her this evening, I said, "There's no good your being mulish, my girl. You're going to the hospital first thing tomorrow morning and getting yourself ultra-violated!"

BRINDSLEY Well, hadn't you better be getting back to poor little Rosie! She must need you, surely?—And there's really nothing you can do here tonight.

CLEA (*Meaningfully*) Are you sure of that, sir?

BRINDSLEY Positive, thank you.
(*They are close now*)

CLEA I mean, I know what this place can be like after one of your evenings. A gypsy caravan isn't in it. Gin bottles all over the floor! Bras and panties in the sink! And God knows what in the——
(BRINDSLEY *muzzles her with his hand. She bites it hard, and he drops to his knees in silent agony*)

COLONEL Please watch what you say, madam. You don't know it, but you're in the presence of Mr. Miller's fiancée.

CLEA Fiancée?

COLONEL Yes, and I am her father.

CLEA Well, I never . . . Oh, Mr. Miller! I'm so 'appy for you! . . . Fiancée! Oh, sir! And you never told me!

BRINDSLEY I was keeping it a surprise.

CLEA Well, I never! Oh, how lovely! . . . May I kiss you sir, please?

BRINDSLEY (*On his knees*) Well yes, yes, of course . . .

(CLEA *gropes for his ear, finds it and twists it*)

CLEA   Oh sir, I'm so pleased for you! And for *you*, Miss, too!

CAROL   Thank you.

CLEA (*To* COLONEL MELKETT)   And for *you*, sir.

COLONEL   Thank you.

CLEA   You must be Miss Clea's father.

COLONEL   Miss Clea? I don't understand.

> (*Triumphantly she sticks out her tongue at* BRINDSLEY, *who collapses his length on the floor, face down, in a gesture of total surrender. For him it is the end. The evening can hold no further disasters for him*)

CLEA (*To* CAROL)   Well, I never! So you've got him at last! Well done, Miss Clea! I never thought you would—not after four years . . .

BRINDSLEY   No—no—no—no. . . .

CLEA   Forgive me, sir, if I'm speaking out of turn, but you must admit four years is a long time to be courting one woman. Four days is stretching it a bit nowadays!

BRINDSLEY (*Weakly*)   Mrs. Punnet, *please!*

CAROL   Four years!

CLEA   Well, yes, dear. It's been all of that and a bit more really, hasn't it? (*In a stage whisper*) And of course it's just in time. It was getting a bit prominent, your little bun in the oven. (CAROL *screeches with disgust.* BRINDSLEY *covers his ears*) Oh, Miss, I don't mean that's why he popped the question. Of course it's not. He's always been stuck on you. He told me so, not one week ago, in this room. (*Sentimentally*) "Mrs. Punnet," he says, "Mrs. Punnet, as far as I'm concerned you can keep the rest of them— Miss Clea will always be on top of the heap for me." "Oh," I says, "then what about that debutante bit, Carol, the one you're always telling me about?" "Oh, 'er," he says, "she's just a bit of Knightsbridge candyfloss. A couple of licks and you've 'ad 'er."

> (*There is a long pause.* CLEA *is now sitting on the table, swinging her vodka bottle in absolute command of the situation*)

COLONEL (*Faintly; at last grappling with the situation*)   Did you say four years, madam?

CLEA (*In her own voice, quiet*)   Yes, Colonel. Four years, in this room.

HAROLD   I know that voice. It's Clea!

MISS FURNIVAL (*Surprised*)   Clea!

CAROL (*Horrified*)   Clea!

BRINDSLEY (*Unconvincingly surprised*)   Clea!

CLEA   Surprised, Brin?

CAROL   (*Understanding*)   Clea! . . .

COLONEL   I don't understand anything that's going on in this room.

CLEA   I know. It is a very odd room, isn't it? It's like a magic dark room, where everything happens the wrong way round. Rain falls indoors, the Daily comes at night and turns in a second from a nice maid into a nasty mistress.

BRINDSLEY   Be quiet, Clea!

CLEA   At last! One real word of protest! Have you finished lying, then? Have you eaten the last crumb of humble pie? Oh you coward, you bloody coward! Just because you didn't want to marry me, did you have to settle for this lot?

CAROL   Marry!

COLONEL   Marry?

CLEA   Four years of meaning to end in this triviality! Miss Laughingly Known As and her Daddipegs!

CAROL   Stop her! She's disgusting.

COLONEL   How can I, for God's sake?

CAROL   Well, where's all that bloody resource you keep talking about?

(*The* COLONEL *goes to her but takes* CLEA's *hand by mistake*)

COLONEL   Now calm down, Dumpling. Keep your head . . . There —hold my hand, that's it, now Daddy's here. Everything is under control. All right?

CLEA   Are you sure that is your daughter's hand you're holding, Colonel?

COLONEL   What? Carol, isn't this your hand?

CAROL   No.

CLEA   You must have lived with your daughter for well over twenty years, Colonel. What remarkable use you've made of your eyes.

(*There is another pause. The* COLONEL *moves away in embarrassment*)

CLEA (*Wickedly*)   All right! Kinky game time! . . . Let's all play Guess the Hand.

HAROLD   Oh good God!

CLEA   Or would you rather Guess the Lips, Harold?

CAROL   How disgusting!

CLEA   Well, that's me, dear. (CAROL's *accent*) I'm Queen Disgustipegs! (*She seizes* CAROL's *hand and puts it into* HAROLD's) Who's that?

CAROL   I don't know.

CLEA   Guess.

CAROL   I don't know, and I don't care.

CLEA   Oh go on. Have a go!

CAROL   It's Brin, of course: You can't trick me like that! It's Brindsley's stupid hand.

HAROLD   I'm afraid you're wrong. It's me.

CAROL (*Struggling*)   It's not. You're lying.

HAROLD (*Holding on*)   I'm not. I don't lie.

CAROL   You're lying! . . . You're lying!

HAROLD   I'm not.

> (CAROL *breaks away and blunders across the room. She is becoming hysterical*)

CLEA   You try it, Harold. Take the hand on your right.

HAROLD   I'm not playing. It's a bloody silly game.

CLEA   Go on . . . (*She seizes his hand and puts it into* BRINDSLEY's) Well?

HAROLD   It's Brin.

BRINDSLEY   Yes.

CLEA   Well done!

> (*She sits on the low stool*)

CAROL (*Outraged*)   How does he know that? How does *he* know your hand and I don't?

BRINDSLEY   Calm down, Carol.

CAROL   Answer me! I want to know!

BRINDSLEY   Stop it!

CAROL   I won't!

BRINDSLEY   You're getting hysterical!

CAROL   Leave me alone! I want to go home.

> (*And suddenly* MISS FURNIVAL *gives a sharp short scream and blunders out through the curtains*)

MISS FURNIVAL   Prams! Prams! Prams—in the supermarket! . . . (*They all freeze. She is evidently out of control in a world of her own fears. She speaks quickly and strangely*) All those hideous wire prams full of babies and bottles—cornflakes over there, is all they say—and then they leave you to yourself. Biscuits over there—cat food over there—fish cakes over there

—Airwick over there. Pink stamps, green stamps, free balloons
—television dinners—pay as you go out—oh, Daddy it's awful!
And then the Godless ones, the heathens in their leather jackets
—laughing me to scorn! But, not for long. Oh, no! Who shall
stand when He appeareth? He'll strike them from their motor-
cycles! He'll dash their helmets to the ground! Yea, verily, I say
unto thee—there shall be an end of gasoline! An end to cigarette
puffing and jostling with hips . . . Keep off . . . Keep off! Keep
off . . .

    (*She runs drunkenly across the room and collides with*
HAROLD)

HAROLD   Come on, Ferny, I think it's time we went home.

MISS FURNIVAL (*Pulling herself together*) Yes. You're quite right
   . . . (*With an attempt at grandeur*) I'm sorry I can't stay any
   longer, Mr. Miller; but your millionaire is unpardonably late. So
   typical of modern manners . . . Express my regrets, if you please.

BRINDSLEY   Certainly. (*Leaning heavily on* HAROLD's *arms she*
   leaves the room. He shuts the door after them) Thank you, Clea.
   Thank you very much.

CLEA   Any time.

BRINDSLEY   You had no right.

CLEA   No?

BRINDSLEY   *You* walked out on *me*.
   (*He joins her on the low stool*)

CLEA   Is that what I did?

BRINDSLEY   You said you never wanted to see me again.

CLEA   I never saw you at all—how could you be walked out on?
   You should live in the dark, Brindsley. It's your natural element.

BRINDSLEY   Whatever that means.

CLEA   It means you don't really want to be seen. Why is that,
   Brindsley? Do you think if someone really saw you, they would
   never love you?

BRINDSLEY   Oh go away.

CLEA   I want to know.

BRINDSLEY   Yes, you always want to know. Pick-pick-pick away!
   Why is *that*, Clea? Have you ever thought why you need to do
   it? Well?

CLEA   Perhaps because I care about you.

BRINDSLEY   Perhaps there's nothing to care about. Just a fake artist.

CLEA   Stop pitying yourself. It's always your vice. I told you when
   I met you: you could either be a good artist, or a chic fake. You
   didn't like it, because I refused just to give you applause.

BRINDSLEY God knows, you certainly did that!

CLEA Is that what *she* gives you? Twenty hours of ego-massage every day?

BRINDSLEY At least our life together isn't the replica of the Holy Inquisition you made of ours. I didn't have an affair with you: it was just four years of nooky with Torquemada!

CLEA And don't say you didn't enjoy it!

BRINDSLEY Enjoy it? I hated every second of it.

CLEA Yes, I remember.

BRINDSLEY Every second.

CLEA I recall.

BRINDSLEY When you left for Finland, it was the happiest day of my life.

CLEA Mine, too!

BRINDSLEY I sighed with relief.

CLEA So did I.

BRINDSLEY I went out dancing that very night.

CLEA So did I. It was out with the lyre and the timbrel.

BRINDSLEY Good. Then that's all right.

CLEA Fine.

BRINDSLEY Super!

CLEA Duper!

BRINDSLEY It's lovely to see you looking so happy.

CLEA You too. Radiant with self-fulfilment.

(*A pause*)

BRINDSLEY If you felt like this, why did you come back?

CLEA If *you* felt like this, why did you tell Mrs. Punnet I was still at the top of the heap?

BRINDSLEY I never said that!

CLEA You did.

BRINDSLEY Never.

CLEA You *did!*

BRINDSLEY Of course I didn't. You invented that ten minutes ago, when you were *playing* Mrs. Punnet.

CLEA I—Oh! So I did! . . .

(*They both giggle. She falls happily against his shoulder*)

BRINDSLEY You know something—I'm not sure she's not right.

(*During this exchange the* COLONEL *and his daughter have been standing frozen with astonished anger. Now the Father takes over*)

COLONEL No doubt this is very funny to you two.

CLEA It is, quite, actually.

COLONEL   I'm not so easily amused, however, madam.

BRINDSLEY   Now look, Colonel—

COLONEL   Hold your tongue, sir, I'm talking. Do you know what would have happened to a young man in my day who dared to treat a girl the way you have treated my Dumpling?

BRINDSLEY   Well, I assume, Colonel—

COLONEL   Hold your tongue, I'm talking.

CAROL   Oh, leave it, Daddy. Let's just go home.

COLONEL   In a moment, Dumpling. Kindly leave this to me.

BRINDSLEY   Look, Carol, I can explain—

CAROL   Explain what?

BRINDSLEY   It's impossible here.

COLONEL   You understate, sir.

BRINDSLEY   Carol, you don't understand.

CAROL   What the hell's there to understand? All the time you were going with me, she was in the background—that's all there is to it—What were you doing? Weighing us up? . . . Here!

   (*She pulls off her engagement ring*)

BRINDSLEY   What?

CAROL   Your ring. Take the bloody thing back!

   (*She throws it. It hits the* COLONEL *in the eye*)

COLONEL   My eye! My damned eye! (CLEA *starts to laugh again. In mounting fury, clutching his eye*) Oh very droll, madam! Very droll indeed! Laugh your fill! Miller! I asked you a question. Do you know what would have happened to a young lout like you in my day?

BRINDSLEY   Happened, sir?

COLONEL   (*Quietly*)   You'd have been thrashed, sir.

BRINDSLEY (*Nervous*)   Thrashed—

   (*The man of war begins to go after him, feeling his way in the dark—like some furious robot.*)

COLONEL   You'd have felt the mark of a father's horsewhip across your seducer's shoulders. You'd have gone down on your cad's bended knees, and begged my daughter's pardon for the insults you've offered her tonight.

BRINDSLEY   (*Retreating before the* COLONEL's *groping advance*) Would I, sir?

COLONEL   You'd have raised your guttersnipe voice in a piteous scream for mercy and forgiveness!

   (*A terrible scream is heard from the hall. They freeze, listening as it comes nearer and nearer, then the door is flung open*

and HAROLD *plunges into the room. He is wild-eyed with*
rage: a lit and bent taper shakes in his furious hand)

HAROLD   Ooooooh! You villain!

BRINDSLEY   Harold—

HAROLD   You skunky, conniving little villain!

BRINDSLEY   What's the matter?

HAROLD   (*Raging*)   Have you seen the state of my room? My room?
My lovely room, the most elegant and cared for in this entire
district?—one chair turned absolutely upside down, one chair
on top of another like a Portobello junk-shop! And that's not all,
is it, Brindsley? Oh no, that's not the worst by a long chalk, is it,
Brindsley?

BRINDSLEY   Long chalk?

HAROLD   Don't play the innocent with me. I thought I had a friend
living here all these years. I didn't know I was living opposite
a Light-fingered Lenny!

BRINDSLEY   Harold!—

HAROLD   (*Hysterical*)   This is my reward, isn't it?—After years of
looking after you, sweeping and tidying up this place, because
you're too much of a slut to do it for yourself—to have my best
pieces stolen from me to impress your new girl friend and her
daddy. Or did she help you?

BRINDSLEY   Harold, it was an emergency.

HAROLD   Don't talk to me: I don't want to know! I know what you
think of me now . . . "Don't tell Harold about the engagement.
He's not to be trusted. He's not a friend. He's just someone to
steal things from!"

BRINDSLEY   You know that's not true.

HAROLD   (*Shrieking—in one hysterical breath*)   I know I was the
last one to know—that's what I know! I have to find it out in a
room full of strangers. Me, who's listened to more of your mis-
eries in the small hours of the morning than anyone else would
put up with! All your boring talk about women, hour after hour,
as if no one's got troubles but you!—

CLEA   She's getting hysterical, dear. Ignore her.

HAROLD   It's you who's going to be ignored, Clea. (*To* BRINDSLEY)
As for you, all I can say about your engagement is this: you deserve each other, you and that little nit.

   (CAROL *gives a shriek*)

BRINDSLEY   Carol!

HAROLD   Oh, so you're there, are you?—Skulking in the shadows!

BRINDSLEY   Leave her alone!

HAROLD   I'm not going to touch her. I just want my things and I'll be off. Did you hear me, Brindsley? You give me my things now, or I'll call the police.

BRINDSLEY   Don't be ridiculous.

HAROLD   (*Grimly*) Item: One lyre-back Regency chair, in lacquered mahogany with Ormolu inlay and appliqué work on the cushions.

BRINDSLEY   In front of you.

> (*He thrusts the taper at it*)

HAROLD   Ta. Item: One half-back sofa—likewise Regency—supported by claw legs and upholstered in a rich silk of bottle green to match the aforesaid chair.

BRINDSLEY   In the studio.

HAROLD   Unbelievable! Item: One Coalport vase, dated 1809, decorated on the rim with a pleasing design of daisies and peonies.

BRINDSLEY   On the floor.

HAROLD   Ta. (BRINDSLEY *hands it to him*) Ooooh! You've even taken the flowers! I'll come back for the chair and sofa in a minute. (*Drawing himself up with all the offended dignity of which a* HAROLD GORRINGE *is capable*) This is the end of our relationship, Brindsley. We won't be speaking again, I don't think.(*He twitches his raincoat off the table. Inside it, of course, is the Buddha, which falls on the floor and smashes beyond repair. There is a terrible silence. Trying to keep his voice under control*) Do you know what that statue was worth? Do you? More money than you'll ever see in your whole life, even if you sell every piece of that nasty, rusty rubbish. (*With the quietness of the mad*) I think I'm going to have to smash you, Brindsley.

BRINDSLEY   (*Nervously*) Now steady on, Harold . . . don't be rash . . .

HAROLD   Yes, I'm very much afraid I'll have to smash you . . . Smash for smash—that's fair do's. (*He pulls one of the long metal prongs out of the sculpture*) Smash for smash. Smash for smash!

> (*Insanely he advances on* BRINDSLEY *holding the prong like a sword, the taper burning in his other hand*)

BRINDSLEY   (*Retreating*) Stop it, Harold. You've gone mad!

COLONEL   Well done, sir. I think it's time for the reckoning.

> (*The* COLONEL *grabs the other prong and also advances*)

BRINDSLEY   (*Retreating from them both*) Now just a minute, Colonel. Be reasonable! . . . Let's not revert to savages! . . . Harold, I appeal to you—you've always had civilized instincts! Don't join the Army! . . .

CAROL (*Grimly advancing also*) Get him, Daddy! Get him! Get him!

BRINDSLEY (*Horrified at her*) Carol!

CAROL (*Malevolently*) Get him! Get him! Get him! Get . . .

BRINDSLEY *Clea!*

(CLEA *leaps up and blows out the taper. Lights up*)

COLONEL Dammit! (CLEA *grabs* BRINDSLEY's *hand and pulls him out of danger. To* CLEA) Careful, my little Dumpling. Keep out of the way.

HAROLD (*To* CAROL) Hush up, Colonel. We'll be able to hear them breathing.

COLONEL Clever idea! Smart tactics, sir!

(*Silence. They listen.* BRINDSLEY *climbs carefully onto the table and silently pulls* CLEA *up after him.* HAROLD *and the* COLONEL, *prodding and slashing the darkness with their swords, grimly hunt their quarry. Twenty seconds. Suddenly, with a bang* SCHUPPANZIGH *opens the trap from below. Both men advance on it warily. The electrician disappears again below. They have almost reached it, on tiptoe, when there is another crash—this time from the hall. Someone has again tripped over the milk bottles.* HAROLD *and the* COLONEL *immediately swing round and start stalking in the other direction, still on tiptoe. Enter* GEORG BAMBERGER. *He is quite evidently a millionaire. Dressed in the Gulbenkian manner, he wears a beard, an eyeglass, a frock coat, a top hat and an orchid. He carries a large deaf aid. Bewildered, he advances into the room. Stealthily, the two armed men stalk him as he silently gropes his way along and passes between them*)

BAMBERGER (*Speaking in a middle-aged German voice, as near to the voice of* SCHUPPANZIGH *as possible*) Hello, please! Mr. Miller?

(HAROLD *and the* COLONEL *spin round in a third direction*)

HAROLD Oh, it's the electrician!

BAMBERGER Hello, please?

COLONEL What the devil are you doing up here? (SCHUPPANZIGH *appears at the trap*) Have you mended the fuse?

HAROLD Or are you going to keep us in the dark all night?

SCHUPPANZIGH Don't worry. The fuse is mended.

(*He comes out of the trap.* BAMBERGER *goes round to the right*)

HAROLD   Thank God for that.

BAMBERGER (*Still groping around*)   Hallo, please? Mr. Miller— vere are you? Vy zis darkness? Is a joke, yes?

SCHUPPANZIGH (*Incensed*)   Ah, no! That is not very funny, good people—just because I am a foreigner, to imitate my voice. You English can be the rudest people on earth!

BAMBERGER (*Imperiously*)   Mr. Miller! I have come here to give attention to your sculptures!

SCHUPPANZIGH   *Gott in himmel!*

BAMBERGER   *Gott in himmel!*

BRINDSLEY   God, it's him! Bamberger!

CLEA   He's come!

HAROLD   Bamberger!

COLONEL   Bamberger!

(*They freeze. The millionaire sets off, left, toward the open trap*)

BRINDSLEY   Don't worry, Mr. Bamberger. We've had a fuse, but it's mended now.

BAMBERGER (*Irritably*)   Mr. Miller!

CLEA   You'll have to speak up. He's deaf.

BRINDSLEY (*Shouting*)   Don't worry, Mr. Bamberger! We've had a fuse but it's all right now! . . . (*Standing on the table, he clasps* CLEA *happily.* BAMBERGER *misses the trap by inches*) Oh, Clea, that's true. Everything's all right now! Just in the nick of time!

(*But as he says this* BAMBERGER *turns and falls into the open trap door,* SCHUPPANZIGH *slams it to with his foot*)

SCHUPPANZIGH   So! Here's now an end to your troubles! Like Jehovah in the Sacred Testament, I give you the most miraculous gift of the Creation! Light!

CLEA   Light!

BRINDSLEY   Oh, thank God. *Thank God!*

(SCHUPPANZIGH *goes to the switch*)

HAROLD (*Grimly*)   I wouldn't thank Him too soon, Brindsley, if I were you!

COLONEL   Nor would I, Brindsley, if I were you!

CAROL   Nor would I, Brinnie Winnie, if I were you!

SCHUPPANZIGH (*Grandly*)   Then thank *me!* For I shall play God for this second! (*Clapping his hands*) Attend all of you. God said: "Let there be light!" And there was, good people, suddenly!

—astoundingly!—instantaneously!—inconceivably—inexhaust-ibly—inextinguishably and eternally—LIGHT!

(SCHUPPANZIGH, *with a great flourish, flicks the light switch. Instant darkness. The turntable of the phonograph starts up again, and with an exultant crash the Sousa march falls on the audience—and blazes away in the black*)

End

Visitor from Mamaroneck

from *Plaza Suite*

BY

Neil Simon

Neil Simon

In less than a decade Neil Simon has risen to the theatrical summit as America's foremost writer of comedies. The roseate series of events began in 1961 with his first Broadway play, *Come Blow Your Horn*, which ran for 677 performances. This was followed by the book for the musical *Little Me* (1962); *Barefoot in the Park* (1963); *The Odd Couple* (1965); the musical *Sweet Charity* (1966); and *The Star-Spangled Girl* (1966).

When *Plaza Suite* opened on February 14, 1968, it was immediately apparent that Mr. Simon had added another golden link to his extraordinary chain of successes. It is the opening play of this trio of short comedies (each transpires, at different times, in the identical suite at the Plaza Hotel, New York) that appears in this anthology.

Mr. Simon was born in the Bronx, New York, on July 4, 1927. He attended New York University and the University of Denver. His first theatrical affiliation came as a sketch writer (in collaboration with his brother Danny) for resort revues at Camp Tamiment, Pennsylvania. From there he moved on to television, supplying material to Sid Caesar, Phil Silvers and other comedians. An accomplished hand at pointed comedy, Mr. Simon later contributed sketches to two Broadway revues, *Catch a Star* (1955) and *New Faces of 1956*.

During the season of 1966–67 Mr. Simon had four hit shows (*Barefoot in the Park, The Odd Couple, Sweet Charity* and *The Star-Spangled Girl*) running concurrently on Broadway—and as this is being written he is represented by two of New York's leading successes, *Plaza Suite* and the musical—based on the film *The Apartment—Promises, Promises*.

In 1965 he won the Tony Award for best author for *The Odd Couple*, and in 1968 he was the recipient of the Sam S. Shubert Award in recognition of his outstanding contribution to the American theatre.

The author recently completed an original screenplay, *The Out-*

of-Towners (to co-star Jack Lemmon and Sandy Dennis) and in December, 1969, his newest comedy, tentatively titled *The Last of the Red Hot Lovers* will open on Broadway under the auspices of Saint Subber.

Plaza Suite was first presented on February 14, 1968, by Saint Subber at the Plymouth Theater, New York City. The cast of *Visitor from Mamaroneck* was as follows:

(*In order of appearance*)

BELLHOP	Bob Balaban
KAREN NASH	Maureen Stapleton
SAM NASH	George C. Scott
WAITER	Jose Ocasio
JEAN MCCORMACK	Claudette Nevins

Directed by MIKE NICHOLS
Scenic Production by OLIVER SMITH
Lighting by JEAN ROSENTHAL
Costumes by PATRICIA ZIPPRODT

VISITOR FROM MAMARONECK

The scene: A suite at the Plaza Hotel on the seventh floor, over-looking Central Park. The set is divided into two rooms. The room at stage right is the living room. It is a well-appointed room, taste-fully furnished with an entrance door at the extreme right and windows that look out over the park. A door leads into the bed-room, which has a large double bed, etc., and a door that leads to the bathroom. The room also contains a large closet.

It is about four in the afternoon in mid-December. The door of the suite opens and a BELLHOP *enters and switches on the lights in the living room. He carries one small overnight bag.*

KAREN NASH *enters behind him. She wears a six-year-old mink coat which could use a bit of restyling, and a pair of galoshes. Un-derneath she wears an expensive suit which unfortunately looked better on the model in Bendel's than it does on* KAREN. KAREN *is forty-eight years old, and she makes no bones about it. C'est la vie. She is a pleasant, affable woman who has let weight and age take their natural course. A mink hat is plopped down on her head. She carries a box from Bendel's with her afternoon's purchases and a small bouquet of flowers.*

The BELLHOP *closes a half-open window in the living room, switches on the lights and puts the bag on the luggage tray.* KAREN *looks around the living room, crosses to the bedroom and puts her packages down on a chair. The* BELLHOP *goes to the bathroom and turns a light on in there.*

KAREN *follows him to the bathroom. The* BELLHOP *comes out of the bathroom, crosses the living room, opens the door to leave and hesitates in the doorway.*

BELLHOP   Everything all right, ma'am?
KAREN   Wait a minute, I want to make sure this is the right room.
   (*She crosses back into the living room*) I know this is Suite 719, but was it always 719?

BELLHOP   Yes, ma'am—719.

KAREN   No, you don't understand. I know sometimes hotels change the numbers around, and this could have been 723 or 715. And it's very important I get 719.

(*She returns to the bedroom for the flowers*)

BELLHOP   I'm here two years, it's always been 719.

KAREN   Because you know about 826 at the Savoy-Plaza?

BELLHOP   No, ma'am.

KAREN   (*Unwrapping the flowers at a table behind the sofa in the living room*)   Oh, well, they had a famous murder in 826. Then the next year there was a fire, and the year after that a husband and a wife committed suicide. Then no one wanted 826. So they turned it into a linen closet. It's a fact, there is no more 826 at the Savoy-Plaza.

BELLHOP   There's no more Savoy-Plaza either. They tore it down two years ago.

KAREN   (*Looks at him incredulously, then goes to look out the window*)   Oh, my God, look at that. There's no Savoy-Plaza . . . What's that monstrosity?

BELLHOP   It's the new General Motors building.

KAREN   (*Still looking out the window*)   Shows you how often I get into the city. Well, listen, that's what they're doing today. If it's old and it's beautiful, it's not there in the morning . . .

BELLHOP   (*Indicating the other windows*)   Well, you still have a nice view from here.

KAREN   (*Crosses to the other windows and looks out*)   Mmmm, for how long? I guarantee you Central Park comes down in five years.

BELLHOP   You think so?

KAREN   (*Starts to put the flowers in a vase on the sofa table*)   I *know* so. Five years from now you'll look out this window and you'll see one little tree and the world's largest A and P.

BELLHOP   I don't think I'll be working here five years from now.

KAREN   You mean the rumor is true?

BELLHOP   What rumor?

KAREN   That the Plaza is coming down too!

BELLHOP   *This* Plaza?

KAREN   (*Puts the vase on the chest between the windows*)   I don't want to worry you or anything. It's just a rumor. No one knows for sure . . . But it's definitely coming down.

BELLHOP   I didn't hear that.

KAREN   (*Crossing to the bedroom, she takes a bag from the luggage*

rack and puts it on the dresser in front of the bedroom window)
Well, I'm sure they want to keep it quiet from the staff. The story
is that they're going to tear down the Plaza and put up a fifty-
two-story luxury hotel.

BELLHOP   Why? *This* is a luxury hotel.

KAREN   Yeah, but it's an *old* luxury hotel. Today it has to be new.
Old is no good any more. (*Picks up the phone on the chest in the
living room*) Well, all I really care about is tonight.

BELLHOP   Yes, ma'am. Is there anything else?

KAREN   Oh, wait a minute. (*She puts down the phone, runs to the
bedroom for her purse and looks for change*) Don't tell me I don't
have any change.

BELLHOP   That's all right, ma'am.

KAREN (*Crossing back into the living room*)   It's not all right. This
is your living. (*Takes out a dollar bill*) Here you are.

BELLHOP (*Taking it*)   Thank you very much.

KAREN   I'll be honest with you. I don't usually give dollar tips.
But it's my anniversary. So I can be a sport.

BELLHOP (*With his hand on the door. He'd really like to go*)   Oh,
well, congratulations.

KAREN   Thank you, dear. Twenty-four years ago tonight I spent
my honeymoon in this room. This *is* 719, isn't it.

BELLHOP   Yes, ma'am—719.

KAREN   I bet you weren't even born twenty-four years ago, right?

BELLHOP   No, I was born . . .

KAREN   You know what I was? I was twenty-five. You know what
that makes me today? . . . Some old lady.

BELLHOP   Well, you certainly don't look like an old lady. (*Smiles*)
. . . Well . . . have a pleasant stay, ma'am . . . and happy anniversary.

   (*He starts out the door*)

KAREN   Thank you dear . . . and take my advice. Don't rush . . . but
look around for another job. (*The* BELLHOP *nods and exits.* KAREN
*crosses to the bedroom and looks at herself in the full-length
mirror on the closet door. She takes off her hat and puts it on the
dresser*) . . . You are definitely some old lady. (*She crosses to the
phone on the night table next to the bed, takes it and sits on the
bed, still wearing her mink coat*) . . . Room service, please. (*She
groans as she bends over to take off the galoshes*) . . . Ohhhhh . . .
(*Into the phone*) . . . No, operator. I was groaning to myself . . .
(*Taking off her coat*) Hello, room service? . . . Listen, room
service, this is Mrs. Sam Nash in Suite 719 . . . I would like a nice

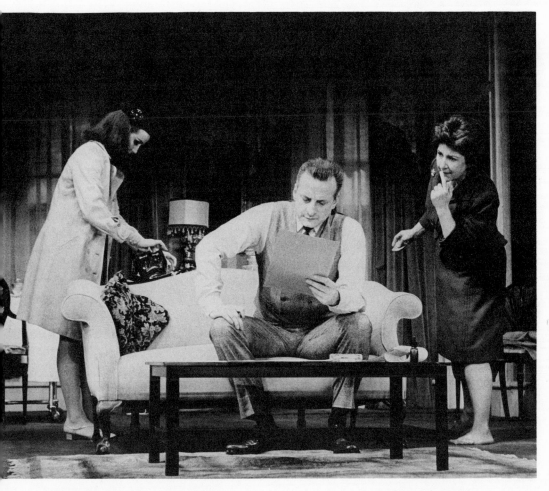

VISITOR FROM MAMARONECK   *Martha Swope*

cold bottle of champagne . . . That sounds good, is it French? . . .
with two glasses and a tray of assorted hors d'oeuvres . . . but
listen, room service. I don't want any anchovies . . . They always
give you anchovy patties with the hors d'oeuvres and my husband doesn't eat anchovies and I hate them, so don't give me any
anchovies . . . Instead of the anchovies, give me some extra
smoked salmon, or you can split them up . . . half smoked salmon
and half caviar . . . That's right. Mrs. Nash. 719 . . . No anchovies
. . . (*She hangs up*) They'll give me anchovies. (*She puts the
phone back on the night table*) Look at that. No more Savoy-
Plaza. (*Starts to take off the galoshes again. The telephone rings.
There is one in each room. She gets up and picks up the one
next to the bed*) Hello . . . (*The phone in the living room rings
again. Hastily she hangs up the bedroom phone and rushes to
answer it*) Hello? . . . Oh, Sam. Where are you? . . . Good. Come
up. I'm here . . . What room do you think? . . . 719 . . . Remember? 719? Suite 719 . . . That's right! (*She hangs up*) He doesn't
remember . . . (*She rushes to the Bendel box and takes out a
sheer negligée. She crosses to the mirror on the closet door and
looks at herself with the negligée in front of her. She is not completely enchanted. The telephone rings. She puts down the
negligée and rushes to the living room to answer it*) Hello
. . . (*The phone in the bedroom rings again. She hastily hangs up
the living room phone and rushes to answer it*) Hello? . . . Oh,
hello, Miss McCormack. . . . No, he's not, dear. He's on his way
up. Yes, I will . . . It's not important, is it? . . . Well, he seemed so
tired lately, I was hoping he wouldn't have to think about work
tonight. (*Glancing down at her feet*) . . . Oh, my God, I still have
my galoshes on . . . All right, I'll tell him to call. Yes, when he
comes in. Good-by. (*She hangs up and quickly bends over in an
effort to remove her galoshes. She is having difficulty. The doorbell rings*) . . . Oh, damn it. (*Calls out*) Just a minute! (*The doorbell rings again. She is having much trouble with the right
galosh*) . . . You had to wear galoshes today, right? (*She pulls
her right galosh off but her shoe remains in it. The doorbell rings
impatiently*) Oh, for God's sakes . . . (*She tries to pull her shoe
out of the galosh but it is imbedded in there*) All right, all right,
I'm coming. (*She throws down the galosh with the shoe still in
one galosh and her stockinged foot. She crosses into the living
room*) Look at this, my twenty-fourth anniversary. (*She "limps"
to the door and opens it.* SAM *stands there.* SAM *has just turned
fifty but has made every effort to conceal it. He is trim, impec-*

cably neat. His clothes are well tailored, although a bit on the junior-executive side. He carries an attaché case, a fine leather Gucci product. Everything about SAM *is measured, efficient, economic. She smiles warmly*) Hello, Sam.

    (SAM *walks brusquely past her, surveying the room*)

SAM An hour and fifteen minutes I was in the goddamned dentist's chair . . .

    (*He puts down his attaché case on the chair downstage of the door to the bedroom, and takes off his coat*)

KAREN (*Closes the door, still warmly*) How do you feel, Sam?

SAM Between his lousy jokes and WQXR-FM, I got some headache. (*He crosses to the mirror over the chest in the living room and looks at his teeth*) Did anyone call?

KAREN Sam, do you remember this room?

    (*Moving to him*)

SAM (*Still examining his teeth*) Well, two more caps and I'm through. (*He turns, baring his teeth at her*) What do you think?

KAREN (*Put her hands in front of her eyes to shield the glare*) Ooh, dazzling!

SAM You don't think they're too white, do you? (*Turns and looks in the mirror again*) Do they look too white to you?

KAREN No, no. Perfect. Very nice with the blue shirt.

SAM (*Still looking*) These don't stain, you know. A hundred years from now when I'm dead and buried, they'll be the same color.

KAREN Oh, good. You'll look wonderful. You don't remember this room, do you?

SAM (*Looks at his watch*) Four thirty already? The meeting must be over . . . Didn't anyone call?

    (*Takes his coat and attaché case into the bedroom, putting the coat on the chest and the case on the bed*)

KAREN Miss McCormack, from the office . . . She wants you to call back.

SAM (*Looks at her, annoyed*) Why didn't you tell me?

KAREN We were busy talking about your white teeth. Happy anniversary, Sam.

    (*Picks up a vase and crosses to the bedroom*)

SAM (*Not hearing her, into the phone*) Judson 6-5900 . . . What did you say? (*Sees her limp into the bedroom*) What's the matter with your leg?

KAREN (*Limps into the bathroom*) One is shorter than the other. Didn't you ever notice that? I've had it for years.

SAM (*Into the phone*) Lorraine? Mr. Nash. Let me have Miss McCormack, please. (SAM *looks at himself in the closet mirror*) . . . Well, that kills my barber's appointment today. Oh, could I use five minutes under the sun lamp. (*Into the phone.* KAREN *begins to sing in the bathroom*) Miss McCormack? Did Henderson call? . . . Did he send the contracts? (*Places his hand over his ear to shut out* KAREN's *singing*) . . . What about Nizer? . . . I see . . . (*He quickly takes a note pad from the night table and places it on the attaché case on the bed in front of him. He can't find a pencil. He snaps his fingers at* KAREN. *Still into the phone*) What does it look like? . . . Ah huh . . . ah huh . . . (*He snaps his fingers at* KAREN *again*) A pencil . . . pencil . . . (KAREN, *rushing in from the bathroom, searches through the night tables on both sides of the bed and dresser.* SAM *is still on the phone*) Very good. All right, give me the figures. (*He nods into the phone.* KAREN *still can't find a pencil. She limps hurriedly over to her purse on the sofa table in the living room.* SAM, *into the phone*) . . . It sounds right, but I've got to go over the estimates . . . Tomorrow morning? That doesn't give us much time . . . Wait a minute, give me those figures again . . . (*He puts his hand over the phone, and whispers angrily*) Karen, for God's sakes, *a pencil!* (KAREN *is frantically looking through her purse.* SAM, *into the phone*) . . . One seventy-five escalating up to three and a quarter . . . (KAREN *takes a lipstick out of her purse and hobbles quickly to* SAM. *She hands it to him*) Hold it. (*He writes on the pad*) One seventy-five up to three and a quarter . . . (*He stops writing and looks at* KAREN) That's a lipstick.

KAREN (*Taking the empty Bendel box from the chair*) I don't have a pencil.

SAM Then why do you give me a lipstick?

KAREN Because I don't have a pencil. It's shocking pink but it writes.

    (*Puts the box into the wastebasket next to the dresser*)

SAM (*He glares at her. Into the phone*) All right, I'm going to go over my figures here. If Henderson calls or the contracts come in, bring them right over. What's that? (*He laughs*) Yes! Well, it's like we were saying the other night, it's the old badger game. (*He laughs again.* KAREN *mocks his private joke with* MISS MC-CORMACK *as she hobbles back into the bedroom*) . . . All right, I'll speak to you later. And thank you, Miss McCormack. (*He hangs up*) A hundred and seventy-five thousand dollar contract, you give me a lipstick.

(Puts the lipstick down on the table next to the chair)

KAREN *(Hobbles out of the bathroom with the vase)* I'd have given you blood but it isn't blue.

SAM All right, don't test me, because I've got enough of a headache. *(He rubs his eyes with his thumb and index finger, opens the case and takes out a bottle of aspirin. She limps into the living room and places the vase on the desk. He looks at her)* And for God's sakes, Karen, stop hobbling around. I don't feel like listening to thump, thump, thump!

KAREN *(She sighs)* And happy anniversary to you.

SAM What?

KAREN Forget it.
(Sits at the desk and takes off her other galosh and shoe)

SAM *(Moving to the bathroom with the aspirin)* What are you talking about? . . . It's not our anniversary.

KAREN Today is December fourteenth, isn't it?

SAM Yes.

KAREN So. We're married twenty-four years today.

SAM *(Looks at her incredulously)* Are you serious?

KAREN We're not married twenty-four years today?

SAM No.
(Comes out of the bathroom with a glass of water and takes an aspirin)

KAREN We're not married twenty-four years?

SAM No.

KAREN . . . We're not married?

SAM Tomorrow is our anniversary and we're married twenty-three years.
(Puts the glass down on the dresser and moves into the living room)

KAREN *(Looks at him)* . . . Are you sure?

SAM What do you mean, am I sure? I know when our anniversary is. December fifteenth, we're married twenty-three years. How can you make a mistake like that?

KAREN All right, don't get so excited, and it's not such a big mistake because I didn't get you a present . . . You're sure it's not the fourteenth?

SAM I go through this with you every year. When it comes to money or dates or ages, you are absolutely unbelievable. *(Turns, exasperated, and goes to the bedroom)* We were married December fifteenth, nineteen forty-five . . .

KAREN Then I'm right. Twenty-*four* years.

SAM Forty-five from sixty-eight is *twenty-three!*

KAREN Then I'm wrong. (*Shrugs*) Math isn't one of my best subjects.

SAM (*Hanging his jacket over the dresser chair*) This isn't math, this is people's *lives!* (*Moves back to* KAREN) How old are you?

KAREN What?

SAM It's a simple question. How old are you?

KAREN (*She's reluctant to answer and moves to the window*) I don't want to play.

SAM I can't believe it. You really don't know how old you are.

KAREN I know how old I am. But you get me nervous. Promise you won't leave me if I'm wrong . . . I'll be forty-nine in April. (SAM *stares at her in disbelief, crosses back into the bedroom and wearily leans against the closet door.* KAREN *follows him*) . . . Isn't that right?

SAM No, but you're close.

KAREN I'm not going to be forty-nine?

SAM Not *this* April. *This* April you're going to be forty-eight. How the hell can you make a mistake like that? Can't you add? (*Taking several contracts out of the attaché case*)

KAREN All right, don't talk to me like I'm a child. I'm a forty-eight-year-old woman.

SAM But the thing that infuriates me is that you make the mistake the wrong way. Why don't you make yourself younger instead of older, the way other women do?

KAREN Okay, I'm forty-seven. (*Throws herself on the bed and poses sexily*) So how do I look to you now?

SAM I've got work to do. I've got a very important meeting at eight o'clock in the morning. (*Crosses to the desk and sits*)

KAREN (*Sitting up in bed*) Oh, come on, Sam, where's your sense of humor? I think it's cute as hell that I don't know how old I am.

SAM (*Starts to look over the papers*) I can't even think straight. I've had five meetings this morning, four teeth capped, and I haven't even had my Metrecal. (*He crosses to the phone in the living room*) I'd better eat something. (*Picks up the phone*)

KAREN I just ordered hors d'oeuvres.

SAM Not for me. You know I'm on nine hundred calories a day. (*Into the phone*) Room service, please. (*He turns and looks in the mirror*) . . . My God, who the hell is that? Will you look at my eyes? I have no pupils left. (*He turns to* KAREN) Come here. Look at this. Do you see any pupils?

KAREN (*Crosses and looks into the mirror*)   Yes, Sam. I see two gorgeous pupils . . .

SAM (*Still looking in the mirror*)   Where? Where? I don't have a pupil in my head. Would you get my eye drops out of the case . . .

KAREN (*Crossing to the case on the bed*)   I think you've been overworking, Sam. I haven't seen you two nights this month.

SAM (*Stretches his arms*)   I really could use some sun. And about a month of sleep.

KAREN (*Searching through the case*)   Hey, why don't we go down to Jamaica for a couple weeks? Just the two of us. We haven't done that in years.

SAM (*Into the phone, pacing*)   Oh, hello, room service, where were you? . . . Listen, I'd like a plate of cold roast beef, medium rare, very lean. You know what very lean is? . . . No, it doesn't mean no fat . . . It means *absolutely* no fat . . . and I want a salad, *no dressing,* a half grapefruit and a pot of black coffee . . . And I'd appreciate it as soon as possible . . . Wait a second. (*To* KAREN, *who has entered the living room with eye drops*) Where are we again?

KAREN   719, Plaza Hotel, New York, twenty-three, New York.

SAM (*Into the phone*)   719 . . . As soon as you can. (*He hangs up, moves down to* KAREN *at the couch*) What's wrong with you today?

KAREN   You wouldn't believe it, but fifteen minutes ago I was the happiest woman on earth . . . Sit down, I'll put your pupils back in.

SAM (*Hand extended*)   I can do it myself.

KAREN   I know you can, Sam, but I like to put your eye drops in. (*He lies down on the sofa with his head on the arm and she moves to look down at him from the side of the sofa*) It's the only time lately you look at me.
      (*She poises the eye dropper*)

SAM (*Looks up at her*)   . . . I'm sorry.

KAREN   You are?

SAM   I haven't been nice to *anyone* the past couple of weeks.

KAREN   You sounded swell to Miss McCormack.

SAM   Put the eye drops in.

KAREN (*Bending down over the arm of the sofa*)   First give an old lady a kiss.

(*He gives her a soft, gentle kiss*)

SAM I give you my permission to hate me.

KAREN (*Straightens up*) I'll save it for later. Open your gorgeous pupils.

(KAREN *fills the dropper with fluid*)

SAM Eight months I've been working on this deal and suddenly today my two top men in the office come down with the flu and I've got to do everything myself. (*She puts the drops in his eye. He jumps up*) Aaghh!

(*He grabs his eye in pain*)

KAREN What's the matter?

SAM (*Sitting up*) You *drop* them in, you don't *push* them in.

KAREN I'm sorry, you moved your head.

SAM I moved my head because you were stabbing my eyeball. (*Gets up and peers in the mirror over the fireplace*) Oh, damn it!

KAREN All right, don't panic, Sam, I'm sorry.

SAM Why do you think they call it a dropper? If they wanted you to stab people, they would call it a stabber. (*Grabs it from her*) Give it to me, I'll do it myself.

(*Lies back down on the sofa and begins to put drops in both eyes*)

KAREN You mean that's the end of being nice to each other?

SAM I don't know what we're doing in a hotel anyway.

KAREN What's the Plaza got to do with my stabbing your eyeball?

SAM Because it's insane being here, that's why. I've got work to do tonight, I don't know how I'm going to concentrate.

KAREN You've got to sleep *some*place tonight. The painter says it's going to take two days for the house to dry.

SAM Yes, but why *now?* Do it in the spring. This is my busy time of the year.

(SAM *puts the eye drops on the coffee table and crosses to the bedroom*)

KAREN I know, but it's not the painter's busy time of the year. In the spring he doesn't want to know you.

SAM Why didn't you ask me first?

(KAREN *follows him into the bedroom*)

KAREN I never see you . . . I saw the painter.

SAM You could have checked with my secretary.

(*He goes into the bathroom*)

KAREN I did. She said go ahead and paint the house. (*She takes his coat from the bed and hangs it in the closet*)

SAM'S VOICE   Of all times of the year. Did you bring my things?
Toothbrush? Pajamas?

KAREN   I brought your toothbrush.

SAM'S VOICE   You forgot my pajamas?

KAREN   (*Plops down on the bed*)   I didn't forget them, I just
didn't bring them.
> (SAM *comes out of the bathroom wiping his eyes on the
> towel*)

SAM   Why not?

KAREN   Because this is Suite 719 at the Plaza and I just didn't
think you'd want your pajamas tonight.

SAM   You know I can't sleep without pajamas.
> (*He returns to the bathroom*)

KAREN   (*Yelling after him*)   I took that into consideration . . .

SAM   What?

KAREN   Never mind. They've got shops in the lobby. (*Gets up and
picks up the phone next to the bed*) Should I send for their
catalog or will you take pot luck?

SAM   Heh. You know what a pair of pajamas would cost at the
Plaza? Forty, fifty dollars.

KAREN   You want me to send a bellhop to Bloomingdale's?
> (*Hangs up the phone*)

SAM   (*Comes out of the bathroom*)   I don't understand you. One
lousy little bag is all you had to pack.

KAREN   Forgive me. It's my busy time of the year.

SAM   Karen, do me a favor. Don't get brittle. (*Crosses to the desk
in the living room*) I'm very shaky right now and one good
crack and I go right to the dry cleaner's . . . Boy, could I use
a nice, big, cold double martini.
> (*He sits and begins to examine the contracts*)

KAREN   (*Follows him into the living room and leans on the chest of
drawers*)   Don't get angry, but can I make a suggestion? Why
don't you have a nice, big, cold double martini?

SAM   Are you serious? You know how many calories are in a
double martini?

KAREN   (*Shrugs*)   Four or five million?

SAM   You know my metabolism. One double martini, and right
in front of your eyes I get flabby.

KAREN   You used to get sexy.
> (*She takes a sheet from a pile of stationery in the chest*)

SAM   (*Gets up with the papers to sit in more comfort on the sofa*)
Well, now I get flabby. Unless I watch myself like a hawk . . .

(*As he passes the fireplace mirror, he pauses, admiring his waist-line*) which I think I manage to do.
   (*Sits on the sofa*)

KAREN (*She starts to fold the piece of stationery*)   I like you flabby.

SAM   What does that mean?

KAREN (*Still folding the paper*)   It means I like you flabby. I admit you look like one of the Pepsi generation, but it seems a little unnatural to me. A man of your age ought to have a couple of pounds of skin hanging over his belt.

SAM   Well, I'm sorry to disappoint you.

KAREN   I'm not disappointed, I'm uncomfortable. I watch you when you get undressed at night. Nothing moves. You're vacuum packed. When you open your belt I expect it to go like a can of coffee—*Pzzzzzz!*
   (*She continues folding*)

SAM   Do you think it's easy with my metabolism to keep my weight down? Do you know what it's like to have a business luncheon at the Villa Capri and watch someone slop down a bowl of spaghetti and I'm munching on a hearts of lettuce salad?

KAREN   My compliments to your restraint.

SAM   I go through torture to maintain my weight.

KAREN   I have nothing but admiration for your waistline.
   (*She is through folding*)

SAM   But you like me flabby.

KAREN   We all have our little perversions.

SAM   Can we drop the subject?

KAREN   Like a baked potato.

SAM   Thank you.

KAREN   You're welcome.
   (*She aims her finished paper airplane across the room and lets it fly*)

SAM (*Gets up and paces angrily*)   . . . Why do you like me flabby?

KAREN   Is the floor open again?

SAM   No. Forget it.

KAREN   It's forgotten.

SAM   What was I just doing?

KAREN   Watching yourself like a hawk.
   (*She crosses to the bedroom and begins to fold her negli-gée at the dresser.* SAM *returns to the sofa. There is a silence. Finally*)

SAM Look, I just want to say one more thing and then the discussion is closed. (KAREN *puts down the negligée and crosses back to the sofa in the living room*) I'm at the athletic club three, four times a week watching men at least ten years younger than me huffing and puffing trying to sweat off a couple of ounces that goes right back on after the cocktail hour. Now maybe you don't consider it a monumental achievement, but my weight hasn't changed in six years. I'm still one seventy-seven on the scale.

KAREN So am I. (*Crosses to the bedroom and puts the negligée away in the chest*) Now you know why I like you flabby . . . The subject is closed.

> (*She crosses to the.chair and sits.* SAM, *upset, remains in the living room. They contemplate the floor a few seconds*)

SAM . . . Hey, Karen.

KAREN Yah, Sam . . .

SAM Let's not fight.

KAREN It's all right with me, Sam.

SAM . . . Let's be nice to each other.

KAREN Okay . . . Who goes first?

> (SAM *gets up and starts for the bedroom. He stops at the door . . . trying to find words*)

SAM Karen . . .

KAREN (*Looks up*) Yes, Sam?

SAM (*This doesn't seem to be the time to bring up whatever is on his mind*) Nothing . . . I'm going to do a little work, okay?

> (*He goes back into the living room and sits on the sofa*)

KAREN (*Still sitting. Without malice*) You don't even remember this room, you louse.

SAM What's that?

KAREN (*Gets up and crosses into the living room*) I may not know how old I am, but I sure as hell remember we spent our honeymoon night in Suite 719 at the Plaza Hotel and this is definitely 719 because I just tipped the bellhop an entire dollar.

SAM (*Looks at the room for the first time*) Was this the room?

KAREN Oh, Christ.

> (*She sits on the arm of the sofa*)

SAM (*Gets up and looks about*) Wait a minute, I think you're right. (*He looks into the bedroom*) Sure, this looks like the suite. Only it was decorated differently. This room was blue.

KAREN (*Going into the bedroom*) That was you. You were in the Navy. The bedroom was green.

SAM I think you're mistaken. The bedroom was blue.

KAREN You're probably confusing it with some other honeymoon . . . (*Sitting on the bed*) Hey, Sam, remember we had dinner here in the bedroom?

SAM No.

KAREN Yes. We had dinner here in the bedroom. Do you remember what we had?

SAM For dinner? Twenty-three years ago?

KAREN *I* remember. You remember too. Take a guess.

SAM Karen, I don't remember.

KAREN Yes, you do. Think about it a second.

SAM I thought about it. I don't remember.

KAREN We had a bottle of champagne and a tray full of hors d'oeuvres. And we left all the anchovies in the drawer.
(*Indicates the night table*)

SAM Oh.
(*Crosses and looks out the living room window*)

KAREN See. It's coming back to you. (*Notices him looking out the window*) If you're looking for the Savoy-Plaza, it's not there.
(*She goes to the bedroom window and follows his gaze*)

SAM (*Looking out the window*) I'm looking at the Pierre.

KAREN There it is.

SAM . . . Karen.

KAREN What?

SAM (*Still looking out the window*) It was 819. (KAREN *steps back from the window and looks at* SAM. SAM *turns and looks at her*) We were in 819, not 719.

KAREN (*She glares at him and grits her teeth with hostility*) You're wrong!

SAM I'm not wrong, I'm right. We were in 819. I'm right.

KAREN (*Angry*) Don't keep saying you're right like you're right. You're wrong. We were in 719.

SAM I'll prove it to you. Come here. (KAREN *joins him at the living-room window*) Remember, I had my binoculars, we were watching that couple getting undressed in the Pierre? They were on the eighth floor. I remember because we were looking for them the next night. We called them "The Couple on the Eighth Floor."

KAREN I don't know what you called them, I called them "The Couple on the Seventh Floor."
(*She walks away angrily into the bedroom*)

SAM Look, it's pointless to argue about it. It's not important.

KAREN (*From the bedroom*) If it's pointless, then why are you pointing it out?

SAM Because you made an issue of it.

KAREN (*Crossing to the bedroom door*) Maybe I made an issue of saying we were in 719, but *you* made an issue of proving to me we *weren't* in 719.

SAM All right, Karen.
(*He walks away to the fireplace*)

KAREN Don't tell me, "All right, Karen." If I thought it was 719, why didn't you have the decency to let me just go on in my ignorance and think it was 719?

SAM Okay. Okay. I'm sorry. It was 719.

KAREN Aw, forget it. It was 819.
(*Moves back into the bedroom*)

SAM (*Rushing into the bedroom*) No, no. As a matter of fact, you're right. I just remembered. It really was 719.

KAREN I don't want it 719. I want it 819 . . . Look, why don't you go inside and lose some weight? (*That was a nasty remark.* SAM *glares at* KAREN, *then goes into the living room, reassures himself with a glance at his waistline in the fireplace mirror, picks up his work papers and sits.* KAREN *realizes what she's done. She crosses to the living room and embraces him*) I'm sorry, Sam. (SAM *nods his head and looks at his papers.* KAREN *moves around the sofa*) . . . We're some lousy couple, aren't we? . . . Aren't we?

SAM (*Doesn't look up*) Mmm.

KAREN Mmm what?
(*Sitting on the arm of the sofa*)

SAM (*Looks up*) Mmm, yes, we're some lousy couple.

KAREN (*Without malice*) That's what I said. First thing we agreed on today.

SAM Look, Karen, I really don't mean to be rude, but I *must* work on these estimates tonight. You understand.

KAREN Sure, I understand.

SAM I explained to you that Sid and Walter suddenly came down with the flu—

KAREN It's all right, Sam. You're excused . . . (*She wanders aimlessly about the room. Catching sight of herself in the mirror over the chest, she examines her figure and then decides to do some exercises, which she quickly gives up. She sits on the arm of the sofa next to* SAM) Do you have any good estimates for me to read?

SAM Isn't there anything to read in the bedroom?

KAREN (*Shrugs*) "Check-out time is three o'clock." That's all I could find . . . Don't worry about me. I'll find something to do. (SAM *goes back to his papers.* KAREN *puts her arms around his shoulders and rocks him playfully from side to side, much to* SAM's *displeasure. Suddenly she releases him, goes to the front door, opens it and goes into the hall*)

SAM What are you doing?

KAREN (*Coming back into the room*) Looking for the waiter.

SAM Call him up.

KAREN I thought I'd look in the hall first. Gives me something to do. (*She goes back out into the hall*) Nope, don't see him. (*Comes back in and closes the door*) In five minutes I'll call. See? I'll alternate them.

SAM Karen, please.

KAREN (*Crosses to him and takes his arm*) Oh, come on. Forget your crummy old papers and take me to a dirty movie. (*Tries to pull him out of the sofa*) Come on, Sam. Let's go.

SAM Stop it, Karen.

KAREN You know what's playing on Sixth Avenue? *Cat House Confidential* and *Ursula the Slut*. I passed it in the cab, I swear on my mother's life.

SAM Don't be ridiculous.

KAREN (*Kneeling by the sofa*) Are you afraid we'll be recognized? We'll buy beards in the five-and-ten.

SAM If you want to go, go yourself.

KAREN What happens if I get picked up?

SAM Call me and I won't wait up for you.

KAREN (*Hugging him*) Oh, good, you've got your sense of humor back. All right, just take a walk with me. A ten-minute walk and I'll leave you alone.

SAM Maybe later. We'll see.

KAREN (*Getting up and pacing*) No movies . . . no walk. (*She sits on top of the chest of drawers and picks up* What to Do in New York *magazine and skims through it. There is a silence. Finally*) Feel like going back to the house and watching the paint dry? (SAM, *at the end of his patience, gets up with the papers and moves into the bedroom*) . . . I'm just trying to think of something we can do together.

(*The doorbell rings*)

SAM (*Pacing in the bedroom*) Shall I get it, or is that something you'd like for us to do together?

KAREN   Listen, I'll even take nastiness. It's not much, but it's a start.

> (KAREN *crosses to the door and opens it. It's the* WAITER *with the food on a roller table. He is a middle-aged Puerto Rican*)

WAITER   Good evening.

KAREN (*Smiles*)   Hello.

> (*The* WAITER *rolls the table in*)

WAITER   Would you like the table near the window?

KAREN (*Moves toward the bedroom*)   Sam, would you like the table near the window?

SAM (*Disinterested*)   It doesn't make any difference.

KAREN (*Sweetly, to the* WAITER)   It doesn't make any difference.

WAITER (*Leaving the table up near the window*)   Shall I leave it here?

KAREN   Sam, should he leave it there?

SAM (*Throwing the contract on the bed and moving to the door-way*)   Here, there, anywhere, it doesn't make any difference.

KAREN (*Shrugs, smiles at the* WAITER)   Here, there, anywhere. It doesn't make any difference.

WAITER (*Takes a chair from the desk and puts it to the right of the table*)   Yes, Ma'am.

> (*He gets the armchair from the right of the sofa and brings it to the table*)

SAM (*To the* WAITER)   You don't have to set up the chairs.

KAREN (*To the* WAITER)   You don't have to set up the chairs.

WAITER   Yes, Ma'am.

> (*He starts to put the armchair back*)

SAM   All right, leave them, you've done it already.

KAREN   Yes, why don't you just leave the chairs. They're all set up.

> (*The* WAITER *puts the chair back at the table*)

SAM   Can I have the bill, please?

WAITER   Yes, sir.

> (*Takes the bill and a pencil to* SAM. KAREN *looks at the tray of hors d'oeuvres on the table*)

KAREN (*Sweetly*)   Oh, look at all the anchovies.

SAM (*Signing the bill*)   Didn't you tell them you didn't want anchovies?

WAITER (*To* KAREN)   You didn't want anchovies?

KAREN (*Doesn't want more trouble*)   No, no. I asked for anchovies. I'm a very big fan of anchovies.

SAM (*Hands the bill to the* WAITER)   That'll be all, thank you.

KAREN   Yes, that'll be all, thank you.

WAITER   And thank you.
   (*Crosses to the door*)

KAREN (*Looks at the table*)   Wait a minute. The champagne. Where's the champagne?

WAITER   No champagne? (*Looks at the check*) You're right. They forgot the champagne.

KAREN   But the anchovies they remembered.

SAM (*Returning to the bedroom*)   I can't drink anything now, I've got work to do. What do you need a whole bottle of champagne for?

KAREN   It's our anniversary. (*To the* WAITER) It's our anniversary.

WAITER   Oh, congratulations.

KAREN (*Sitting on the arm of the chair at the table*)   Thank you. We're married twenty-three or twenty-four years today or tomorrow.

WAITER   Then you want the champagne?

KAREN   With two grown children in college.

WAITER   Oh? That's wonderful.

KAREN (*Shrugs*)   You think so? He's flunking out and she's majoring in dirty clothes.

SAM (*Greatly irritated, moves back to the living room*)   He's not flunking out. Why do you say he's flunking out? (*Controls himself. To the* WAITER) That'll be all, thank you.

WAITER   If you don't want the champagne, I'll cross it out of the bill.

SAM   She doesn't want the champagne. Cross it off the bill.
   (*Crosses back to the bedroom*)

KAREN (*To the* WAITER)   I *want* the champagne. Don't cross it off the bill. Bring me a bottle and *one* glass.

WAITER   Yes, Ma'am.

SAM (*From the bedroom*)   That'll be all, thank you.

KAREN   Yes, that'll be all, thank you.

WAITER (*Opening the door*)   When you want me to take the table, just ring.

KAREN (*Moving to the* WAITER)   Yes, I'll ring when I want you to take the table.

WAITER   Thank you . . . And again, congratulations.
   (*He exits.* SAM *crosses to the table and takes the cover off a dish*)

KAREN (*At the mantel*)   . . . Did you hear that, Sam? We're being congratulated on being married to each other.

SAM (*Disgusted, slams the cover back on the dish*)   I asked for lean roast beef. That is not lean roast beef. (*Moves to the sofa and sits, taking a contract from the coffee table*)

KAREN (*Contemplatively*)   You know how many people we know who are still married as long as us? One other couple. The Shelleys . . . The most boring people I ever met.

SAM (*Cannot contain himself any more*)   Why do you talk to the waiter like that?

KAREN   Like what?
(*Sits at the table and begins to serve herself*)

SAM   Like you've known him for twenty years. You just met him. He walked in here two minutes ago with fatty roast beef. It's none of his business how our son is doing in school.

KAREN   I was just having a conversation. I get lonely, I like to talk to people.

SAM   He's a waiter. Talk to him about food.

KAREN   I did something wrong again. I'm sorry, Sam. When he brings the champagne I'll hide behind the drapes.

SAM   You don't have to hide. Just don't tell him our personal problems, that's all.

KAREN   What should I do, lie?

SAM   Certainly, lie. Everybody else does. Tell them you have a beautiful and devoted daughter. Tell them you have a brilliant son who's on the dean's list. Tell them you're only forty-two years old.

KAREN   There's no point to it. In two years I'll be fifty. Who's going to like me better if I'm only forty-two?

SAM   You don't have to revel in it like it's some kind of an accomplishment.

KAREN   I'm not insane about getting older. It happens to everyone. It's happened to you. You're fifty-one years old.

SAM (*Nods his head in exasperation*)   That's the difference between us. I don't accept it. I don't have to accept being fifty-one. (*Getting up and moving to her*) I don't accept getting older.

KAREN   Good luck to you. You'll be the youngest one in the cemetery.

SAM   We can't even have a normal discussion any more.
(*He stalks into the bedroom, closes the door and stretches out on the bed*)

KAREN   Accept being fifty-one and I'll have a normal discussion. (*Stops as* SAM *closes the door*) . . . Aren't you going to have your dinner? (*Gets up and examines the plate of meat. Holds up a piece to the bedroom door and calls to* SAM) Sam, I found some very lean roast beef. (*She nibbles on a piece*) Come inside and see how thin I'm getting. (*The doorbell rings*) . . . Hey, come on. The champagne is here. (*She opens the door to the bedroom and calls in*) If you don't come out, I'll tell the waiter you wear dentures. (*She crosses and opens the front door.* JEAN MCCORMACK *stands there. She is* SAM's *secretary. She is a trim, attractive woman about twenty-eight. She is neatly dressed, bright, cheerful and smilingly efficient*) . . . Oh! Hello, Miss McCormack.

JEAN   Hello, Mrs. Nash. I hope I'm not disturbing you.

KAREN   No, no, not at all. Mr. Nash and I were just sitting around, joking. Come in.
     (*Still holding the roast beef in her hand*)

JEAN   Thank you. (*She enters the room, closing the door behind her*) I hate to barge in this way, but I have some papers that need Mr. Nash's signature immediately.

KAREN   Certainly. (*Calls out*) Sam. It's Miss McCormack. (*To* JEAN) It is *Miss* McCormack now, isn't it?

JEAN (*Taking several contracts out of her brief case*)   It *was* Mrs. Colby last year. This year it's Miss McCormack again.

KAREN (*Sitting on the arm of the sofa*)   Oh. You're lucky you can remember. I've been married so long, if I got divorced, I'd have to make up a maiden name . . . Have you had your dinner yet?
     (*Indicates the roast beef in her hand*)

JEAN (*Laying out some contracts on the coffee table in front of the sofa*)   I don't have dinner, thank you.

KAREN   No dinner? Ever?

JEAN (*Getting her glasses and a pen from her purse on the console* table behind the sofa)   I have a large breakfast, a moderate lunch and a snack before going to bed. On this job I've worked late so often, I had to readjust my eating routine. Now I'm used to it.
     (SAM *gets up from the bed and moves into the living room*)

KAREN   Oh. Well, I can understand that. I miss a lot of dinners with Mr. Nash too.

SAM   Oh, hello. You got them, huh?
     (*Sits on the sofa and examines a contract*)

JEAN   Just came in. All ready for signature.

KAREN (*To* JEAN)   How about some black coffee? Or would that fill you up?

JEAN   Black coffee would be fine, thank you.

KAREN   One black coffee coming up. Sam, would you like some black coffee?

SAM   No.

KAREN   That's no black coffee and one black coffee.

> (KAREN *crosses to the table;* SAM *is looking over the contracts.* JEAN *sits next to him.* KAREN *pours coffee*)

SAM   Why is there an adjustment on this figure?

JEAN   (*Looks at it*)   There was a clerical omission on the Cincinnati tabulations. It didn't show up on the 1400 but I rechecked it with my own files and made the correction. (*Points to respective pages of the contract*) So that item 17B should read three hundred and twenty-five thousand and disregard the figure on 17A.

KAREN   Cream and sugar?

JEAN   No, thank you.

SAM   But this should have been caught on the IBM.

JEAN   It should have, but it wasn't. Obviously it wasn't fed properly.

KAREN   No cream and no sugar or no cream and yes, sugar?

JEAN   No cream and *no* sugar.

KAREN   So it's yes, no cream and no sugar.

SAM   Did you call this to Purcell's attention?

KAREN   (*Handing a cup to* JEAN)   Would you like some pastry or cookies? I could call down. They have beautiful pastry and cookies here.

JEAN   This is fine, thank you. (*To* SAM) Mr. Purcell says this happened once before this month. He can't pin it down until he rechecks the whole 66 file.

KAREN   (*Leaning on the console table behind the sofa*)   You're sure? A sandwich? A Welsh rarebit?

JEAN   No, I'm really quite happy, thank you.

> (*Takes saccharine from her purse and puts it in the coffee*)

SAM   Well, I'm just going to have to go over this whole thing tonight with Howard. If we give Henderson any room for doubt, we can blow our entire presentation.

JEAN   (*Sips the coffee*)   I told him there was a possibility of this, so he made plans to stay in town tonight.

SAM   Damn! Of all nights to have this happen. (*Putting down the contract*) What time is it now?

JEAN   (*Looks at her watch*)   Ten past five.

KAREN (*Looking over* JEAN's *shoulder*) Ten past five.

SAM All right, you tell Howard I'll meet him in the office between six fifteen and six thirty. Tell him I want to see every one of last year's 1400 forms.

KAREN (*Moving around the sofa to* SAM) You're going to the office? Tonight?

SAM It can't be helped, Karen. (JEAN *puts her coffee cup down*) We're having that same damned trouble with the computer again.

KAREN I could go with you. Maybe all it needs is a little dusting.

SAM Something in that office sure as hell needs dusting. (*Getting up and moving to the bedroom.* JEAN *gathers up the contracts and moves to put them in the brief case at the console table*) All right, Miss McCormack, why don't you hop in a cab now and get started on these figures with Howard? I just want to clean up and I'll meet you in about twenty minutes.

JEAN Yes, sir.

SAM I hope I'm not ruining any plans you had for tonight.

JEAN When I saw the figures this morning, I expected it. (*Closes the case.* SAM *takes a bottle of pills from his attaché case and crosses to the bathroom*) Mrs. Nash, thank you very much for the coffee.

KAREN You really should eat something. You'll faint right over the IBM machine.

JEAN (*Opening the front door*) I'll be all right.

KAREN (*Moving to her above the sofa*) It's a pity you can't stay two more minutes. I just ordered champagne. Can I tell her why, Sam?

SAM (*Returns from the bathroom, having taken pills. Throws the pills back into his case*) What's that?
(*Drinks from a glass on the dresser. Takes his jacket from the back of the chair and puts in on*)

KAREN Well, I'm not supposed to go around blurting these things out, but it's our twenty-third anniversary . . .

JEAN Oh? I didn't know. Congratulations.

KAREN (*To* JEAN, *but for* SAM's *benefit*) Thank you . . . Yes, life has been very good to me. I have a beautiful and devoted daughter, a brilliant son who's on the dean's list, I'm forty-two years old, what more can I ask?

SAM (*Moving into the living room*) Karen, Miss McCormack has to get back to the office.

(SAM *goes back into the bedroom, takes hair-brushes from an overnight bag and brushes his hair in front of the closet mirror*)

KAREN   Oh, I'm sorry. (*To* JEAN) Don't let him work you too late.

JEAN   It's all right. I'm used to it now. Best wishes again, Mrs. Nash.

KAREN (*As* JEAN *starts out*)   Thanks, dear. And see that he buys me a nice gift.

JEAN (*Smiles*)   I definitely will.
(*Closes the door*)

KAREN (*To* SAM)   What a sweet girl. That's a very sweet girl, Sam.

SAM   Karen, listen, I'm very sorry about tonight. It just can't be helped.
(*Puts the brushes back*)

KAREN   That's a sweet, young, skinny girl.

SAM (*Takes a cordless electric razor from his attaché case and crosses to the bathroom*)   The thing is, if I leave now maybe I can still get back in time for us to have a late dinner.

KAREN (*Enters the bedroom and sits in the armchair*)   Oh, don't worry about me, Sam. (SAM *begins to shave*) I understand. I just feel badly for you. You could have really relaxed tonight, and instead you'll be cooped up in that stuffy office until all hours working over some boring contracts with your smooth-shaven face.

SAM (*Still shaving, moves into the bedroom*)   Well, I can't very well walk through the lobby of the Plaza Hotel with a stubbly chin.
(*Returns to the bathroom*)

KAREN   They wouldn't let you into the elevator. Don't forget your Jade East.

SAM'S VOICE   My what?

KAREN   Your sexy cologne. The doorman will never get you a cab if you don't smell nice.

SAM (*Enters the bedroom. Looks at* KAREN *for a moment and then shuts the razor off*)   What are you doing, Karen?

KAREN   Oh, I'm just joking. Can't you tell when I'm kidding around any more, Sam?

SAM   No, I can't.
(*Crosses around the bed and puts the razor back in the case*)

KAREN (*Playfully pats his fanny, and then sits on the bed*)   Well, of course I am. I'm just teasing you by intimating you're having an affair with your secretary.

SAM   I see.

> (*Takes his overcoat from the top of the bureau and puts it on*)

KAREN   Are you, Sam? Is sweet, skinny Miss McCormack your mistress?

SAM   For God's sakes, Karen, what kind of a thing is that to say?

KAREN   If you're not, it's a lousy thing to say. If you are, it's a hell of a question.

SAM   I'm not even going to dignify that with an answer.

KAREN   (*On her knees, bouncing up and down like a child*)   Oh, come on, Sam, dignify it. I'm dying to know. Just tell me if you're having an affair with her or not.

SAM   And you'll believe me?

KAREN   Of course.

SAM   No, I'm not having an affair with her.

KAREN   (*Giving a big smile*)   Yes, you are.

SAM   Curses, trapped again. (*Looks out the window*) It looks like snow. I hope I can get a cab.

KAREN   (*Starting to take off her hairpiece*)   Even if you're not, Sam, it's all right if you do. I approve of Miss McCormack. She's a nice girl.

SAM   (*Getting his attaché case from the bed*)   Thank you. She'll be pleased to know. Look, I could call downstairs and get you a ticket for a show tonight. There's no reason for you to sit alone like this. Is there something you'd like to see?

KAREN   (*Smiles*)   Yeah. What you and Miss McCormack will be doing later.

SAM   Really, Karen, I find this in very poor taste.

> (*Moving to the living room, puts the attaché case down on the console table behind the sofa*)

KAREN   (*Getting a brush from the overnight case*)   Why? I'm just being honest again. I'm saying that if at this stage of your life you wanted to have a small, quiet affair with a young, skinny woman, I would understand.

> (*Sits back on the bed and begins to brush out her hairpiece*)

SAM   (*Stops abruptly in his gathering of the contracts from the coffee table and returns to the bedroom*) What do you mean, at this stage of my life?

KAREN   (*Continues her brushing*)   Well, you're blankety years old. I would say the number but I know you don't accept it. And I realize that when a man becomes blankety-one or blankety-two, he is feeling insecure that he's losing his virility (*Smiles broadly at* SAM), and that a quiet fling may be the best thing for him. I know, I read the New York *Post*.

SAM   I'm glad to know I have Rose Franzblau's permission.

KAREN   And mine if you really want it.

SAM (*Yells*)   Well, I don't want it and *I'm not having an affair!*

KAREN   Then why are you yelling?

SAM (*Crosses to the living room*)   Because this is an idiotic conversation.

KAREN (*Collapses on the bed*)   Oh, Sam, I'm so glad.

SAM (*Takes the contracts from the coffee table and puts them in his case*)   Now you're happy? You're happy because *now* you don't think I'm having an affair?

KAREN   Well, of course I'm happy. You think I'm some kind of a domestic mental case? I don't want you having an affair. I'm just saying that if you *are* having one, I understand.

SAM (*Crosses to the bedroom and picks up a contract from the bed*)   Karen, I have a hard night's work ahead of me. I'll be back about twelve.

     (*Starts to leave*)

KAREN   Sam, stay and talk to me for five minutes.

SAM   They're waiting for me at the office. I've got work to do.

KAREN   You've got help in the office. I've been with the firm longer than all of them . . . (*After a moment,* SAM *sits on the edge of the bureau*) Sam, I know we haven't been very happy lately. I know you've been busy, you may not have noticed it, but we have definitely not been very happy.

SAM   Yes, Karen, I've noticed it.

KAREN (*Continues to brush her hairpiece*)   What's wrong? We have a twelve-room house in the country, two sweet children, a maid who doesn't drink. Is there something we're missing?

SAM   I—don't know.

KAREN   Can you at least think about it? I need hints, Sam . . . (*Quoting*) "Is there something else you want?" (SAM *doesn't answer*) "Is there something I can give you that I'm not giving you?" (*Again no answer*) . . . Could you please speak up, we're closing in ten minutes.

SAM   It's me, Karen, it's not you.

     (*Crosses to the living room, puts the contract in his case, closes it*)

KAREN (*Puts her hair and brush on the dresser and follows him into the living room*) I'll buy that. What's wrong with you, Sam?

SAM (*There is a long pause*) I don't know . . . (*Moves to the mantel and then paces in front of the sofa*) I don't know if you can understand this . . . but when I came home after the war . . . I had my whole life in front of me. And all I dreamed about, all I wanted, was to get married, and to have children . . . and to make a success of my life . . . Well, I was very lucky . . . I I got it all . . . Marriage, the children . . . more money than I ever dreamed of making . . .

KAREN (*Sitting on the sofa*) Then what is it you want?

SAM (*Stopping by the fireplace*) I just want to do it all over again . . . I would like to start the whole damned thing right from the beginning.

KAREN (*Long pause*) I see. Well, frankly, Sam, I don't think the Navy will take you again.

SAM (*Smiles ruefully*) Well, it won't be because I can't pass the physical. (*Takes his case and starts for the door again*) I told you it's stupid talking about it. It'll work itself out. If not, I'll dye my hair.

(*He opens the door*)

KAREN You know what I think? I think you want to get out and you don't know how to tell me.

SAM (*Stops in the door. Turns back to* KAREN) That's not true.

KAREN Which isn't? That you want to get out or that you don't know how to tell me?

SAM Why do you always start the most serious discussions in our life when I'm halfway out the door?

KAREN If that's what you want, just tell me straight out. Just say, "Karen, there's no point in going on." I'd rather hear it from you personally, than getting a message on our service.

SAM Look, we'll talk about it when I get back, okay?

(*He starts out again*)

KAREN (*Can no longer contain herself. There is none of that "play-ful, toying" attitude in her voice now. Jumping up*) No, god-damnit, we'll talk about it now! I'm not going to sit around a hotel room half the night waiting to hear how my life is going to come out . . . If you've got something to say, then have the decency to say it before you walk out that door.

(*There is a moment's silence while each tries to compose himself . . .* SAM *turns back into the room and closes the door*)

SAM   . . . Is there any coffee left?

KAREN   It's that bad, huh? . . . All right, sit down, I'll get you some coffee. (*She starts to cross to the table and stops, looking at her hands.* SAM *crosses to the sofa. He puts down his attaché case by the coffee table and sits*) Look at this. I'm shaking like a leaf. Pour it yourself. I have a feeling in a few minutes I'm not going to be too crazy about you.

　　　(KAREN *crosses and sits on the ottoman next to the sofa, hands clasped together.* SAM *finds it difficult to look at her*)

SAM   . . . No matter what, Karen, in twenty-three years my feelings for you have never changed. You're my wife, I still love you.

KAREN   Oh, God, am I in trouble.

SAM   It has nothing to do with you. It's something that just happened . . . It's true, I am having an affair with her . . . (SAM *waits for* KAREN *to react. She merely sits and looks at her hands*) . . . It's been going on for about six months now . . . I tried stopping it a few times, it didn't work . . . After a couple of days I'd start it again . . . And then—well, what's the point in going on with this? You wanted honesty, I'm giving it to you. I'm having an affair with Jean, that's all there is to it.

KAREN   (*Looks up*)   Who's Jean?

SAM   Jean! Miss McCormack.

KAREN   Oh. For a minute I thought there were two of them.

SAM   I'm not very good at this. I don't know what I'm supposed to say now.

KAREN   Don't worry about it. You're doing fine. (*She gets up and moves to the table*) You want that coffee now? I just stopped shaking.

SAM   . . . What are we going to do?

KAREN   (*Turns back to* SAM)   Well, you're taken care of. You're having an affair. I'm the one who needs an activity.

SAM   Karen, I'll do whatever you want.

KAREN   Whatever *I* want?

SAM   I'll leave. I'll get out tonight . . . Or I'll stop seeing her. I'll get rid of her in the office. I'll try it any way you want.

KAREN   (*Moves to the sofa*)   Oh. Okay. I choose "Stop Seeing Jean" . . . Gee, that was easy. (*Snaps her fingers*) Now we can go back to our old normal life and live happily ever after. (*Starts to pour coffee, but stops and puts the pot down*) It's not my day. Even the coffee's cold.

SAM   Oh, come on, Karen, don't play "Aren't we civilized." Call me a bastard. Throw the coffee at me.

KAREN   You're a bastard. You want cream and sugar?

SAM   It's funny how our attitudes have suddenly changed. What happened to "I think a man of your age *should* have an affair"?

KAREN   It looked good in the window but terrible when I got it home.

SAM   If it's any solace to you, I never thought it would go this far. I don't even remember how it started . . .

KAREN   Think, it'll come back to you.

SAM   Do you know she worked for me for two years and I never batted an eye at her?

KAREN   Good for you, Sam.

SAM (*Angry*)   Oh, come on.
(*Crosses to the bedroom and stretches out across the bed*)

KAREN (*She follows him into the bedroom*)   No, Sam, I want to hear about it. She worked for you for two years and you didn't know her first name was Jean. And then one night you were both working late, and suddenly you let down your hair and took off your glasses and she said, "Why, Mr. Nash, you're beautiful" . . .

SAM (*Takes a pillow and places it over his head*)   That's it, word for word. You must have been hiding in the closet.

KAREN (*Tears the pillow away and throws it back down on the bed*)   All right, you want to know when I think the exact date your crummy little affair started? I'll tell you. It was June nineteenth. It was your birthday, and you just turned fifty years old. Five-oh, count 'em, folks, and you were feeling good and sorry for yourself. Right?

SAM   Oh, God, here comes Doctor Franzblau again.

KAREN   And the only reason you picked on Miss McCormack was because she was probably the first one you saw that morning . . . If she was sick that day, this affair very well could have been with your elevator operator.

SAM   Wrong. He's fifty-two and I don't go for older men.

KAREN (*Breaks away and crosses to the living room*)   You were right before, Sam. Let's discuss this later tonight.

SAM (*Sitting up on his side of the bed*)   No, no. We've opened this up, let's bring it all out. I've told you the truth, I'm involved with another woman. I'm not proud of it, Karen, but those are the facts. Now what am I supposed to do about it?

KAREN (*Moves back to the bedroom doorway*)   Well, I *would* suggest committing suicide, but I'm afraid you might think I meant *me* . . . (*Goes back to the living room*) I have one other suggestion. Forget it.

SAM (*Sharply*) Forget it?

KAREN (*Pacing above the sofa*) I understand it, Sam. It's not your fault. But maybe I can live with it until it's over. What else can I do, Sam, I'm attached to you. So go out, have a good time tonight and when you come home, bring me the *Daily News,* I'm getting sick of the *Post.*
(*Sits on the sofa*)

SAM If I lived with you another twenty-three years, I don't think I'd ever understand you.

KAREN If that's a proposition, I accept.

SAM (*Gets up and moves to* KAREN) Damn it, Karen, stop accepting everything in life that's thrown at you. Fight back once in a while. Don't understand me. Hate me! I am *not* going through a middle-aged adjustment. I'm having an affair. A cheating, sneaking, sordid affair.

KAREN If it helps you to romanticize it, Sam, all right. I happen to know better.

SAM (*Crossing above the sofa to the fireplace*) You don't know better at all. You didn't even know I was having an affair.

KAREN I suspected it. You were working three nights a week and we weren't getting any richer.

SAM (*Leaning on the mantelpiece*) I see. And now that you know the truth I have your blessings.

KAREN No, just my permission. I'm your wife, not your mother.

SAM That's indecent. I never heard such a thing in my life. For crying out loud, Karen, I'm losing all respect for you.

KAREN What's the matter, Sam, am I robbing you of all those delicious guilt feelings? Will you feel better if I go to pieces and try to lash back at you?

SAM (*Crosses below the sofa*) At least I would understand it. It's normal. I don't know why you're not having hysterics and screaming for a lawyer.

KAREN (*Getting up to confront him*) All right, Sam, if it'll make you happier . . . I think you stink. You're a vain, self-pitying, deceiving, ten-pound box of rancid no-cal cottage cheese. How'm I doing?

SAM Swell. Now we're finally getting somewhere.

KAREN Oh, you like this, don't you? It makes everything nice and simple for you. Now you can leave here the martyred, misunderstood husband. Well, I won't give you the satisfaction. I take it back, Sam. (*Sits on the sofa. Pleasantly, with great con-*

trol) You're a pussycat. I'll have milk and cookies for you when you get home.

SAM (*Sits on the ottoman*)   No, no. Finish what you were saying. Get it off your chest, Karen. It's been building up for twenty-three years. I want to hear everything. Vain, self-pitying, what else? Go on, what else?

KAREN   You're adorable. Eat your heart out.

SAM (*Furious*)   Karen, don't do this to me.

KAREN   I'm sorry, I'm a forgiving woman. I can't help myself.

SAM (*Gets up, takes his case and crosses to the door*) You're driving me right out of here, you know that, don't you?

KAREN   There'll always be room for you in my garage.

SAM   If I walk out this door now, I don't come back.

KAREN   I think you will.

SAM   What makes you so sure?

KAREN   You forgot to take your eye drops.
> (SAM *storms to the coffee table, snatches up the drops and crosses back to the door. He stops*)

SAM   Before I go I just want to say one thing. Whatever you think of me is probably true. No, not probably, *definitely*. I have been a bastard right from the beginning. I don't expect you to forgive me.

KAREN   But I do.

SAM (*Whirling back to her*)   Let me finish. I don't expect you to forgive me. But I ask you with all conscience, with all your understanding, not to blame Jean for any of this.

KAREN (*Collapses on the couch. Then pulling herself together*) I'll send her a nice gift.

SAM (*Puts down his case beside the sofa*)   She's been torturing herself ever since this started. *I'm* the one who forced the issue.

KAREN (*Moving away from him on the sofa, mimics* JEAN)   "It didn't show up on the 1400 but I rechecked it with my own files and made the correction on the 640" . . . You know as well as I do that's code for "I'll meet you at the Picadilly Hotel."

SAM (*Kneeling beside the sofa*)   You won't believe me, will you? That she's a nice girl.

KAREN   Nice for you and nice for me are two different things.

SAM   If it's that Sunday supplement psychology you're using, Karen, it's backfiring, because you're just making it easier for me.

KAREN   Well, you like things easy, don't you? You don't even have an affair the hard way.

SAM   Meaning what?

KAREN (*Getting up*)   Meaning you could have at least taken the trouble to look outside your office for a girl . . . (*Picks up an imaginary phone*) "Miss McCormack, would you please come inside and take an affair!" . . . Honestly, Sam.
       (*Moves above the sofa*)

SAM   Karen, don't force me to say nice things about her to you.

KAREN   I can't help it. I'm just disappointed in you. It's so damned unoriginal.

SAM   What did you want her to be, a fighter pilot with the Israeli air force?

KAREN   *Everyone* cheats with their secretary. I expected more from *my* husband!

SAM (*Shaking his head*)   I never saw you like this. You live with a person your whole life, you don't really know them.

KAREN (*Crossing below the sofa to the bedroom*)   Go on, Sam, go have your affair. You're fifty-one years old. In an hour it may be too late.
       (*Sits at the dresser and brushes her hair*)

SAM (*Getting up and crossing to her in the bedroom*)   By God, you are something. You are really something special, Karen. Twenty-three years I'm married to you and I still can't make you out. You don't look much different than the ordinary woman, but I promise you there is nothing walking around on two legs that compares in any way, shape or form to the likes of you.

KAREN (*Drops the brush and turns to him. Laughing*)   . . . So if I'm so special, what are you carrying on with secretaries for?

SAM   I'll be goddamned if I know . . .
       (*They look at each other. He turns and starts to the front door, taking his attaché case*)

KAREN (*Following him into the living room*)   Sam! (SAM *stops*) Sam . . . do I still have my two choices? (*He turns and looks at her*) Because if I do . . . I choose "Get rid of Miss McCormack." (*He looks away*) I pick "Stay here and work it out with me, Sam." (KAREN *turns her back to him and leans against the arm of the sofa*) . . . Because the other way I think I'm going to lose. Don't go to the office tonight, Sam . . . Stay with me . . . Please.

SAM (*Leaning on the console table, he looks at her*)   I swear, I wish we could go back the way it was before. A couple of years ago, before there were any problems.

KAREN   Maybe we can, Sam. We'll do what you said before. We'll lie. We'll tell each other everything is all right . . . There is nothing wrong in the office tonight, there is no Miss McCormack and I'm twenty-seven goddamned years old . . . What do you say, Sam?

SAM (*Moves about indecisively*) . . . Maybe tomorrow, Karen . . . I can't—tonight! I'll—I'll see you.

KAREN When? (*He exits, leaving the door open*) Never mind. I love surprises.

(*As* SAM *leaves, the* WAITER *appears with a tray with an ice bucket filled with a bottle of champagne and two glasses*)

WAITER The champagne . . . I brought two glasses just in case. (*He closes the door and places the ice bucket and glasses on the desk. He glances back*) Is he coming back?

KAREN (*Remains leaning on the sofa*) . . . Funny you should ask that.

(*He begins to open the bottle*)
Curtain

Losers

from *Lovers*

B Y

Brian Friel

Brian Friel

Brian Friel recently told an interviewer: "There are two kinds of Irishmen. There is the garrulous swashbuckling Brendan Behan type and then there is the black morose kind. I am not of the first sort." Whatever their personality differences, however, there is little doubt that both Friel and Behan are Ireland's two most valued export-dramatists of the mid-twentieth century.

Mr. Friel (who lives in County Donegal with his wife and four daughters) taught in sundry public schools "around the Irish countryside" until 1960, then declared he'd had enough of pedagogery and turned an avocation—writing—into a full-time profession. Although his short stories frequently have appeared in *The New Yorker* magazine and two collections of stories (*The Saucer of Larks* and *The Gold in the Sea*) have been published in the United States, his primary recognition has come through the stage.

Mr. Friel's first sortie in the American theatre came with *Philadelphia, Here I Come!* in February, 1966, under the auspices of David Merrick. The presentation won five nominations for Tony Awards (the New York theatre's highest honor) and *Variety's* Poll of New York's Drama Critics cited the author as the year's "most promising new Broadway playwright." Later in 1966 he was again represented on the Broadway stage with *The Loves of Cass McGuire*.

Mr. Friel's most popular success, *Lovers,* inaugurated the 1968–69 New York theatre season. Once again the critics acclaimed him as "a lovely writer, funny and compassionate." *Life* magazine commented that "Although Friel's dialogue is not in verse—except insofar as anything these Irish actors utter sounds like poetry—he writes so beautifully and his ear for Irish speech is so faultless that he has written a kind of poem, touching and often hilarious."

Originally, the double bill (comprised of *Winners* and *Losers*) opened at the Vivian Beaumont Theatre as part of the Lincoln Center Festival '68, then transferred to the Music Box Theatre. As this is being written, *Lovers* has been nominated for three 1968–

69 Tony Awards—for best play, best male dramatic star (Art Carney) and best featured or supporting actress (Anna Manahan). The play is at present on a national tour, and also is scheduled for early filming by producers Helen Bonfils and Morton Gottlieb.

Mr. Friel's previous plays, produced in Belfast and Dublin, are *This Doubtful Paradise, The Blind Mice* and *The Enemy Within,* the last-named at the Abbey Theatre.

The author has just completed a new work, *Crystal and Fox,* which deals with itinerant actors in the hinterlands of present-day Ireland. The enterprise will again unite the dramatist and Hilton Edwards, director of *Lovers* and *Philadelphia, Here I Come!* and co-founder with Micheál MacLiammóir of the famed Dublin Gate Theatre. The new play will be brought to Broadway by Miss Bonfils and Mr. Gottlieb after its Dublin engagement.

Lovers was first presented in New York City on July 25, 1968, by Helen Bonfils and Morton Gottlieb (by arrangement with Oscar Lewenstein), at the Vivian Beaumont Theatre, Lincoln Center. The cast of *Losers* was as follows:

(In order of appearance)

ANDY TRACEY	Art Carney
HANNA	Anna Manahan
CISSY	Beulah Garrick
MRS. WILSON	Grania O'Malley

An Edwards-MacLiammóir Dublin Gate Theatre Production

Directed by HILTON EDWARDS
Scenery by WILLIAM RITMAN
Costumes by NOEL TAYLOR
Lighting by THARON MUSSER

LOSERS

The action takes place in the town of Ballymore, Ireland. The time is the present.

The stage is divided into three equal areas: The portion on the right is the backyard of a working-class terrace house; the center portion is the kitchen-living room; the area on the left is the bedroom. There should be no attempt at a realistic division of the stage areas, no dividing walls, no detailed furnishings; frames will indicate doors, etc.

The backyard is suggested by a trash can and by two high stone walls. It is a gray, grimy, gloomy, sunless place.

The kitchen is furnished with a table and a few chairs, and with a disproportionately large black horsehair couch. The couch sits along the imaginary wall between the kitchen and the backyard. There are three doors leading out of the kitchen: one to the yard, one to the scullery (unseen) and one to the hall and stairs (unseen).

The bedroom area is raised on a shallow platform which is approached by two steps (because this room is supposed to be directly above the kitchen). It is furnished with a big, iron double bed, a chest of drawers (the "altar"), and a few chairs. Except where indicated, the bedroom will be hidden from the audience by a large draft screen.

When the curtain rises, ANDY TRACEY *is sitting upright and motionless on a kitchen chair in the backyard. He is staring fixedly through a pair of binoculars at the gray stone wall, which is only a few yards from where he is sitting. It becomes obvious that he is watching nothing: there is nothing to watch. When he becomes aware of the audience, he lowers the glasses slowly, looks at the audience, glances cautiously over his shoulder at the kitchen to make sure that no one in the house overhears him, and then speaks directly and confidentially down to the audience.*

He is a man of fifty, a joiner by trade, heavily built. His work-

mates look on him as a solid, decent, reliable, slightly dull man. Because his mind is simple, direct, unsubtle, he is unaware of the humor in a lot of the things that he says.

ANDY   I'll tell you something: I see damn all through these things. Well, I mean, there's damn all to see in a backyard. Now and again maybe a sparrow or something like that lands on top of the wall there but it's so close it's only a blur. Anyway, most of the time I sit with my eyes closed. And Hanna—she probably knows I do 'cos she's no dozer; but once I come out here—I'll say that for her—she leaves me alone. A gesture I make, and she —you know—she respects it. Maybe because her aul fella used to do the same thing; for that's where I learned the dodge. As a matter of fact, these are his glasses. And this is where he was found dead, the poor bugger, just three years ago, slumped in a chair out here, and him all happed up in his cap and his topcoat and his muffle and his woolen gloves. Wait—I'm telling you a lie. Four years ago—aye—that's more like it, 'cos he passed away that January Hanna and me started going, and we won't be married four years until next summer. Not that I knew the man, beyond bidding him the time of day there. Maybe he'd be inside in the kitchen, there or more likely sitting out here, and I'd say to him, "Hello there, Mr. Wilson"—you know the way, when you're going with a woman, you try to be affable to her aul fella —and he'd say, "Oh, hello there, Andy," or something like that back. But you know yourself, a man that's looking through binoculars, you don't like interrupting him. Civil wee man he was, too. Fifty years a stoker out in the general hospital. And a funny thing—one of the male nurses out there was telling me—all his life he stuck to the night shift: worked all night and slept all day, up there in that room above the kitchen. Peculiar, eh? All his life. Never saw the wife except maybe for a couple of hours in the evening. Never saw Hanna, the daughter, except at the weekends. Funny, eh? And yet by all accounts the civilest and decentest wee man you could meet. Funny, too. And the way things turn out in life; when the mother-in-law found him out here about seven o'clock that evening, she got such a bloody fright that she collapsed and took to the bed for good and hasn't risen since, not even the morning we got married. The heart. But that's another story. Anyway, Hanna and me, as I say, we were

only started going at the time; and then with the aul fella dying
and the aul woman taking to the bed, like we couldn't go out to
the pictures nor dances nor nothing like any other couple; so I
started coming here every evening. And this is where we done
our courting, in there, on the couch. (*Chuckles briefly*) By God,
we were lively enough, too. Eh? I mean to say, people think that
when you're . . . well, when you're over the forty mark, that
you're pacified. But aul Hanna, by God, I'll say that for her, she
was keen as a terrier in those days. (*Chuckles at the memory*)
If that couch could write a book—Shakespeare, how are you!
(*He rises from the chair*) Every evening, after I'd leave the
workshop, I'd go home to my own place at Riverview and wash
myself down and make a cup of tea and put on the good suit and
call in at Boyce's paper shop and get a quarter of clove rock—
that's the kind she liked—and come on over here and there she'd
be, waiting for me, in a gray skirt and a blue jumper, and when
she'd open the door to me, honest to God the aul legs would
damn near buckle under me. (HANNA *comes into the kitchen
from upstairs. She is dressed in a gray skirt and blue sweater.*
ANDY *walks through the invisible walls, through the hall, and taps
on the kitchen door.* HANNA *is in her late forties. She works in a
local shirt factory, lives alone with her invalided mother, and
until* ANDY *came on the scene has not been out with a man for
over twenty years. And this sudden injection of romance into a
life that seemed to be rigidly and permanently patterned has
transformed a very plain spinster into an almost attractive
woman. With* ANDY *she is warm; with her mother she reverts to
waspishness. Because neither* ANDY *nor* HANNA *is young, there is
a curious and slightly dated diffidence between them. And yet,
when they begin courting, it is* HANNA *who takes the initiative
and caresses him with a vigor and concentration that almost
embarrass him*) Well, Hanna.

HANNA   Hello, Andy.

ANDY   Not a bad evening.

HANNA   There's a cold wind, though.

ANDY   It's sharp—sharp.

HANNA   But it's nice all the same.

ANDY   Oh, very nice—very fresh. (*Pause*) Nothing startling at
the factory?

HANNA   Not a thing. Working away.

ANDY   Suppose so.

LOSERS

Bert Andrews / Dorothy Ross Associates

HANNA   Cutting out shirt collars this week. And you?

ANDY   Still at the furniture for the new hotel. Going to cost a fortune, yon place.

HANNA   I'll bet you.

ANDY   Only the very best of stuff going into it: maple and pine and mahogany. Lovely to work with.

HANNA   D'you see that now.

ANDY   Lovely. (*Pause. Then* ANDY *produces the small bag of sweets from his pocket*) Here. Catch.

(*He throws them to her*)

HANNA   Oh, Andy . . .

ANDY   They don't even ask me in the shop any more. They just say, "Quarter pound of clove rock, Mr. Tracey. Right you are."

HANNA   You have me spoiled.

ANDY   How's the mother?

HANNA (*Sharp*)   Living. And praying.

ANDY   Terrible sore thing, the heart, all the same.

HANNA   I come home from my work beat out and before I get a bite in my mouth she says, "Run out like a good child and get us a sprig of fresh flowers for Saint Philomena's altar."

ANDY   Did you go?

(HANNA *points to the flowers wrapped in paper lying on the kitchen table*)

HANNA   But she can wait for them.

ANDY   She'll miss you when you leave, Hanna.

HANNA   Hasn't she Cissy Cassidy next door? And if she hadn't a slavey like me to wait hand and foot on her, her heart mightn't be just as fluttery! (*From behind the screen comes the sound of a bell—not a tinkling little bell, but a huge brass bell with a long wooden handle*) We're early at it the night! There's the paper. Have a look at it.

(*With a bad grace she goes to answer the summons*)

ANDY (*As she is about to exit*)   The flowers. (*She grabs them, grimaces, and leaves.* ANDY *calls after her*) Tell Saint Philomena I was asking for her! (*He chuckles at* HANNA's *bad humor. Then he moves forward and addresses the audience*) That bloody bell! And nine times out of ten, you know, she didn't want a damn thing: Who's at the door? Is the fire safe? Did the Angelus ring? Is it time for the Rosary? Any excuse at all to keep Hanna on the hop, and at the same time making damn sure we weren't going to enjoy ourselves. But we got cute to her. You see, every sound

down here carries straight up to her room; and we discovered
that it was the long silences made her suspicious. That's the way
with a lot of pious aul women—they have wild dirty imagina-
tions. And as soon as there was a silence down here, she thought
we were up to something and reached for the bloody bell. But if
there was the sound of plenty chatting down here, she seldom
bothered you. But I mean to say, if you're courting a woman
there, you can't keep yapping about the weather all night. And it
was the brave Hanna that hit on the poetry idea. Whenever we
started the courting, she made me recite the poetry—you know
there, just to make a bit of a noise. And the only poetry I ever
learned at school was a thing called *Elegy Written in a Country
Churchyard* by Thomas Gray, 1716 to 1771, if you ever heard
tell of it. And I used to recite that over and over again. And
Hanna she would throw an odd word in there to make it sound
natural. And, by God, we'd hammer away at it until we'd stop
for breath or for a sup of tea or something; or else we'd get
carried away and forget the aul woman altogether—and then
the bloody bell would go and the session would be destroyed.
But they were good times . . . Funny thing about that poem, too:
it had thirty-two verses, and as long as I could bull straight at it
—you know, without thinking what I was saying—I could rattle
it off like a man. But stop me in the middle of it or let me think
of what I was saying, and I had to go right back to the beginning
and start all over again. Christ, they were rare times, too . . .
(HANNA *returns*) Well?

HANNA   "Is that Andrew I hear?" "No," says I, "it's Jack the Rip-
per."

ANDY   And how's Saint Philomena?

HANNA   You can laugh. "The pair of you'll be up later for the
Rosary, won't you?"

ANDY (*Mock devotion*)   With the help of God.

HANNA   One of these days I'll do something desperate.
         (*She sits dispiritedly beside him on the couch. He wants to
         say something tender and consoling to her, but feels he is
         past the age for effusive, extravagant language*)

ANDY   You're looking nice, Hanna.

HANNA   It's the jumper. (*Pause. Then he takes her hand in his and
         strokes it. She raises his hand to her lips and kisses it gently
         again and again. He puts his arm round her shoulder. They sit
         like this for some time*) We'd better keep talking.

ANDY   There's a nice smell of you.

HANNA   Soap.

ANDY   Nice soap.

HANNA   (*Dreamily*)   Her bloody ear'll be twitching like a rabbit.

ANDY   Hanna...

(*Pause. They speak the next eight lines as if they were in a trance*)

HANNA   Say something, Andy.

ANDY   I don't want to.

HANNA   Please, Andy. She'll know.

ANDY   I don't give a damn.

HANNA   Andy...

ANDY   Nice...

HANNA   Please, Andy...

ANDY   Very nice . . . (*Very suddenly, almost violently,* HANNA *flings herself on him so that he falls back, and she buries her face in his neck and kisses and caresses him with astonishing passion. He is momentarily at a loss. But this has happened before, many times, and he knows that this is his cue to begin his poem. His recitation is strained and too high and too loud—like a child in school memorizing meaningless facts. Throughout his recital, they court feverishly*)

"The curfew tolls the knell of parting day,

The lowing herd wind slowly o'er the lea,

The plowman homeward plods his weary way,

And leaves the world to darkness and to me.

Now fades the glimmering landscape on the sight—"

HANNA   (*To ceiling*)   It's a small world, isn't it?

ANDY

"Now fades the glimmering landscape on the sight,

And all the air a solemn stillness holds,

Save where the beetle wheels his droning flight,

And drowsy tinklings lull the distant folds—"

Oh, God, Hanna—

HANNA   Just imagine. Fancy that. Keep going, man.

ANDY

"Save that from yonder ivy-mantled tow'r

The moping owl does to the moon complain

Of such as, wand'ring near her secret bow'r,

Molest her ancient solitary reign."

HANNA   Andy—Andy—

ANDY
   "Beneath those rugged elms, that yew-tree's shade—"
   (HANNA *groans voluptuously*)
ANDY   Steady on—steady on—say something—
HANNA   Mm?
ANDY   She'll be listening to—
HANNA   I don't give a damn.
ANDY (*To ceiling*)   Fine. Yes, indeed. Imagine that. Where in the name of God was I?
HANNA
   "That yew-tree's shade—"
ANDY   What, where?
HANNA
   "Beneath those rugged elms."
ANDY
   Oh. "Beneath those rugged elms, that yew-tree's shade,
   Where heaves the turf in many a mould'ring heap,
   Each in his narrow cell for ever laid,
   The rude Forefathers of the hamlet sleep."
Speak, woman! (*She kisses him on the mouth*) Say something!
HANNA   Kiss me.
ANDY   For God's sake, woman—
HANNA   Andy, kiss me. (*He kisses her. They forget everything. The clanging of the bell shatters the silence—and* HANNA *breaks away roughly from him, jumps to her feet, and is almost trembling with fury. Her jumper and skirt are twisted*) Bitch! The aul bitch!
ANDY   Sure you're only after leaving her! What the hell can she want?
HANNA   Stuffed!
ANDY   Your jumper.
HANNA   Agh! My . . . !
   (*She pulls the sweater right up and then pulls it back into place.* ANDY *laughs at her anger*)
ANDY   Go on—go on—go on. A girl's best friend is her mother.
HANNA   Shut up, will you.
   (*She adjusts her skirt and brushes back her hair, and charges out of the room.* ANDY *looks after her and smiles contentedly. Then he addresses the audience*)
ANDY   By God, she had spunk in those days, eh? Suited her, too: gave her face a bit of color and made her eyes dance. But what-

ever it was that happened to her—well, I mean to say, I think I know what happened . . . But, like, to see a woman that had plenty of spark in her at one time and then to see her turn before your very eyes into a younger image of her mother, by God it's strange, I'll tell you, very peculiar . . .

But I was going to tell you about the aul woman and the altar and the Rosary and Saint Philomena and Father Peyton and all that caper. The routine was this. At the stroke of ten every night wee Cissy Cassidy—her and the aul woman's well met; two lisping Lizzies—she came down and asked Hanna and me to go up for the nightly Rosary. Fair enough. Why not? And there's the aul woman lying in the bed, smiling like an angel, and there, smiling back at her from the top of a chest of drawers, is this big statue of Saint Philomena. And you know, you got this feeling, with the flowers and the candles lit and with all the smirking and smiling and nodding and winking, you got the feeling by God that you were up to the neck in some sort of a deep plot or other. Like I knew damn well what the aul woman was up to: if she couldn't break it up between Hanna and me, at least she was going to make damn sure that I wasn't going to take Hanna away from her. And *she* knew that *I* knew what she was up to with her wee sermons about Father Peyton and all the stuff about the family that prays together stays together. And there was the pair of us, watching and smiling, each of us knowing that the other knew, and none of us giving away anything. By God, it was strange. Eh? 'Cos she thought that every time I got down on my knees in that bedroom to join in the Rosary I was cutting my own throat. But because I knew what she was up to, I was safe . . . or at least I thought I was. She's crafty, that aul woman. You've got to hand it to her. By God she's crafty.

(*He goes upstage and casually lifts the newspaper to glance over it.* HANNA *enters on her way through to the scullery. She is carrying her mother's soiled tray*)

HANNA   Look at—the invalid tray! Not a crumb on it! Six rounds of a sliced-pan and a boiled egg! Thanks be to God she gets no fresh air or she'd eat up the town! (*Knock at the front door*) That'll be prissy Cissy.

(*She goes off to the scullery.* ANDY *goes to open the door.* CISSY *and* ANDY *come back to the kitchen briefly before* CISSY *goes upstairs.* CISSY *is a small, frail wisp of a woman in her late sixties. She lives next door, is a daily visitor, and be-*

cause of the close friendship between herself and MRS. WIL-
SON *she has a proprietary air in this house. A lifetime spent
lisping pious platitudes has robbed them of all meaning.
The sickly piousity she exudes is patently false*)

ANDY   Hello, Cissy.

CISSY   Good night, Andrew. You're not alone, are you?

ANDY   Hanna's inside. How's things, Cissy?

CISSY   Struggling away, Andrew, thanks be to God. Sure as long as we have our health.

ANDY   That's it, Cissy.

CISSY   Thanks be to God, indeed. I'll go on up then, Andrew.

ANDY   Right—right.

CISSY   You'll be up later for the prayers?

ANDY   Aye.

CISSY   Thanks be to God.

     (HANNA *enters from the scullery. She is abrupt with* CISSY)

CISSY   Hello, Hanna. How's Mammy tonight?

HANNA   As ever.

CISSY   Sure that's grand.

ANDY (*Winking at* HANNA)   Thanks be to God.

CISSY   Just, Andrew—thanks be to God. Well . . . I'll see you both at ten.

ANDY   Joyful mysteries tonight, Cissy, isn't it?

CISSY   Thursday—so it is! Oh, you're coming closer and closer to us, Andrew Tracey!

     (*She leaves.* ANDY *laughs*)

HANNA   Sweet wee wasp!

     (HANNA *flops down on the couch.* ANDY *sits beside her. He sees she is in bad form and tries to coax her out of it*)

ANDY   Tired?

HANNA   Done out.

ANDY   D'you think was Cissy ever courted?

HANNA   Who cares?

ANDY   Imagine a man putting a hand on her knee. "Thanks be to God, mister." (*She does not laugh*) You're in bad aul form, Hanna.

     (*He puts his arm round her. She jumps to her feet*)

HANNA   Not now.

ANDY   What's wrong? Is there something the matter?

HANNA   Sick—sick—sick—sick of the whole thing; that's what's the matter! I can't stand it much longer!

ANDY Take a clove rock, Hanna.

HANNA What in the name of God are we going to do?

ANDY I've asked you half a dozen times to—

HANNA It's her I'm talking about! Her up there! What do we do with her?

ANDY When we're married she can come with us to Riverview. I've said that all—

HANNA Never! Never! The day I get married I'm getting shot of her for good (ANDY *spreads his hands: "What can I reply to that," the gesture says*) And no matter what you say now, you know fine well you don't want her hanging round your neck either.

ANDY I hear they took old Maggie Donaldson into Saint Patrick's.

HANNA She's not sick enough for hospital. And they've no spare beds for cranks.

ANDY The Nazareth nuns! Let her sell this place and go into the Nazareth House with the money.

HANNA She wouldn't go to them above all people.

ANDY What else is there?

HANNA I don't know, Andy. Honest to God, I just don't know.
(*Pause, and it dawns on* ANDY *that an offer is expected from him. He reacts strongly to the unspoken idea*)

ANDY Well, damnit all, you don't expect me to come in here, do you? I mean to say, I have a place and all of my own, ready and furnished and everything! And leaping sky-high every time you hear a bloody bell isn't my idea of married bliss! My God, you don't expect that of me, do you? Well, do you?

HANNA Bitch! That's what she is—an aul bitch!

ANDY We're getting no younger, Hanna, you know.

HANNA Tomorrow—I'll tell her tomorrow that we're going to clear out and she can damn well forage for herself!

ANDY You'll like it over at Riverview. It's—it's—(*He sees that she is crying*) Hanna, Hanna—aw, God, you're not away crying, are you—(*He puts his arm round her and leads her to the couch. They sit. She blows her nose while he tries to console her*) Come on, come on, there's no need for that. You know I can't stand seeing you crying. And you know I'd do anything to make you happy. We'll solve it some way or other. Don't you worry about it—we'll get some solution to it all. (*Pause*) . . . some solution to it all.

HANNA   No, we won't.

ANDY   I'm telling you we will.

HANNA   No, no. And only this morning I found myself singing at my work. And sure I can't even sing in tune.

ANDY   I could listen to you all day.

HANNA   But sure nobody goes through life singing all the time.

ANDY   We will, Hanna. (*Very suddenly, almost violently—exactly as before—*HANNA *flings herself on him and smothers him with kisses. And as before, he is taken unawares. Then he responds. But after a few seconds he realizes that they are being silent and he launches into his poem*)

> "The curfew tolls the knell of parting day,
> The lowing herd wind slowly o'er the lea,
> The plowman homeward plods his weary way,
> And leaves the world to darkness and to me."

Hanna...!

> (*She does not hear him. Pause. Then he goes on*)
> "Now fades the glimmering landscape on the sight,
> And all the air a solemn stillness holds,
> Save where the beetle wheels his droning flight,
> And drowsy tinklings lull the distant folds."

Say something, woman!

HANNA   A loaf of bread costs 1/3½ and a pound of tea 6/8.

ANDY

> "Full many a gem of purest ray serene
> The dark unfathom'd caves of ocean bear:
> E'en from the tomb the voice of Nature cries—"

I've bucked it!

HANNA

> "Can storied urn or animated bust—"

ANDY   What—what—what is it?

HANNA

> "Back to its mansion call the fleeting breath."

ANDY

> "... call the fleeting breath?
> Can Honour's voice provoke the silent dust,
> Or Flatt'ry soothe the dull cold ear of death?
> Perhaps in this neglected spot is laid
> Some heart once pregnant with celestial fire;
> Hands, that the rod of empire might have swayed..."

> (*But he fades out because he can no longer resist the bar-*

rage of her passion. Their mouths meet. A long kiss. Silence. Then—the bell. HANNA *springs to her feet. This time* ANDY *is angry too*)

HANNA   Christ!

ANDY   For God's sake!

HANNA   Bitch! Bitch! Bitch! Bitch! Bitch!

ANDY   It's your fault! You make no attempt at all!

HANNA   I don't know no poems!

ANDY   Well . . . bloody shopping lists . . . multiplication tables . . . anything! (*Again the bell*) What the hell can she want? Isn't Cissy with her?

HANNA   (*Evenly*)   One of these days I'm going to strangle that woman . . with her Rosary beads.

   (*She marches off.* ANDY *grabs a paper and tries to read it. We now see* HANNA *enter the bedroom and we hear* MRS. WILSON'S *voice*)

MRS. WILSON   We're going to say the Rosary a bit earlier tonight, dear. Cissy has a bit of a headache.

   (HANNA *removes the screen and puts it to the side of the set. In the large iron bed, propped up against the pillows, lies* MRS. WILSON. *Like* CISSY, *she is a tiny woman, with a sweet, patient, invalid's smile. Her voice is soft and commanding. Her silver hair is drawn back from her face and tied with a blue ribbon behind her head. She looks angelic.* CISSY, *her understudy, is sitting beside her, watching her with devotion. Directly facing* MRS. WILSON *is a chest of drawers, on which are a white cloth, two candles, a large statue of a saint, and a vase of flowers—a miniature altar.* MRS. WILSON *frequently nods and smiles to the statue and mouths "Thank you, thank you."* HANNA *clumps around the room, doing her chores with an ungracious vigor and with obvious ill-will*)

HANNA   Whatever suits Cissy suits me!

CISSY   She's looking lovely tonight, Hanna, isn't she? It must be the good care you're taking of her.

MRS. WILSON   I'm blessed, Cissy dear, and I know it. A good daughter is a gift of God. (*To the statue*) Thank you. (*To* HANNA, *who is fixing the bedclothes too robustly*) That's fine, dear, thank you. Just fine.

HANNA   Pillows.

MRS. WILSON   What's that, dear?

HANNA   D'you want me to beat up the pillows?

MRS. WILSON   No, I'm grand. A wee bit of discomfort's good for me.

CISSY   Invalids is all saints—that's what I say.

MRS. WILSON   Here's the matches, dear. (HANNA *goes and lights the candles*) Cissy, could I trouble you to give Andrew a call?

CISSY   Pleasure.

MRS. WILSON (*To* HANNA)   And maybe you'd be good enough to move Saint Philomena round a wee bit so that she's facing me . . . just a little to the left . . . so that we're looking at each other . . . That's it. Lovely. Thank you, dear.

(CISSY *off and unseen*)

CISSY   Andrew!

MRS. WILSON   God be praised a thousand times. Saint Vibiana, Virgin and Martyr, protect us. Saint Hyacintha de Mariscottis, look after us this day and this night.

CISSY   The Rosary!

ANDY   Coming.

MRS. WILSON (*To* HANNA)   And my jewels, dear.

HANNA   What are you saying?

MRS. WILSON   Could you hand me my beads, please? (HANNA *does this*) God bless you. Another day is nearly o'er. A journey closer to the heavenly shore.

(*Enter* CISSY)

CISSY   He's coming. Thanks be to God.

MRS. WILSON   Amen to that. Poor Hanna's run off her feet, isn't she?

CISSY   A labor of love.

(ANDY *enters. He tries to be brisk and matter-of-fact in this cloying feminine atmosphere*)

MRS. WILSON   Ah, Andrew!

ANDY   How are you tonight, Mrs. Wilson?

MRS. WILSON   Grand, Andrew, thanks. I have Saint Philomena during the day and I have you all at night.

ANDY   Very nice.

MRS. WILSON   Are you going to join us in the prayers?

HANNA   Didn't you send down for him!

MRS. WILSON   Thank you, Andrew. As Father Peyton says: the family that prays together stays together.

HANNA   Get started.

MRS. WILSON   And Father Peyton is right, isn't he, Andrew?

ANDY   Right, Mrs. Wilson.

MRS. WILSON   If you only knew the consolation it is for me to have you all kneeling round my bed.

CISSY   It's what you deserve.

MRS. WILSON   Thank you, Saint Philomena. Thank you.

HANNA   Who's giving it out?

MRS. WILSON   Aren't the flowers pretty, Andrew?

ANDY   Very nice.

MRS. WILSON   Hanna got them for me. But then—why wouldn't she? Didn't she take the name Philomena for her confirmation.

HANNA   Lookat—are we going to say the prayers or are we not?

CISSY   Hanna dear, you're talking to a sick woman.

(MRS. WILSON *lays a restraining hand on* CISSY)

MRS. WILSON   She's tired, Cissy. I know. I don't mind. Maybe you'd give it out tonight, Andrew, would you?

ANDY   I—I—I—

HANNA   He will not, then. I will. (MRS. WILSON *mouths her thanks to the statue.* HANNA *begins at top speed*) In the name of the Father and of the Son and of the Holy Ghost. We fly to thy protection, O holy mother of God. Despise not our prayers in our necessity, but deliver us from all dangers, O glorious and ever blessed virgin. Thou O Lord will open my lips.

MRS. WILSON, CISSY and ANDY   And my tongue shall announce thy praise.

HANNA   Incline unto my aid, O God.

MRS. WILSON, CISSY and ANDY   O Lord, make haste to help me.

HANNA   Glory be to the Father and to the Son and to the Holy Ghost.

MRS. WILSON, CISSY and ANDY   As it was in the beginning, is now, and ever shall be, world without end, Amen.

(*They are all on their knees around the bed, facing the altar now. While the prayers continue,* ANDY *gets to his feet and places the screen in its opening position—that is, completely hiding the bedroom. He then goes behind the screen to continue the Rosary. The lights come down slowly and the prayers fade. Total black for about a minute. When the lights go up,* ANDY *is sitting as we first saw him, in the backyard, with his binoculars. He puts down the binoculars, glances cautiously over his shoulder at the kitchen to make sure that no one in the house overhears him, and then speaks to the audience*)

ANDY   The big mistake I made was to come back here after the honeymoon—*even* for the couple of weeks that it was supposed to be at the beginning. I should have put the foot down then. But, like, everything happened so sudden. One bright morning the firm turns round and says "All the single men in the joinery room are being sent to Belfast on a contract job." So there was nothing for it, like, but to get married. And that's what we done. And then when we got back from the three days in Dublin, there's the damn painters still hashing about in Riverview, and the aul woman has a bit of a flu, and Hanna's kind of worried about her, and damnit, between one thing and another we find ourselves back here. But it was to have been only for a couple of weeks—that was the arrangement—aw, no, there was no doubt about that. Two weeks, she said. And a funny thing, you know, looking back on it, there was a change in the tune even then. No, not so much with the aul woman—she's too crafty—Christ, you've got to hand it to the aul woman—but with Hanna. Like, you know, before we got married, she was full of fight, there: let the aul woman step out of line or say something sharp to me and by God she jumped at her like a cock at a gooseberry. But somehow the spirit seemed to drain out of her from the very beginning. Of course, when the bloody bell would go, she would still say, "The aul bitch!" But, you know, even the way she said it now, like kind of weary, and almost as if it wasn't anger at the aul woman at all but more to please me. That sort of thing. And a funny thing about that bloody bell, too. You know, before, if there was no noise coming from downstairs, that ringing would be enough to waken the dead. But *after* we got married, it only went when Hanna and me started talking. Wasn't that perverse now, eh? Oh, a deep one; deep as a well. We could sit, by God, for a whole night and not say a word to each other, and there wouldn't be a cheep from upstairs. But let us start chatting and the clanging would damn near shake the house! You know there, that sort of thing.

And then there was the Rosary caper. Well, I mean to say, a man has to draw the line somewhere. Oh, no, says I; we may have to stay together of necessity, says I, but by God it won't be because we pray together; I'll say my own mouthful of prayers down here. And that settled that. I mean to say, a man has to take a stand some time. No harm to Father U. S. A. Peyton, says I; but all things in their proper place, and the proper place for me and my missus is in Riverview. I'll manage rightly down here, says I; and Father Peyton and Saint Philomena and the three sorrowful mysteries can hammer away upstairs. She didn't like that, the aul woman, I'll tell you. Didn't speak to me for weeks. And would you believe what she done on me to get her own back: it was Cissy told me with a wee toss of her head. "She offered you up to Saint Philomena," says she. Crafty? Oh, man! Hanna's thick—there's no denying that; but she'll never have the craft of the aul woman.

But I got her! By God I got her! . . . or I damn near got her. It was this day in the works—a Friday—I'll never forget it— and George Williamson comes sidling up to me with a newspaper in his hand and a great aul smirk on his jaw, and says he, "So the Pope's not infallible after all, Andy," says he. Oh, a bad bitter Protestant, the same Williamson. "What's that?" says I, you know there, very quiet. "According to the paper here," says he, "even the Pope can make a mistake. What d'you make of that now, eh? Isn't that a surprise?" And he hands me the paper. So I pulls out the glasses, very calm, and puts them on, and takes the paper from him and looks at it. And true as Christ, when I seen it, you could have tipped me over, I was that weak. Like, for five seconds, I couldn't even speak with excitement; only the heart thumping like bloody hell in my chest. For there it was in black and white before my very eyes: THE SAINT THAT NEVER WAS. "Official Vatican sources today announced"—I know it by heart —"that the devotion of all Roman Catholics to Saint Philomena must be discontinued at once because there is little or no evidence that such a person ever existed." Like I never knew I was a spiteful man until that minute; and then, by God, my only thought was to stick that paper down the aul woman's throat. Poor Williamson—Christ, I shot past him like a scalded cat and out of the workshop like the hammers of hell.

What I should have done—like, I know now—my God, no need to tell me; instead of coopering the thing up the way I done—but what I should have done was wait until after the tea and then go upstairs nice and calm, you know there, and sit down on the side of the bed very pleasant, and say, "Have a look through the paper there, Mrs. Wilson," and watch, by God, watch every wee flicker of her eye when she'd come to the big news . . . but I bollixed it. I know. I know. I bollixed it. Straight from the workshop into a pub. And when closing time comes, there I am—blotto. And back to the house singing and shouting like a madman.

(HANNA, *who has been in the bedroom, now removes the screen. And, as she does this,* ANDY *goes off.* MRS. WILSON *is in bed.* CISSY *is sitting on the edge of the bed.* HANNA *has been crying for some time and shuffles around the room, vaguely touching different things. The candles are lit. The atmosphere is subdued and doleful and expectant. Trite words of consolation are being spoken. And one gets the sense of feminine solidarity and of suffering womanhood)*

MRS. WILSON I promise you, dear: he's all right. I know he is.

HANNA But where *is* he?

MRS. WILSON Maybe he met some of his companions.

HANNA He has no companions.

MRS. WILSON Maybe he's doing overtime.

HANNA There's no overtime this week.

MRS. WILSON Or maybe he's gone to confession.

CISSY Ah! Indeed!

HANNA At half past ten? For God's sake!

MRS. WILSON Well, we'll say the Rosary; that's what we'll do; and we'll ask God and Saint Philomena to look after us all. And before we're finished, you'll find he'll be home safe and sound to us.

CISSY Thanks be to God.

MRS. WILSON All down on your knees. God and his holy mother guide all our thoughts and actions this day and this night. In the name of the Father and of the Son and of the Holy Ghost. The five sorrowful mysteries of the most holy Rosary—

(*Remote sounds of* ANDY *singing*)

HANNA Sshhh!

MRS. WILSON The first sorrowful mystery—the agony in the garden—

HANNA Sh! Sh! Listen! Listen!

(*The women freeze. Downstairs* ANDY *staggers into the kitchen, singing "God Save Ireland." The women are horrified*)

MRS. WILSON Is it—?

HANNA Shut up!

CISSY Singing! Andrew?

MRS. WILSON He's not—?

HANNA He is!

CISSY A drunk man!

(ANDY *flings his coat on the couch and reels to the bottom of the stairs. Calls up*)

ANDY Mrs. Wilson! Hello there, old Mammy Wilson! I've got news for you . . . big, big news.

(HANNA *is terrified.* MRS. WILSON *takes control*)

HANNA   What in the name of God—?

MRS. WILSON   Leave him to me.

ANDY   Stay where you are till I come up . . . very important, old Mammy . . . very important.

MRS. WILSON   Don't say a word. Leave everything to me.

CISSY   Drunk—the dirty animal!

MRS. WILSON   Quiet.

HANNA   But what if he—?

MRS WILSON   Don't worry. I'll settle him. And stop whinging!
   (ANDY *enters and surveys the three alarmed faces. He has the newspaper in his hand*)

ANDY   By God if it's not the Dolly Sisters! (*He gives them a grand bow*) And Saint Philomena! (*Grand bow to the statue*) All we need now is Father Peyton . . . Where's Father Peyton? . . . I'll tell you something: the family that drinks together sinks together.

MRS. WILSON   Andrew!

ANDY

   "The cock's shrill clarion, or the echoing horn—"

CISSY   Dirty animal!

ANDY

   "No more shall rouse them from their lowly bed.
      For them no more the blazing hearth shall burn,
      Or busy housewife ply her evening care—"
   Thomas Gray, 1716 to 1771.

HANNA   Mother, please—!

MRS. WILSON   Listen to me, Andrew!

ANDY   She (*Indicating* HANNA) knows what I'm talking about 'cos she's my wife—

MRS. WILSON   If you don't behave yourself—

ANDY   As for prissy Cissy here—

CISSY   All for Thee—all for Thee—

ANDY   You'll go down with the white bobbins. Know what that means, prissy Cissy? The white bobbins? It means you'll never know your ass from your elbow.

HANNA   Andy!

MRS. WILSON   I'll give you one minute to get out of this house—!

ANDY   News for you, old Mammy—here, in this paper. (*To the statue*) And news for you, darling, too.

MRS. WILSON   Get out!

ANDY   You've (*Indicating* PHILOMENA) been sacked.

MRS. WILSON   I said get out!

ANDY (*To statue*)   You and me—both sacked.
   (*He comes over to the bed with the paper*)

HANNA   Stop it, Andrew! Stop it!

ANDY   In black and white . . . Read it . . . It says: We don't stay
   together—that's what it says. Father Peyton, it says, your head's
   a marly. That's what it says.

CISSY   Dirty, dirty animal.

MRS. WILSON   I warned you! I gave you ample warning! And if
   you think you can profane in this room—
   (*She breaks off and clutches her heart and cries out*)

CISSY   What—what is it?

HANNA   Mother! Mother?
   (ANDY *staggers back to the altar. On his way he kicks over
   the bell. He laughs*)

ANDY   "The curfew tolls no more the knell of parting day." (*He
   lifts the statue and waltzes with it*) Come on, darling; we know
   when we're not wanted.

MRS. WILSON   Don't—touch—that—

CISSY   The statue!

HANNA   Andrew!

CISSY   Oh, my God!

MRS. WILSON   Stop him! Stop him!
   (*Chaos and confusion as* HANNA *and* CISSY *rush at* ANDY *and
   wrest the statue from him. Everyone is shouting at the same
   time.* MRS. WILSON *gets out of bed and* CISSY *puts a coat
   around her*)

CISSY   Come on! Come on! Into my place!

HANNA   Are you all right, Mother?

ANDY
   "Large was his bounty, and his soul sincere,
      Heav'n did a recompense as largely send—"

MRS. WILSON   Take all—statue—candles—cloth—

CISSY   Brute animal!

MRS. WILSON   Oh, my heart—

HANNA   Out—quick—(CISSY *and* HANNA *each take an arm of* MRS.
   WILSON *and they support her out.* HANNA *also takes the altar
   things.* MRS. WILSON *groans loudly and pathetically.* CISSY *con-
   soles her.* ANDY *reels over to the bed and sits on it. He is muttering
   to himself.* HANNA *leaves the others, goes to him, and sticks her*

face into his, and hisses) You'll regret this day, Andrew Tracey! You'll regret this day as long as you live!

> (*She then pulls over the screen, hiding* ANDY *from view, and joins* CISSY *and her mother, who go off chattering hysterically*)

ANDY (*Shouts after them from behind the screen*)   We're sacked, Philomena—both of us—both sacked! What the hell are we going to do now? What the hell are we going to do now?

> (*The three women have struggled downstairs and pause in the kitchen before escaping to* CISSY's *house*)

MRS. WILSON   O my heart! O my God!

HANNA   How are you, Mother?

CISSY   All men is animals—brute animals.

HANNA   Come on, Mother. I'll look after you.

CISSY   Brutes of the field.

MRS. WILSON   God have mercy on us this day and this night.

HANNA   He'll pay for this. By God, he'll pay for this!

> (*The three ladies go off.* ANDY *appears, in cardigan and house slippers, and comes into the kitchen. He addresses the audience*)

ANDY   I don't think I told you about the tenant I have over in Riverview. Retired accountant. Quiet couple. No kids. He pays me on the first Saturday of every month. Sometimes if the weather's good I take an odd walk over there and look at the outside of the house. He has rose trees in the front and vegetables at the back. Very nice. Very cozy. But by the time you get home from work and get washed, you don't feel like going out much. So I usually sleep at the fire for a while and then come out here for a breath of air. Kills an hour or two. And then when the bell rings I go up to the aul woman's room for the prayers. Well, I mean to say, anything for a quiet life. Hanna sleeps there now, as a matter of fact. Just in case the aul woman should get an attack during the night. Not that that's likely. The doctor says she'll go on forever.

And a funny thing, you know: nothing much has changed up there. Philomena's gone, of course. And she never mentions Father Peyton any more. But she still has the altar and she still lights the candles and has the flowers in the middle and she still faces it when she's praying and mouths away to it. I asked Cissy about it one night when she came in—who the hell they were supposed to be praying to.

(*Enter* CISSY *in a coat and hat. She is about to go straight upstairs but sees* ANDY *and pauses. She is very formal with him*)

CISSY Good night, Andrew.

ANDY 'Night, Cissy.

CISSY The crowds for confession! You should see them. The poor priests must be mortified.

ANDY Cissy—

CISSY You'll be up later for the prayers?

ANDY I will. I will. Cissy—

CISSY Well?

ANDY Cissy, you've no statue up there now.

CISSY I'm not blind.

ANDY Well, I mean to say, what does she think she's at?

CISSY We've no statue, true enough; but we have a saint in our mind even though we've no figure for it.

(HANNA *enters.* ANDY *does not see her at first*)

ANDY What saint?

CISSY Aha, that's something you'll never know, Andrew Tracey! Wild horses wouldn't drag that out of us. You robbed us of Saint Philomena but you'll never rob us of this one, for you'll never be told who it is!

(CISSY *marches upstairs and* ANDY *turns with embarrassment to* HANNA. *Her coldness to him is withering*)

ANDY Damnit, she's fighting fit . . . isn't she? Hanna—

HANNA What?

ANDY Hanna, things are . . . we're not making . . . you and me, Hanna, we're not . . . Here, have a clove rock, Hanna.

(*She moves toward him as if she were going to take one, hesitates*)

HANNA No. They'd put me off my supper.

ANDY I suppose you're right.

HANNA You'll be up for the prayers?

ANDY I will . . . I will . . .

(HANNA *goes upstairs.* ANDY *turns to the audience and speaks with strained joviality*)

ANDY And that's the way things are now. (*He goes slowly out toward the yard*) And when I go into the bedroom she smiles and nods at me and you can see her lips saying *Thank you, thank you,* to the altar. And when we kneel down, she says, "It's nice for me to have you all gathered round my bed. As a certain

American cleric says: the family who prays together stays together."

By God, you've got to admire the aul bitch. She could handle a regiment.

(*He lifts the binoculars, puts them in front of his eyes, and stares at the wall in front of him. The lights slowly go down until the stage is totally black*)

Trevor

from *Little Boxes*

B Y

John Bowen

John Bowen

John Bowen was born in Calcutta, India, in 1924, and reared by "various relatives in various parts of England." He returned to India in 1940, served in the Indian Army during World War II, and was demobilized in 1947. He obtained a place at Pembroke College, Oxford, where he studied modern history as an under-graduate; graduated and was awarded the Frere Exhibition in Indian Studies by the University; and from there went on to do some postgraduate work at St. Anthony's College.

He was in the United States from the fall of 1952 to 1953, "partly teaching Freshman English at Ohio State University, partly hitch-hiking and partly on a scholarship to the Kenyon School of Letters at the University of Indiana." He returned to Oxford, promptly ran out of money, and took a job as assistant editor with a fort-nightly magazine, *The Sketch*. To augment his income, he also worked at intervals in advertising, as an actor, and reviewing ballet for the British Broadcasting Corporation ("After a while I couldn't think of anything more to say").

Mr. Bowen has written six novels, of which four—*After the Rain, The Centre of the Green, The Birdcage* and *A World Else-where*—have been published in the United States.

His first play, *I Love You, Mrs. Patterson*, was produced at St. Martin's Theatre, London, in 1964. As the author recalls the event, "It was sort of Ibsenish, about marriage. It ran for five weeks—in a heat wave."

His second work for the stage, *After the Rain*, was decisively more impressive. A "very free adaptation" of his novel of the same title, the drama originally was presented in 1966 at the Hamp-stead Theatre Club, then transferred to the Duchess Theatre in the West End. It was highly praised by the press; the *Daily Express* cited it as "the most fascinating new play in London."

After the Rain opened on Broadway (with Alec McCowen re-peating his London role) in the fall of 1967 and although it ran for only 64 performances, the New York first-night jurors hailed both author and play for "providing theatregoers with the first solid food for thought of the season." The drama garnered additional honors when Otis L. Guernsey, Jr., editor of the theatre yearbook, selected it as one of the "ten best plays of the New York theatre season, 1967–1968." A French translation of *After the Rain* has been performed at the Théâtre de l'Athénée, Paris, and a German one in the Kammerspiele, Frankfurt.

Trevor and its companion piece, *The Coffee Lace,* comprise John Bowen's double bill, *Little Boxes,* which initially opened in London at the Hampstead Theatre Club on February 26, 1968. Its success was immediate and again Mr. Bowen was acclaimed by the critical gentry. Harold Hobson wrote in the *London Sunday Times:* ". . . a major talent, disturbing, brooding and despite its humour, essentially tragic, has come into the British theatre." The critic for the British magazine, *Plays and Players,* described *Trevor* as "a brilliant theatrical idea . . . a play that I found extremely funny. In fact, Mr. Bowen seems to me to belong with Peter Shaffer and Robert Bolt as one of the best dramatists we've got writing within the inherited tradition of the well-made play." Clive Barnes, covering the London presentation for the *New York Times,* joined in the chorus of international praise: "This is a remarkably funny and adroit work. In *Trevor,* Bowen is still being provocative, but he has written a farcical comedy that is as neat and as deft as you could wish."

After completing *Little Boxes* (at present scheduled for production in New York next year), Mr. Bowen made a "piratical raid" into the texts of the various medieval mystery plays, selecting and adapting to create a play called *Fall and Redemption* which he himself directed at the London Academy of Music and Dramatic Art, and which he is to stage again for the Pitlochrie Festival Theatre in 1969.

Mr. Bowen, who lives in South Kensington, also has written extensively for television, and is a regular contributor to the *London Sunday Times* and the *New York Times Book Review.*

Little Boxes was first performed on February 26, 1968, at the Hampstead Theatre Club, London. The cast of *Trevor* was as follows:

(*In order of appearance*)

JANE KEMPTON	Anna Cropper
SARAH LAWRENCE	Angela Thorne
TREVOR	David Cook
MRS. LAWRENCE	June Jago
MR. LAWRENCE	Frank Middlemass
MRS. KEMPTON	Maureen Pryor
MR. KEMPTON	Peter Howell
MR. HUDSON	Larry Noble

Directed by PHILIP GROUT

Designed by J. HUTCHINSON SCOTT

On April 1, 1968 *Little Boxes* transferred to the Duchess Theatre. The part of SARAH was there played by Elizabeth MacClennan.

TREVOR

*The scene: The top-floor flat (two rooms, kitchen and bathroom)
shared by* JANE *and* SARAH, *two young upper-middle-class women
in their late twenties, both earning a good salary.*

*The two lower-floor rooms are divided by a passage that runs
the full depth of the stage. There is a short winding staircase,
opening off the passage, that leads to a small kitchen which is at a
higher level than the other rooms. A door at the far end of the
passage opens to a well-furnished bathroom. Next to it, but opening to the right off the passage, is the door to the downstairs world.*

*The flat has been fairly recently decorated—the furniture, pic-
tures and objects have been collected over the last three years, so
that they express a unity of taste in a pleasant* Sunday Colour
Magazine *way. Books. Record player. Television. Indirect lighting.
Central heating. Wall-to-wall carpets in downstairs rooms and hall.
An intercom set in the wall of the hall by the door, and an ordinary telephone on a hall table.*

*There is one rather odd aspect of the set which will not be im-
mediately obvious, but will appear—what are normally a bedroom
and living room have been hastily rearranged to look like two bed-
sitters.*

*The time is the present. It is about 3:30 on a Saturday afternoon
in February.* JANE *is lying on the studio couch in the room on the
right, smoking a cigarette and reading a book. A table is laid for
tea—cups and saucers, knives, forks and spoons, milk jug, jam in a
pottery dish, butter in a saucer, a Fullers cake.*

The door to the outside is opened by a latchkey. JANE *looks up
and listens.* SARAH *brings* TREVOR *into the hall. He is a young actor
with traces of North Country in his speech.*

SARAH Shall I take your coat?

TREVOR What? . . . Yes . . . Thank you.

SARAH (*She hangs up his coat together with her own, which she
removes without his help*) Straight in. It's the door on the left.

(TREVOR *goes into the room at the left. He looks around, ad-*

miring the room, clearly a stranger to it. Having hung up the coats, SARAH *follows, closing the door behind her*)

TREVOR   You've got a nice place here.

SARAH   I share it with another girl.

TREVOR   You've each got your own room?

SARAH   Yes, and we share the kitchen and bathroom.

TREVOR   Where is she?

SARAH   She's gone out. (JANE *looks at her watch. Then she returns to reading*) Would you like a drink?

TREVOR   I'm not used to this.

SARAH   To what?

TREVOR   This ... (*Gesture*) luxury.

SARAH   Oh, really!

TREVOR   And I'm not used to being taken home by girls, as a matter of fact.

SARAH   Who usually takes you home?

TREVOR   That's not what I meant. (*Pause*) Of course ... my own place ...

SARAH   Yes?

TREVOR   It's not much to take anyone back to.

SARAH   Why not?

TREVOR   I haven't got much money.

SARAH   Then why fritter it away, hanging around pubs?

TREVOR   You've got to do something.

SARAH   You could try work.

TREVOR   I told you; I'm an actor.

SARAH   Sorry. I forgot.

TREVOR   What do *you* do?

SARAH   I told you; I design fabrics.

TREVOR   That's right; you did. (*Pause*) Shall we ... (*Indicates studio couch*) I mean, do you want to sit down?

SARAH (*Sits in a chair*)   Thank you.

(TREVOR *hovers, uncertain whether he is expected to share the chair with her*)

TREVOR   Shall I sit down with you?

SARAH   No.

(*Pause.* JANE *looks up, looks at her watch again, half gets up, decides against it, and returns to reading*)

TREVOR   You're a funny girl.

SARAH   Why?

TREVOR   I mean, you picked *me* up. Standing there in your plastic mac, rubbing yourself up against me.

SARAH   I was not rubbing—

TREVOR   Asking me to come home with you.

SARAH   For a drink.

TREVOR   I thought you wanted to make all the running. Well, I didn't mind. Only now it looks as if I've got to do it. I'm not very good at that, as a matter of fact, because I'm a bit shy. I've got no instinct for it. I never know when it's time to put my hand on your leg—I mean, what the right moment is. Every girl I've ever been with has had to—sort of let me know—you know, tactfully —they move tactfully. I always have to know it's all right before I can go on to the next step.

SARAH (*Rises*)   I'll get you that drink.

TREVOR   Don't bother. I'm not much good if I've had too much to drink, as a matter of fact.

SARAH (*Goes to drinks cupboard*)   There's vodka and tonic.

TREVOR (*Sits in the chair she's left*)   Thank you. (JANE *looks at her watch again, gets up, opens her door cautiously, goes into the hall, and on up to the kitchen. From the cupboard, she takes a bowl and a packet of Scone Mix. She lights the oven. A buttered tin tray is already on the kitchen table. She starts to make scones. Meanwhile,* SARAH *has given* TREVOR *his drink—he thanks her— and goes to sit on the studio couch, leaving* TREVOR *in the chair.* JANE *makes some slight noise in the kitchen.* TREVOR *hears it*) What was that?

SARAH   What?

TREVOR   I thought I heard something.

SARAH   It's an old house. It makes noises.

TREVOR   Oh.

SARAH   Built by Gianino Pisco in 1824. You'll find it in *The A to Z of Historic London* if you're interested. Under P.

TREVOR   Ah.

        (*Pause*)

SARAH (*Speaks at the same time as* TREVOR)   Do you—

TREVOR   *You* aren't—

        (*Both stop*)

SARAH   I'm sorry.

TREVOR   *You* aren't having a drink.

SARAH   No. I had more than I wanted in the pub. (*Pause. He puts down his drink. There is another noise from the kitchen. He looks up, but* SARAH *seems to have noticed nothing. He gets up, and goes toward her*) Don't *touch* me!

TREVOR   What?

TREVOR

SARAH   I don't want you to touch me.

TREVOR   I'm sorry.

SARAH   No, it's my fault. I'm sorry, Trevor. I'm very nervous.

TREVOR   My name's not Trevor.

SARAH   Never mind.

TREVOR   Why did you think I was called Trevor?

SARAH   It doesn't matter.

TREVOR   Did you go to that pub to meet someone called Trevor? Have you made a mistake?

SARAH   I did, and I haven't.

TREVOR   What?

SARAH   I did go to that pub to meet someone called Trevor, and I haven't made a mistake.

TREVOR   I don't understand you.

SARAH   (*Notices his slight accent*) You're from the north, aren't you? You're what they call a new wave actor.

TREVOR   Yes. There's a lot of us. That's why I'm not in work.

SARAH   Please sit down. Finish your drink. I'm sorry I snapped at you.

> (TREVOR *goes back to his chair.* JANE *puts the scones into the oven. Then she looks at her watch again, and comes back into the hall*)

TREVOR   I wish I knew what you're talking about.

> (JANE *hesitates, then enters the room they are in*)

JANE   Well?

SARAH   Trevor, this is Jane.

JANE   Have you told him?

SARAH   Not yet.

JANE   It's three forty-five. I've just put the scones in.

TREVOR   Er . . .

> (*He crosses his legs*)

JANE   There's only half an hour.

SARAH   How long do they take? the scones?

JANE   Don't worry about it. I'll see to it.

SARAH   Is there anything you want me to do?

JANE   No. I did it all while you were out. (TREVOR *crosses his legs the other way. They look at him, considering how to start.* JANE *begins*) Trevor—

TREVOR   I'm sorry. I told your friend. My name's not Trevor.

JANE   Yes, it is.

TREVOR   She made a mistake.

SARAH   (*To* JANE) He was on his own. He's an out-of-work actor.

He needs money. I'm sorry about the accent, but a lot of people have accents now, you know they do.

JANE The accent doesn't matter. If they take against him, they'll be all the more pleased when I break it off.

TREVOR Look—

(*Recrosses his legs uncomfortably*)

JANE Don't worry. We're just going to explain.

TREVOR Then, if you wouldn't mind . . .

SARAH Yes?

TREVOR I mean, if it's going to take a bit of time—

JANE (*Looks at her watch*) It can't take much.

TREVOR I had a lot of beer in that pub, and—

SARAH It's at the end of the hall.

TREVOR (*Gets up*) Thank you.

(*He leaves the room and goes up the hall into the bathroom*)

JANE You took your time.

SARAH It wasn't easy.

JANE All you had to do was go up to someone and—

SARAH You can't just approach a man like that. I had to stand there for hours, rubbing myself up against him.

JANE Rubbing yourself up!

SARAH Metaphorically. Then when we got back, he thought—

JANE I know what he thought.

SARAH Well, he was bound to. I had to discourage him.

(*Pause*)

JANE Love, I'm sorry. I am sorry, love. I was here . . . reading . . . wondering.

SARAH I know. I could feel you wondering all the way from the pub. Wonder and jealousy. They were very thick on the stairs when we came in.

JANE Jealous! Of him?

SARAH You'd be jealous of the *Manchester Guardian* if it was delivered every day.

JANE I'll tell him. I'll just put it to him. He can only say no.

SARAH I wish we didn't have to.

JANE We do have to.

SARAH Couldn't we say Trevor had a business conference or something?

JANE Script conference. My Trevor writes for television—do try to remember. *Your* Trevor's in ICI.

SARAH Sorry. Couldn't we say he had a script conference, and couldn't get here? Then I'd ring up from a phone box, and pretend to be him. (JANE *gives her a look*) Well, they wouldn't hear my end of the conversation.

> (*The WC is flushed in the bathroom.* TREVOR *appears, and comes down the hall*)

JANE   We'll have to do that anyway if he refuses.

> (TREVOR *returns*)

TREVOR   Who uses Arpège? I took some. I like using other people's things: it's a kind of kleptomania. I thought I might brush my teeth with your toothbrush, but I don't really know you well enough, do I?

SARAH   I can smell the Arpège. It's very strong.

TREVOR   That's the trouble. When it belongs to somebody else, I always put too much on.

JANE   Trevor—

TREVOR   I told you—

JANE   That's the first thing. You've got to get used to answering to the name.

TREVOR   Why?

JANE   Just listen. You're not very well off, are you?

TREVOR   No.

JANE   And you're an actor. (*To* SARAH) That's a bonus, Sarah, getting an actor. It's worth the extra time. (*To* TREVOR) We want you to act.

TREVOR   What in?

JANE   Just for this afternoon. My parents are coming to tea. They live in Paignton, and I hardly ever see them, but once a year they make a family tour—a weekend in Maidenhead with my married sister, during which they visit me, then up to Buxton to my brother—

SARAH   He's a mining engineer. You might have met him.

TREVOR   I'm from Bolton.

SARAH   It's all the north, isn't it?

JANE   Then back home. They'll be here in (*Looks at her watch*) fifteen minutes. They must think you're my fiancé.

TREVOR   Where is your fiancé?

JANE   I haven't got a fiancé. But I'm twenty-seven. My parents think I should have one.

TREVOR (*To* SARAH)   But why did *you*—

SARAH   I picked you up because Jane's a friend of mine. She had to get things ready here. Finding you was the best way to help her.

TREVOR (*To* JANE) But twenty-seven's nothing. People get engaged at any age.

JANE That's what I tell my parents. But my mother is rather a
bossy woman, Trevor. She doesn't want me to become a dried-up
spinster, and she does want to see some positive evidence of my
intention to avoid that. (*Pause*) But don't worry. I shall certainly
break it off. It won't come to anything.

SARAH We thought if you played up your accent a bit, and took
milk first in tea, and dribbled your scones, Jane's mother might
break it off herself.

TREVOR But why couldn't you get one of your friends to do it?

JANE We'll pay you five pounds for the afternoon. Do you agree?
(*Pause*)

TREVOR I see.

JANE What do you see?

TREVOR If this is a bed-sitter, where's the dressing table?

JANE In the other room.

TREVOR The bedroom?
(*Pause*)

JANE Yes. (*To* SARAH) He's quick, isn't he? It must come from
working in the theatre.

TREVOR (*To* SARAH) And *your* mother?

SARAH My mother's the President of the local Liberal Party, and
she runs the Welfare Clinic, and she does part-time teaching of
retarded children. She doesn't care if I get married or not, but
she says she'd like me to be sexually fulfilled. Consequently *my*
Trevor is a married man who works for Shell.

JANE ICI.

SARAH ICI. (*To* TREVOR) But you don't have to bother about *my*
Trevor.

TREVOR What a pity!

SARAH Do you need work that badly?

TREVOR I didn't mean that. I meant . . . What a pity! I'm sorry.

JANE We don't need your pity. Will you take the job? (*The doorbell rings. Looks at her watch*) They're early. Quickly—Will
you do it?

TREVOR Yes.

JANE (*Going*) Sarah, fill him in.
(*She goes to answer the door by means of the intercom.*
SARAH *hastily briefs* TREVOR)

SARAH You're Trevor Hudson. You live in JANE (*Conversation*
Chelsea—quite near here—in Paultons   *not really*

Square—a flat. Christ, I can't remember the number. Never mind; they won't ask. You're a staff writer for the BBC: that's why you never get your name in the *Radio Times*. You do research and linking bits for programs about animals and the Common Market. You're writing a novel. It takes you ages because you can never think of the right words. You had some poems published when you were at the university.

heard) Mother? . . . What? . . . I can't hear— . . . Oh! . . . Yes . . . (*Thinks*) I'm sorry; the door buzzer isn't working. She'll have to come down.

TREVOR Which?

SARAH Any you like.

TREVOR Oxford, then. I did *Charley's Aunt* at Southport two years ago.

(JANE *returns, appalled*)

JANE It's *your* parents.

SARAH What?

JANE It's your parents. They wanted to surprise you. I told them the buzzer wasn't working. You'll have to go down and let them in.

SARAH Jesus! (*Going quickly*) Fill him in.

(*She runs into the hall, and out through the door*)

JANE Trevor works for ICI. He's married.

TREVOR What about the scones? Shouldn't we take them out of the oven?

JANE (*Looks at her watch*) Oh God! God! Come on! (*They go quickly upstairs to the kitchen to get the scones out of the oven*) Trevor has two children. Twins. They were an accident. He doesn't like them much.

TREVOR What's his name?

JANE Hudson.

TREVOR But that's—

JANE They're both called Hudson. Both Trevors. Hers and mine.

TREVOR Convenient.

JANE It's the landlord's name.

TREVOR Trevor?

JANE Hudson. Trevor, do listen! Trevor's an economist. He—

TREVOR What's the landlord's first name?

JANE How do *I* know? Landlords don't have first names. Put the scones in that basket, and cover them with a napkin. I'd better make some more.

TREVOR He's an economist?

JANE Very brilliant and young. He was married at eighteen. That's where the twins came from. It was a shotgun wedding in the chapel of Dulwich College. He and Sarah met at the National Gallery one lunchtime. He picked her up in front of a Study of Small Children Being Mobbed by Apes.

TREVOR He did?

JANE No. *I* did.

    (*The door to the outside opens.* SARAH *is heard. Both react*)

SARAH Go straight in. (MR. *and* MRS LAWRENCE, *both in their late fifties, enter.* SARAH *follows*) I'll take your coat, Mother. It's the room on the left.

TREVOR There they are.

JANE You'd better take the scones down.

MRS. LAWRENCE I thought you said Trevor was here.

SARAH He is.

    (MRS. LAWRENCE *goes into* SARAH's *room*)

MRS. LAWRENCE No, he isn't.

TREVOR Hey!

JANE Yes?

TREVOR What do I do when *your* parents come?

JANE I'll have to tell them Trevor had a script conference.

TREVOR I could drop in for a drink later.

JANE *You* could?

TREVOR Trevor could.

MRS. LAWRENCE He's not here, Sarah.

    (SARAH *joins her in the room, leaving* MR. LAWRENCE *to hang up his coat, take his scarf off, etc.*)

SARAH Well, he should be. (*Calls from the door*) Trevor!

TREVOR (*Calls*) I'm in the kitchen, making some scones. (*He comes downstairs, carrying the scones in a basket, with a napkin over them. In the kitchen,* JANE *puts the kettle on and lays a tray for tea.* TREVOR *stops to speak to* MR. LAWRENCE) How do you do?

MR. LAWRENCE Very well, thank you.

TREVOR Stock Market's recovering, I see.

MR. LAWRENCE What?

TREVOR Stocks and shares. They're very buoyant.

MR. LAWRENCE Oh . . . Good.

TREVOR You have to keep a sharp eye on the state of the market in my job. I'll take these in. (*He goes into* SARAH's *room with the scones.* MR. LAWRENCE *has begun to get the full aroma of the*

Arpège. He gazes after TREVOR, *and sniffs the air, surprised*)
Scones. Eat them while they're hot.

SARAH   Mother, this is Trevor.

TREVOR   How do you do? Your husband and I have just been discussing stocks and shares.

MRS. LAWRENCE   I'm so glad to meet you, Trevor. I've heard a lot
about you. (*To* SARAH) Sarah dear, you're wearing a very heavy
perfume. I didn't notice it when we came in.

TREVOR   No, it's me. I put too much on. (*Sudden thought*) Oh
my Gawd, I forgot the kettle.

> (*He goes swiftly out again, passing* MR. LAWRENCE *at the
> door of the room, and on up the stairs into the kitchen.*
> MR. *and* MRS. LAWRENCE *look after him, and then at each
> other*)

MRS. LAWRENCE   *That's* Trevor?

SARAH   I told you so, mother.

MRS. LAWRENCE   My dear, I hope you haven't made a mistake.

SARAH   Don't be ridiculous.

MR. LAWRENCE   What was that about stocks and shares?

SARAH   He takes an interest in them.

> (TREVOR *has reached the kitchen, and sees the kettle already
> on*)

TREVOR   Oh, you've done it. What about cups and saucers?

JANE   There's the tray. How's it going?

TREVOR   Early to say. I'm concentrating on making a good impression. No cake?

JANE   There's a cake in the other room. You'd better cut it in half.

> (TREVOR *gathers up the tray*)

TREVOR   I'll come back when it whistles.

JANE   No. Let Sarah do it.

TREVOR   Oh, I don't—(*Realizes* JANE *wants reassurance*) Rightyho. (*Ready to go downstairs*) I'd start making those extra
scones if I were you.

> (JANE *takes a packet of Scone Mix from the cupboard, and
> begins on the scones*)

MRS. LAWRENCE   Now we *are* here, we can take you and Trevor
out for the evening. Your father's brought his Barclaycard.

SARAH   But Trevor's married. He has a family in Blackheath.

MRS. LAWRENCE   Then what's he doing here, baking scones?

SARAH   He comes round on Saturday afternoons sometimes.

MRS. LAWRENCE   Don't be silly, Sarah. If you only had the afternoon, you'd spend it in bed, not up to your elbows in dough.

MR. LAWRENCE   Steady on, Hetty.

SARAH   As a matter of fact, we—

MRS. LAWRENCE   Don't say you've been. That bed's not even rumpled.

MR. LAWRENCE   Hetty!

MRS. LAWRENCE   I've no time for prudery about sex, Harold. You ought to know that, if anyone does.

MR. LAWRENCE   I do, dear; I do.

　　　(TREVOR *comes in*)

MRS. LAWRENCE   Trevor, my husband and I thought you and Sarah might like to come out with us this evening. There was a Hungarian film in the Sunday papers.

TREVOR (*Begins to set the table*)   Hungarian?

SARAH (*Helps*)   I'll help you.

MRS. LAWRENCE   We hardly ever see Hungarian films in Bury St. Edmunds. If one has to come to London, one oughtn't to waste the trip. (*To* SARAH) I've already taken your father round the Victoria and Albert Museum.

MR. LAWRENCE   I'll sit down for a bit if I may, and take my shoes off.

MRS. LAWRENCE   We'll see the six o'clock show, and have dinner afterwards. Then we'll be able to catch the 10:45 home. Harold, what did you do with the *Good Food Guide?* We'd better find somewhere to eat between King's Cross and the Curzon Cinema.

TREVOR   That'll be lovely.

SARAH   But Kathy's expecting you. (*Slight emphasis*) At home.

TREVOR   Who? . . . Oh, Kathy. Yes, that's right; Kathy's expecting me. I've got a wife and family. (*To* MR. LAWRENCE) Twins. But I don't like them very much. If it hadn't been for them, I wouldn't be married. It's hard to forgive a thing like that.

SARAH   You're not trying, are you?

TREVOR   I'd better get the cake. (*To* MRS. LAWRENCE) We're only having half a cake because Jane's expecting *her* parents. (*Bell rings.* JANE *hears it, and begins to come downstairs, leaving the scones on the baking tray*) That's them now. (*He meets* JANE *in the hall*) Getting the cake.

JANE   I haven't had time to put the scones in.

　　　(*He goes on into the room on the right.* JANE *answers the intercom. Overlapping:*)

MRS. LAWRENCE   Jane? That's the girl—?　JANE   Mother? . . . Do come up. Push the door when it

SARAH   The girl I share with.　buzzes.

MR. LAWRENCE (*Has his shoes off*)   That's better. That's much better.

> (JANE *pushes the buzzer that lets people in downstairs.* TREVOR *fusses with cutting the cake in half and looking for another plate to put his half on. He finds one under a plant*)

MRS. LAWRENCE   How do you get on with her? You never say.

SARAH   Oh, very well. We don't really see much of each other. She has her friends, and I have mine. She's engaged, as a matter of fact.

> (JANE *has the door open, and is looking down the stairs. The kettle whistles in the kitchen.*)

TREVOR (*Shouts*)   Sarah, can you go?

SARAH   I won't be a moment, Mother.

> (*She goes into the hall.* JANE *turns to her for a moment.* SARAH *takes* JANE's *hand, and squeezes it, then goes quickly up into the kitchen*)

MRS. LAWRENCE   There's something wrong with that young man.

MR. LAWRENCE   Lots of men wear scent nowadays.

MRS. LAWRENCE   If one's going to be somebody's mistress, it's not up to *him* to bake the scones. It's not the basis of a satisfactory relationship. I think we'd better find out a little more about him.

> (JANE *has turned to look after* SARAH. *Consequently her attention is off the door, through which* MRS. KEMPTON, *a woman in her late fifties, now comes sailing*)

MRS. KEMPTON   Jane, dear!

JANE   Hullo, Mother.

> (MRS. KEMPTON *folds* JANE *in her arms, as* TREVOR *comes out of the room stage right with half a cake on the plant plate.* MRS KEMPTON *drops* JANE *and advances to him*)

MRS. KEMPTON   And you're Trevor.

TREVOR   Yes.

JANE   No! (*Moves behind her mother to sign to* TREVOR)

TREVOR   Eh?

> (MRS. KEMPTON *sniffs, and turns to* JANE)

MRS. KEMPTON   Jane, you're wearing too much perfume.

TREVOR   No, it's me.

MRS. KEMPTON   I beg your pardon.

TREVOR   I went a bit mad with the Arpège. Nerves, I expect. Knowing I was going to meet you.

JANE   Mother, you've made a mistake.

MRS. KEMPTON   No, no, Jane dear, it's quite all right. (*To* TREVOR) I understand.

JANE No, you don't.

MRS. KEMPTON Trevor wished to make a good impression on his fiancée's parents, and accidentally put on too much after-shave lotion. That's not hard to understand. (MR. KEMPTON, *a man in his late fifties, appears, exhausted by the stairs*) Harold, this is Trevor. (*To* TREVOR) My husband takes longer to come upstairs than I because he likes to have a little rest on every landing.

TREVOR How do you do, Mr. . . . er . . .

MR. KEMPTON How do! She ought to have a lift. You tell her. (*To* JANE) You ought to have a lift, Janey. Get one put in.

JANE Mother, this isn't Trevor.

MRS. KEMPTON What?

JANE This isn't Trevor.

MRS. KEMPTON (*Turns to* TREVOR) But—

TREVOR Well . . . maybe I'm not.

MRS. KEMPTON Then why did you say you were?

        (SARAH *comes downstairs from the kitchen with the teapot*)

SARAH Trevor—

        (*Stops dead as they all look at her. Pause*)

MRS. KEMPTON I don't know what's got into you, Jane.

SARAH I'm so sorry. I interrupted.

MRS. KEMPTON (*To* TREVOR) Are you Trevor or are you not?

TREVOR Sort of yes and no, in a manner of speaking.

JANE Mother—

MRS. KEMPTON Just a minute, Jane. (*To* SARAH) You're the girl my daughter shares the flat with. How do you do?

SARAH Yes, I am. How do you do?

MRS. KEMPTON Sarah Lawrence.

SARAH Yes. You're Mrs. Kempton.

MRS. KEMPTON Exactly. (*Indicates* MR. KEMPTON) My husband.

MR. KEMPTON How do you do?

MRS KEMPTON I know your name, Miss Lawrence. Little else. Jane writes very little about you.

SARAH I'm sorry.

MRS. KEMPTON Don't apologize. You have your life to lead; that's as it should be. Sharing a flat is a matter of convenience. I don't approve of close friendships between young women.

TREVOR I'll just take the cake in.

MRS. KEMPTON (*To* SARAH) You know Mr. Hudson, of course?

SARAH Trevor? Yes.

MRS. KEMPTON Thank you. (*To* TREVOR) Take the cake in, Trevor, by all means. I shall join you in a moment. Jane dear, no doubt

you wish to show me where to wash my hands. Harold, follow
Trevor.

JANE (*Indicates the door*)   In here, Mother.

TREVOR (*Gives* SARAH *the cake*)   For you.

SARAH (*Forestalls surprise in* MRS. KEMPTON)   My parents have
come to tea unexpectedly. Trevor thought I ought to have half
the cake.

MRS. KEMPTON   Ah! . . . I am glad my daughter bought one large
enough.

JANE   This *way*, Mother.

(MRS. KEMPTON *and* JANE *go into the bathroom.* SARAH *and*
TREVOR *look at* MR. KEMPTON)

SARAH   Will you be coming in to say hullo to my parents?

TREVOR   I think I'd better, don't you?

SARAH   I'm sure you'd better.

TREVOR (*To* MR. KEMPTON)   Sarah's father's very interested in
writing for television. We don't often get the chance to talk.

MR. KEMPTON   Which is Jane's room?

TREVOR (*Points*)   That one.

MR. KEMPTON   I'll just take my shoes off. We've been to see Queen
Mary's dolls. My wife likes to keep active.

(*He goes into* JANE's *room, sits, and takes his shoes off*)

SARAH   What happened?

TREVOR   She thought I was Jane's Trevor.

SARAH   So I gather. And Jane?

TREVOR   Wanted *you* to have me.

SARAH   Yes . . . Blast! I mucked it up.

TREVOR   Now you've both got me.

SARAH   But hardly both at once.

TREVOR   It's just like *The Corsican Brothers* I must say. I've always
wanted to play twins. I'd better come in with you for a bit, and
then get back to the others.

SARAH (*Giving it*)   Take the cake

(SARAH *opens the door and enters her own room,* TREVOR
following)

MRS. LAWRENCE (*As she sees him*)   Trevor—

(*The bathroom door opens and* MRS. KEMPTON *comes out*)

MRS. KEMPTON   Trevor—

(*A frozen moment. Then the phone rings*)

TREVOR (*Gives* SARAH *the cake quickly*)   I think it's for me. (*He
answers the phone*) Hullo? . . . What? . . . This is Trevor
Hudson speaking. Yes, it's I. (*Signs to* JANE *who closes the door.*

Gives a conciliatory smile to MRS. KEMPTON. *Then, unseen by her, but seen by the audience if possible, cuts himself off from the caller at the other end, while continuing to speak*) No, you tell Huw Wheldon I can't do it for that. He'll have to get Jonathan Miller . . . No, I'm sorry. Not a penny under two thousand . . . That's right. You tell him. (*He puts down the phone, and his smile to* MRS. KEMPTON *is much more confident*) I'm so sorry. Do forgive me. It's really not at all important, but my agent gets distraught if he doesn't know where to find me. Do please go in. Jane, did you put the kettle on?

JANE No.

TREVOR I'll do it. (*Opens the door for* MRS. KEMPTON) With you in a moment. I just want to whip up some scones to supplement the cake.

MRS. KEMPTON Whip?

TREVOR Only a manner of speaking. Nothing kinky.

    (MRS. KEMPTON *enters the room, giving another sniff at the reek of* TREVOR's *Arpège.* MR. KEMPTON *looks up at her*)

MR. KEMPTON I thought I'd take my shoes off.

MRS. KEMPTON There's something odd about that young man.

MR. KEMPTON Oh, I don't know. Lots of men wear scent nowadays. I thought it was rather attractive.

MRS. KEMPTON That will do, Harold.

MR. KEMPTON He's a writer, isn't he? Bound to be artistic.

MRS. KEMPTON I don't want Jane getting into the newspapers. I think we'd better find out a little more about him (*Looks around*) Why isn't there a wardrobe in here?

    (TREVOR *has been leaning against the wall of the hall with his eyes closed, recovering, watched by* JANE)

JANE Who was on the phone?

TREVOR I don't know. Someone with asthma.

JANE What?

TREVOR Heavy breathing.

JANE Oh . . . him.

TREVOR You know him?

JANE All the women in this district know him. He's called the Chelsea Breather. I usually put the phone down.

TREVOR Well, let him breathe a bit next time. You owe him something. He saved my life. (*Moves*) I'll get the scones in. That should give me a few minutes with Sarah's parents while they're baking. (*As he goes*) I hope you noticed that two thousand quid's my minimum fee for scripts.

JANE Yes. As far as my parents know, that's how much you make in a year.

TREVOR (*Going*) Ah! . . . Well, you can't win them all.

> (JANE *goes in to her parents.* TREVOR *goes to the kitchen, and puts scones in the oven. He looks round for something to serve them on, and finds a plate and napkin. Meanwhile* SARAH *has been pouring tea for the* LAWRENCES, *handing scones, jam, butter, etc.*)

MRS. LAWRENCE Where's Trevor?

SARAH He had a phone call. Business.

MRS. LAWRENCE He's gone?

SARAH No. He'll be in in a minute.

MR. KEMPTON Where's Trevor?

MRS. KEMPTON He had a phone call. Something about two thousand pounds.

MR. KEMPTON Good God!

MRS. KEMPTON He refused it.

MR. LAWRENCE (*Biting*) He makes a good scone.

SARAH He enjoys cooking.

MRS. LAWRENCE (*Looks at* MR. LAWRENCE) I suppose he doesn't get the opportunity at home.

SARAH No, his wife does it all.

MRS. LAWRENCE Is that why he comes here?

SARAH No, he comes to see me. As you know.

MRS. KEMPTON I suppose men's after-shaving lotion is designed to linger nowadays.

JANE Why do you say that?

MRS. KEMPTON If Trevor shaved this morning, it's still rather strong.

JANE It's not after-shave; it's scent. It belongs to Sarah. Trevor found it in the bathroom, and put some on just before you arrived.

MRS. KEMPTON Did he?

JANE He told you; he was nervous.

MRS. KEMPTON It's all right, dear; I said I understood. (*Looks around*) There's something odd about this room. I'll put my finger on it in a minute.

> (TREVOR *puts the scones in the oven and comes downstairs to join the* LAWRENCES, *going quietly past the* KEMPTONS' *door*)

TREVOR (*Makes an entrance*) Everybody happy?

MRS. LAWRENCE What was your phone call?

TREVOR   Oh . . . financial matters.

MRS. LAWRENCE   On Saturday afternoon?

TREVOR   Well, you know how it is.

MRS. LAWRENCE   No, I don't.

MR. LAWRENCE   I don't either.

SARAH   Trevor does a lot of free-lance work in his spare time.

TREVOR   That's right. I've got a wife and family to support.

SARAH   He's a consultant.

TREVOR   Yes.

SARAH   Firms consult him.

TREVOR   Always at it.

SARAH   He advises them.

TREVOR   They pay for my advice.

MRS. LAWRENCE   He must be very brilliant.

TREVOR   Yes, I am.

MRS. LAWRENCE   Tell me, Trevor, what exactly do you do at ICI?
        (*Pause*)

TREVOR   I'm glad you asked that question.

MRS. KEMPTON   Jane dear, how much do you really know about
        Trevor?

JANE   I've told you. He's a scriptwriter. He's—

MRS. KEMPTON   We know what he does for a living; that's not the
        point.

JANE   What is the point?

MRS. KEMPTON   How well do you really know him?

MR. KEMPTON   Your mother's afraid he might be a nancy boy.

JANE   What?

MR. KEMPTON   Homosexual. You know the sort of thing. Exposing
        himself in public lavatories.

JANE   Why?

MR. KEMPTON   Just because he wears scent and likes cooking. I
        told her everybody wears scent these days. She said she didn't
        want you getting into the papers.

JANE   (*To* MRS. KEMPTON) You don't approve of my fiancé,
        Mother?

MRS. KEMPTON   I never said that. I just don't want you to rush into
        things and be sorry afterwards.

JANE   But you told me I ought to get married.

MRS. KEMPTON   To the right man. Yes.

JANE   I wish you'd make your mind up. Last time, you said that
        at my age I couldn't afford to be choosy.
        (*Pause*)

MRS. KEMPTON He's a long time with the scones, dear. Do you think you ought to go and—

JANE —see what he's up to? Don't worry, mother. He's hardly likely to be exposing himself in the kitchen.

TREVOR And that's it really.

MRS. LAWRENCE It doesn't seem very clear to me.

SARAH Of course it is, Mother. It's quite clear.

MRS. LAWRENCE But *do* large commercial corporations work like that?

TREVOR Of course they do. If you watched television as much as I do, you'd know they do.

MRS. KEMPTON (*Gets up*) He shouldn't be doing the cooking. It's not a man's job. I'll help him.

JANE No.

MRS. KEMPTON It will give us the chance for a little talk. (*Opens the door*) Trevor—

JANE Mother, I said no. (*At the door*) I won't have you making Trevor nervous.

MRS. KEMPTON Really, Jane, what—

JANE Trevor gets nervous very easily. I'll go.

(*She goes into the hall, closing the door firmly behind her*)

MRS. KEMPTON (*Sitting*) I don't like this, Harold. I don't care for it at all.

MRS. LAWRENCE Was that someone calling?

SARAH No, I don't think so.

MRS. LAWRENCE Somebody wanted Trevor. I heard them distinctly.

SARAH Jane's parents are here. I told you.

MRS. LAWRENCE But what should they want with Trevor?

TREVOR I give them advice sometimes. On financial matters.

(*JANE has gone upstairs to the kitchen, looked for* TREVOR *and seen he isn't there. She comes downstairs into the hall, and hovers outside the bathroom door*)

JANE Trevor?

MRS. LAWRENCE There!

SARAH That was Jane.

MRS. LAWRENCE But why should Jane—

SARAH Mother, don't be so suspicious of everything.

MRS. LAWRENCE Suspicious? I don't know what you mean. What is there to be suspicious about?

TREVOR (*To* SARAH) Don't you have a cat called Trevor?

SARAH (*Angry*) No.

TREVOR   Just trying to be helpful.
   (JANE *still undecided, looks at door of* SARAH's *room, then smells the scones burning in the kitchen*)
JANE   Oh Christ! The scones!
MRS. KEMPTON   What are they talking about up there? They're a very long time.
MR. KEMPTON   Dammit, they're engaged.
MRS. KEMPTON   He's supposed to be meeting us, not gossiping with Jane in the kitchen. Besides, I don't want Jane talking about me to that young man.
MR. KEMPTON   She's obviously done that already. That's why he put on all that scent.
   (JANE *has shot upstairs to the kitchen, and taken the scones out of the oven. She puts them on the plate* TREVOR *has left out, and covers them with a napkin. While:*)
TREVOR   I suppose I ought to say Hullo to Jane's parents. I mean, they might be a bit hurt if I ignored them.
SARAH   They're very fond of Trevor.
MRS. LAWRENCE   I thought you said you saw very little of Jane.
SARAH   I don't see much of her. Trevor just happens to get on with her parents. He collects people.
TREVOR   I'm terribly good with older women. (*Going*) Do excuse me. I shan't be a moment.
   (*He crosses the hall, opens the door, and goes in to* MR. *and* MRS. KEMPTON, *just missing* JANE *as she comes downstairs with the scones on a plate*)
TREVOR   I'm so sorry. The scones won't be a moment.
MRS. KEMPTON   But where's Jane?
TREVOR   Jane?
MRS. KEMPTON   She went to fetch you.
TREVOR   Did she? That's right, she did. (*To* MRS. KEMPTON) Jane went to fetch me.
MRS. KEMPTON   Then where is she?
TREVOR   She hasn't come back yet.
   (JANE *hesitates, then knocks at* SARAH's *door, and goes in. She is surprised not to see* TREVOR)
JANE   Er . . . (*Pause. All look at her*) I . . . er . . .
MRS. LAWRENCE   Are you looking for my daughter's lover?
MR. LAWRENCE   Hetty!
JANE   No . . . No . . . I . . . (*Indicating the scones*) I just brought you these.
MRS. LAWRENCE   But we have scones already.

JANE   These are hot.

MRS. KEMPTON   And where are the scones?

TREVOR   Scones?

MRS. KEMPTON   You went to "whip them up."

TREVOR (*At the door*)   That's right. They're ready. I'll get them.

MRS. KEMPTON   Can't Jane bring them?

TREVOR   Oh, she'll need a bit of help. My scones are terribly heavy.

> (*He goes quickly into the hall, and up into the kitchen, sees* JANE *isn't there, goes to take the scones out of the oven, and finds they're gone*)

JANE   Well . . . I'd better get back.

SARAH   Thank you for the scones.

JANE   That's quite all right.

MR. LAWRENCE (*Eating one*)   They're very good.

MRS. LAWRENCE   I have a great deal of difficulty keeping my husband away from starchy foods.

JANE (*Going*)   I'm so glad to have met you, Mrs. Lawrence.

MRS. LAWRENCE   You will find Trevor with your parents. He is giving them advice on financial matters.

> (JANE *is out and crosses the hall.* TREVOR *has looked for Scone Mix, found none, and is haphazardly mixing flour, milk and eggs in the mixing bowl.* JANE *is surprised not to find* TREVOR *with her parents*)

MRS. KEMPTON   And where is Trevor?

JANE   Trevor?

MR. KEMPTON   He went to help you.

JANE   Oh . . . Trevor. He's making scones.

MRS. KEMPTON   Again!

JANE   The first lot didn't take.

> (*The phone rings.* JANE *and* SARAH *both respond to it as a welcome diversion*)

JANE   I'll go.

SARAH   I'll go.

> (*Both go into the hall, where* TREVOR *is already on his way down to answer the phone. Pause. They look at each other. Both shut the doors to their rooms behind them. The phone is still ringing.* TREVOR *picks it up, and holds it a moment*)

TREVOR   Just letting him breathe. (*Puts down the phone*)

SARAH   I can't keep it up.

TREVOR   *You* can't?

SARAH   We should never have started. It's ridiculous. Like a farce.

JANE   We can't tell them.

SARAH   I'm sick of it. I'm sick of deceit.

JANE   Love, we've started the deception. We have to go on. If they find out now—

TREVOR   That's right. If you hadn't invented *me*, you could just be two friends sharing a flat.

SARAH   Well, we've got to do something.

JANE   What?

TREVOR   If you could just get rid of one set of parents, we could manage.

JANE   How?

TREVOR   Unless you'd rather get rid of me. I don't mind suicide in a good cause. I've often thought of it.

(*Doors to both rooms are opened simultaneously.* MRS. KEMPTON *and* MRS. LAWRENCE *have grown impatient*)

MRS. KEMPTON and MRS. LAWRENCE (*Together*)   Who was—

MRS. KEMPTON   I beg your pardon.

MRS. LAWRENCE   Not at all. (*To* SARAH) Who was it, dear?

TREVOR   Wrong number. (*Looks from one to another*) Ah well, back to the kitchen.

MRS. KEMPTON (*As he goes*)   Why?

SARAH (*Quickly*)   Oh Mother, I don't think you know Jane's mother. Mrs. Kempton . . . this is my mother.

MRS. KEMPTON   How do you do?

MRS. LAWRENCE   I'm so glad to meet you. (*To* SARAH) Sarah, why did Trevor—

JANE   And *we* haven't really been introduced, have we? I brought you some scones just now, but we never really met.

SARAH   Mother, this is Jane.

MRS. LAWRENCE   How do you do? I was just telling my daughter, she never mentions you. Though apparently Trevor—

JANE   We lead rather separate lives, I'm afraid.

MRS. KEMPTON   I'm sure Mrs. Lawrence understands that, Jane.

MRS. LAWRENCE   Sarah tells me your daughter's engaged to be married.

MRS. KEMPTON (*Looks toward kitchen*)   Yes, we—

SARAH (*Jumps in almost hysterically*)   And Mr. Kempton, Mother. You haven't met Mr. Kempton.

MRS. KEMPTON   Trevor—

SARAH (*Waving through door*)   Hullo, Mr. Kempton! Hullo! This is my mother.

MR. KEMPTON   What? . . . What? . . .

SARAH (*To* MRS. KEMPTON)   It's so nice to have met you. (*Pulling* MRS. LAWRENCE *back into her own room*) Come along, Mother. Mustn't let the scones get cold.

MRS. LAWRENCE (*As she goes*)   Will Trevor be long?

MRS. KEMPTON   Is that girl right in the head?

JANE   Of course she is.

MRS. KEMPTON   There's no of course about it.

JANE   She's having . . . rather a difficult love affair at the moment. It makes her nervous.

MRS. KEMPTON   What did that woman mean?

JANE   What woman?

MRS. KEMPTON   "Will Trevor be long?"

JANE   Sarah's mother is not "that woman," Mother. Her name is Mrs. Lawrence.

MRS. KEMPTON   What did she mean: "Will Trevor be long?"

JANE   You must have misheard her.

MRS. KEMPTON   Nonsense. I hope she understands that Trevor—

JANE   He advises her husband on scripts. It's a free-lance thing he does.

MRS. KEMPTON   But she didn't know you. She had to be introduced to you.

JANE   She knows Trevor. I . . . (*Inventing*) I met Trevor through Sarah.

MRS. KEMPTON   Indeed!

JANE   She gave a party, and of course she had to ask me. Trevor was one of the guests.

MRS. KEMPTON   But you told me you met Trevor at the National Gallery in front of a picture—

JANE (*In an outburst*)   Mother, for God's sake will you stop questioning everything I say?

(*Pause*)

MRS. KEMPTON   I don't know what's got into you today.

(*She goes back into* JANE's *room.* JANE *is left in the hall. She would like to join* SARAH, *looks at the door to that room, takes a step, but of course she can't go in. At this point,* TREVOR, *in the kitchen, drops the mixing bowl and says, "Blast!" Since his arrival there, he has looked doubtfully at his mixture, lit the oven, and kept himself unobtrusively occupied in scone preparation until this moment.* JANE *hears him, is undecided whether to go up, but decides against, and follows her mother.* TREVOR *picks the bowl off the floor, and attempts to roll out the mixture which has got very sticky*)

SARAH   I'm sorry. I really can't bear Jane's mother.

MRS. LAWRENCE   But—

SARAH   I don't want to talk about it. If you can't bear someone you can't.

MRS. LAWRENCE   Where's Trevor?

SARAH   In the kitchen. Making—

MRS. LAWRENCE   (*Holds up two brimming plates of scones*) Scones?

SARAH   I don't know what he's making.

MRS. LAWRENCE   Harold, go and find out.

SARAH   No. Leave Trevor alone.

MRS. LAWRENCE   Run along, Harold.

SARAH   Why?

MRS. LAWRENCE   Because I want to talk to you privately, dear.
    (*Pause*)

MR. LAWRENCE (*To* SARAH)   Back soon.
    (*Goes*)

SARAH   Father, you've forgotten your shoes.

MR. LAWRENCE (*In hall*)   Can't get them on. My feet have swollen.
    (*As* MR. LAWRENCE *gets into hall, the phone rings*)

SARAH   I'll go.

MRS. LAWRENCE (*Calls*)   Answer it, Harold, will you?
    (*She closes the door firmly.* MR. LAWRENCE *answers the phone*)

MR. LAWRENCE   Hullo? . . . Hullo?

MRS. KEMPTON   Harold dear, why don't you have a word with Trevor?

MR. KEMPTON   Eh?

JANE   What about?

MR. LAWRENCE   Hello? . . . Hello? . . .

MRS. KEMPTON   If you intend to marry Trevor, dear, then naturally your father ought to get to know him. In the kitchen, Harold.

MR. KEMPTON   Oh . . . All right.

MR. LAWRENCE   Speak up. What do you want? This is (*Looking*) —one of those number things. Used to be Freemantle, but they changed it.

JANE   Why does Father have to go? Trevor'll be back in a moment.

MRS. KEMPTON   Because I want to have a little talk with you.

JANE   Why—

MRS. KEMPTON (*Straight over her*)   And I don't want your father to be embarrassed.

MR. LAWRENCE   Hello? . . .

MR. KEMPTON (*To Jane*) Back soon, Janie.
   (*Going*)

JANE Father, you've forgotten your shoes.

MR. KEMPTON Never mind.
   (*Closes the door behind him*)

MR. LAWRENCE Hello? . . . (*Puts the phone down. Sees* MR. KEMPTON) Nobody there.

MR. KEMPTON Wrong number?

MR. LAWRENCE Don't know. He didn't say.

MR. KEMPTON How do you know there was anybody there at all?

MR. LAWRENCE Asthma.

   (TREVOR *puts the new tray of scones in the oven, and comes downstairs. Seeing the fathers, he tries to back out but is spotted*)

MR. KEMPTON There you are, young man. I was just coming to have a word with you.

MR. LAWRENCE So was I.

MR. KEMPTON Were you? Why?

TREVOR *Were* you? Ah, you were. Yes, of course you were. You both were. But you won't both want to have a word with me at the same time, will you? No, you won't.

MR. KEMPTON My wife says we've got to get to know each other.

MR. LAWRENCE (*Puzzled*) But you do know each other.

TREVOR Better. We should know each other better. We all should. Everyone should.

MR. LAWRENCE Trevor gives you advice.

MR. KEMPTON No, that's what he gives you.

MR. LAWRENCE He gives you advice about—

TREVOR I give everyone advice. It's a fault. Can't mind my own business. Mr. Kempton—Mr. Lawrence. Mr. Lawrence—Mr. Kempton.

MR. KEMPTON and MR. LAWRENCE (*Together*) How do you do?

TREVOR (*To* MR. KEMPTON) I expect you'd like to go to the loo, wouldn't you?

MR. KEMPTON No, I wouldn't.

TREVOR Your wife went. It's nice in there.

MR. KEMPTON No, I don't think so, thanks.

MR. LAWRENCE Wait a minute. There's something I don't understand.

TREVOR Never miss an opportunity, because you don't know when you'll get another chance. Royalty do it. They're always doing it. And President de Gaulle and everybody.

MR. KEMPTON   No, thanks.

TREVOR   You could be out walking. Any minute you'd pass a fountain. Or a mountain stream. Trickle, trickle! Imagine it.

MR. KEMPTON   I said, no thank you.

TREVOR   They've got blue bleach in the cistern. It colors the bowl when you flush. You pull the chain, and the water goes zzzzzz.

MR. LAWRENCE   My wife wanted me to find out what you were doing in the kitchen.

TREVOR   Making scones.

MR. LAWRENCE   Again? Bit obsessional isn't it?
  (*The phone rings*)

MR. KEMPTON (*To* TREVOR)   That for you?

TREVOR   No. Why?

MR. KEMPTON   Thought it might be another of your—

TREVOR   No. It isn't.

MR. LAWRENCE   Probably that fellow with asthma.

TREVOR   The Chelsea Breather. (*To* MR. KEMPTON) It's someone who breathes.

MR. KEMPTON   I'll take it, then. (*Picks the phone up*) Hello? . . . (*Listens then nods to the others*) Now look here, breather—

MR. LAWRENCE   My wife says you've got to understand these people.

MR. KEMPTON   They need a shock. A sharp shock. (*Into the phone*) Breather, you need a shock.

MR. LAWRENCE   They did some experiments at the Howard League. Got a lot of them in a group, breathing at each other. Found they preferred that to using the phone.

MR. KEMPTON (*Into the phone*)   You run along and find some other breathers. We've had enough of you here. We—Hah! (*To the others*) Hung up. (*Puts the phone down*) We shan't hear from him again. What was that about scones? (*To* MR. LAWRENCE) He's always making scones, this fellow, but you never see any.

MR. LAWRENCE   Never *see* any?
  (*Phone rings*)

MR. KEMPTON   I'll leave it off.
  (*Does so*)

TREVOR (*To* MR. KEMPTON)   Look, sir, whatever you wanted to chat about, it's probably a bit personal, isn't it? So (*Indicating the door*) if Mr. Lawrence wouldn't mind—

MR. LAWRENCE   Oh, I can't go back in there.
  (*Smoke has begun to emerge from the oven door*)

TREVOR   Ah! ... (*Turns to* MR. KEMPTON) Er ...

MR. KEMPTON   Nor can I.

TREVOR   Oh.

MR. LAWRENCE   My wife sent me out of the room. I can't go back.

MR. KEMPTON   So did mine. Wanted to have a heart-to-heart with Jane.

MR. LAWRENCE   Mine wanted to have a heart-to-heart with Sarah.

TREVOR   What about? (*Quick second thoughts*) Wait! Don't tell me.

MR. KEMPTON   Can you smell anything burning?

(TREVOR *sniffs. Then he returns to the kitchen, the other two following. Thick smoke from oven. He opens it, looks inside, then closes the door again, and turns the oven off*)

TREVOR   You have to watch them.

MR. KEMPTON   No scones, eh?

MR. LAWRENCE   You could have some of ours. We've got lots.

TREVOR   There's some brandy in the cupboard.

MR. KEMPTON   Ah. Wonder which of the girls it belongs to.

MR. LAWRENCE   Sarah wouldn't mind.

MR. KEMPTON   Or Jane.

TREVOR   Let's have some. (*Getting the bottle*) Where do they keep the glasses?

MR. KEMPTON   If you don't know, who does?

TREVOR   How true! Of course, they're downstairs, aren't they in the—in Sarah's ... Jane's ...

MR. LAWRENCE   What?

TREVOR   In the chiffonier.

MR. KEMPTON   (*Finds them in the kitchen cupboard*)   Here you are.

TREVOR   Oh, *those* glasses. (*Filling them*) You don't mind it neat. (*Toasting*) Cheers. (*All drink*) I needed that.

MR. KEMPTON   Must be a bit of a strain.

TREVOR   You don't know how much.

MR. LAWRENCE   Meeting the parents.

TREVOR   Exactly.

MR. KEMPTON   Silly business. Unnecessary.

TREVOR   Yes.

MR. KEMPTON   What young people do nowadays; it's nothing to do with their parents.

TREVOR   No.

MR. LAWRENCE   You can't get Sarah's mother to see that, though.

MR. KEMPTON   Or Jane's.

MR. LAWRENCE   If two people want to live together—

MR. KEMPTON   Oh, I don't know about living together.

MR. LAWRENCE (*To* TREVOR)   Anyway, you're not living together.

MR. KEMPTON   No, he's not.

TREVOR   No, I'm not.

MR. LAWRENCE   But the point is, if you did want to, you'd do it. Please yourselves.

MR. KEMPTON (*To* TREVOR)   Would you?

MR. LAWRENCE   Your love life is your own affair. Nothing to do with your parents. (*To* MR. KEMPTON) Our generation should stay out of it.

MR. KEMPTON (*To* TREVOR)   But you're not going to live together?

TREVOR   No, I'm not.

MR. KEMPTON   Jane's not that kind of girl. I'm sure she's not.

TREVOR (*Pouring*)   Let's have another drink.

MR. LAWRENCE   Jane?

MR. KEMPTON   My daughter.

MR. LAWRENCE   Oh, Jane! Well, Jane would move out, I assume.

MR. KEMPTON   Why?

MR. LAWRENCE   Well, you weren't thinking—

TREVOR   No, he wasn't.

MR. KEMPTON   What?

TREVOR   You weren't thinking.

MR. LAWRENCE   No, I didn't imagine Jane would stay here if you were living together. Even my wife isn't that broad-minded.

MR. KEMPTON   She wouldn't want to stay here. No room, for one thing.

MR. LAWRENCE   Exactly.

MR. KEMPTON   I don't understand this. (*To* TREVOR) You're not going to live together.

MR. LAWRENCE   I don't see why *you're* so bothered, Kempton.

TREVOR   Cheers.

MR. KEMPTON and MR. LAWRENCE (*Together*)   Cheers.

MR. LAWRENCE   Funny.

TREVOR   What is?

MR. LAWRENCE   My wife thought you might be queer.

TREVOR   Queer?

MR. LAWRENCE   You know . . . homosexual. That kind of thing.

MR. KEMPTON   A nance. So did my wife.

TREVOR   Oh, I don't think people say "nance" nowadays, do they?

MR. LAWRENCE   I told her everyone wears scent in 1968.

MR. KEMPTON   I don't. Never have.

TREVOR   Don't you?

MR. KEMPTON   I wouldn't mind, though. I like scent. I respond to it.

TREVOR (*Shifts a little away uneasily*)   Do you?

MR. LAWRENCE   I've never been attracted to scent. Smell, yes. Not scent. Sweat. I've always found sweat attractive.

TREVOR (*Wipes his hands nervously*)   Let me fill your glass.

MR. KEMPTON   My wife wears Yardley's Lavender. It's not the same.

MR. LAWRENCE   My wife hardly sweats at all.

MR. KEMPTON   Funny my wife thought you were a nance.

TREVOR   Hilarious.

MR. KEMPTON   Cheers.

   (*All drink*)

MR. LAWRENCE   Of course she used to sweat when she was younger. We went to Antibes for our honeymoon, and she sweated like a horse. Now she buys one of those roll-on deodorants.

   (*Conversational focus shifts downstairs. The men continue to drink in the kitchen*)

SARAH   This is ridiculous. I won't have this conversation.

MRS. LAWRENCE   He's not at all suitable.

SARAH   Suitability's got nothing to do with it. I'm not marrying him. You wanted me to be fulfilled. Well, I am fulfilled. Trevor fulfills me every Saturday afternoon, and now you're complaining.

MRS. LAWRENCE   A man like that couldn't fulfill anyone.

SARAH   What do you want?—A blow-by-blow account?

MRS. LAWRENCE   Sarah!

SARAH   That shocks you, doesn't it? But you're supposed to be unshockable, Mother; you're the one that understands people. All my life you've told me to understand people, and now I'm understanding you.

MRS. LAWRENCE   What's that supposed to mean?

SARAH   Try working it out. Why you've nagged at me to find a lover, and why you don't like it now I've found one.

TREVOR   If your feet have swollen, you could put them in the fridge.

MR. LAWRENCE   Cheers.

TREVOR and MR. KEMPTON (*Together*)   Cheers.

MRS. LAWRENCE   I don't want you to be unhappy.

SARAH   Don't you?

MRS. KEMPTON   I don't want you to be unhappy, Jane. A man like that—

JANE   Like that?

MRS. KEMPTON   You know what I mean.

JANE   No. Tell me.

MRS. KEMPTON   I don't say Trevor's . . . effeminate.

JANE   Then?

MRS. KEMPTON   He's clearly unstable. He's not stable, dear. Not the sort of man you could rely on.

JANE   What if I'll settle for someone who'll rely on *me?*

MR. KEMPTON   Don't make debating points.

JANE   Damn you, Mother. I've had enough.

MRS. KEMPTON   What?

SARAH   I've had enough.

JANE   You come here, meet someone—

SARAH   —for the first time. You don't really know—

JANE   —a single bloody thing about him—

SARAH   —and in fifteen minutes—

JANE   —you've written him off.

SARAH   You tell me you're concerned about my future.

JANE   You don't give a damn for anyone but yourself.

SARAH   Just because Trevor wears scent—

JANE   —and bakes scones—

MRS. KEMPTON   Jane! Please!

MRS. LAWRENCE   Sarah!

SARAH   Oh, you're so broad-minded, Mother, so understanding—

JANE   Narrow-minded! Intolerant!

MRS. LAWRENCE   But, Sarah, if you love him—

MRS. KEMPTON   —if you really love him that's a different matter.

MRS. LAWRENCE   If you're sure you love him.

(*Pause*)

SARAH   What?

JANE   Oh . . .

MR. KEMPTON   I'll tell my wife, "You've got it all wrong," I'll say.

MR. LAWRENCE   Yes, *I'll* say that. (*To* TREVOR) Don't you worry. I'll have a word with her.

MR. KEMPTON   "He's not in the least queer. He's just a very obliging fellow."

MR. LAWRENCE   Cheers.

MR. KEMPTON and TREVOR (*Together*)   Cheers.

JANE   I'm sorry. I got carried away.

SARAH   I got carried away, Mother. I didn't mean to hurt you.

MRS. LAWRENCE   No, no, dear. I've no right to interfere.

SARAH   I was cruel. I didn't mean—

MRS. LAWRENCE   You did, dear.

SARAH   No.

MRS. LAWRENCE   And you were right. I look at myself, and what do I see? Prurient curiosity. And jealousy afterwards. I'm ashamed, Sarah.

MRS. KEMPTON   I've been a bossy woman all my life. Of course, your father encourages it.

JANE   But, mother—

MRS. LAWRENCE   Hearing you defend Trevor, "Lord, lord!" I thought, "I've had the impertinence to talk to this girl about fulfillment!"

SARAH   But I didn't mean to defend him. I just lost my temper.

MRS. KEMPTON   You wouldn't be my daughter if you didn't pick someone unsuitable to marry.

JANE   But, Mother, if he *is* unsuitable—

MRS. LAWRENCE   Your father used to be a very passionate man.

MR. LAWRENCE   I think she'd been reading the BO advertisements.

MRS. LAWRENCE   I forgot who spoke to me about it.

MR. LAWRENCE   I couldn't very well tell her, "I *like* BO."

MR. KEMPTON   Cheers.

MR. LAWRENCE and TREVOR (*Together*)   Cheers.

JANE   I'm trying to say, you may be right.

SARAH   I have had . . . doubts about Trevor.

JANE   If you really think I should give him up—

MRS. KEMPTON   No, dear, no.

MRS. LAWRENCE   No, Sarah. It's your own life.

SARAH   Perhaps if I didn't see him for a while—

JANE   If we tried a separation until I feel clearer in my mind.

SARAH   I could talk to him. If he really loves me—

JANE   —he'd want me to be certain of what I feel; I'm sure of that.

MRS. LAWRENCE   Perhaps later . . .

SARAH   No, I'll do it now.

MRS. LAWRENCE   He's still in the kitchen with your father.

MRS. KEMPTON   Your father's talking to him in the kitchen.

JANE   Yes, that's right. (*Going*) I'll send daddy down.

SARAH (*Going*)   I shan't be long. I think it's better if he leaves straightaway.

MRS. LAWRENCE   Oh, my dear, if you're sure.

SARAH   I am.

JANE   I shan't bring Trevor back. He's bound to be a bit upset.

MRS. KEMPTON   My brave girl!
    (*Both girls go into the hall, closing doors behind them. Both mothers sigh exhausted sighs. Pause*)

MR. LAWRENCE   Cheers.

MR. KEMPTON   Cheers.

TREVOR (*Stands*)   Excuse me.

JANE   I've promised to give him up.

SARAH   So have I.

JANE   I said I'd talk to him, and he'd leave right away.

SARAH   Have you got the five pounds?

JANE   In my bag.

SARAH   Oh, love! Love!
    (*They kiss, as* TREVOR *comes downstairs*)

JANE   Trevor—

TREVOR   I don't feel well.

SARAH   No!

TREVOR   I had a lot of beer in the pub. And then vodka. And I've been drinking brandy with your fathers. I feel very strange.

JANE   Get him into the bathroom. (*As they do so*) You'll be all right, Trevor. You'll be all right.

TREVOR (*Last words*)   I'm not Trevor.
    (*Upstairs the two fathers sip brandy*)

MR. LAWRENCE   Think he's all right?

MR. KEMPTON   My wife doesn't care for him.

MR. LAWRENCE   Looked a bit shaky, I thought.

MR. KEMPTON   Oh . . . that. Probably not used to it.

MR. LAWRENCE   Used to what?

MR. KEMPTON   Drinking brandy in the afternoon. Got out of the habit. (*The door leading downstairs is opened with a latchkey. It is the landlord,* MR. HUDSON, *a man in his late fifties. He enters, looks round, sees the phone is off the hook and replaces it censoriously. He looks about him, then crouches to peer through the keyhole of the door on the right*) Tell you a devil for the brandy. Old Johnny Chinaman.

MR. LAWRENCE   Johnny?

MR. KEMPTON   Manner of speaking. Old Johnny Chink.

MR. LAWRENCE   Ah!

MR. KEMPTON   Used to see a lot of those fellows during the war. Chiang Kai-shek's fellows. Devils for brandy. They'd knock it back by the tumblerful. "Banzai," they'd say—

MR. LAWRENCE (*Pouring*)   Couldn't have been "Banzai."

MR. KEMPTON   By George, you're right there. What *did* they say.
I wonder? Neat brandy. Tigers for it. (*Raising his glass*) Banzai.

MR. LAWRENCE   Cheers.

MR. KEMPTON   No, no, old boy. It was something Chinese. Something colloquial. You'd learn it off a record nowadays, but in my
time we actually had to meet these fellows.

> (MR. HUDSON *has been puzzled by what he's seen through
> the keyhole of* JANE's *room. He has left that door, looked
> about him, and tried the door of* SARAH's *room. Nobody
> there but an old woman on her own. Equally puzzling. Now
> there is a gurgle from* TREVOR *in the bathroom*)

JANE (*Heard from the bathroom*)   Get his head under water.

> (HUDSON *goes to the bathroom door, and peers through*)

MR. LAWRENCE   I suppose he is all right. Trevor.

MR. KEMPTON (*Stands*)   I'll go and see. I could do with a leak. Too
much talk about fountains. (*He descends the stairs, and sees*
HUDSON) Ah, bit of a queue, is there?

MR. HUDSON (*Startled*)   What?

MR. KEMPTON   Bit of a queue. (*Notices the phone*) That's funny.
Thought I left it off. (*Takes it off again*) I hope he won't be long
in there. At my age, the old kidneys—

MR. HUDSON   You shouldn't leave the telephone off the hook.

MR. KEMPTON   Why not?

MR. HUDSON (*Replaces it*)   The Post Office don't like it.

MR. KEMPTON   You're from the Post Office, are you?

MR. HUDSON   Er—

MR. KEMPTON   Thought I hadn't seen you before. (*Toward the
bathroom*) Tell you what; let's bang on the door. He might have
passed out.

MR. HUDSON   Who?

MR. KEMPTON   I had to climb over a lavatory door once in Dehra
Dun. Been knocking it back a bit with a friend of mine. Brother
officer, you know. In he went, locked the door, never came out.
Couldn't let him down, so over the top I went. It was pretty to
see him lying there, curled around the bowl.

MR. HUDSON   *Who* may have passed out?

MR. KEMPTON   But it was rather difficult to explain to the briga-
dier, when we both came out together.

MR. HUDSON   *Who*—

MR. KEMPTON   You wouldn't know him. Lumley—Mahratha Light
Infantry. Oh—in there? My daughter's fiancé.

(MRS. KEMPTON *opens the door to* JANE's *room, and looks out*)

MRS. KEMPTON Harold, to whom are you talking?

MR. KEMPTON Fellow from the Post Office come in for a bit of a leak.

MRS. KEMPTON From the *Post Office!* In here?

MR. KEMPTON (*To* HUDSON) By George, that's true. Just because you're in the government service, that doesn't give you the right to barge into a private flat every time you want to—

MR. HUDSON I am not—

MR. KEMPTON Bloody Trade Unions throwing their weight around again. Dammit, you've got pillar boxes for that sort of thing.

MRS. KEMPTON Why should a man from the Post Office—

MR. KEMPTON I'd left the phone off the hook. (*To* HUDSON) Had to. One of those breathers kept ringing up. Dring! Dring! Couldn't hear yourself speak. He'll ring again in a minute.

MR. HUDSON No, he won't.

MRS. KEMPTON How did he get in?

(MRS. LAWRENCE *opens the door of* SARAH's *room, and looks out*)

MRS. LAWRENCE Harold!

MR. KEMPTON Yes? (*Comes to her*) How do you do? I'm Jane's father; I don't think we've met. And this is a man from the Post Office come in for a—

MRS. KEMPTON That will do, Harold.

MR. KEMPTON (*Goes on into* SARAH's *room*) You don't mind if I sit down? Not much point in standing around when you're not even first in the queue.

(*Sits*)

MRS. LAWRENCE I was calling my husband.

MR. KEMPTON (*Gets up*) Ah! (*Crosses to the door; calls*) Lawrence, your wife wants you.

(*He returns to his seat.* MR. LAWRENCE *hears the call and stands*)

MR. LAWRENCE What?

MRS. KEMPTON (*To* MRS. LAWRENCE) I have been trying to discover how this man gained entry to the flat. (*To* HUDSON) If you're from the Post Office, why aren't you in uniform?

MR. HUDSON I'm not from the Post Office.

MRS. LAWRENCE A burglar? (*To* MRS. KEMPTON) Is he a burglar?

MR. HUDSON   I'm the landlord.

MR. KEMPTON (*Makes a discovery*)   I say! Lots of scones here!

MR. HUDSON   I came to put the phone back on the hook.

(MR. LAWRENCE *descends the stairs from the kitchen*)

MRS. LAWRENCE   Harold, where is Trevor?

MR. LAWRENCE   Kempton went to find out. (*Passing* HUDSON) How do you do? (*Sees* MR. KEMPTON) Kempton, where's Trevor?

MR. KEMPTON   Still in there. Probably passed out.

MR. LAWRENCE (*Joins him in the room*)   You've found the scones, I see.

MR. KEMPTON (*Passing them*)   Have one.

MR. LAWRENCE   Not allowed. Tea?

MR. KEMPTON   God, no.

MR. LAWRENCE   Ah! You haven't . . . ?

MR. KEMPTON   Not yet. I told you. He's still in there.

MRS. LAWRENCE (*From the door*)   Harold, this man says he's the landlord.

MR. KEMPTON   How did he get in, then?

MRS. LAWRENCE (*To* MR. HUDSON)   How did you—

MR. HUDSON (*Passes her and comes into the room. Indignantly to* MR. KEMPTON)   I have a key. I let myself in. I have the right to do so. (*Looks round*) And now I shall go.

(MRS. KEMPTON *joins* MRS. LAWRENCE, *so that they bar his way back into the hall*)

MRS. KEMPTON   There's no proof of that.

MR. KEMPTON   That's right. He could be a damned thief, come sneaking in here, pretending he wants to use the loo. (*Stands*) Come here, sneak thief; I'm going to search your pockets.

MRS. LAWRENCE   He said he wanted to put the phone back on the hook.

MR. KEMPTON   How did he know the phone was off the hook?

(*Pause.* HUDSON *is now uneasy.* MRS. LAWRENCE *and* MRS. KEMPTON *come into the room, so that he is surrounded*)

MRS. KEMPTON   Well, my man?

MRS. LAWRENCE   How did you know the phone was—

MR. LAWRENCE   It *was* off, though.

MR. KEMPTON   What?

MR. LAWRENCE   I mean, he is right. The phone was off the hook.

MRS. LAWRENCE   But how could he know that?

(*Pause*)

MR. HUDSON   I have . . . ways of knowing.

MR. LAWRENCE   What ways?

MR. HUDSON   Mind your own business.

    (*Pause*)

MR. KEMPTON   By George, you're not the landlord at all; you're
that breather. You've been ringing up and breathing at us, and
when I took the phone off the hook, you couldn't bear it.

MR. HUDSON   I'm the landlord. I have the keys. It's natural for me
to be here.

MR. KEMPTON   You stole them, you breather.

MR. HUDSON   No.

MR. LAWRENCE   I suppose he could be both.

MRS. LAWRENCE   What, Harold?

MR. LAWRENCE   Landlord and breather. He could be both.

    (*Pause.* MRS. KEMPTON *closes the door of the room*)

MRS. KEMPTON   Do you mean that a man who breathes at women
on the telephone has the key to my daughter's flat?

    (*The bathroom door opens.* TREVOR, SARAH *and* JANE *come
into the hall cautiously*)

SARAH   It's all right. There's nobody here.

MR. HUDSON   But I never use it.

TREVOR   Shouldn't I say Goodbye to *anyone?*

JANE   No.

MRS. KEMPTON   Never use it? Of course you use it. You're using
it now.

JANE   Just go. Quietly. We'll explain.

TREVOR   It's so impolite. Both of me just creeping off like this.

MR. HUDSON   Only because the telephone was off the hook.

SARAH   Goodbye, Trevor.

JANE   Good*bye*, Trevor.

TREVOR   Wait a sec. I forgot something.

    (*He returns to the bathroom*)

MR. HUDSON   You can ask your daughters. I never come here.

    (TREVOR *flushes the WC*)

MR. KEMPTON   By George, he's out. (*Quickly to the door*) Excuse
me.

MR. HUDSON   But—

MR. KEMPTON   No, old boy. You've forfeited your turn. (*Opens
the door*) Jane, there's a breather in here, says he's your landlord.
(*Passing* TREVOR) There you are, Trevor. Feeling better?

TREVOR   Much better.

MR. KEMPTON   You took your time.

TREVOR Sorry.

(MR. KEMPTON *goes into the bathroom, and closes the door*)

SARAH Trevor! Go!

MRS. LAWRENCE (*Looks through the open door*) Sarah dear, just come in for a moment, will you please? Oh, is Trevor going? Just a minute. I'll have a word with him.

SARAH Mother, I've already had a word with him.

TREVOR Yes, she has, and I quite understand. Goodbye, Mrs. Lawrence. Goodbye, Sarah. Goodbye, Jane.

(*He has the front door open*)

MRS. KEMPTON (*Calls*) Is that Trevor?

TREVOR (*Calls*) Goodbye, Mrs. Kempton.

MRS. KEMPTON (*Comes into hall*) I'll have a word with him before he goes. (*To* JANE) Go in, Jane dear; I just want a word with Trevor.

MRS. LAWRENCE Run along, Sarah.

SARAH Mother, you *don't* want a word with him.

MRS. LAWRENCE Just to show there are no hard feelings, dear.

(JANE *and* SARAH *look at each other, and at* TREVOR. *Then they go into* SARAH's *room.* HUDSON *regards them piteously*)

MR. HUDSON There's been a mistake.

SARAH Yes.

(MRS. KEMPTON *closes the door*)

MRS. KEMPTON Now, Trevor—

TREVOR Please, please! I know what you both want to say.

MRS. LAWRENCE All *I* wanted to tell you—

TREVOR No need to put it into words.

MRS. KEMPTON There are no hard feelings.

TREVOR Just say goodbye. Believe me, I do understand. It's better.

MRS. LAWRENCE (*To* MRS. KEMPTON) No hard feelings?

MRS. KEMPTON None.

MRS. LAWRENCE But I have no hard feelings for Trevor. I'm the one with no hard feelings.

MRS. KEMPTON Why should *you* have no hard feelings?

TREVOR Surely if neither of you has any hard feelings, there's no need to go on about it.

MRS. LAWRENCE Because Sarah is going to give him up.

MRS. KEMPTON No, no, my dear, Jane is going to give him up.

MRS. LAWRENCE Sarah's going to give the affair time to cool.

MRS. KEMPTON Jane wants to be certain what she feels for him.

TREVOR Mrs. Lawrence—

MRS. KEMPTON   Trevor is Jane's fiancé, Mrs. Lawrence.

TREVOR   Mrs. Kempton—

MRS. LAWRENCE   Trevor is Sarah's lover, Mrs. Kempton.

> (*Pause*)

TREVOR   Anyway, if they're both going to give me up, there's no harm done, is there?

> (*The WC is flushed.* MR. KEMPTON *comes out of the bathroom*)

MRS. KEMPTON   Harold, take Trevor into Miss Lawrence's room.

MR. KEMPTON   *Take* him?

> (TREVOR *looks from* MR. KEMPTON *to the women, then closes the door*)

TREVOR   I'll come quietly.

> (*He follows* MR. KEMPTON *into* SARAH's *room*)

SARAH   They know?

TREVOR   Yes.

MR. LAWRENCE   Hello, Trevor. We've caught your breather.

MR. HUDSON   I do not breathe. I have a right to telephone my own tenants.

MR. KEMPTON   I don't understand this.

> (MRS. KEMPTON *and* MRS. LAWRENCE *follow them in, closing the door*)

MRS. KEMPTON   Now.

MR. HUDSON   I am not obliged to explain to you. All my tenants are single women. I have a duty—

MRS. KEMPTON   What is this person talking about?

MR. HUDSON   I do not breathe at women.

MRS. LAWRENCE   No time for that now. Well, Sarah?

MRS. KEMPTON   Well, Jane?

MR. LAWRENCE   What's up?

MR. KEMPTON   Don't ask me.

SARAH   Mother's found out that Trevor's Jane's fiancé as well as my lover.

MR. LAWRENCE   What?

MR. KEMPTON   Steady on.

SARAH   He's single as well as married, and he works for the BBC as well as Shell.

JANE   ICI.

MRS. KEMPTON   Mr. Hudson—

MR. HUDSON   *My* name's Hudson.

TREVOR   Not Trevor?

MR. HUDSON Wallace.

MRS. KEMPTON I'm waiting for an explanation.

JANE We put him up to it.

MRS. LAWRENCE Why?

JANE You wanted Sarah to have a lover. (*To* MRS. KEMPTON) You wanted me to be engaged. You both went on about it. We invented Trevor. Both of him. Then you wanted to meet him. Well, you only come up to London one day a year; it didn't seem too difficult. We couldn't know Sarah's parents would arrive on the same day.

MRS. KEMPTON But why?

MR. HUDSON You've moved the furniture. That wardrobe belongs in the bedroom.

MR. LAWRENCE I thought you said you never used your key.

MRS. KEMPTON The bedroom?

SARAH We don't have two bed-sitters. We have a bedroom and a living room. The two couches push together.

TREVOR Sarah, love, enough's enough.

SARAH No, I'm sick of it. I'm sick of deception.

JANE Sarah!

SARAH I told you. I'm sick of deception. (*To* MRS. LAWRENCE) Jane and I live together, Mother.

MRS. LAWRENCE Yes, dear. You share a flat.

SARAH We *live* together. There isn't any Trevor. There's just Jane and me.

MRS. KEMPTON Yes, my dear; you told us. It was a stupid deception, but I'm sure your mother won't hold it against you.

SARAH Jane, *tell* them.

JANE Sarah means—

MRS. KEMPTON We know what she means, dear. You and Sarah share a flat.

SARAH Yes.

MRS. KEMPTON Naturally you're friends—

SARAH Yes, we are friends.

MRS. KEMPTON (*Riding on*) It would be very inconvenient if you weren't. And since you're both a little shy. (*To* MRS. LAWRENCE) Jane's always been shy.

MRS. LAWRENCE And Sarah. Ridiculous. Pathologically.

MRS. KEMPTON Naturally you're embarrassed that you've neither of you found a young man yet.

SARAH Yet!

MRS. KEMPTON   I blame myself. (*To* MRS. LAWRENCE) I push Jane
too much; I know I do. I had to push her when she was a girl,
or she'd never have done anything.

MRS. LAWRENCE   They're a more puritanical generation now. We
were very frank about sex in the thirties. Perhaps I'm too out-
spoken. I brought Sarah up on D. H. Lawrence.

MRS. KEMPTON   Did you?

MRS. LAWRENCE   So she invents a lover. Then she's ashamed.

MRS. KEMPTON (*To* JANE)   You chose to play a joke on us, my dear.
Not in very good taste, but perhaps we deserved it.

SARAH   Daddy . . . Mr. Kempton . . . do you believe this?

MR. KEMPTON (*Fiddling with shoes*)   I can't get these shoes on.

MR. LAWRENCE   They're mine.

MR. KEMPTON   Oh, is that it?

    (*He gives the shoes to* MR. LAWRENCE *who puts them on.*)

MRS. KEMPTON   I don't know whose particular friend Trevor happens to be.

SARAH   Nobody's. I picked him up in a pub.

MRS. LAWRENCE   There! You do go out and meet people.

SARAH   We never go out.

MRS. KEMPTON   Anyway, now you have met Trevor, I'm sure you'll
get to know each other better.

TREVOR   My name's not Trevor.

MRS. LAWRENCE   You must bring him down to Bury St. Edmunds,
Sarah.

MRS. KEMPTON   Jane, you must bring him to Torquay. (*To* MR.
KEMPTON) Harold!

    (MR. KEMPTON *gets up*)

SARAH (*To Jane*)   They're going. They won't listen.

MR. KEMPTON (*Kisses* JANE *awkwardly*)   Bye, Janey . . . Er . . .

JANE   Yes?

    (MR. KEMPTON *looks at his wife, then decides against what
he was going to say*)

MR. KEMPTON   I'll just get my shoes.

    (*He goes into* JANE's *room, and puts them on*)

MRS. KEMPTON   Will you get the coats, Jane?

SARAH   You don't want to know, then?

MRS. KEMPTON   Goodbye, Sarah my dear. I'm so glad to have met
you at last. (*To* MRS. LAWRENCE) Goodbye, Mrs. Lawrence. (*To*
MR. LAWRENCE) Goodbye.

    (*She and* JANE *go out into the hall, and* JANE *gets the coats.*
MR. KEMPTON *joins them*)

SARAH Mother, you've been open-minded all your life. You've boasted of it. Your mind was so open, I used to fall in.

JANE Here are your coats.

(MRS. KEMPTON *kisses her.* JANE *is entirely unresponding*)

MRS. KEMPTON Goodbye, my dear. You know we always enjoy seeing you.

MR. KEMPTON Bye, Janey.

JANE Goodbye, Daddy.

(MRS. KEMPTON *opens the front door*)

MRS. KEMPTON You're such a silent sulky little thing when you're upset.

(*She goes, her husband following*)

JANE Goodbye, Mother.

(*She remains, gazing after them, then closes the door*)

SARAH I was cruel to you just now, do you remember, when we were arguing about Trevor? I was nervous and hating everything, and I lost my temper. I mocked you for being unshockable, and always understanding people. I said you ought to understand yourself for a start. And you took it, Mother. You shamed me by seeing what I saw, and accepting it. Now accept me.

MRS. LAWRENCE You overdramatize, dear. (*To* JANE, *who returns*) Doesn't she overdramatize, Jane?

SARAH Do you remember that Easter I didn't come home. Jane didn't go home either. We'd just met—picked each other up in the National Gallery.

MRS. LAWRENCE You met in the National Gallery?

TREVOR In front of a picture of small children—

SARAH We went away together that Easter, to a cottage near Cirencester. It was down a long muddy path. We took Jane's haversack, full of healthfood bread and salami and tins of stuffed vine leaves and a pheasant in jelly, and we bought eggs and cream from the farm. We'd lie in bed very late, and one of us would wash up while the other chopped wood for the fire, and we'd go for long walks in the afternoons. It was warm spring weather. We walked through wild anemones and celandines, through primroses and bluebells and wild garlic. We hunted for fossils in the quarry. At night, we'd pile the fire high with wood, and sit in front of it, playing bezique and eating chocolates.

MRS. LAWRENCE We must get our coats.

SARAH I'm trying to explain something to you, Mother. I'm trying to get you to feel something.

MRS. LAWRENCE Sarah dear, you don't need to explain to me about friendship. It's very rare. (*To* JANE) Real friends are very rare, and much to be prized. (*To* MR. LAWRENCE) Harold!

MR. LAWRENCE (*Stands*)   Off now, are we?

SARAH   I wasn't talking about friendship, Mother. I was talking about love. We made love.

MRS. LAWRENCE   Goodbye, Jane. I'm so happy to have met you. (*Into the hall*) Goodbye, Trevor.

MR. LAWRENCE (*Following*)   Bye, Trevor . . . Jane . . .

TREVOR   Goodbye.

> (SARAH *follows her parents into the hall, as they get their coats*)

MRS. LAWRENCE   If you do want to bring Trevor down for a week-end, dear, we've plenty of room.

SARAH   Mother, if you're going to understand people, you'd better begin with what they do in bed.

MRS. LAWRENCE (*Going*)   Sarah, Sarah, *how* you exaggerate!

MR. LAWRENCE (*Going*)   I like Trevor, you know. And your mother's quite come round to him.

> (*They have gone.* SARAH *returns to the others*)

SARAH   Oh . . .

> (*Here follows the most extreme obscenity that the Lord Chamberlain will permit a British actress to say on the stage in the late 1960's. Whatever the word is, she says it several times*)

TREVOR   What did you expect?

> (SARAH *sits in the armchair*)

JANE   Shut up, Trevor.

MR. HUDSON   If I understand you . . .

JANE   Yes?

MR. HUDSON   There will be no question of . . . young men.

JANE   What?

MR. HUDSON   In the flat. Visiting. (*Looks at* TREVOR) Well, they may visit. From time to time. But—

JANE   We have few visitors, and no young men. You understand correctly.

MR. HUDSON   Ah! I let all my properties to single women, you see. I like to feel . . . in a fatherly relationship. One can do very little to discourage young men, but I dislike them visiting.

TREVOR   What *can* you do?

MR. HUDSON   If there are too many, I don't renew the lease.

JANE   We shall be model tenants in that respect.

MR. HUDSON   Thank you. You won't object if I . . . ring up from time to time? I shan't speak, of course.

JANE   We'll know who it is.

HUDSON   I'll say farewell then. Miss Kempton . . . Miss Lawrence . . . Mr.—

TREVOR   Goodbye.

MR. HUDSON (*Going*)   I'll show myself out.

TREVOR (*As he goes*)   You know your way. (HUDSON *goes. Pause*) It's just us, then. (*Pause*) Not my most successful performance, I'm afraid.

JANE   It wasn't your fault.

TREVOR   They do know, you know.

JANE   Yes.

TREVOR   It's just that they don't want to put it into words.

JANE   No.

TREVOR   You can't blame them.

JANE   I don't.

TREVOR   Sarah does.

JANE   Yes.
      (*Pause*)

TREVOR   I don't suppose you'll be taking me down to Bury St. Edmunds. Or Torquay.

JANE   No.

TREVOR   Thank you for the five pounds.

JANE   You earned it.

TREVOR   No, really, I enjoyed—Well, I did enjoy it actually. (*Pause*) Shall I see you around? (*Pause*) If you were going out for a drink or anything. I'm often in that pub when I'm not working.

SARAH   We don't go out, Trevor. We hardly ever go out.
      (*Pause*)

TREVOR   My name's not Trevor.
      (*He goes into the hall, and out by the front door. They listen to it close.* JANE *sits on the arm of* SARAH's *chair, and puts a hand round* SARAH's *shoulders. Lights fade leaving a single box of hard, white light, then all front lights fade, leaving them backlit. They are sitting very still. Hold it*)
                    Curtain

The Shock
of Recognition

*from You Know I Can't Hear You
When the Water's Running*

B Y

Robert Anderson

Robert Anderson

Robert Anderson was born in New York City in 1917, attended Phillips Exeter Academy, and was graduated from Harvard University in 1939. While at Harvard, he wrote, acted in and directed plays, wrote drama criticism, and taught drama and writing courses. He served as a naval officer in World War II, and during this period wrote *Come Marching Home,* a drama which won the National Theatre Conference prize for the best play written by a serviceman on overseas duty.

Following his discharge from the Navy, Mr. Anderson buckled down to a writing career and turned out more than seventy radio and television scripts. In September, 1953, he made his debut as a Broadway playwright with *Tea and Sympathy,* directed by Elia Kazan and starring Deborah Kerr. Named a "best play" of the season, the drama ran for 712 performances and later reappeared as a successful film, for which Anderson wrote the screenplay.

Tea and Sympathy was the longest-running play in the twenty-one-year history of The Playwrights' Company. Just before the opening of his play, Mr. Anderson was invited to join the management of that noted production company, founded in 1938 by Robert E. Sherwood, Sidney Howard, S. N. Behrman, Maxwell Anderson and Elmer Rice ". . . to make a center for ourselves within the theatre, and possibly rally the theatre as a whole to new levels by setting a high standard of writing and production."

The organization produced his next two Broadway scripts: *All Summer Long* (1954) and *Silent Night, Lonely Night* (1959), the latter co-starring Henry Fonda and Barbara Bel Geddes.

In the season of 1965–66, Mr. Anderson's play, *The Days Between,* was chosen by the American Playwrights Theatre circuit for production in college and community theatres throughout the nation.

In March, 1967, Robert Anderson once again achieved extraordinary Broadway success with his program of four one-act comedies, *You Know I Can't Hear You When the Water's Running—*

described by *Time* magazine as "a blizzard of hilarity," and by Richard Watts, Jr., of the New York *Post* as "an evening of pleasure and distinction." *The Shock of Recognition,* the opening play of this delightful and illuminating quartet, appears in this collection of modern short comedies.

Mr. Anderson's next Broadway venture was considerably more serious; it was a powerful drama, *I Never Sang for My Father,* which opened at the Longacre Theatre in 1968, with a superb company headed by Hal Holbrook, Teresa Wright, Alan Webb and Lillian Gish.

The author's screenplay credits include *The Nun's Story* (nominated for an Academy Award), *Until They Sail* and *The Sand Pebbles.*

Prior to the production of *Tea and Sympathy,* Mr. Anderson initiated the playwriting classes at the American Theatre Wing and the Actors Studio. He also was one of the original members of The New Dramatists Committee, organized in 1950 to assist in the development of outstanding new playwrights. In addition to Mr. Anderson, who also served as president of the group for a year, the now-celebrated alumni include William Inge, Paddy Chayefsky, William Gibson, Joseph Kramm, James Baldwin, Michael Stewart, Joe Masteroff, Burt Shevelove and Joseph Hayes, among many others.

Robert Anderson and his wife, actress Teresa Wright, live in a New England farmhouse, built in 1825, in Bridgewater, Connecticut.

You Know I Can't Hear You When the Water's Running was first presented on March 13, 1967, by Jack Farren and Gilbert Cates at the Ambassador Theatre, New York City. The cast of *The Shock of Recognition* was as follows:

(*In order of appearance*)

JACK BARNSTABLE	George Grizzard
HERB MILLER	Joe Silver
DOROTHY	Melinda Dillon
RICHARD PAWLING	Martin Balsam

Directed by ALAN SCHNEIDER
Scenery designed by ED WITTSTEIN
Costumes designed by THEONI V. ALDREDGE
Lighting designed by JULES FISHER

THE SHOCK OF RECOGNITION

The action takes place in the office of a producer. There are doors to the left and right.

JACK BARNSTABLE, *the playwright—slight and intellectual—is waiting. In a moment,* HERB MILLER, *the producer, enters through the door on the right in a hurry. He is large, a rough diamond. He smokes a cigar.*

HERB   Sorry to keep you waiting, Jack. How are you?
        (*They shake hands warmly*)
JACK   I'm fine, Herb.
HERB   Good trip?
JACK   Great.
HERB   I'm damned excited about producing this play of yours.
        (*He picks up a manuscript and waves it*)
JACK   Good.
HERB   Did you order coffee? The girl can get you coffee.
JACK   No, thanks. I just finished breakfast.
HERB (*Snaps on the intercom on his desk*)   Dorothy?
DOROTHY (*Her voice is heard*)   Yes, Mr. Miller?
HERB   Any calls?
DOROTHY   No, Mr. Miller.
HERB   I don't want to be disturbed.
DOROTHY   Yes, Mr. Miller . . .
HERB (*Sits at the desk*)   Now, Jack . . . I've been talking to that agent of yours, and he says you mean it when you say in your script here . . . (*He reads*) "Patrick, age forty-three, enters from the bathroom naked."
JACK   Well, sure. It's in the script.
HERB   I know. But I thought maybe it was there just to give an indication for the actor or director.
JACK   No. I mean it.
HERB   Well, Jack . . . I mean, hell! You've written a lot of plays. You know we can't do that.

JACK   Why not?

HERB   We'd be put in jail. You'd offend people.

JACK   Why should people be offended by a naked man?

HERB   Oh, come on . . .

JACK   Damn it, Herb, it's about time our theatre grew up . . . We got to let some air in here someplace . . . It's not as though I were trying to do something sexy. Far from it . . . Look, when Ibsen put a real-life scene on the stage in 1889, the audience recognized their own lives and stood up and cheered.

HERB   Well, if you put a naked man onstage, they're gonna stand up and go home.

JACK   I'm not asking you to show a couple making love onstage.

HERB   That'll come next.

JACK   I just want the audience to get that shock of recognition . . . to feel at home . . . to say, "My God, that's just like us." Look, the wife's lying there in bed reading the morning news-papers . . . (HERB *suddenly looks at the script frantically*) What's the matter?

HERB   I just thought I'd better check. Is she naked too?

JACK   No, Herb. For God's sake! She's lying there. She can be dressed six layers deep, as far as I'm concerned . . . and she's reading the papers and chattering away to her husband, who is in the bathroom . . . water running. Suddenly the water is turned off. Husband appears in the bedroom, . . . with tooth-brush in his hand, naked, and says, "Honey, you know I can't hear you when the water's running." He stands there a mo-ment . . .

HERB   Just long enough for everyone to faint.

JACK   . . . goes back in, and the next time we see him, he has a robe on, and that's that.

HERB   Why?

JACK   I told you. The shock of recognition. For the same reason they put running water onstage in *The Voice of the Turtle*.

HERB   Jack, baby, that was twenty-five years or more ago. We're in a different kind of theatre now.

JACK   Okay . . . I'll release you from your contract. What the hell . . .

HERB   Wait a minute, Jack . . .

JACK   It's important to me, Herb. This is not a sexy, muscular man . . . bare to the waist and full of erotic implications as to what he's got in his bulging blue jeans. I want to show man as he is . . . you . . . me . . .

HERB   Speak for yourself . . .

JACK   . . . what Shakespeare called a poor forked radish . . . with no implications except of mortality and ridiculousness.

HERB   You find a naked man ridiculous?

JACK   Mostly, yes. And so do you. I think the males in the audience will howl with delight and recognition.

HERB   At seeing this guy flapping in the breeze?

JACK   Yeah. A real man, naked. And, of course, in the play he's quite a guy. He's our hero.

HERB   (*Looking at the script*)   You know, you didn't say in the script that not only do you want a naked man . . . you want a ridiculous-looking naked man.

JACK   That's the whole point. I don't want an Adonis onstage. That's what the movies and the other boys are getting at, the thing I'm trying to get away from.

HERB   (*Reads*)   "He is touching in his nakedness . . ." Do you find a naked man "touching"?

JACK   Well . . . actually that was Sarah's expression. She finds a naked man . . . especially his rear end . . . "touching." When she said it, she called my attention to it, I took a look in the mirror.

HERB   And did you find your . . . tail . . . touching?

JACK   Look—

HERB   I think it's Sarah needs the analyst, not you. "Touching." Sounds kind of maternal, as though she wanted to use some baby powder on it . . . The last time I looked, I didn't find my behind touching . . . Nor does Gloria. She just finds it big . . . Mr. Big-Ass she calls me, if you'll excuse the expression. And I say, "Honey, you can't drive a spike with a tack hammer." Now, that's our relationship. Yours is obviously something else again.

JACK   Look, Herb—

HERB   Wait a minute, now. Let me suggest a compromise. If it's the rear end that's so touching, I mean . . . maybe we could get away with just showing that. They did that in *Marat-Sade* and got away with it.

JACK   No.

HERB   You want the whole works?

JACK   Yes.

HERB   I hesitate to ask you how your wife characterizes your . . . uh . . . your . . . Does she find that touching, too?

JACK   She finds it no work of art . . . nor does any woman, as I understand it, though I haven't done a house-to-house poll on it.

THE SHOCK OF RECOGNITION   *Friedman-Abeles*

It's the boys who find it a work of stunning magnificence . . .
And I want to blast that. I want every man in the audience to
want to reach out and shake my hand.

HERB   And every woman to reach out and pat your fanny.

JACK   I knew you'd give me a fight on this, Herb . . . so I brought
some pictures.

HERB   (*Starts for the door, left*)   Should I lock the door?

JACK   Come on now, look. (*He takes two pictures from a brief-
case*) Now that's what we're used to seeing . . . the idealized
image of a naked man . . . fantasy! This is a normal, real man,
naked.

HERB   (*Winces at the second picture*)   I may be queer, but I like
the first one better . . . Look upon this, dear mother . . . and on
this . . . where the hell did you ever find a guy looked that pathetic? It's not you, is it? (*He steps back and looks*) You take
these pictures?

JACK   No.

HERB   I tell you what I think . . . I think the men are not going to
reach out and shake your hand. They're gonna want to reach
out and belt you one for showing up how ridiculous they are.
Because no matter what your wife thinks, I don't think any man
feels that his . . . thing . . . is ridiculous. I think he feels it's a
formidable weapon, an awesome . . . thing.

JACK   Is that the way you think of it, something to attack with . . .
aggressive . . . battering?

HERB   Well, I don't think of it as ridiculous.

JACK   I wonder what Gloria thinks of it.

HERB   I'm not going to ask her.

JACK   No. I wouldn't take the chance.

HERB   You know, Jack, I had Hank in mind for this part.

JACK   I think he'd be great.

HERB   You don't foresee any obstacle? Any eensy, weensy, ridiculous, pathetic obstacle?

JACK   How do you know that Hank wouldn't think it about time—

HERB   That someone saw him naked onstage? Somehow I don't
think it's ever entered his mind. It's you who have this compulsion to exhibit yourself via some poor actor bastard . . . before
the admiring public.

JACK   I don't want them to admire.

HERB   You want them to laugh. What masochism!

JACK   Okay, we'll get some unknown who'll leap at the chance to
play a part like this.

HERB   I'm afraid if he leaps at the chance to appear naked on the stage, he's exactly the kind you don't want.

JACK   Well, somebody . . . My God.

HERB   I think an unknown would be ill-advised to do it, even for the chance to play the lead in a play of yours. Can't you see him for the rest of his career? Supposing he goes on to play Shakespeare, Hamlet, Lear, Oedipus. Nobody will ever be able to wipe out that touching image of him standing there naked with his toothbrush in his hand, saying, "Honey, you know I can't hear you when the water's running."

JACK   Look, Herb, haven't I earned the right to ask for this? The public knows me as a serious playwright . . . not someone just out for kicks and shocks. And if I feel that it's an important step forward in my playwriting, for all playwrights . . . I mean, are we going to let all the daring things be done in the wrong name because we're scared?

HERB   Jack, old friend, you have a fine play here. It's that rare combination . . . the public will love it, and the intellectuals won't be too contemptuous.

JACK   Why the hell should we in the theatre be so far behind the times? Have you read a book recently . . . what they put in books? Or seen a movie?

HERB   Look, it's already hard enough putting on a serious play this day and age. People say, "I got enough troubles in my life. Why come to the theatre to see the same thing?" Now you'll have them saying, "Look, I see my poor, pathetic, ridiculous husband walking around naked all the time. I don't want to come to the theatre to see another ridiculous naked man I don't even know."

JACK   (*Vehemently*)   I want to say to that plain, ordinary man, her husband, I want to say to him in the audience . . . "Hello. We haven't forgotten you."

HERB   And he'll call back and say, "I wish the hell you would."

JACK   I want to say, "Hello. You're sick of seeing bizarre, way-out problems of men who aren't men and women who aren't women. Here you are!"

HERB   This is your life! Right down to your bare ass and pathetic—

JACK   Herb, you don't want to do this play?

(*He heads for his overcoat and starts to put it on*)

HERB   Take it easy. Have you thought of the . . . uh . . . problem of casting . . . of auditioning for this part if Hank doesn't play it? I mean, actors are used to being turned down because they're too short or too tall. But to be turned down because their equipment is not ridiculous enough.

JACK   You're so damned prudish, you won't even call it by its right name . . . all these euphemisms . . . Equipment . . . Thing . . .

HERB   What would you like me to call it?

JACK   The technical word . . . the correct word . . . is penis.

HERB   If you go around calling it that, I understand why you think of it as pathetic and ridiculous. It's a ridiculous and belittling name. You call it what you want to call it, and I'll call it what I want to call it. But I've got to tell you something . . . I called it what I did partly because of you.

JACK   What do you mean?

HERB   All the years I've known you, I still find myself apologizing when I use a dirty word in front of you.

JACK   Oh, come on.

HERB   It's the truth. There's something about you. I always find myself saying "Sorry" . . . "Excuse it" . . . And that's another reason I think you're wrong to do this. The public doesn't see you as that kind of writer.

JACK   I'm sorry as hell I've been inhibiting you all these years, Herb. That's one of the most insulting things anyone has ever said to me.

HERB   I can't help it. It's true. Just something about you.

JACK   Would you care to explain that?

HERB   (*At the intercom*)   Dorothy?

DOROTHY   (*On the intercom*)   Yes, Mr. Miller.

HERB   Will you step in a minute? (*To* JACK) You met her, didn't you?

JACK   (*Puzzled as to what this is all about*)   When I came in, yes.

HERB   She's a Bennington girl doing her three months' stint of learning about real life.
(DOROTHY *enters*)

HERB   Dorothy, you know Mr. Barnstable . . . (*To* JACK) She's a great fan of yours. (DOROTHY *is embarrassed*) She played in one of your plays at college.

DOROTHY   Oh, Mr. Miller. Really!

JACK   (*Trying to be pleasant*)   Which one?

DOROTHY   Oh, I was terrible!

JACK   I'm sure you weren't.

DOROTHY (*Insistent*) I was! I was just horrible!

JACK What part?

DOROTHY If I told you, you'd drop dead right on the spot. Just awful!

HERB Dorothy, tell me something. You read Mr. Barnstable's play?

DOROTHY Yes.

HERB You liked it?

DOROTHY (*Beams on* JACK) Oh, yes, I did.

HERB You read the stage directions?

DOROTHY Well . . . yes.

HERB The one in the beginning where the man comes out of the bathroom naked . . . You see, she's blushing just from my reading the stage directions.

DOROTHY I wasn't blushing.

HERB You were. Mr. Barnstable here has the idea he actually wants the man to come out naked in that scene . . . (DOROTHY *giggles*) You see, deeper blushes.

DOROTHY (*Giggling and angry*) I'm *not* blushing.

HERB Now here's a broad-minded educated girl . . . Her mind accepts the idea, but her soul blushes.

DOROTHY (*Put out*) Oh, Mr. Miller. I'm not blushing.

HERB Okay. Would you like to pay your six-ninety to see a naked man onstage?

DOROTHY (*Confused, she giggles*) It's not a fair question.

HERB Why not?

DOROTHY Well, it just isn't.

HERB Sounds like you got some kind of conflict going there. You would like to see him, but you don't want to admit it.

DOROTHY Oh, no.

HERB Do women get a boot out of seeing naked men?

DOROTHY Oh, Mr. Miller.

HERB Do they or don't they? (DOROTHY *squirms*) Do you . . . or don't you?

DOROTHY Mr. Miller!
       (*She heads for the door, left*)

HERB (*To* JACK) She's an incompetent witness. She's never seen a naked man.

DOROTHY (*Stops*) Mr. Miller!

HERB Oh, then you have?

DOROTHY You certainly don't expect a person to answer that.

HERB   All right, go out and pull yourself together . . . I just wanted to demonstrate to our playwright here what even the idea of a naked man does to you.

DOROTHY   That's not fair.

HERB   There go your matinées . . .

JACK   Nonsense. I gave this to my grandmother to read, and her only comment was, "Let me know when it opens and I'll be there with my opera glasses." . . . Women are bored with this respectability which red-blooded but prudish men have forced on them . . . They want to be let in on the joke.

HERB   Dorothy, do you find a man's sexual equipment ridiculous and pathetic?

DOROTHY   Mr. Miller!
        (*She runs out gasping and in confusion*)

HERB   Do you think she meant "yes" or "no"?

JACK   You're a cruel bastard. That's a cheap way of getting your kicks.

HERB   She's kind of cute, isn't she?

JACK   Getting yourself all worked up, talking about the great Forbidden. That's what I'm driving at.

HERB   I'm sorry if I didn't keep it on a high intellectual plane . . . But people just aren't going to. A baby . . . a naked male boy, age two . . . they'll goo-goo over, blush a little and say "Isn't it cute?" But by age three it's already indecent.

JACK   (*Good-naturedly annoyed*)   You insist on thinking of it as sexy.

HERB   And you insist on pretending we're in a laboratory where everyone is going to be so high-minded. Look, we'll get the designer to do the set so that the bathroom is downstage . . . and there's this piece of furniture just below it . . . and he comes out just above it . . . and he's covered to just below his belly button. But we'll know he's naked, because she says, "For God's sake, put something on."

JACK   You can hear a man's wife saying that?

HERB   Yes.

JACK   What would her motive be?

HERB   She just wants him to put something on.

JACK   Come on, Herb . . . you've called me often enough on motivation . . . It would mean that the thing is some kind of monstrosity frightening to the eye . . . or that she's prudish and doesn't like her husband appearing naked in front of her. Neither of these things is true of my couple . . . You see, Herb . . .

HERB   Look, you got a lovely, sensitive play here, except for this one moment.

JACK   This one moment is what makes the whole play real . . . Look, people go to European movies, or art movies . . . not because of art but because of Life. They know there's some chance that the story will break through to the absurdities and truth of life . . . You want to know a scene I've got in my notebooks that I've never seen? I've lived it, but I've never seen it . . . A guy is giving a girl a snow job. He's almost got her where he wants her . . . and the timing is everything. He can't let a moment pass, or the mood change, or he's lost her. It's the end of the evening, and he's kissing her and fondling her . . . and she's smiling "yes" but telling him to run along home like a good boy. The only trouble is that this guy is running a race with his bladder . . . And he's finally got to go, and he's lost it . . . Didn't that ever happen to you? (HERB *gives him a look and turns away*) Now that's real life . . . But when are we gonna see that scene in an American movie or in the American theatre? I feel like going to the edge of the stage, like Mary Martin in *Peter Pan* . . . and saying to the audience . . . "Do you believe in life as it is lived? . . . Don't you want to see it?" I think they want to see the ironies, the paradoxes . . . the absurdities . . . Hell, Life is a tragedy played by comedians. They know it. Let them see it onstage.

HERB   Look, Jack, you know more about tone than I do . . . TONE . . . You can't shift tone like that in a play.

JACK   You do it in life . . . at least in my house. One moment we're making love . . . the next minute we're wrangling about something . . . and then the dog gets excited and pees on the carpet . . . and we break up laughing.

HERB   That's your house! Your assumption is that what you experience in your house, they experience. I don't go around naked in my house. This is your assumption.

JACK   I would assume that at least in a man's bedroom and bathroom he goes naked occasionally. I don't walk around the living room or the kitchen, as a rule . . . I've done it a couple of times in the summer when the kids are away. It's okay . . . Gave me a feeling . . .

HERB   (*Flips on the intercom*)   Dorothy.

DOROTHY   (*Over the intercom*)   Yes, Mr. Miller?

HERB   Any actors out there?

DOROTHY   (*Over the intercom*)   Yes, Mr. Miller.

HERB   Send one in.

JACK   What's this all about?

HERB   If we're gonna get this show on the road, we're gonna have to start seeing actors.

(JACK *takes off his coat*)

DOROTHY (*Enters from the door, left*)   Mr. Richard Pawling. (*He doesn't follow at once. She calls him*) Mr. Pawling!

(RICHARD PAWLING *enters. He is thirty-five. He is overeager, self-explaining, and anxious.* DOROTHY *exits*)

HERB (*Shaking hands*)   Hello, Mr. Pawling.

PAWLING   How do you do?

HERB   This is Mr. Jack Barnstable.

PAWLING (*Awed and pleased*)   Oh . . . (*Crosses to shake hands very appreciatively with* JACK) How do you do, Mr. Barnstable. It's a pleasure. A *real* pleasure! I . . . uh . . . didn't really expect to be seen by anyone . . . I was just bringing some new pictures of myself around for your files.

HERB   That's all right, Mr. Pawling. Please sit down.

PAWLING   Thank you . . . I've got my hair long because I'm up for a part in a Western series . . . but I can cut that . . . And the mustache is temporary . . . for a commercial. I'm a doctor, and I guess they feel it gives more dignity, you know. (*He rises*) "One out of every two doctors recommends . . ." (*He laughs nervously and sits again*) I . . . uh . . . worked for you once, Mr. Miller.

HERB   Oh?

PAWLING   About five years ago. I understudied Steiger . . .

HERB (*Not registering at all*)   Oh, yes.

PAWLING (*There is awkward silence, as* JACK *watches* HERB *and* HERB *waits*)   Uh . . . what kind of part is it, if I may ask?

HERB   It's a very good part . . . the lead.

(JACK *is aghast and goes to sit at one side of the room*)

PAWLING (*Worried that he is giving the wrong impression, he follows* JACK)   I can be taller . . . I don't have my elevator shoes on . . . Or shorter. I mean . . . I can pretty well adapt. The hair is dark now, but you may remember, Mr. Miller, it was blond when I worked for you last.

HERB   Oh, yes.

PAWLING (*Going on nervously*)   I'm pretty well tanned up because of this Western . . . I told you . . . but if I stay away from the sunlamp for a couple of days . . . I . . . well . . . look more . . . intellectual, Mr. Barnstable . . . if that's what you're looking for. Also, I have my contact lenses in now, but I do have glasses, if that's closer to the image. (*He whips his glasses out and puts them on. He is thrown off balance by the two sets of lenses. After a moment, he takes them off*) And, of course, I do have other clothes ... And my weight's variable ... I mean, if you're looking for someone thinner.

HERB   Actually, we're looking for someone rather . . . well, someone who can look a little pathetic and ridiculous.

PAWLING (*Without a moment's hesitation*)   That's me . . . I mean, put me in the right clothes . . . a little big for me . . . and I look like a scarecrow . . . I can shrink inside my clothes.

HERB   The question is, can you shrink inside your skin?

PAWLING (*Looks from one to the other, smiling*)   I can if I think it. If I can think it, I can be it . . . You see, here's my composites, the pictures I was leaving with the girl. (*Whips out a photo sheet and shows it to* HERB *at the desk*) A doctor . . . a cowboy . . . a soldier . . . businessman . . . small-town grocer . . . You can't notice it, probably, but I'm wearing a hairpiece . . . I look quite different without it. Do you want me to . . .

   (*He makes a move to strip off the very obvious hairpiece*)

HERB   No, no. You don't have any pictures of you in a bathing suit, do you?

PAWLING   No. I . . . uh . . . When are you planning on doing the play?

HERB   No dates yet.

PAWLING   I could work out in a gym from now until then. I can put on quite a bit of muscle in a few months.

HERB   That wouldn't be necessary. "Ridiculous," I said.

PAWLING   Oh, yes. I forgot. Well, as I said, I *do* look ridiculous.

HERB   Jack, why don't you fill Mr. Pawling in? Take over. After all, it *is* your idea.

JACK   I don't think Mr. Pawling is exactly the type.

PAWLING (*Coming to* JACK)   I can look a lot younger.

   (*He "acts" younger*)

JACK   It isn't that.

PAWLING   Or older.

   (*He slumps*)

HERB (*Egging* JACK *on*)   I think you owe it to Mr. Pawling to go into the part and the requirements. I mean, I don't think we should jump to any conclusion as to whether he's right or wrong. Particularly in this part, with its special requirements . . . I don't see how we can know until we've really seen Mr. Pawling.

PAWLING   Perhaps if I could read the script, I could come in looking more like . . . I mean, you know . . . dressed more for the part.

HERB (*Seeing that* JACK *is not going to do anything*)   Well, Mr. Pawling . . . this is an unusual part. It's a husband and . . .

PAWLING   Well, I've been married three times.
(*He laughs nervously*)

HERB   And in the opening scene, it's right after breakfast, and his wife's in bed, with the newspapers and coffee, and the husband is in the bathroom, which is adjacent to the bedroom . . . where the wife is lying in bed, having coffee, reading the papers. It's morning, you see, and she's having her morning coffee . . . and the husband is in the bathroom, and he's brushing his teeth, and the water's running . . . you know, while he's brushing his teeth . . . and she's talking to him . . . Why are you smiling?

PAWLING   Well, I mean . . . that's a situation I know like the back of my hand. My wives . . . they could never get it through their heads that you can't hear when the water's running.

HERB   That's his first line. He turns off the water, and he comes out and says, "Honey, you know I can't hear you when the water's running."

PAWLING   Well, you've got every husband with you from then on . . . I didn't say "honey," but I remember distinctly saying "For Christ's sake, how many times do I have to tell you I can't hear you when the goddamned water's running?" (*Turns to* JACK) Excuse me, Mr. Barnstable.

JACK (*Burning*)   Why did you say "excuse me" to me?

PAWLING   I don't know.
(*Shrugs as if to say "Did I do something wrong?"*)

HERB   So the scene is familiar to you? (PAWLING *makes a gesture* —"*of course*") What did you wear when you brushed your teeth?

PAWLING (*Immediately*)   I can wear anything you want.

HERB   But what did you wear?

PAWLING   It depends. Sometimes I sleep in my underwear . . . sometimes pajamas.

HERB   In this play the character wears nothing. He's brushing his teeth bare-assed.

PAWLING   I can do that. I've done that. Naturally. In the bathroom. Of course. Very good. Why not? The bathroom's offstage. Why not? But why is it important what the man is wearing if it's offstage?

HERB (*Motions for* JACK *to take over*)   Uh . . . Jack.

PAWLING   I mean, excuse me, I'm not questioning it. I can see where it helps the actor to understand the character. He's the kind of guy who brushes his teeth . . . (*He looks at* JACK) in the nude. Yes. I can handle that . . . because I've done that.

HERB   He turns off the water, comes into the bedroom, and says the line you said . . . Only without the blasphemy, because Mr. Barnstable doesn't like blasphemy onstage.

PAWLING   Of course . . . I see, yes. He says the line . . .

HERB   Bare-assed. (PAWLING *looks from one to the other*) How would you feel about that? The actor has to stand there naked . . . and say the line.

JACK (*Getting angry, realizing that* HERB *is making a test case with this nonentity*)   Look, let me explain it. This is not just for shock effect, or for thrills. There's nothing sexy about it. I just think that it's an added value for an audience to relate to a situation they know. The only shock would be the pleasurable shock of recognition . . . the honesty and truthfulness of it. The man then goes back in the bathroom, and next time we see him, he's in a bathrobe, and we never see him naked again . . . I think it can be one of the great moments in the history of the theatre . . . Like Nora slamming the door in *A Doll's House.*

   (PAWLING *has never heard of* A Doll's House)

HERB (*To* PAWLING)   How would you feel about that?

PAWLING (*Looking from one to the other*)   I have to apologize.

HERB (*Thinking he has won his point, he speaks kindly*)   I understand, Mr. Pawling.

   (*He turns to smile his satisfaction at* JACK)

PAWLING   I've got a hole in my sock. (*He takes off his coat and tie*) I told you, I really didn't expect to see anyone. I was just dropping by to leave some new pictures . . . I didn't expect an interview. (*Goes on undressing. He takes off his shirt*) How ridiculous do you want this man to look? I mean, I'm not a ninety-eight-pound weakling, but if I didn't eat anything for a while, and if I shaved the hair on my chest . . . is this guy supposed to be funny?

   (JACK *won't answer; he looks at* HERB)

HERB   No, he's the leading man. It's just that Mr. Barnstable wants to puncture this idea of the muscular and hefty man. He wants, in a sense, everyman.

PAWLING (*In his undershirt*)   Well, that's me . . . I'm really the original anonymous man. People are all the time coming up to me and thinking they've met me . . . I got a face looks like everybody else's. (*Pulls off his undershirt*) You see, I haven't got much muscle on my arms . . . and if I stand in a certain way, it even looks like less. (*He moves around demonstrating*) The hair on the chest . . . I can shave that off and powder it down . . . and if I stand right . . . But then, they won't see that, I suppose. If I come in from downstage and look up at her in the bed (*He acts it out, going downstage and walking up*) they'll only get a view of my tail and side . . . (*He is standing, trying this view out*) Still, we ought to have that shaved.

HERB   But you see, Mr. Pawling, you don't come in from downstage. You come in from upstage. I believe that's Mr. Barnstable's idea.

PAWLING (*Stares out at the audience full-face, gradually getting the idea of what this involves*)   Well . . .

   (*He starts to take off his trousers*)

JACK (*Embarrassed*)   I think that will be all, Mr. Pawling.

PAWLING (*Sits down, slipping off his shoes so that he can get his trousers off. We see the hole in the sock*)   My chest is misleading. That hair. But you see, my legs . . . (*As he strips off his trousers*) I mean, I wouldn't want you to count me out because of that hair on my chest.

HERB (*Watching* JACK's *embarrassment*)   I think you're quite right, Mr. Pawling. Mr. Barnstable is out after a certain uncompromising effect, and I think we should see the whole works.

PAWLING (*The trousers are off; he stands there*)   Well, the legs, as you see, are . . . well . . . ridiculous.

HERB   I think you're being modest, Mr. Pawling. But you see, I don't think the legs, or the hair on the chest, or anything like that really matters . . . Because when you come out onstage absolutely skinny, nobody is going to be looking at your legs, or your chest. So the question is . . . is the rest of you ridiculous? You see, Mr. Barnstable has the interesting theory that most women look upon that part of their men as ridiculous and pathetic . . . and he wants to present his man not as a stud, not as a romanticized phallic symbol, but as the miserable, laughable thing it is. Now, Mr. Pawling?

PAWLING   Well, I . . . It's embarrassing discussing this sort of thing, but . . . girls have sometimes . . . uh . . . laughed, or giggled . . . at first. Of course, it's not the look that counts. I mean we all know that. (*They are all silent for a moment*) Well, I've been turned down for parts because I was too short or too tall . . . too fat or too thin . . . too young or too old . . . But I never did or didn't get a part because of . . . (*He swings his arms in embarrassment*) What the hell!

(*He starts to unbutton his shorts*)

JACK Hold it, Mr. Pawling!

(*He gathers up Pawling's clothes*)

PAWLING But I agree with you completely, Mr. Barnstable. It's time the American theatre grew up.

JACK (*Holding out his clothes to him*) Thank you for your co-operation, Mr. Pawling. You can dress in the next room. There's a door into the hall from there . . . (*Indicating the door, right*) And we'll be in touch with you.

PAWLING (*Not giving up*) But, I mean, if that's going to be the whole point of the thing . . .

JACK (*Heading for the door, left*) I'm sure that that's as adaptable as the various other parts of your body . . .

HERB But, Jack, I don't see how you're ever going to—(JACK *has turned and gone into the secretary's office, left.* PAWLING *looks after him, standing there in his shorts and socks, with his arms full of clothes*) Well, thank you, Mr. Pawling. There's not much point without Mr. Barnstable.

(*He holds the other door for* PAWLING)

PAWLING (*Crossing to follow* JACK) I didn't say anything to . . . uh . . . ? I mean . . .

(*Catching him at the left door and ushering him back across to the right door*)

HERB No. Thank you very much. And I'd keep this all very much to myself, if I were you. We're thinking of you very seriously for the part.

PAWLING You are! Well . . . Gee . . . Thank you for seeing me. It was a great honor meeting Mr. Barnstable . . . and to see you again.

(*There is a certain confusion with shaking hands with all the clothes, and saying goodbye, but finally* PAWLING *is out.* HERB *closes the door; he looks satisfied. He goes to the other door and opens it*)

HERB Ollie, Ollie, ocksin, all in free.

JACK (*Comes in, mad; he goes for his coat*) I suppose you think you've won your point.

HERB Theory is theory. Life is life.

JACK   That was no test. A man taking off his clothes in front of two guys is one thing—

PAWLING (*Opens the door and steps in. He is still in shorts and socks*)   Oh, Mr. Miller. Oh, excuse me.

(*He holds his undershirt to his bare chest.* JACK *stares at him and instinctively puts his overcoat over his chest*)

HERB   Yes, Mr. Pawling?

PAWLING   Excuse me, but I've just had an idea. I've got a Polaroid camera . . . and I'll get my agent to take some pictures of me . . . uh . . . the way you want them, and I'll send them to you.

HERB   Not through the mails, please.

PAWLING   I'll bring them around, then.

HERB   "Attention Mr. Barnstable" . . . in a plain wrapper.

PAWLING   Right. Sorry about the holes in the socks.

(*He goes back into his room*)

JACK (*Putting on his coat*)   You're a cruel bastard. You know we wouldn't even think of reading that guy . . .

HERB   Where you going?

JACK   I've got to have lunch with my lawyer and accountant.

HERB   Jack, I'll tell you what I'll do for the American theatre. What about a naked woman? Now, we put the man in bed, and the woman in the bathroom . . . naked. The water's running. And she's talking to him . . . And when she gets no answer from him, she comes out of the bathroom and says, "Did you hear what I said?" And she's naked.

JACK   And he says, "Honey, you know I can't hear you when you're naked."

(*He starts out the same door* PAWLING *used, checks himself, and crosses to the other door*)

HERB (*Acting as the businessman*)   Okay, Jack. Let's quit the kidding around. Hank wants to do this part.

JACK (*Stops in his tracks*)   He does?

HERB   But he won't appear naked. I got an offer from Warner Brothers to pay $300,000 on a pre-production deal *if* Hank plays the part. Now you haven't had a hit in a while . . . Your share of $300,000 is . . .

JACK   That's insulting, Herb. You know that?

HERB   Yeah, I know. But how about it?

JACK (*Ranting*)   I turned down two movies could have earned me a fortune to write this play.

HERB   True. True.

JACK For the privilege of saying what I want to say, the way I want to say it, in the only place I *thought* where you could still say it with some freedom.

HERB You're right.

JACK I mean, Herb . . . If we can't be bold in the theatre . . . where else? (*He calms down a moment.* HERB *waits*) You asked Hank if he'd play the scene as written?

HERB No. I just took it for granted what his answer would be. Anyway, I didn't know you really meant to play it . . . as written.

JACK He didn't say anything about the scene?

HERB Maybe he doesn't read stage directions.

JACK On the other hand, Hank's a pretty gutsy guy. Maybe he just assumed we'd play it as written . . . You know, you bastard, you did prove one thing to me here just now . . . we couldn't play the scene with just anybody. It would have to be someone of Hank's stature . . . He'd bring his authority onstage with him . . .

HERB So it really comes down to whether Hank with his authority . . .

JACK (*Comes to* HERB) Will you put it on, as written, if Hank'll play it that way?

HERB Sure.

JACK Okay . . . I gotta get out of here, but after lunch, I'll call Hank. Let *me* talk to him . . . let me give him the background of my thinking . . . (*Heads for the door, stops, and turns*) My God, we still got a problem.

HERB What now?

JACK We haven't any idea what Hank looks like naked.

HERB Well, before we sign the contract, we could invite him to the Y for a swim. (JACK *thinks about this a second, nods in assent, and leaves.* HERB *shakes his head, smiling. He reaches for the phone and dials a number*) Hello, Hank . . . Herb Miller here . . . Sorry to call you at home, but I wanted to get to you fast. I'm going ahead with the play for sure this season . . . Barnstable's crazy to have you do it . . . He just left here . . . And he may be getting in touch with you, so I thought I ought to warn you about one thing and ask for your help. He's a kind of nut about that first scene. I don't know if you read all the stage directions, but the guy is supposed to be standing there in the bedroom naked . . . Oh, you did read that? Well, Barnstable's got the crazy idea he wants it played just like that . . . Naked. What? (*He rises*) But good God, Hank. We can't do that! (*He continues to listen, consternation on his face*) The shock of recognition.

(He nods dully. The right door bursts open)

PAWLING *(His voice is heard)* Hey, Mr. Miller. Look! *(PAWL-ING's right hand can be seen on the edge of the door.* HERB *dully motions* PAWLING *to go away, and barely gives him a glance. Then suddenly he realizes what he's seen. His head jerks up, straight front; then he does a slow turn to check out what he's seen.)* I told you . . . Ridiculous!

(HERB's eyes close, shutting out the sight of what he has seen. He is sinking to his chair as the lights go out)

Curtain

Shadows
of the Evening

from *Suite in Three Keys*

B Y

Noël Coward

Noël Coward

Since 1924, when he sprang to international prominence with *The Vortex*, Noël Coward has symbolized glistening sophistication, trenchant wit, and impeccable style in the theatre. Few can match his prolificacy as dramatist, composer, lyricist, director and performer.

Born near London in 1899, Mr. Coward made his stage debut at the age of ten as Prince Mussel in a children's play, *The Goldfish*. When he was twenty-one, his first produced play, *I'll Leave It to You*, opened in the West End. As he personally has described the event: "The first night was a roaring success, and I made a boyish speech. The critics were mostly enthusiastic, and said a lot about it having been a great night, and that a new playwright had been discovered, etc., but unfortunately their praise was not potent enough to lure audiences to the New Theatre for more than five weeks; so the run ended rather miserably . . ."

In the four decades that followed, however, the unique theatrical wizardry of Noël Coward *did* lure hundreds of thousands into theatres throughout the world. Among his forty plays, musicals, and revues are such landmarks of their respective eras as: *The Vortex; This Year of Grace; Hay Fever; Fallen Angels; Private Lives; Design for Living; Cavalcade; Bitter Sweet; Conversation Piece; Set to Music; Quadrille; Present Laughter* and *Blithe Spirit*. His memorable series of nine short plays, *Tonight at 8:30*, with himself and the radiant Gertrude Lawrence as co-stars, brightened a depression-clouded world in the mid-1930's.

A Renaissance man of the theatre, Mr. Coward also has made some notable contributions to films (*In Which We Serve; Brief Encounter; This Happy Breed*), and has added substantially to international library shelves with four volumes of memoirs, five collections of short stories, three of revue sketches and lyrics, a popular novel, *Pomp and Circumstance*, and of course his forty or so published plays.

In spite of the fact that he occasionally has come under critical fire from some disciples of the "new wave," for persistently cling-ing to traditional—and ignoring exploratory—forms in the theatre, Mr. Coward still maintains his undeniable status as one of the giants of the twentieth-century theatre. This was affirmed un-equivocally in 1964, when Britain's celebrated National Theatre Company, under the leadership of Sir Laurence Olivier, trium-phantly revived Mr. Coward's indestructible comedy, *Hay Fever*, with Dame Edith Evans as star. Its success with press and public sparked an extraordinary resurgence of interest in the author and his plays, with additional West End revivals (*Private Lives; Pres-ent Laughter*) coming close upon the heels of the precursive *Hay Fever*. ("People have constantly written me off and are surprised that I've come back," Coward wryly observes. "Now, I wish they would tell me where I am supposed to have been.")

In 1966 London again welcomed him as author and co-star (with Lilli Palmer and Irene Worth) of *Suite in Three Keys*. Lauded by the London *Daily Express* as "Coward at his zenith," *Suite in Three Keys* represents the omnibus title for three individ-ual plays designed to be performed by the same players in two evenings. The program consists of the full-length *A Song at Twi-light,* and the brace of short plays, *Shadows of the Evening* and *Come into the Garden, Maud.* While they are entitative, they are linked together by a mutual frame of action: the sitting room of a private suite in a luxury hotel in Switzerland.

The inclusion of *Shadows of the Evening* in an anthology de-voted to comedy may stir the cauldron of curiosity. Intrinsically, it is a serious play, but like almost all of Coward, there is a pre-dominance of style, wit and levity in the face of tragedy, and for this reason alone the editor believes it deserves a prominent niche in this collection.

Noël Coward frequently has been likened to the nineteenth-century master of "artificial comedy," Oscar Wilde; for he, too, is a supreme precisionist at entertainingly tearing away at social pre-tensions. For beneath the surface of Coward's characteristically witty, cutting and pointed dialogue, there is invariably a flow of pertinent commentary on contemporary society and its values.

Would his plays—particularly the early plays—be very differ-ent if he started writing them now? The author, who now makes the world his home, favoring Jamaica and New York as his two most frequented locales, reflected: "I would continue to write what I wanted to write and about people who are interesting . . . and both peers and charwomen are interesting to me."

Suite in Three Keys was first presented on April 14, 1966, by H. M. Tennent Ltd. at the Queen's Theatre, London. The cast of *Shadows of the Evening* was as follows:

(*In order of appearance*)

LINDA SAVIGNAC	Lilli Palmer
FELIX	Sean Barrett
ANNE HILGAY	Irene Worth
GEORGE HILGAY	Noël Coward

Directed by VIVIAN MATALON
Setting by BRIAN CURRAH
Costumes by MOLYNEUX-PARIS
Lighting by JOE DAVIS

SHADOWS OF THE EVENING

Scene One

The scene is the sitting room of a private suite of the Hotel Beau Rivage in Lausanne-Ouchy, Switzerland. On the right of the audience there is a door opening into a bedroom. In the center are double doors leading to a small lobby and thence to the corridor. The furniture is conventional and what one would expect to find in an expensive European hotel. On the left of the audience there are French windows opening onto a balcony which overlooks the Lake of Geneva. On the opposite side of the lake the high mountains of France stand against the sky.

The time is the present.

When the curtain rises, late afternoon sun is flooding through the open windows. It is a day in early summer.

LINDA SAVIGNAC *is sitting on a sofa playing "Patience" on a small table in front of her. At her right is a teacart upon which is a tea tray.* LINDA *is a handsome well-dressed woman in her forties. There is a knock on the double doors.*

FELIX, *the floor-waiter, enters. He is a very good-looking young Italian.*

FELIX   Madame rang the bell?

LINDA   Yes, Felix. You can take away the tea table now.

FELIX   Very good, madame.

LINDA (*As he begins to wheel the table away*)   And will you bring some ice in a few minutes?

FELIX   With pleasure, madame.

> (*He bows and goes out with the table.* LINDA *goes on with her "Patience" then, after a moment, she rests both her elbows on the table and buries her face in her hands. She stays like this for a little and then glances anxiously at her wristwatch. She gives a deep sigh and begins listlessly to play again. The telephone on the desk behind her rings. She flings down the pack of cards and goes hurriedly to answer it*)

LINDA (*Into the telephone*) Allo, allo . . . Oui . . . *Voulez-vous demander à Madame de monter tout de suite.* (*She hangs up the telephone and stands quite still for an instant with her eyes closed. Then she nervously takes a cigarette out of a box, lights it, and almost immediately stubs it out in an ashtray. She wanders over to the window, stares at the view briefly and then comes back to where she was. There is a knock on the door.* LINDA *responds in rather a strangled voice*) Come in.

    (ANNE HILGAY *enters. She is a tall, distinguished Englishwoman. Her age might be anywhere between forty-five and fifty-five. She is dressed in a traveling suit and a light coat. She advances into the room. She and* LINDA *stand looking at each other unsmilingly for a moment.* ANNE *finally breaks the silence*)

ANNE   How are you, Linda?

LINDA   I'm all right, I think. (*She makes a movement toward her but* ANNE *steps back.* LINDA *halts where she is*) It was good of you to come—so—so promptly.

ANNE   It was a bit of a scramble getting up from the country and one thing and another, but Gillie organized it all with her usual efficiency. I expect you remember Gillie, she was George's secretary for years.

LINDA   Of course. I remember her quite well.

ANNE (*After a pause*) You don't seem to have changed a bit.

LINDA   Neither do you.

ANNE   These are the sort of things people always say when they meet again after a long time. It's almost exactly seven years, isn't it?

LINDA (*Mechanically*) Yes. Seven years.

ANNE   Considering that this isn't a particularly comfortable moment, don't you think we'd better sit down?

LINDA   Of course—forgive me. (*She motions* ANNE *to a chair*) Would you like a drink?

ANNE (*Sitting down*) Not quite yet, thank you.

LINDA (*Her voice is strained*) I've ordered ice—I mean I told him to bring it in a few minutes. I didn't think you'd get here quite so soon.

ANNE   Your chauffeur is an excellent driver and, of course, the new autoroute makes a great difference. In my day we used to have to weave along by the lake. It was kind of you to send the car.

LINDA   It was the least I could do.

ANNE   Yes. In the circumstances I suppose it was.

LINDA   (*With an effort*)   I apologize for being so hysterical and incoherent on the telephone last night. I was in rather a state.

ANNE   You were certainly incoherent, however I managed to gather that something fairly serious had happened. I presume it concerns George.

LINDA   Yes. Yes it does.

ANNE   Has he had an accident?

LINDA   No, he hasn't had an accident.

> (FELIX *knocks and enters, carrying a bucket of ice. He takes it over to the drink table*)

FELIX   Madame requires anything else?

LINDA   No thank you, Felix, that will be all for the moment.

FELIX   Very good madame.

> (*He bows and goes out*)

ANNE   (*After a pause*)   He hasn't run off with anyone else, has he?

LINDA   No, Anne. He hasn't run off with anyone else, and even if he had, you would hardly be the one I should send for to comfort me. I am not entirely devoid of taste or common sense.

ANNE   It is such a long time since I have seen you that I seem to have forgotten both your assets and your defects.

LINDA   I would be the last to complain of your perfectly natural antagonism towards me, but I think you would be wise to submerge it for the moment.

ANNE   I would prefer to decide that for myself when you have explained to me what has happened.

LINDA   Your manner makes it difficult for me to explain anything at all. You must have realized that it wasn't for my sake that I telephoned you last night and asked you to come here, it was for George's.

ANNE   Why?

LINDA   Because he is going to die.

ANNE   (*After a long pause*)   How do you know?

LINDA   The doctor told me last night. His name is Pasquier. He is a brilliant man. It was he who gave George the check-up last spring and advised him to have the operation.

ANNE   (*Sharply*)   Operation! What operation?

LINDA   Didn't George tell you about it when he was in England last summer?

ANNE   No. He did not.

LINDA   It was apparently quite trivial, a small cyst under his left arm. Pasquier said that it would be a good idea to get rid of it, so

SHADOWS OF THE EVENING   *Angus McBean*

George went into the clinique for a couple of days and had it cut
out. Nobody seemed to attach much importance to it. We stayed
on here for about a week so that it could be dressed, then it
healed up and we went to Corsica as we had planned.

ANNE   I remember. He sent me the usual routine postcards.

LINDA (*With an edge in her voice*)   Would you rather he hadn't?

ANNE   Mind your own business.

LINDA   If I were you, I wouldn't indulge your personal bitterness
now, Anne. There's very little time. You will have to make an
effort to forgive me my trespasses, outwardly at least, for his
sake. He will need you.

ANNE   How flattering of you to be so sure.

LINDA (*Angrily*)   Once and for all, will you stop talking like that
and even feeling like that. This is a desperate emergency.

ANNE   In the circumstances, isn't it a little arrogant of you to
dictate to me how I should speak or feel?

LINDA   No, it is not. In these particular circumstances there is no
room for wounded pride or remembered heartbreaks or any
other form of self-indulgence. The situation between you and
George and me has existed for seven years. I said a moment ago
that you would have to make an effort to forgive me my trespasses and I added "outwardly at least." That was the operative
phrase. I don't give a damn whether or not you truly forgive me
or despise me or hate me or love me. You've made your gesture
by coming here when I asked you to. For God's sake carry it
through.

ANNE   What did this Dr. Pasquier say exactly?

LINDA   He said that there was no hope whatever. That George
will die within nine months, possibly sooner.

ANNE   What is the disease? What is he to die of?

LINDA   It's something called "melanoma." He explained it to me
carefully but I'm not very good at medical technicalities. It has
something to do with "secondaries" occurring as a result of the
cyst being removed.

ANNE   Is Dr. Pasquier infallible? Has he suggested calling in any
other consultant?

LINDA   Several doctors have been consulted. George has been in
the clinique for the last three days. They performed a minor
exploratory operation. The findings were malignant.

ANNE (*Looking down*)   I see.

LINDA   That is what Pasquier came to tell me last night. He was
fairly blunt and absolutely definite.

ANNE   Has George any idea of this, any suspicion?

LINDA   No—I don't think so.

ANNE   When is he coming out of the clinique?

LINDA   Tomorrow morning.

ANNE   How is he now? I mean—is he in any way ill?

LINDA   No. He feels perfectly all right. I talked to him on the telephone just before lunch. He had had an anaesthetic yesterday for the exploratory examination, but they gave him a sleeping pill last night and he said he'd slept like a log. I asked him if he wanted me to come and see him this afternoon, but he said he'd rather be left alone to relax and get on with his James Bond. He was actually being considerate, I think. He knows hospitals and cliniques give me the horrors. I'm—I'm—glad he was considerate—it would have been a bit difficult after seeing Pasquier last night. I suppose I should have managed all right but I *am* feeling rather strung up and George is awfully quick at sensing people's vibrations and I—I—(*She bursts into tears. Fumbling in her bag for her handkerchief*) I'm sorry. I've been so determined *not* to do this. (ANNE *lights a cigarette. It is apparent that her hand is trembling slightly.* LINDA *continues to sob convulsively for a moment or two and then, with a determined effort, controls herself. She takes a compact out of her bag and dabs her face with a powder puff*) It won't occur again, I promise you.

ANNE   I'd like to see Dr. Pasquier.

LINDA   Yes. I think you should. We'll telephone him at his home number. I have it written down. He said he'd be in between seven and eight.

ANNE   What's the time now?

LINDA   (*Glancing at her watch*)   Just six-thirty.

ANNE   (*Returning to her chair*)   It is absolutely certain, isn't it? I mean there isn't any hope of them being wrong?

LINDA   He's a wise man, and sensible. I'm sure he wouldn't have been so—so definite if he weren't quite sure.

ANNE   Does he speak English?

LINDA   Yes, perfectly.

ANNE   Did he give any opinion as to whether George ought to be told or not?

LINDA   No. We talked about that. He said it was one of the most difficult problems that doctors have to cope with. Sometimes, apparently, mortal illness carries with it a sort of compensating illusion, a subconscious refusal to face the fact of dying. He said that in such cases it was unwise and cruel to shatter the illusion. With certain people, however, he said that not knowing was worse than knowing. Obviously it all depends on character, on individual temperament.

ANNE   I would be inclined to place George in the latter category.

LINDA   You mean you think he should be told.

ANNE   Yes. I suppose that is what I mean.

LINDA   Would you be prepared to tell him?

ANNE   Is that why you sent for me?

LINDA (*Steadily*)   No, Anne. That is not why I sent for you. I am perfectly capable of telling him the truth alone if it is necessary. But you surely couldn't expect me to make such a decision without consulting you? You would never have forgiven me if I had.

ANNE   I should have thought that by now my forgiveness was immaterial to you one way or the other.

LINDA   You are quite right, it is. It is also irrelevant. What is relevant is that you are still his wife. I am merely his mistress.

ANNE   If I had agreed to divorce him, years ago, when both you and he wished me to, would you still have sent for me? Would you still have needed my help?

LINDA   If I considered that you still loved him enough to be of use, yes.

ANNE   Whether I love George or not has nothing whatsoever to do with you, Linda.

LINDA   On the contrary, it has everything to do with me. Your love for him, coupled with mine, is all he has to hang on to. For the next few months, all he has left of his life, he is going to need us both, and he's going to need us both on the best behavior we are capable of. I am well aware that from the obvious, conventional point of view all the rights are on your side. You are his lawful wife and the mother of his children but if, in this intolerable situation, you attempt to trade on those rights, you will not only be cruel but stupid.

ANNE   And what rights are *you* intending to trade on?

LINDA   None. Beyond the fact that he is still in love with me and I with him.

ANNE   Are you quite sure this romantic passion you feel for each other will survive the imminence of death?

LINDA (*Steadily*)   Yes. I hope it will and I think it will. However if I am proved wrong that will be my problem and I will deal

with it as best I can. In the meantime you and I have got to come
to some sort of an arrangement. When George is dead, when he
is no longer here for either of us, we can indulge in orgies of
recrimination if you wish to. You can accuse me of taking your
husband away from you and breaking up your happy marriage.
I can accuse you of vindictive self-righteousness in refusing to
divorce him so that he could marry me. We can go through all
the hoops and give vent to all the mutual bitterness that has
been fermenting in us for years. But not now. Not yet. For so
long as George lives, we are going to establish a truce. We are
going to be friends, close, intimate, loving friends. Is that clear?

ANNE   Yes. Quite clear. But out of the question. I have no intention of pretending something that I don't feel for George's sake
or anyone else's.

LINDA   I think that that sort of stubbornness indicates weakness
rather than strength.

ANNE   It is a matter of supreme indifference to me what you think.

LINDA   It isn't what you or I think that counts. It is what George
feels.

ANNE   You said just now that he was still in love with you and you
with him. That surely should be enough to comfort him.

LINDA   That was cheap and unworthy of you. You had George's
wholehearted love for fifteen years, and even now you still have
part of it.

ANNE   I really don't care for this sort of conversation, Linda. It's
embarrassing.

LINDA   I don't care for it either, but we've got to come to an understanding. You still love George and you always will, otherwise
you wouldn't have come here when I asked you to. I love George
and I always will. In a way we're both in the same boat and in
a moment as tragic and desolate as this, it would be shameful
for either of us to allow our personal animosity to rock it. We
have no way of knowing how he is going to react to this situation,
but we do know that we are the two people he loves most. Surely
you must see that if we can make him realize that we are friends
again rather than enemies, it will be a little easier for him to face
what he has to face. Please, Anne, give in.

ANNE   (*After a long pause*)   Very well. I'll give in. There really
doesn't seem anything else to do.

LINDA   Is it a deal?

ANNE   Yes. It's a deal (*She closes her eyes miserably for a moment*) What do we do—kiss?

LINDA   We may need to later on. At the moment I think a strong drink would be more sensible.

ANNE   I agree.

LINDA   What would you like?

ANNE   Brandy, I think, with a lot of ice.

LINDA   Good idea. I'll have the same.
(*She proceeds to pour the drinks*)

ANNE   I suppose I'm beginning to accept the truth of the matter. I don't think I did quite, at first. (LINDA *brings* ANNE *her drink*) What do you think they told him—the doctors, I mean?

LINDA   (*Bringing her own drink and sitting down*)   I don't know. I expect they just said that the exploratory examination had been satisfactory.

ANNE   He must suspect something. He has a sharp mind. He isn't the type to accept evasions without question.

LINDA   I suppose it all depends on whether he really wants to know or not. Perhaps his subconscious has already started the resistance process.

ANNE   I doubt that. Don't you?

LINDA   Yes—yes I do—but we can't tell for certain, can we?

ANNE   I must talk to that damned doctor.

LINDA   (*Going to the telephone*)   I'll call him now.

ANNE   Shall I go to him or will he come here?

LINDA   Whichever you prefer.

ANNE   I think I'd like to see him alone anyhow.

LINDA   Of course. (*Into the telephone*) Mademoiselle, voulez-vous me donner trente-six-quarante-deux-vingt-trois . . . Merci.

ANNE   (*Rising and walking about the room*)   I suppose he's aware of the situation, between you and George, I mean?

LINDA   Oh yes. We haven't discussed it, obviously, but—(*Into telephone*) Allo. Puis-je parler avec le docteur, s'il vous plaît? Il n'est pas encore rentré de la clinique? Oui. Dans une demi-heure? Quand il arrive, voulez-vous lui demander de téléphoner à Madame Savignac au Beau Rivage? Oui, c'est assez urgent . . . merci beaucoup. (*She hangs up*) He'll be back within half an hour, I've asked for him to call me here. (*Coming away from the telephone*) You'd better go to him, I think. My car will take you. It isn't very far.

ANNE   (*She takes a cigarette from a box and lights it*)   How are we to explain to George about me being here? He'll suspect something's up the moment he sees me.

LINDA   I've thought of that. You stopped off here for a few days

on your way to Italy and we ran into each other by chance in
the foyer downstairs and had a sort of *"rapprochement."*

ANNE   Why should I stop off here on my way to Italy? If I wanted
to go to Italy, which I don't, I should go straight there.

LINDA   You came to see Professor Boromelli.

ANNE   Who on earth is Professor Boromelli?

LINDA   He's the new miracle man here. People come from all over
the world to see him. He's a highly controversial figure. Most
doctors hate him and say he's a charlatan, but he has had a few
spectacular successes with his injections, it's a special formula of
his own apparently.

ANNE   What sort of injections?

LINDA   I don't know exactly, hormones or something—
     (*She tails off*)

ANNE   You mean rejuvenation?

LINDA   (*Weakly*)   Yes—something of the kind.

ANNE   What nonsense. George wouldn't swallow that for an instant. He knows perfectly well that I'd never go in for that sort
of thing.

LINDA   You might have been run-down and overtired and in sudden need of some sort of physical reassurance.

ANNE   No, Linda, it won't do, really it won't. We shall have to
think of something else.

LINDA   What? What do you suggest then?

ANNE   When in doubt, stick to the truth, or as near to the truth
as possible.

LINDA   You mean tell him I telephoned you and asked you to
come?

ANNE   Why not? You were naturally upset and worried about
him, and on a sudden impulse you called me.

LINDA   He'd know I wouldn't do that unless it were something
really serious.

ANNE   You can't fool George for long. I'm perfectly prepared to
believe that in certain cases Dr. Pasquier's theory about the subconscious building a deliberate barricade against the truth is
accurate, but George would never be one of those cases. He'll
see through any foolish little conspiracy we cook up. You must
know this as well as I do.

LINDA   Yes, of course I do—but we can't be sure, can we—really
sure?

ANNE   Of course we can't, therefore we can make no decisions as to whether we should tell him or not. He must take the lead. He must dictate how we are to behave.

LINDA I'm so desperately frightened of taking a wrong step, of making a false move.

ANNE Well, don't be. Keep your mind clear. Be vigilant.

LINDA After you've seen Pasquier, you'll come straight back, won't you?

ANNE Yes. I'll come straight back.

LINDA Would you like to dine up here in the suite or shall we go out somewhere?

ANNE I don't care one way or the other.

LINDA I think I would rather go out if you don't mind. I'm feeling rather overstrained and there'll be less likelihood of sudden flurries of tears in a public place. There's a little restaurant perched high up in the vines between here and Vevey. The food's good and there's a lovely view across the lake.

ANNE All right. We'll go there. (*With a wry smile*) We can talk over old times.

LINDA (*Turning away*) Oh, Anne!

ANNE Don't worry, I wasn't trying to dig up the hatchet again, I gave you my word that it was buried for the time being. (*She holds out her glass*) I think I'd like a freshener.

LINDA (*Taking it*) A good idea. I think I would too.

ANNE (*Lighting a cigarette*) As a matter of fact I meant it quite genuinely.

LINDA (*At the drink table*) Meant what quite genuinely?

ANNE That we could talk over old times.

LINDA Oh—Oh I see.

ANNE The future is miserable, the immediate present appalling, so ghastly in all its implications that we can't go on discussing it indefinitely without undermining our self-control. The past will be almost a relief, even the painful parts of it.

LINDA (*Handing* ANNE *her drink*) I find it difficult to imagine anything undermining your self-control.

ANNE I shouldn't bank on that if I were you.

LINDA I'm sorry. It was a disagreeable thing to say.

ANNE There's nothing to be sorry about. I quite see your point.

LINDA I see that this isn't going to be very easy for either of us.

ANNE I agree. That is why I proffered that rather withered little olive branch. You could hardly expect it to be in full bloom.

LINDA (*With a slight smile*) I didn't expect it at all. It took me by surprise.

ANNE   I was trying to remember that we were friends once, long
    ago.

LINDA   Not so very long ago.

ANNE   You made this drink extremely strong.

LINDA   Mine is the same. I thought it might uninhibit us a little.

ANNE   Are you certain that that would be an entirely good idea?

LINDA   It's worth trying. It might at least lighten the atmosphere
    between us a little. We can't spend the whole evening hating
    each other at full blast.

ANNE   It might on the other hand work the other way and unin-
    hibit us too much.

LINDA (*Holding up her glass*)   A risk worth the taking.

ANNE (*Perfunctorily raising hers*)   Have it your own way.

LINDA   Can you remember the very first time we met?

ANNE   Certainly I can. I pulled you out of the Suez Canal in 1943.

LINDA   You always boasted that you did, but it wasn't really as
    dramatic as that. The brakes failed and I just slid in, lorry and
    all. I admit that if you hadn't suddenly appeared with that Major
    What's-his-name, I might have been sitting there now.

ANNE   His name was Edgar Hethrington.

LINDA   It couldn't have been!

ANNE   I was driving him from Suez to Cairo. It was at Ismailia
    that you skidded. Actually he was rather nice, in a way.

LINDA   I remember he lent me a pair of slacks because mine were
    sodden and made roguish jokes while I put them on behind the
    car.

ANNE   I can also remember the orderly's face when we dropped
    you off at your base and you were trying to hold the trousers up
    with one hand and return the salute with the other.
    (*She laughs*)

LINDA (*Also laughing*)   What happened to him—Major Edgar
    Hethrington?

ANNE   The poor beast got mumps three days later and everything
    swelled up—they're liable to, you know, if you get it when you're
    an adult—and he had to be sent home. It's called hydrosome-
    thing-or-other, I believe.

LINDA (*Laughing helplessly*)   Cele I think—it can't be phobia be-
    cause that's mad dogs, so it must be cele.

    (*At this moment* GEORGE HILGAY *comes into the room. He is
    a tall man in the early fifties. He stares at* LINDA *and* ANNE
    in astonishment. For a moment they don't see him. When*

they do, their laughter ceases abruptly. LINDA *jumps up and goes to him.* ANNE *remains seated*)

GEORGE Anne! What in the name of God are you doing here?

ANNE (*Rising slowly*) Hallo, George.

GEORGE Is there anything wrong with Brian or Margaret?

ANNE No. Brian's with Andrew in Scotland and Margaret went off to Spain with the whole Chisholm family. They've rented a house near Malaga for a month. I was left alone at home so I thought I'd take a little jaunt.

GEORGE (*Looking swiftly from her to* LINDA) Well, I'll be damned!

LINDA Are you all right?

GEORGE I couldn't stand that damned clinique for another minute, so I nipped out when nobody was looking, got a taxi and came home. What were you both laughing at?

LINDA Anne pulling me out of the Suez Canal and Major Hethrington having mumps.

GEORGE I don't know what the hell you're talking about.

ANNE We were reminiscing—war experiences—that's when Linda and I first met, you know, during the war. We were both driving people about Egypt.

GEORGE (*With a puzzled frown*) I see. At least I think I see.

LINDA Sit down and have a drink. You must be tired.

GEORGE I'm not particularly tired, but I should certainly like a drink.

(*The telephone rings.* LINDA *shoots* ANNE *an agonized look and goes to it*)

ANNE (*Calmly*) If it's for me, say I'm out and will call back later. It's probably Mariette de Castries. I ran into her in the foyer when I came in. She threatened to telephone about seven-thirty. I'll get George his drink. (*To George*) Whisky or gin or vodka?

GEORGE (*Still puzzled*) Whisky please, with plain water.

ANNE (*At drink table*) Ice?

GEORGE No ice—thank you.

LINDA (*At the telephone*) 'Allo—*Oui à l'appareil*—Oh good evening—how nice of you to call—yes indeed, I did leave a message, but it doesn't matter now. Will you be at home later in the evening? Oh I see—Just one moment while I take down the number—(*She scribbles on a pad*) *Soixante-six-seize-cinquante-trois.* Thank you so much. Yes—yes I'll call later on or early in the morning.

(*She hangs up*)

GEORGE   That was a mysterious little conversation.

LINDA   It was poor Mr. Brevet at the American Express. I think I'm driving him mad. I keep on canceling air tickets and then wanting them again.

> (*She lights a cigarette and sits down on the sofa*)

GEORGE   Well, you've got his number in case you want to cancel anything else.

LINDA   Have you seen Dr. Pasquier?

GEORGE   Yes.

LINDA   What did he say?

GEORGE (*Sipping his drink*)   Quite a lot of things.

LINDA (*Bravely*)   Did they find out what was wrong?

GEORGE   Yes. He was very uncompromising.

ANNE (*After a slight pause*)   Don't keep us in suspense, George. It's rather nerve-wracking.

GEORGE   Linda asked you to come, didn't she?

ANNE (*Meeting his eye*)   Yes. She telephoned to me.

GEORGE   When?

ANNE   Last night. I caught the afternoon plane.

GEORGE (*To* LINDA)   That was after you had talked to Pasquier?

LINDA (*Biting her lip*)   Yes.

GEORGE (*Getting up and kissing* ANNE)   It was dear of you to come, Anne. I'm very grateful—(*He leaves her and goes over to the window, patting* LINDA *reassuringly on the shoulder as he passes her. He stands with his back to them both, looking out over the lake. They watch him mutely. After a moment or two he comes back to them. He is smiling, as convincingly as he can*) What had you decided? Which of you was going to tell me?

ANNE   We hadn't decided anything. We didn't know. We were waiting for you—to—to show us what to do.

LINDA (*Firmly*)   What did Pasquier tell you?

GEORGE   Exactly what he told you last night. That I am going to die. Within the next nine months possibly, but probably within the next three. I will not confuse and sadden you with the details, but there will be no pain. He promised me that. He's a kindly man and I believe him.

LINDA   He told you all this just now, this afternoon?

GEORGE   I forced him to, because I had already guessed, before they did the examination, while I was waiting to have the anaesthetic I suddenly knew, with all my nerve centers, with all my instincts. It was a curious sensation, remote, detached and without fear, then. I've had a few bad moments since, but I think I'm all right now.

ANNE You're absolutely certain that Dr. Pasquier is right, that there is no chance of wrong diagnosis?

GEORGE Absolutely certain. Several doctors were involved. Of course Pasquier was extremely reluctant to pronounce my sentence. He was faced, poor man, with the most recurrently difficult problem that a doctor has to face, whether or not to tell the truth when a patient insistently demands it. Nine out of ten people believe sincerely that they wish to know their fate, but it is only the tenth who really means it. I finally managed to convince him that I was genuinely one of those tenth men. When he gave in and told me I was shocked beyond measure, and at the same time infinitely relieved. After he'd gone I had a glass of water and smoked a cigarette and lay there staring at the white ceiling, and thought harder than I've ever thought before. You see, I felt it was essential to arrive at a point of view to offer you, Linda—naturally I didn't know that Anne was going to be here too—and I think I've succeeded, temporarily at least. (*He pauses and walks about the room*) The point of view I want to give you both is that I consider myself to be fortunate rather than misfortunate. These are not merely brave words to comfort you with, but to comfort myself as well. I have had a reasonably happy life, much happier and more secure than the lives of millions of my fellow creatures. I have done my job to the best of my ability . . . and being a publisher has kept me in touch with all the things I love most. I have been neither a spectacular success nor a dismal failure. I have tried to live my life with passable dignity. I have tried to be kind rather than cruel. I have a few regrets, a few remembered follies, but I have no complaints. And now, while I have been told that my life must end specifically in such and such a time, I have also been guaranteed that I shall cease upon the midnight with no pain. What more can I ask than that? Of course, I should have liked a little longer but I have at least been allowed time to rally my forces, and so to hell with it. That's all there is left for me to do.

LINDA (*Choked*) I'll be back in a minute, don't be cross with me.
(*She goes swiftly into the bedroom*)

GEORGE Everything forgiven and forgotten?

ANNE (*Wearily*) Forgiven at any rate.

GEORGE I see so clearly why I married you.

ANNE Can you see equally clearly why you left me?

GEORGE Yes—that too. Except that I didn't actually *leave* you. I just happened to fall in love with Linda.

ANNE It's more or less the same thing, isn't it?

GEORGE No it isn't, and you know it. We went through it all at the time. You accepted the situation.

ANNE I hadn't much choice, had I?

GEORGE You could have divorced me.

ANNE Never.

GEORGE Why not? I've often wondered why you were so stubborn.

ANNE The children for one thing, and my pride too.

GEORGE Wouldn't your pride have been less humiliated if you'd got rid of me once and for all?

ANNE I didn't want to get rid of you once and for all.

GEORGE Oddly enough you won your point.

ANNE That's good news anyhow, a trifle bleak perhaps, but better than nothing.

GEORGE We should have had this scene before. After all we've seen each other several times over the last years . . . I've been back and forth between my two loves.

ANNE That's a nauseating little phrase and you ought to be ashamed of such facile vulgarity.

GEORGE (*Raising his glass*) I salute you.

ANNE Keep your damned salutes to yourself.

GEORGE This is quite like old times, isn't it?

ANNE (*Suddenly heartbroken*) Oh no, it isn't.
(*She turns blindly away from him*)

GEORGE (*Gently*) I would like you to know that, in spite of all betrayals, you are still a necessary part of my life.

ANNE Fine words, but curiously arid. They should have been spoken earlier. Seven years is a long time.

GEORGE Longer than three months.

ANNE That was cruel of you. I don't need to be reminded that you have so little time left. I am here to help, and I have no intention of confusing the issues by allowing emotion to override my common sense. I'll leave that to Linda. She's bellowing her heart out in the bedroom at this very moment.

GEORGE I suppose I should be grateful for such stinging astringency.

ANNE Certainly you should. It will contract your spiritual tissues and help to keep your mind clear. You have to set your house in order. There's no time to sit up in the attic opening up old trunks and sorting out dusty, nostalgic souvenirs.

GEORGE   Were you still in love with me when I upped and left you?

ANNE   What does it matter if I were or not?

GEORGE   I really should like to know.

ANNE   I see that you insist on the attic and the old trunks and the shabby disintegrated gollywogs.

GEORGE   Please, Anne, stop being so defensively articulate and answer my question.

ANNE   Very well. I'll set your mind at rest. The answer is No. I was not in love with you when you "upped and left me." Perhaps I was never in love with you in the way that you mean. But I cared for you deeply. There are so many different degrees of loving. How can one tell? One loves as much as one can. As you know I have never been a particularly passionate woman. I see now, in fact I've realized for a long time, that that was where I failed you. But never believe that my heart was frigid. I gave you all I was capable of giving. When you went away from me I was more unhappy than I have ever been in my life. Naturally, after a while, I got over it to a certain extent, but I missed you sadly, I still do. Perhaps I shall miss you less when you are dead.

GEORGE   Fair's fair. But try not to consign me to the limbo too soon. I know I shan't mind then but I do mind now. It makes me feel lonely.

ANNE   None of that, George, none of that. Like the reeds at Runnymede, I may bend but I will not break. So don't waste your time trying to make me.

GEORGE   Have you loved anyone else—since me?

ANNE   Do you mean, have I been to bed with anyone else?

GEORGE   If you choose to put it that way.

ANNE   Yes. Three times.

GEORGE   With different men, or the same one?

ANNE   Different. Three times in seven years isn't an abnormally high percentage.

GEORGE   Maybe not, but it seems oddly out of character.

ANNE   Yes. I suppose it was. But it was a sort of search really. I was trying to find out something.

GEORGE   What were you trying to find out?

ANNE   Where I had gone wrong. Why it was that I let you down.

GEORGE   You never let me down.

ANNE   (*With a faint smile*)   Of course I let you down, sexually, I mean.

GEORGE   That simply isn't true. I loved your body for many years.

ANNE   Perhaps. But it didn't love you—enough. That's why I went to bed with the others, to discover where the fault lay, with you or with me. But it didn't work really. I proved nothing. I felt nothing, beyond a momentary fleeting physical excitement. I still missed you, and somehow resented you at the same time. I am sure that any psychiatrist could explain it to me in a minute, but I don't want to know, not any more. It's all too far away and the search is over.

GEORGE   I must come back home again soon. To see the house and the garden. How is it all looking?

ANNE   Flourishing. I've planted a row of tamarisks along the lower lane. They're doing very well.

GEORGE   How's old Tom?

ANNE   Old Tom's been gathered. Just as well really, he was crippled with arthritis and very feeble. Young Tom has taken over, shining with good will and more idiotic than ever.

GEORGE   When was I last there? Time goes so quickly.

ANNE   (*Evenly*)   Nearly two years ago. You came for Brian's twenty-first birthday and we had a cocktail party on the lawn. Later we dined on the flagged terrace outside the dining-room window, just us and that awful girl friend of Margaret's.

GEORGE   . . . the one with the lisp?

ANNE   . . . Yes . . . It was a lovely warm evening.

GEORGE (*Suddenly sitting down*)   Oh Christ! (*He covers his face with his hands*) Fear is an ignoble enemy. It strikes at you suddenly, unexpectedly. (*He looks up*) I've always rather despised people who were afraid of the dark. Now I begin to see their point. When I was a little boy I was outstandingly brave. I used to force myself to grope my way about the house in the middle of the night touching familiar things, the round silver tray in the hall where people used to leave their visiting cards, the Chinese lacquer cabinet in the drawing room, the china horse on the mantelpiece in my father's study, I had to climb up onto a leather armchair to reach it. I had to prove to myself that these things were still there, although I couldn't see them. I wasn't commended for my bravery because one night my hand slipped and the china horse fell into the fireplace and broke. I was severely whacked for it the next day. But I had at least proved that I wasn't frightened. Now it's different. There'll be no familiar, friendly objects to touch, no china horses to break.

ANNE   Maybe the eternal darkness will be lighter than you think.

GEORGE   No, Anne. That won't wash, you know it won't, not for me. I know you still believe, up to a point, in the things you were brought up to believe in, but I don't—I can't. I've occasionally paid lip service to religious superstition for the sake of appearances and to spare other people's feelings, but my mind refuses to accept hazy, undefined promises of life after death.

ANNE   There is always a chance that you may be wrong.

GEORGE   Of course there is. But I'm quite content to die believing only in life itself which seems to me to be quite enough to be going on with, and I have no complaints either except an immediate resentment that I am only to be allowed to go on with it for such a little while longer.

ANNE   If that's how you feel, hang on to it. No words can help, from me or anybody else.

GEORGE   On the other hand if, in three months' time, I suddenly find myself in some tinsel heaven or some gaudy hell, I shall come back and haunt you. But don't let go my hand—don't let go my hand.

The Lights Fade

Scene Two

*An hour has elapsed since the preceding scene. It is dusk outside
and lights can be seen glimmering across the lake. There is still a
slight glow behind the high mountains.*

*FELIX comes in with a bottle of champagne in an ice bucket, and
a tray of glasses. He puts the ice bucket and the tray down, and
proceeds to tidy up the drink table.*

*After a moment or two LINDA comes out of the bedroom. She is
wearing a dinner dress and carrying an evening coat over her arm,
and a pair of white gloves. These she puts on the window seat. She
is in perfect control and her face is calm.*

LINDA   Is it the Lanson, Felix, or the Pol-Roget?

FELIX   The Lanson, madame. Signor Luigi considered it to be the
wise choice because it is a most good year.

LINDA   Thank you, Felix.

FELIX   If Madame would wish some canapés, I have them prepared.

LINDA   I'll ring if we need them.

FELIX   *Va bene, signora.*

LINDA   Has your friend recovered?

FELIX   *Sì, signora.* It was only a small concussion. They made three
stitches in his head and sent him away, but he is most low in
spirits because the police have taken from him his driving license.

LINDA (*With a smile*)   Perhaps that is not entirely a bad idea.

FELIX   But it is not quite just, madame, because it was not all his
fault. The young lady in the Alfa Romeo drove across the red
lights.

LINDA   Did she get a concussion, too?

FELIX   No, madame, she was not hurt at all, but she was most
deeply angry. It was because of her great rage that they took

away his license. She is a Swiss young lady and he is an Italian,
so there was no true justice.

LINDA   True justice is a rare thing. It is foolish to expect it.

FELIX (*Sadly*)   *E vero—la signora a ragione.* You would wish anything more, madame?

LINDA   No, that will be all for the moment, Felix. Wish your friend
well for me.

FELIX   Madame is most kind—*à votre service.*

(FELIX *bows and goes out.* LINDA *looks at herself pensively
in the mirror and gives her hair a reassuring pat, then she
lights a cigarette.* GEORGE *comes in. He is wearing a dinner
jacket and there is a red carnation in his buttonhole. He
looks at* LINDA *with an appreciative smile and then goes over
and kisses her*)

GEORGE   You look wonderful.

LINDA   Thank you, darling. So do you, red carnation and all.

GEORGE   I always wear a red carnation when I'm going to gamble.
I have a feeling that it brings me luck. What time does the boat
leave?

LINDA   Nine o'clock. I've ordered the car for a quarter to.

GEORGE   It doesn't take more than three minutes to go from here
to the Embarcadere.

LINDA   There might be a crowd. I always like to play safe.

GEORGE   Did you ring up and reserve a table?

LINDA   Of course. I also ordered a bottle of champagne. We might
just as well go the whole hog. Shall we open it now or wait for
Anne? She'll be here in a minute.

GEORGE (*Sitting down*)   Let's wait a while. There's no hurry.

LINDA   Poor Felix has had a trying day. His great friend, the bar-
man at the Hotel de la Paix, bumped into an Alfa Romeo on his
motor-bicycle and had three stitches in his head and his license
taken away.

GEORGE   Italians shouldn't be allowed to ride motor-bicycles.

LINDA   Neither should anyone else. (*There is a silence*) Do you
think this is really going to work?

GEORGE   We must persevere.

LINDA   I'll do my best. I'm quite determined to. But I can't guarantee how long it will last. I'm glad Anne is here. She'll keep me
in order.

GEORGE   We must all keep each other in order.

LINDA   She's stronger than I am.

GEORGE   In some ways perhaps, but in others she is more vulnerable.

LINDA   What makes you say that?

GEORGE   Possibly because I've only just realized it. As a matter of fact, I've been realizing quite a number of things during the last twenty-four hours. It's extraordinary how swiftly the mind works when faced with sudden urgency.

LINDA   We're on dangerous ground. It may open at our feet and swallow up our little charade.

GEORGE   (*Gently*)   It's more than a little charade, Linda. Don't underrate it. The only alternative is to knuckle under, to abandon ourselves to wasteful tears and emotional chaos. And even that wouldn't last. Grief is no more durable than happiness. We should merely exhaust ourselves and each other. We can't snivel our way through the next few months just because one of us is going to die. We're all going to die eventually. There's too much spiritual defeat in the world today, too much shrill emphasis on fear. Let's stay away from that particular bandwagon. Let's, in fact, try to behave ourselves.

LINDA   Perhaps we'd better open the champagne after all.

GEORGE   (*Getting up*)   I'll do it.

LINDA   I expect Felix has loosened the wire a bit. He's very efficient.

GEORGE   (*Taking the bottle out of the bucket*)   You're quite right. He has.

LINDA   Shall we be going back to London immediately?

GEORGE   No. We'll have our two weeks in Capri, as planned. I shall have to be back on the second of next month anyhow. There's a general directors' meeting. Also, I shall have to do some settling up. I shall take old Fielding into my confidence. I can trust him not to betray it. I don't want to have to face commiserating looks and tight-lipped sympathy.

LINDA   Will part of the settling up include going back to Anne?

GEORGE   Of course. I want to see Brian and Margaret and look through some old trunks in the attic.

    (*He laughs*)

LINDA   Why do you laugh?

GEORGE   It was something Anne said. She has a deep-dyed distrust of ancient souvenirs. (*He opens the champagne bottle with a loud pop*) There. That sounds all right . . . (*He looks up at her while he is pouring the champagne into two glasses*) Don't look so stricken. I've been back before. Nothing is changed.

LINDA (*Vehemently*) Everything is changed and you know it.

GEORGE (*Handing her a glass of champagne*) Heightened perhaps, but not changed. Here you are.

LINDA (*Taking it*) I minded you going back before. I shall mind more than ever now.

GEORGE Don't fuss, darling. I'm still in love with you.

LINDA (*Before she can stop herself*) You still love Anne too?

GEORGE (*Fetching his own glass from the table*) I've never pretended that I didn't. Have a swig of champagne.

LINDA I must say something to you, now, urgently, before Anne comes back. You must bear with me. It will be a little sentimental but I promise not to go too far.

GEORGE Fire away, fire away. I'm steeling myself.

LINDA I know we made a pact a little while ago, the three of us, after I'd been crying and making a fool of myself. I know we all agreed that the only sensible way to behave was to go on as though there were no shadows closing in on us. I swear I'll keep my part of the bargain for so long as I am capable of it, but I must tell you now, before the performance really gets under way, that the last seven years have been the happiest of my whole life. Before we met and became lovers, I lived in a vapid, over-social vacuum. I went everywhere and I knew everybody and I never once looked clearly at myself. My marriage was a failure, my child miscarried and my divorce was sordid and humiliating. But the fact of you loving me changed everything. It gave me a new point of view and something to believe in. I want you to know that I shall be grateful to you until the end of my days. This is really a sort of spoken bread-and-butter letter and look—I'm not even crying.

GEORGE Thank you, my love, thank you indeed. (*He hands her his glass*) You might pop a lump of ice into my drink. It's getting a bit tepid. (LINDA *takes his glass to the drink table and puts some ice in it.* ANNE *comes in. She is wearing a dinner dress and she, too, has an evening coat over her arm.* GEORGE *rises and takes it from her*) You haven't forgotten your passport, have you? We have to show it when we land.

ANNE I have it in my bag.

LINDA Would you care for a little expensive champagne?

ANNE Very much indeed.

GEORGE (*Bringing* ANNE *her champagne*) How are we for time?

LINDA (*Glancing at her watch*) Fine. There's no hurry.

ANNE (*Sitting down*) I haven't been inside a casino for years. I'm quite looking forward to it. You'll have to give me some money, George. I hadn't time to get any traveller's cheques.

GEORGE Are you going to stick to Roulette or have a bash at Chemin-de-fer?

ANNE Roulette. I can never read the cards at Chemin-de-fer. I get too flustered. At any rate, I'm much happier just watching. I wish now I'd brought a more glamorous dress. Next to Linda I look like somebody's governess.

LINDA I know comparatively few governesses who are dressed by Molyneux.

ANNE It's about a hundred years old.

GEORGE We shall be the only ones in the casino who are dressed up to the nines. It isn't a Gala night. We shall stick out like sore thumbs.

ANNE I've always wondered why sore thumbs are supposed to stick out.

GEORGE For the matter of that, I see no reason why we should be dressed "up to the nines" as opposed to the tens or the twenties.

ANNE I expect there *is* a reason for it somewhere. I'm sure Mr. Fowler or Mr. Partridge would know.

GEORGE It's curious that our two leading authorities on English idiom should both sound so ornithological.

LINDA There's always marmalade, for instance.

ANNE What on earth do you mean?

LINDA I was thinking of the origins of words that have become common usage. Marmalade goes straight back to Mary Stuart.

ANNE How?

LINDA When she was Queen of France she was ill and took a fancy to orange preserve and everyone said "*Marie est malade!*"

ANNE (*Vaguely*) How fascinating.

GEORGE Do you imagine that we shall be able to keep the conversation up to this level for the whole evening?

ANNE You mustn't be crushing, dear. We're doing our best.

LINDA We agreed to try to behave as usual.

GEORGE I know we did, and it was a brave resolution, but like so many brave resolutions it is liable to prove impracticable. Heroic gestures, unless they are immediately carried out in the heat of battle with all flags flying, have a nasty habit of degenerating into anticlimax. We are all three of us far too intelligent not to realize that soon, very soon, the pretense may become more of a strain than reality.

ANNE   The reality has struck at us with dreadful suddenness, George. We have had little time to prepare our defenses.

GEORGE   I know, darling, I know. But even so, to attempt to silence the enemy's guns by throwing puff-balls is worse than useless. If we try to maintain an attitude of artificial casualness, the tension will become intolerable. The supply of puff-balls will soon run out and the silences between us will lengthen.

ANNE   What do you suggest? A summit conference on life and death?

GEORGE   Not necessarily, but I am definitely against a policy of evasion.

ANNE   We should be going to Geneva instead of Evian.

GEORGE   What about another nip of champagne, there's a lot left in the bottle.

ANNE   (*Holding out her glass*)   Certainly.

LINDA   I'll do it. (*She fetches the bottle of champagne and refills their glasses*) Shall I ask Felix to bring another bottle?

ANNE   Oh no, please not. I'm not very good at drinking a lot. It makes me sleepy and dull and sometimes rather disagreeable, and I don't want to be any of those things tonight.

LINDA   Quite right. Tonight's going to be difficult enough anyway. Perhaps it would be wiser to go up to that little restaurant in the mountains, after all. To have decided on Evian and gambling seems to me now to be overambitious, running before we can walk. We're sure to meet someone we know and have to smile and make conversation; also we may feel claustrophobic, shut up in a hot casino waiting for the boat to bring us back.

ANNE   A quiet, romantic restaurant in the mountains would be more dangerous still. Beautiful views can be melancholy. Moonlight and stars and infinite distance are all right for young lovers, but for three middle-aged people trying to be brave they might be even more claustrophobic than a crowded casino.

LINDA   All right, Anne—I give in. It was only an idea—like the champagne.

GEORGE   I hate to insert a harsh note into this gallant conversation, but your ghastly politeness to each other is driving me mad.

LINDA   Would you rather we snarled at each other?

GEORGE   It would certainly be more convincing, and more honest.

ANNE   Don't place too much value on honesty. In certain circumstances, it can be a very overrated virtue.

GEORGE   It happens to be one of the things I'm fighting to hang on to, and I certainly can't win if I have to face you both cooing at each other like doves. For God's sake, let's chuck this bloody performance and get down to brass tacks.

ANNE   What particular brass tacks had you in mind?

GEORGE   (*Suddenly near the breaking point*) I don't know—I don't know—and I'm not even sure that I care. All I do know is that this is wrong, deeply wrong. I can't spend the last two months of my life watching you two acting out a loving affection for each other which neither of you feel and which, considering the situation between the three of us, you could never *possibly* feel. I resent being treated like an imbecile and I also resent your treacly compassion. I'm going to die—I'm going to die— and, what is more, I'm going to die alone, because everybody dies alone. This fact is hard enough for me to face without your God-damned loving-kindness and pity and synthetic heroics.

LINDA   (*Emotionally*)   You're not to say such things—it isn't fair. Anne and I agreed to a compromise because we considered that our feelings for you were more important than our feelings for each other. There was nothing heroic about it. We did it for your sake, because we wanted to help.

GEORGE   But it won't work! Can't you see? It could never possibly work. I know you both too well and I also love you both too well. I will not put up with tactful deceptions. The moment for me is too bitter.

ANNE   (*Calmly*)   Why, George. You're positively driving us into each other's arms.

GEORGE   Excellent. A little Lesbian frolic might take the burden of emotionalism off my shoulders.

LINDA   (*Near tears*)   You're certainly gone a long way away from us already.

GEORGE   Of course I have. It's train-fever, I expect. I'm on my way to the station.

ANNE   If that's not synthetic heroics I should like to know what is.

LINDA   I don't think I can bear any more of this, I really don't.

ANNE   You could always retire to the bedroom again in tears.

LINDA   I know I could, Anne, but however much it may disappoint you, I am not going to.

GEORGE   Things are looking up.

ANNE   What more does your obstinate masculine vanity require, George? What do you really want of us?

GEORGE   Truthfulness, a realistic view. Less tender womanly understanding and more horse sense.

LINDA Do all men who love women despise them so utterly?

GEORGE That is a generalization that I am not prepared to analyze at the moment. I have more important things to think about.

ANNE Are we going to this damned casino, or aren't we?

GEORGE Of course we are. What else is there to do?

ANNE Well, I could go back to England, for one thing. I expect there's a night plane.

GEORGE Do you want to?

ANNE In one way, yes. But the decision is up to you. You're the dying Gladiator.

LINDA (*Violently*) Anne!

GEORGE What do you think, Linda? Would you like Anne to go back to England and leave us on our own?

LINDA This is the first time since we've been together that I have ever known you to be really cruel.

GEORGE That doesn't exactly answer my question.

ANNE Your question was contemptible.

GEORGE (*Inexorably to* LINDA) Would you like Anne to go back to England, now—tonight?

LINDA (*After a pause*) No. No, I wouldn't. I'd rather she stayed.

ANNE What on earth made you say that?

LINDA (*Meeting her eye*) Because I'm too miserable and exhausted to be able to cope with this situation by myself. Whether you go back to England tonight or not, George and I will *not* be "on our own." I don't think we shall ever be on our own again. That's all over. You will be with us if you're here or not. Therefore, you might as well stay. The charade's over and everybody has guessed the word.

GEORGE You're wrong, Linda, you're wrong. You've neither of you guessed correctly. You think the word is "Death" but it isn't, it's "Life." If only I could make you see this there would be no necessity for any more pretense between us at all. Just now, I deliberately destroyed the pattern of behavior we had set for ourselves because I suddenly realized how completely false it was, and that it could only lead us further and further away from facing honestly the ultimate truth that we have to face. Not only me and you and Anne, but every living human being on this God-forsaken planet. We are all united in the fear of death, we all share it, because, like eternity, it is beyond the grasp of the human mind. It is the unfathomable, the unimaginable and the unknown. But while death is the ultimate reality, it is also a negative one. Courage and honesty and humor on the other hand are positive because they belong to life and life, up until that last bewildering second, is all we have and all we know. It is also our most important responsibility. The heroic figures of our world were not great because of their strength and nobility, but because they had the imagination to deal with their weaknesses. I happen to believe that fear is the most insidious weakness of all, and if you two, during the next few months, can help me to battle with that and conquer it, I shall be grateful to you, literally, to my dying day.

ANNE   How do you suggest that we set about it?

GEORGE   By divorcing your emotions from me as much as possible and being yourselves.

ANNE   An interesting performance. I trust you will be ready to correct us when we say the wrong lines.

GEORGE   Why are you so angry?

ANNE   Because I find the situation infuriating.

GEORGE   No longer heartbreaking?

ANNE   No—no longer heartbreaking at all ...
(*Her voice quivers, she makes a tremendous effort to control herself, but can't quite manage it. She sinks into an armchair, buries her face in her hands, and bursts into tears.* LINDA *and* GEORGE *look at her in silence for a moment.* GEORGE *goes to her*)

GEORGE   Oh, Anne, don't, please don't. Forgive me for being so bloody selfish. I didn't mean to be unkind.

ANNE (*In a muffled voice*)   I think I'd like a cigarette.

LINDA   Would you care for a nip of brandy, too? The champagne's all gone.

ANNE   Yes, please. I would.
(GEORGE *lights a cigarette and gives it to her.* LINDA *goes to the drink table, pours out some brandy and brings it over*)

GEORGE   It isn't unappreciated, really it isn't. All the effort, I mean.
(ANNE *searches in her bag, produces a handkerchief and blows her nose*)

ANNE   Good. I'm glad.

GEORGE   Do as you want to do, behave as you want to behave, I didn't mean to preach. (*With an effort at lightness*) You should never have married a publisher in the first place. You always said I was too in love with words.

ANNE   It wasn't your words that defeated me, it was a sudden feeling of hopelessness. Please don't worry. I'm perfectly all right now. Thank you for the brandy, Linda. This isn't strained politeness, it's wholehearted gratitude. (*She pauses and sips her brandy*) Are the children to be told?

GEORGE   Not yet I think; a little later on.

ANNE   And when the time comes, will you tell them or shall I?

GEORGE   You. You are closer to them than I am. They will be startled and saddened, but no more than that. I have seen little of them during the last few years.

ANNE   I think you underrate their feeling for you.

GEORGE   Brian will mind more than Margaret, which is curious really. It is usually daughters who are nearest to their fathers, but Margaret has never quite forgiven me for going away. Brian has. This is one of my deeper regrets. I love my son and I shall never see what is to become of him.

ANNE   Don't waste any time on guilt, George, what is done is done. Brian will survive, so will Margaret, so will I. We have all three become used to your absence.

LINDA   I envy you, you are better off than I am.

ANNE   Yes. I suppose I am. I have become accustomed to my own kind of loneliness, yours will be a different kind, but it won't last long.

LINDA   (*With an edge in her voice*)   Why do you say that?

ANNE   Because your temperament is more resilient than mine and your character more adventurous. It always was. Once your immediate grief is over you will begin to look about you, the world for you is still full of a number of things. You will always ask more of life than I shall. My children will eventually marry, I expect, and leave me alone and, oddly enough, the prospect doesn't depress me unduly. I shall be content to pull up a few weeds in the garden, do the *Times* crossword and look at the sea. You will make more flamboyant demands and reap more dramatic rewards, one method is as valid as the other and there is no blame attached to either. It is merely the fundamental difference in our characters.

LINDA   (*With a hint of mockery*)   Scarlet women are seldom conceded such patrician tolerance. Your manners are certainly impeccable.

ANNE   What nonsense! You are no scarlet woman, you are merely a compulsive amoureuse. Your heart still yearns for passionate love, mine only longs for peace and quiet.

GEORGE   My God! Moments of truth are clattering around us like hail!

ANNE   Which proves that our summit conference is progressing favorably.

LINDA   Later on, when we are alone, will all these wise words still be available to comfort us? Or shall we have forgotten them and find overselves back where we started, only a few hours ago, when we first knew, when the nightmare began?

GEORGE   Don't minimize the value of words. They are our only currency, our only means of communication.

LINDA   But we can't talk indefinitely. There will be the moments before sleep and the moments just after waking, when realization comes and we shall be without hope.

GEORGE   Those moments will have to be faced, along with everything else. We can't expect to escape scot free. But the sharp impact will soon diminish, sooner than you think.

LINDA   I am sorry to be a weak sister again, but I was brought up as a Catholic and I have a sudden craving for more dogmatic, more professional consolation.

GEORGE   You mean that a priest's mumbo-jumbo would soothe you more than my graceless agnosticism?

LINDA   Not the mumbo-jumbo exactly, but the feeling behind it, the age-old wisdom, the reassurance.

GEORGE   (*Gently*)   I wouldn't mock at your faith, my darling, or stand between you and your hopeful prayers, any more than I would query Anne's sturdy Church of England rectitude. There is much age-old wisdom at the base of all religions, but for me never enough. Human beings are intrinsically cruel, it is part of their inheritance, so it is not to be wondered at that the gods they set up to worship should be equally so. Some of the Old Oriental despots are perhaps a shade less bombastic than our ruthless Christian dictatorship, but they one and all smile benignly on pain and suffering and the blood of human sacrifice. Mother Nature, the Life Force, is just as bad, but at least she doesn't wrap her sadistic inconsistencies in an aura of sanctity.

ANNE   You said this afternoon that you were grateful, that your life had been fortunate. Isn't it an abuse of hospitality to speak so bitterly?

GEORGE   One may be received with the utmost politeness at Gestapo headquarters, but the politeness fails to deaden the screams of the tortured in the rooms below.

LINDA   Oh George, please don't—please don't. I can't bear it.

GEORGE   You mustn't misunderstand me. I am not denying that life can be a wonderful gift. Nor am I denying that man has achieved miracles of ingenuity, courage, and loving kindness. I am only bewailing the fact that these achievements should be so perpetually offset by insensate cruelty, greed, fear, and conceit. I am not pretending to be infallible. I do not consider that I have been singled out by some celestial agency to set the world to rights. I am merely a reasonably observant man who is about to die and who refuses to be fobbed off with mysticism and romantic fallacies.

LINDA   You can't be sure. The mysticism may suddenly become clear and the romantic fallacies true.

GEORGE   So might heaven, hell, purgatory, the bogey man, Santa Claus, and all the other nursery dreams. I make no claim to omniscience. I only know that I *don't* know and that faced with this insoluble mystery all the priests, philosophers, scientists, and witch doctors in the world are as ignorant as I am. I have no time to waste on profitless speculation, less than ever now, and I intend to utilize the days that are left by fortifying my mind against fear. Throughout the course of history, many better men than I have confronted the imminence of death with courage, humor, and equanimity and I would prefer to die, if my will is strong enough, as a member of their distinguished company. Nor will I permit myself the scared luxury of last-minute deathbed repentance. I propose to greet oblivion without apology. I wish for no cringing, subservient prayers for the salvation of my immortal soul. My immortal soul, whether it is an intricate combination of nuclei, chromosomes, and genes, or a spiritual abstraction, will have to take its chance, as my mortal body has had to take its chance for over fifty years. Every schoolboy has to face the last day of the holidays. That is how I feel now. I still have enough time to recapitulate a few past enjoyments, to revisit the cove where we had the picnic, to swim again into the cave where we found the jellyfish, to swing once more in the wooden swing and to build the last sand-castle. I still have time to eat and drink and be reasonably merry, say "Banco" at the Chemin-de-fer table, to turn up a nine and win a few colored plaques. All I ask of you both is perhaps a little additional strength to tide me over a few inevitable moments of weakness. (*From outside, on the lake, three hoots of a siren are heard*)

That's the steamer. It always does that ten minutes before leaving to warn latecomers. Come, my dear ones, you have your passports. I have mine. It is still valid for quite a while.

(GEORGE *helps* ANNE *on with her coat. They collect their handbags, and the three of them go out*)

Curtain

The Sponge Room

BY

Keith Waterhouse
and
Willis Hall

Keith Waterhouse
and
Willis Hall

In September, 1960, a new play, *Billy Liar*, opened at the Cambridge Theatre, London, and its immediate success sparked two significant events in theatrical circles. It brought together two writers, Keith Waterhouse and Willis Hall (both born in 1929 in Leeds, Yorkshire, and lifetime friends), who since have become one of Britain's foremost writing teams; and it brought unequivocal stardom to actor Albert Finney, who scored a personal triumph with his portrayal of the title character of this North Country comedy, the daydreaming Billy Fisher.

Since that eventful year, the coauthors have together fashioned a number of plays that have been produced in London: *Celebration* (1961); *England, Our England; All Things Bright and Beautiful; The Sponge Room* and *Squat Betty* (1962); *They Called the Bastard Stephen* (1964); *Say Who You Are* (1965); and in 1969 their newest comedy, *Whoops-a-Daisy*, was presented at the Nottingham Playhouse.

On his own, Willis Hall achieved an outstanding London success in 1959 with *The Long and the Short and the Tall* (seen on the New York stage in 1962) and in November, 1960, he also scored with his adaptation of François Billetdoux's *Chin-Chin*, at Wyndham's Theatre, with Celia Johnson and Anthony Quayle in the leading roles.

Films written by the Messrs. Waterhouse and Hall include *Whistle Down the Wind; A Kind of Loving; Billy Liar; Man in the Middle* and *Torn Curtain*.

The Sponge Room and *Squat Betty* were performed (under the direction of John Dexter) as a double bill at the Royal Court Theatre (1962). Though they are completely independent plays, their underlying connection is that both are "offbeat" comedies on the subject of sex, and are what the authors term "three-handers" —or plays requiring the acting services of two men and a woman. The collaborators aptly describe *The Sponge Room* as a play "about three dreamers who will never have the courage to carry out their dreams—for the dreams themselves are a substitute for courage." Comedic as the treatment may be, *The Sponge Room* explores the basic truths about loneliness, fear and fantasy.

The play is published for the first time in the United States in *Modern Short Comedies from Broadway and London*.

The Sponge Room was first presented on December 18, 1962, by the English Stage Company and Oscar Lewenstein at the Royal Court Theatre, London with the following cast:

(*In order of appearance*)

LESLIE EDWARDS	George Cole
HILARY SHEPHERD	Jill Bennett
COLIN BROUGHTON	Robert Stephens

Directed by JOHN DEXTER
Designed by KEN CALDER

THE SPONGE ROOM

The scene is the Sponge Room of the Natural History Museum in London. There are glass cases on the walls consisting of neatly labeled sponges of various types. There is a low central showcase in front of which is a padded bench. Arches on either side lead into the room and there is an arch at the back through which we catch a glimpse of the Bird Gallery with stuffed exhibits. A hanging sign pointing toward one of the arches reads: "MARINE BIOLOGY, CRUSTACEANS AND TOILETS."

It is early evening on any Tuesday and the room is empty. After a moment the uniformed attendant, LESLIE EDWARDS, *enters from the Bird Gallery. He is a man in his forties who wears steel-rimmed glasses, and he walks with a slight limp. He glances into both of the other archways to confirm that he is unobserved. He then faces into the Bird Gallery and moves, for inscrutable reasons of his own, two side-steps to the left, back again, and then two side-steps to the right, peering all the time into the Bird Gallery. Arms akimbo, he continues to stare into the Bird Gallery as* HILARY SHEPHERD *enters. She is a girl in her middle-twenties, originally from the provinces, who has been in London for about two years. She is a receptionist and so has to be fairly smartly dressed; she has come here straight from the office. She speaks to* EDWARDS, *who has his back to her.*

HILARY   Good evening, Mr. Balmforth. (*He turns and she sees that she is mistaken*) Oh.

EDWARDS   No, it's not Mr. Balmforth.

HILARY   No.

EDWARDS   He's on his leave. (*Looking at his watch*) Yes, he'll be in Ilfracombe by this time.

HILARY   You look like him from the back.

EDWARDS   So I've been told. (*He glances over his shoulder to con-*

firm the image) No, he's at a summer school. (HILARY *smiles politely and, not anxious to hear about Mr. Balmforth's holiday adventures, moves several steps away and gazes into a glass case.* EDWARDS, *however, is in no hurry to be off and he folds his arms. Chattily*) Local Government. Local Government, its Theory and Practice. That's where he's gone. Fourteen days! (*Another quick, polite smile from* HILARY, *but she looks even more pointedly into the case*) Yes. Ilfracombe. So you'll have a long wait.

HILARY No, I don't want to see him. I just thought you were him.

EDWARDS No, no. (*The exchange apparently over,* HILARY *begins to drift round the exhibits.* EDWARDS *leans back and examines his feet*) I believe I do look like him from the back. (*She takes no notice*) But my name is more in the nature of being Edwards. (HILARY *is now staring fixedly at a large sponge.* EDWARDS *proudly volunteers some information about it*) Spongia agaricina corlosia.

HILARY What?

EDWARDS (*With a little jab of the finger towards the sponge case*) Or Hardhead sponge. An industrial sponge found at tidal level in the Mediterranean area.

HILARY (*Abstractedly consulting the card in the showcase*) Haiti, according to this.

EDWARDS (*Again jabbing his finger*) Correction. Haiti.

HILARY There's no tide in the Mediterranean.

EDWARDS I don't dispute it. I can only tell you what's on the card. I don't set myself up as an expert. Chief Attendant Balmforth's the expert. On sponges. (HILARY *turns back to the sponge case.* EDWARDS *indicates the Bird Gallery*) No, that's my little kingdom through there. The Bird Gallery. (*As* EDWARDS *continues,* COLIN BROUGHTON, *an Air Ministry clerk in his early thirties, enters the Sponge Room. He, too, has come straight from work and wears an off-the-rack brown suit with an R.A.F. tie. He carries a raincoat. He notes that a conversation is going on and rather ostentatiously begins to look in one of the showcases*) You'll be passing through there, I hope.

HILARY Probably.

EDWARDS Be advised by me if you want to get the best of it. Don't spend too much time on cases A to E. They're spectacular, yes— eagles, cormorants, puffins, but they're the bigger birds, you can't do a great deal in the way of display. (*Becoming enthusiastic*) You look at the sandmartins. We've built a river bank for them, and we've arranged them peeping out of their little nests, caught in flight, feeding, mating, their little heads cocked on one side. Look at the owls. Look at the starlings. It's wonderful what you can do with stuffed birds, with a bit of imagination.

(*Since* COLIN's *entrance,* HILARY *has been paying more attention to* EDWARDS, *partly for* COLIN's *benefit and partly to find an opportunity to close the conversation*)

HILARY   I'm sure it is. I'll look out for them.

EDWARDS (*Preparing to move off*)   See if you get the same impression as me. I always feel they're looking out at me. Reproachfully. I might be wrong. Might be wrong.

(EDWARDS, *with a nod toward* COLIN, *wanders off into the Bird Gallery.* COLIN *and* HILARY *turn and look at each other, but do not speak until* EDWARDS *is well out of hearing*)

HILARY (*Reproachfully*)   It's nearly twenty past.

COLIN   Yes, I'm sorry. I went to the Science Museum. I had an idea we said the model coal mine.

HILARY (*Bitterly*)   I thought we'd finished with the model coal mine.

COLIN   Yes. I'd forgotten that.

HILARY   It was only three weeks ago.

COLIN   I'm sorry.

HILARY   It was three weeks last Tuesday.

COLIN   Time flies.

HILARY   I'd rather go anywhere than the model coal mine. (*She broods for a moment*) I'd even go to the Artillery Museum rather than the model coal mine.

COLIN   Don't bring that up again.

HILARY   Anyway, you haven't spent twenty minutes in the model coal mine.

COLIN   No, I was late to begin with. (*She gives him a glance of irritation*) I'm sorry! I had to shake somebody off.

HILARY (*Coldly*)   Had you?

COLIN (*Discursively, almost as if giving evidence*)   I was coming down the steps of the Air Ministry when I noticed a thick-set man in a trench coat—

HILARY (*Breaking in, even more coldly*)   I don't really want to know about it.

COLIN   You used to be interested.

HILARY (*Sharply*)   I've got other things to think about.

(HILARY *turns abruptly and begins pointedly wandering*

THE SPONGE ROOM

Sandra Lousada / Whitecross Studio Ltd.

about, looking at the exhibits. COLIN, *with a shrug, does the same. Both of them approach the central showcase from opposite directions. Mistaking each other's move, they almost bump into one another.* COLIN *speaks with elaborate politeness*)

COLIN Excuse me. (*He moves over to one of the showcases on the wall, and after a moment reads out one of the inscriptions*) Zimocca sponge, Adriatic.

HILARY (*Also reading*) Fine Levant sponge, Tunis.

COLIN Did you know that shrimps live in sponges?

HILARY (*Trying to sound interested*) No?

COLIN They go in in pairs. Then they grow up and can't get out, so they have to live there for ever.

HILARY Have you found anything?

COLIN (*As if bearing good news*) I've been waiting for a phone call all day—

HILARY (*Sharply*) Have you found anything?

COLIN No. (*Her face falls*) You? (*She shakes her head*) What about that friend of yours? No developments there?

HILARY No. It fell through.

COLIN It's all right—

HILARY Prawn cocktail, ham omelette and a tangerine sorbet.

COLIN (*Consoling her*) You wouldn't have had the time.

HILARY I'd have got there early. And I was going to buy two oranges. I was going to scoop them out and put the sorbet inside. Thin red candles on the table, two orange sorbets and me. We'd have been waiting for you. It's on the third floor. You press a bell and speak. I'd have pressed the buzzer and let you in. You come bounding up the stairs and I'm waiting for you on the second landing. You had a bottle of wine under your arm.

COLIN (*Humoring her*) Red or white?

HILARY White, I suppose, with ham omelette. Or rosé. I was going to ring you up and ask you.

COLIN (*In alarm*) Don't do that!

HILARY (*Her enthusiasm drained*) No. Anyway, it fell through.

COLIN Never do that. Never ring me up, Hilary.

HILARY (*Sadly*) No. (*A pause. She makes conversation*) Mr. Balmforth's on holiday.

COLIN (*Not interested*) Yes?

HILARY Ilfracombe. (*Nodding toward the Bird Gallery*) That one's Mr. Edwards.

COLIN (*Coldly*) Is he?

HILARY   Yes.

COLIN   How do you know?

HILARY   He told me.

COLIN   I wish you wouldn't strike up conversations with these attendants.

HILARY   (*Incredulously, stung by the implicit accusation*)   What? (COLIN *walks over to one of the arches and glances over-casually into the next room before he speaks*)

COLIN   You mustn't strike up these personal relationships.

HILARY   I did no such thing. I thought he was Mr. Balmforth. He looks like Mr. Balmforth from the back. He says he looks like Mr. Balmforth from the back. Everybody says so.

COLIN   You shouldn't have struck up a personal relationship with Mr. Balmforth in the first place.

HILARY   (*Heavily*)   I have not got a personal relationship with Mr. Balmforth.

COLIN   He knows your name. He knows my name. It's only been a month. I can see this being a case of the Victoria and Albert all over again.

HILARY   Chinese Applied Art.

COLIN   Persian.

HILARY   Chinese! I was the one who had to wait there, hour after hour. I waited forty minutes one day.

COLIN   I was being followed.

HILARY   So you said. But you could hardly blame me for talking to the attendant.

COLIN   You didn't have to tell him your life story. Or mine. What's this one after?

HILARY   Which one? (COLIN *points a sinister finger in the direction of the Bird Gallery*) Nothing. I told him there was no tide in the Mediterranean and he asked me to look at his sand-martins. (*Without change of tone*) Who were you expecting a phone call from?

COLIN   (*Evasively*)A friend.

HILARY   Which friend?

COLIN   You don't know him.

HILARY   Obviously I don't know him. I don't know any of your friends, do I?

COLIN   All right, then, his name's Metcalfe. He's a grade two clerk, he works in the equipment section across the corridor from me and he lives in Holland Park. (*A pause to impress her*) Alone.

HILARY   And—?

(COLIN *does a wavering motion with his hand to show that things are still in the balance*)

COLIN   I'm working on it. I don't want to say much at the present time, because there's always a chance that we might be disappointed.

HILARY   What does it depend on?

COLIN   (*Taking a deep breath*)   Well. Touch wood. (*He does so*) There's a temporary requirement for a civilian clerk at R.A.F. Station Hornchurch, and it's well on the cards that Metcalfe's in line for it.

HILARY   But Hornchurch is on the tube.

COLIN   Oh yes, he'll still be living at home, but the place will be empty until eight o'clock every night.

HILARY   And does he say we can borrow it?

COLIN   He doesn't say we can borrow it, no, because I haven't asked him yet.

HILARY   So who were you expecting a phone call from?

COLIN   (*Airily*)   From Metcalfe.

HILARY   (*Testily*)   About what?

COLIN   Nothing in particular. Took him for a drink yesterday— he'll ring me up, take me for a drink. (*A to-and-fro motion with his hand*) That's how these things work out.

HILARY   So we'll have to wait and see?

COLIN   (*Brightly*)   Mm. Mm.
       (*Again he touches wood*)

HILARY   (*Dramatizing*)   We can't go on like this.

COLIN   No.

HILARY   (*Still dramatically*)   We must get a room.

COLIN   Yes.

HILARY   (*Looking rather neurotically about her*)   I never did trust sponges. Going about pretending to be vegetables. I'm sick of sponges.

COLIN   (*With concern*)   We could meet in Marine Biology.

HILARY   I hate Marine Biology!

COLIN   Why don't we go back to art galleries?

HILARY   I hate Marine Biology, I'm sick and tired of parquet floors and glass cases. The smell of Mansion Polish and disinfectant. And wherever you go, wherever you turn, wherever you look, rows and rows and rows of little small things—stones, moths, kneecaps, bits of bowls. (*With sudden indignation*) Why do they take away your umbrella in the National Gallery? Why have we never had a meal together—except in some subter-

ranean museum cafeteria? Kunzle Cakes and coffee. Shrunken
gingham tablecloths and small women in raincoats. (*With a
wild gesture*) Things leaning against the wall—why don't they
hang them up? (*With a dangerous calm, evenly cataloguing her
aversions*) I hate art galleries. I hate the National Gallery, the
Tate, the Royal Academy and the Wallace Collection. Why is
everything up steps or through turnstiles with shilling cata-
logues and sixpenny postcard reproductions? I've been in love
three months and all I've got to show is a dozen Medici postcards and a gloomy view of the Elgin Marbles. Pinned up on my
bedroom wall—the Hilary Shepherd Collection. How's your
wife, Colin?

> (COLIN *takes the question at its face value and is happy that
> her tirade is finished. With relief he begins quite enthusi-
> astically*)

COLIN   Actually she's not been too well over the last couple of
days.

HILARY (*Venomously*)   Good. And the children?

COLIN   Leueen came out with a good one yesterday. She's got her
own miniature watering-can, you know, and I said where are
you going with that—

HILARY (*Cutting him short*)   And how's little Colin?

COLIN (*Peevishly*)   Don't call him little Colin. You make him
sound like a dwarf. (*Shaking his head reminiscently and smiling,
and for a moment we catch a glimpse of him as the family man*)
He's a character—

HILARY   Why can't we go away?

COLIN (*With a quick nervous reaction*)   How?

HILARY   Just for the weekend. You could manage it somehow.

COLIN (*Giving another of his vague gestures*)   It's difficult—very
difficult. I had hoped she was going up to her mother's. Derbyshire. Seems to have fallen through.

HILARY (*A bright suggestion*)   Some people do it in cars.

COLIN   I know. I know.

HILARY   Couldn't you hire one?

COLIN (*Again vague*)   It's very difficult. (*Steering off the car subject*) It's Metcalfe I'm pinning my hopes on.

HILARY   When does he go to Hornchurch?

COLIN   Could be any time. Two weeks. Month.

HILARY   A month!

COLIN (*Hastily*)   What happened with *your* contact?

HILARY   We had a row.

COLIN (*Shrugging impatiently*) Oh, well, that's marvelous. The only girl you know with a flat of her own and you have a row with her.

HILARY I didn't have a row with her. She had a row with me. She had a row with her boy friend, so, naturally, I was the one to suffer.

COLIN You must have done something.

HILARY I swear I didn't do anything! The alarm didn't go off, that's all. It wasn't my fault I was late for work. Well, you know what it's like at United Fats.

COLIN That's just it, I don't.

HILARY Neither do I, when I come to think of it. It's fantastic. United Fats House. Two thousand four hundred United Fats employees and she's the only one I speak to. Did. I don't speak to her now.

COLIN (*Bitterly*) Marvelous.

HILARY I was only ten minutes late, but someone had been screaming for the Domestic Fats return and she had to make it out. Well, she was very piqued because it put her behind on her Commercial Oils.

COLIN But why were you late?

HILARY (*Snappishly*) I've told you why I was late! The alarm didn't go off.

COLIN (*Probingly*) Why didn't your mother call you?

HILARY (*Lamely inventing*) She was—out.

COLIN (*Coldly*) Huh. (*He paces the room, his hands dug in his pockets, contemplating the injustice of it all. He speaks without looking at her*) You know, it's very funny. (*Pause*) It's a very funny thing. (*Pause*) Here am I, buttering up my contact. Buying him drinks. (*Pointing to his raincoat, which is tossed across a glass case*) I lent him my raincoat yesterday! I don't even like the man! And what do you do with your contact? The only contact you've ever had! The alarm doesn't go off.

HILARY (*Coldly*) Any other little criticisms?

COLIN I'm not criticizing, darling. I'm just looking at the facts. (HILARY *is about to launch into an attack when* EDWARDS *enters from the Bird Gallery. He carries under his arm a cardboard shoebox.* HILARY *is holding herself in readiness for her tirade, but she waits for* EDWARDS *to complete his business. He crosses to one of the low cupboards at the back of the room*)

EDWARDS I've been saying Ilfracombe. It's not Ilfracombe at all.

(*He unlocks the cupboard with a large official bunch of keys, puts the shoebox inside, locks it again, straightens up and addresses* COLIN) It's Robin Hood's Bay. Chief Attendant Balmforth's Summer School. I was just strolling along that gallery there. I was saying, "Ilfracombe, Ilfracombe, that doesn't ring a bell." Just came to me. It's not Ilfracombe at all. It's Robin Hood's Bay.

COLIN   It's near Whitby.

EDWARDS   That's right. (*He strolls round the room in his official capacity*) Don't you find it warm in here?

COLIN   Not too warm.

EDWARDS   I find it stuffy. For any length of time. (*Indicating the Bird Gallery*) 'Course, I've got the fans going in there. (*He reaches up to a switch*) Shall I put a fan on?

HILARY (*Sharply*)   No!

COLIN (*Covering up*)   No, thank you.

    (EDWARDS *nods agreeably and moves off into the Bird Gallery talking to himself*)

EDWARDS   Who went to Ilfracombe then? Somebody went to Ilfracome—

    (HILARY *has held herself in check for so long that her anger is subsiding. She speaks very flatly*)

HILARY   Shall we stop seeing each other?

COLIN (*Surprised*)Why?

HILARY   It's a bit pointless, isn't it?

COLIN   It'll be all right. It'll be different when we've got the room.

HILARY   Which room? What room?

COLIN   We'll get one somewhere.

HILARY (*Reminiscing softly*)   Do you remember the Hotel Victoria?

COLIN (*Also remembering*)   Double room with bath.

    (*They go into a happy reverie which is broken by* HILARY)

HILARY   I don't know why we never went.

COLIN   We couldn't, Hilary.

HILARY (*Still reminiscing*)   We met at the model coal mine. You were carrying an empty suitcase.

COLIN   Yes, I'd bought it that afternoon.

HILARY   We had a whole two hours in front of us. It seemed foolproof. Taxi to the hotel, sign the register—

COLIN   Mr. and Mrs. Rollo Wallace.

HILARY   —pay the bill in advance—

COLIN   —collect the key—

HILARY   —go up to the room
COLIN   —lock the door—
HILARY   Two whole hours!
   (*They think blissfully for a moment*)
COLIN   (*Matter-of-factly*)   They'd have seen us sneaking out. Something would have gone wrong.
HILARY   It's the nearest we've ever been.
COLIN   Yes.
HILARY   I've never been so disappointed or so unhappy. We had a row in the pit-cage, didn't we?
COLIN   (*Trying to laugh it off*)   Yes.
HILARY   I cried, you marched off without speaking. And I stood there with the tears pouring down my face and I thought I was never going to see you again. You barged through a crocodile of schoolboys with the suitcase.
COLIN   Yes!
HILARY   What did you do with it?
COLIN   What?
HILARY   Suitcase.
COLIN   Oh, it came in! I gave it to Beryl.
HILARY   (*Outraged*)   You did what!
COLIN   Yes, well, it was almost her birthday—we needed one. I couldn't throw it away. I thought it was rather a clever thing to do, actually. I had to do something with it.
HILARY   (*Incredulously*)   You gave that suitcase—*our* suitcase— to your wife?
COLIN   Yes!
HILARY   That was my suitcase. It was mine, my trousseau, my honeymoon. It was my suitcase.
COLIN   (*Evenly and logically*)   She was seriously thinking of visiting her mother at the time. We do have a suitcase, a large one in point of actual fact, but that would have been taken up with the kiddies' things. She'd have needed another one before I could have got her out of the house. (*Brightly*) So I was doing it for us in a way. Then, of course, she didn't go.
HILARY   (*Despondently*)   She'll never go. (COLIN, *clutching at optimism, wavers his hand in the familiar touch-and-go gesture*) She'll just sit there, in that house, with those kids and their miniature watering-cans. For ever.
COLIN   (*To get her off the subject of his wife*)   Any, er, possibility of making it up with your contact?
HILARY   (*Her anger flaring up again*)   Why should I?

COLIN   Well—single girl. Flat. Room.

HILARY   It's not my job to find a room! You're supposed to be the man. You find a room! Why do we keep meeting week after week! Every Tuesday and Friday! It's been three months, Colin, three months! And every time we meet it's got to be—(*Waving her arms to embrace the room in a gesture of inadequacy*)—this. Why can't you meet me somewhere else? Why can't we go to the pictures?

COLIN   (*Soothingly*)   It's very difficult, darling—

> (*For a moment the idea of a visit to the pictures looms in* HILARY's *mind as a fantastic luxury superseding even the dream of a room. She cuts* COLIN *short almost in a scream*)

HILARY   I want to go to the pictures! (*After this explosion there is silence between them.* HILARY *is rather ashamed of her outburst and turns away and they both for a moment plod around the exhibits in different directions. When* HILARY *speaks it is in a small, pleading voice*) Or even a teashop.

> (*They have stopped drifting around the room and are looking across at each other. There is a pause and when* COLIN *speaks it is in well-articulated, overreasonable tones*)

COLIN   Nothing would give me greater pleasure than to take you to the pictures or a teashop or both. Often, at the Air Ministry, I am required to take a file of letters into Air Vice-Marshal Abthorpe. They expect even civilians to stand at attention there, you know. But while I am waiting for his signatures I glance out the window and I can see where Kardomah have opened a new branch across the street. And even in the presence of a senior Air Officer I fall into a dream. I picture us blanketed together in the warm air heavy with the smell of coffee. Perched at a counter consuming toast.

HILARY   (*Drawn to him*)   Grilled tomatoes and croquette potatoes.

COLIN   But then I catch a glimpse of a thick-set man in a trenchcoat. Or Air Vice-Marshal Abthorpe brings me back to earth. (*With a bitter impersonation*) "Don't daydream, man!"

HILARY   We've got to get a room.

COLIN   Yes.

HILARY   Who is he?

COLIN   (*Formally*)   He's the Air Officer in charge of all perishable equipment on issue to the Home Commands.

HILARY   Not him. The man in the trenchcoat.

COLIN (*Shrugging*)   The latest. You remember the man in the sports coat?

HILARY   He followed you to the British Museum.

COLIN   This one's taken over from him. I'm sure of it.

HILARY   What does he do? Does he make reports, do you think?

COLIN   No. He's watching.

HILARY   Why?

COLIN   He's waiting.

HILARY   What for?

COLIN   He's waiting till we get a room.

(*And the fear draws them even closer together. They look at each other wide-eyed for a moment*)

HILARY   How much do you think she knows.

COLIN (*Ruminatively, chewing his lip*)   I don't know—don't know. Actually, I've no concrete indication that she knows anything. We've been very careful, after all.

HILARY   She must know something.

COLIN   I don't know. There's something vaguely familiar about that trenchcoat. In my more optimistic moments I sometimes think he might be from Intelligence.

HILARY   Why should he be?

COLIN (*As if giving evidence*)   In the course of my duties I obviously have access to classified and restricted files. When Mulliner was arrested for passing Microfilm to the Russians they'd been tailing him for months.

HILARY   You don't know any Russians.

COLIN   That's not the point. Why should an Air Ministry clerk make assignations in museums on Tuesdays and Fridays? What is he up to? Who is he meeting?

HILARY   Your conscience is clear, Colin.

COLIN (*Stoutly*)   As far as my country is concerned—yes.

HILARY (*Taking slight umbrage*)   But not as far as I'm concerned?

COLIN   I didn't say that.

HILARY   The implication was there.

COLIN   Wasn't.

HILARY   Was.

COLIN (*Stiffly*)   I thought we thrashed this whole matter out at the Courtauld Institute Galleries to our mutual satisfaction? I'm a family man.

HILARY (*Bitterly*)   You have family responsibilities.

COLIN   My wife has never done anything to harm me.

HILARY (*Happily*)   It would kill her if she ever found out.

COLIN (*Impressively*)   The scandal of divorce would harm us all.

HILARY (*Matter-of-factly*)   It would kill my mother, too.

COLIN   We'd have nothing to gain.

HILARY   Everything to lose.

COLIN   Divorce would not bring us closer together.

HILARY   It would drive us farther apart.

COLIN   What we hold at the moment is precious to us both.

HILARY   And unique.

COLIN   Yes. Unique.
> (*They have reached the end of their catechism and are happily back in their private world. There is a pause*)

HILARY   Quite a small room would do.

COLIN (*Desperately*)   Anything.

HILARY   A basement.

COLIN   An attic.

HILARY   A room.
> (*They both think hard*)

COLIN   In Paris, I believe, you can hire a room for the afternoon.

HILARY   The problem wouldn't arise in Paris.

COLIN   Quite.

HILARY   Or for that matter in any continental country.

COLIN   Indeed. (*They both pace the room and finally sit on the bench deep in thought. After some time* COLIN *broaches a question tentatively*) Is Morden on the tube?

HILARY   I believe so. Northern line.

COLIN   It needn't be Morden of course. It could be Walthamstow.

HILARY (*Looking at him expectantly*)   Anywhere.

COLIN (*Slowly*)   What I have in mind is—supposing we advertised?

HILARY (*Incredulously*)   Advertised!

COLIN   Not in the evening papers, of course, because then it's a question of box numbers and you have to give your address.

HILARY   We couldn't do that.

COLIN (*Raising his finger impressively*)   But!

HILARY (*Eagerly*)   Yes?

COLIN (*Triumphantly*)   Shop windows!
> (HILARY *flashes* COLIN *a glance of adulation*)

HILARY   Shop windows!

COLIN   Not in the central area, of course. Not in the West End.

HILARY   Out in the suburbs.

COLIN   All these little shops with the adverts in the windows.

HILARY   Hanging on string like little Christmas cards.

COLIN   I thought Morden.

HILARY   Or Walthamstow.

COLIN   (*At first conceding the point*)   Mmm. Mmm. (*Then reconsidering*) Walthamstow's a bit far out.

HILARY   (*Eagerly*)   Or Morden!

   (COLIN *rises. He takes a mechanical pencil from his breast pocket and paces the room, thoughtfully tapping his teeth with it*)

COLIN   (*Slowly*)   Now. Let's think about this very carefully. (*Beginning to frame the advertisement he jabs out the words in the air with his pencil*) Young couple. (*Pause*) Require. (*Pause*) Occasional Use of Room. (*Pause*) For.

   (*There is quite a long pause while they both think of what conceivable reason they could offer. At last it is* HILARY *who helpfully ventures a suggestion in a small voice*)

HILARY   Experiments?

   (COLIN *gives the suggestion serious consideration*)

COLIN   No. (*Beginning afresh*) Young couple. (*A fresh thought*) Respectable couple. Require. Temporary premises. (*Correcting himself*) Temporary office. Temporary room for use as office.

   (*Again* COLIN *is deep in thought*)

HILARY   (*Raising an objection*)   But supposing it was an office. (COLIN, *thinking hard, frowns at her interruption and waves an impatient hand. Again there is silence before* HILARY *butts in again*) We could say we were a charitable organization.

COLIN   (*Authoritatively*)   No. Just a minute, darling. Paper! (HIL-ARY *fishes in her handbag and takes out a scrap of paper.* COLIN *takes it and examines both sides before leaning on the central showcase and writing carefully.* HILARY *does not watch him, but sits hugging herself excitedly. Finally* COLIN *proudly reads out what he has written*) Small Research Team. Carrying Out Survey. Require Occasional Use of Room. For Collation of Material. Evenings only.

   (HILARY *gazes at her hero in adoration*)

HILARY   I love you, Colin!

COLIN   (*Now master of the situation*)   There'll probably be six or seven replies. Now. There'll be a strong temptation to jump at the first one we're offered. (HILARY *nods dutifully*) There's all sorts of considerations. Is it near the station? Is it reasonably discreet? Can we get in and out without fuss and bother?

HILARY   We'll have to inspect them all. (*Joyfully*) Oh, darling!
(HILARY *is very excited, but* COLIN *remains cool and businesslike. He wets his finger and draws an imaginary line in the air*)

COLIN   Assuming this is Morden High Street. I'll take all the houses on this side and you take the ones on the other. Then we'll meet and compare notes.

HILARY   Is there a museum in Morden?

COLIN (*Slowly*)   I don't think there is. (*Making the best of a bad job*) We may have to meet in the public library. Anyway, that's a minor point at the moment. (*Studying his scrap of paper*) Shouldn't be difficult. Small single room. Usual furniture. Cozy gas fire. (*Indicating the scrap of paper*) Should I specify Tuesdays and Fridays, or leave it open?

HILARY   What have you put?

COLIN   Evenings only.

HILARY   Why not "Two Hours. Evenings only"?

COLIN (*Judiciously*)   Well, it won't be two hours. Got to allow for travel. Say an hour and a quarter—if we're lucky.

HILARY (*Very innocently and in ingenuous contentment*)   We'll manage.

COLIN (*Thoughtfully*)   Research Team. We ought to carry files of some description.

HILARY   Manila folders.

COLIN (*Brushing the subject aside*)   Anyway, some kind of papers. Depends on how inquisitive the landlady is, I suppose. She'll want some sort of name—

HILARY   Mr. and Mrs. Rollo Wallace.

COLIN (*Aghast at her lack of discretion*)   Not Mr. and Mrs.! We're a research team! I can be Rollo Wallace. You'll have to be—
(COLIN *snaps his fingers to summon up inspiration, but* HILARY *comes in with a bright suggestion*)

HILARY   Mr. Rollo Wallace and friend.

COLIN (*Shrugging as though the matter isn't important*)   Oh, assistant, secretary—what about addresses?

HILARY   What about addresses?

COLIN   They'll want addresses, references.

HILARY (*Beginning to get testy at his objections*)   We can make them up.

COLIN (*More and more unsure of himself*)   It's very difficult. Question of transport. We can't travel backwards and forwards together.

HILARY   I'll take the tube, you take the bus.

COLIN   It's much slower by bus.

HILARY   I'll take the bus, you take the tube!

COLIN (*Rubbing his chin doubtfully*)   Yes—yes—

HILARY (*Almost triumphantly*)   You're afraid!

(COLIN *holds* HILARY's *challenging glance and his mood changes to one of determination*)

COLIN   We'll do it!

(COLIN *flops down on to the bench beside her and, having made their decision, they both relax happily. The smile fades on* HILARY's *face and she speaks nervously*)

HILARY   Colin?

COLIN   Yes?

HILARY   I've got an aunt in Morden.

(COLIN, *who is still holding the scrap of paper, rises slowly to his feet and takes a cigarette lighter from his pocket. Holding the paper between finger and thumb, he sets it alight. As it burns away he drops it on the floor and as a final act he rubs the ashes into the floor with his foot.* HILARY *sits huddled in misery, not looking at him. There is nothing to be said and he strolls moodily over to one of the glass cases and stares into it*)

COLIN   So far as I can see, one bloody sponge looks much like another.

HILARY (*After a moment's pause*)   Still, we've had some good times here.

(COLIN, *his hands deep in his pocket, strolls back to the bench and flops down moodily stretching out his legs*)

COLIN   I suppose so.

(HILARY *tries to cheer him up*)

HILARY (*Smiling reminiscently*)   Was it the second or the third time we were here?

COLIN (*Grunting*)   Mmmm?

HILARY   When that nun came in with a camp stool? And she sat just there, for over an hour, sketching sponges. (COLIN, *although still moody, allows himself a smile and a further grunt*) And we daren't speak. We stood at opposite sides of the room, peering at each other through the glass cases. (*An afterthought*) Why should a Little Sister of the Poor draw sponges? (*Conjecturing*) P'raps it was a penance.

(HILARY *has succeeded in winning* COLIN *round again and he joins in a game of reminiscence*)

COLIN   Remember when we were thrown out of the Reading Room of the British Museum for talking?

HILARY   We weren't thrown out!

COLIN   Well, asked to leave. We were escorted to the door, anyway.

HILARY   And when you had a cold and I looked after you. I hung your raincoat and things out to dry on the radiators in the Geological Museum.

COLIN   British Transport Museum, surely?

HILARY   Geological, darling! It was October.

> (*There is a silence while they enjoy their memories. They are sitting a couple of feet apart. Without looking at each other they creep their hands along the bench towards each other until they are holding hands*)

COLIN   We've had some marvelous times.

HILARY   Colin?

COLIN   Yes?

HILARY   Can I ask you something?

COLIN   Of course.

HILARY   I've never dared ask you before. Do you remember that first day? In Leicester Square Post Office?

COLIN (*Teasingly*)   Don't you?

HILARY   I often go back. It's miles from United Fats House, but often in my lunch hour I walk round there. I feel drawn to it. I walk inside, and over there are the phone booths where we met. Sometimes there's someone standing there, and my heart jumps because it might be you.

COLIN   I never go back.

HILARY   I often go back. I go in, there's nothing that I want, but I purchase a stamp or a letter card, for old time's sake. I don't need them—I've no one to write to. Except you.

COLIN (*In alarm*)   Don't do that, Hilary! Never do that! That's the worst possible thing you could do!

HILARY   I once did, but I tore it up.

> (COLIN *shoots her a quick, anxious glance. He is rather ashamed to ask his question*)

COLIN   What did you do with the pieces?

HILARY   Burnt them. But what I wanted to ask—on that first day —when we met—you weren't waiting for another girl, were you?

COLIN (*Incredulously*)   In a post office?

HILARY (*Timidly*) Well, I only—

COLIN (*Cutting her short*) There were scores of people in that post office! You don't think I'd meet anyone in a public place like that, do you! Good God, Hilary, credit me with some sense!

HILARY (*Persisting*) But you weren't, were you?

COLIN (*Soberly*) What we have and what we are to each other is something that only happens once. To the lucky ones. (*Looking round*) We have our own world, Hilary. I could never share it with anyone else.

HILARY (*Simply*) I'm glad.

(*During the above their hands have parted, but now they steal them together again*)

COLIN (*Softly*) A room—

(HILARY *nods slowly. After a moment* EDWARDS *enters leisurely from the Bird Gallery. He is on a tour of inspection and looks idly around the glass cases before addressing* COLIN *and* HILARY, *who have moved self-consciously apart upon his entrance.* EDWARDS *sniffs the air*)

EDWARDS (*Pleasantly*) Someone been in here with a cigarette?

COLIN (*Rising*) No.

EDWARDS They do, you know. I caught one chap with a cheroot last week. (*Apologetically*) Not that I have any personal objection. We live by the rule book here.

(*Over the above* EDWARDS *has discovered the mark on the floor from the piece of paper which* COLIN *burned. He toys with the mark with his foot in silence, waiting for an explanation. The pause is interminable and* HILARY *breaks first*)

HILARY We had to burn some paper.

(COLIN *darts her a warning glance*)

EDWARDS (*Evenly*) I see—Yes—Well, I suppose it's a good job that Chief Attendant Balmforth is in Robin Hood's Bay.

HILARY We're very sorry.

EDWARDS (*Continuing*) Although you seem to know him quite well?

HILARY Well, no actually, we—

EDWARDS (*Cutting in*) Incidentally, it's the Curator who went to Ilfracombe. Sorry, you were saying?

(HILARY *is about to speak, but* COLIN, *afraid of her indiscretions, gets in quickly*)

HILARY He—

COLIN (*With abrupt finality*)   We don't know Mr. Balmforth at all.

EDWARDS   Ah!

HILARY   Well, hardly at all. We talk to him sometimes. (*Correcting herself*) I talk to him sometimes. When I'm waiting for Colin.

EDWARDS (*With roguish familiarity, shaking his head at* COLIN) Shouldn't keep a lady waiting. That's her prerogative.

HILARY (*Now chatty*)   It's not his fault. I've only to come from United Fats House. But he's got to come all the way from the Air Ministry.

> (COLIN *cuts in hastily over* HILARY's *last words, hoping to drown the sound of them*)

COLIN   I work in Woolworth's!

EDWARDS (*Looking from one to the other*)   Air Ministry? Woolworth's?

> (COLIN *flashes* HILARY *a look of disgust.* HILARY *attempts to repair the damage while* COLIN *gives up in defeat. They speak together*)

COLIN (*Dully*)   Air Ministry.

HILARY (*Brightly*)   Woolworth's.

EDWARDS (*Indulgently*)   Makes no difference to me, sir. It doesn't matter two shakes of a pig's bottom, as far as I'm concerned. (*Half-derogatively, indicating that he has come across far more spectacular cases*) I used to have a couple who met in that Bird Gallery. I'm talking about the period nineteen forty-nine to nineteen fifty-five now. Years and years they came in. A middle-aged couple. They had a spiral notebook apiece. And if I strolled through it was scribble, scribble, scribble and "Hello, Mr. Edwards! We're compiling an encyclopedia of British birds!" They were doing no such thing. They'd nowhere else to meet. My two little love-birds I used to call them.

HILARY   What happened to them?

EDWARDS   They vanished—eventually. Flew off. Fly away, Peter; fly away, Paul. Oh, that's nothing to what we do get. (*Pointing to the ceiling*) Go up and have a word with Probationer Attendant Woolerton in Primeval Man. He gets a couple up there, a nursing sister and a West Indian gentleman. It's flasks of coffee and buttered rolls with them. He sets his watch by them: Monday one week, Wednesday the next.

COLIN (*Anxiously*)   You seem to keep your eyes open.

EDWARDS   Oh, we don't miss much. Funny the things you do see.

(*Recitatively, as though delivering a complete non sequitur*)
I am one of the few attendants not yet eliminated from the
Inter-museum Snooker Championships.

HILARY (*Interested*) Really?

EDWARDS The Horniman Cup. So, naturally, I have a constant
opportunity to meet attendants from many museums. Funny the
things you do see here. There's one fellow from the Geological.
Went out in the fourth round. (*He turns to* COLIN *as one man to
another, and as he speaks, demonstrates with an imaginary cue*)
Leading sixty-two, fifty-eight, goes in off the black. (*To them
both*) But he had a couple. Chap comes in soaking wet. Young
lady's waiting for him. She had his raincoat off, jacket off, scarf,
pullover. (*His voice rises hysterically*) She only had them strung
out along the radiators! It was like a launderette!

> (HILARY *and* COLIN *have been looking at each other in grow-
> ing alarm*)

COLIN My God!

> (EDWARDS *continues, noticing their alarm*)

EDWARDS Next door. Science Museum. Model coal mine. I don't
know whether you're familiar with it.

HILARY (*In her small voice*) Slightly.

EDWARDS (*Reminiscently and almost to himself*) Screaming
match they had in there, story I heard. Fellow waving a suitcase about. Her tears streaming down her face. Yelling at the
top of her voice, "Don't leave me! Don't leave me!"

COLIN (*Bitterly*) So much for security.

EDWARDS (*Continuing his recital*) Artillery Museum. Couple in
there. Girl of about twenty-six.

HILARY (*Promptly*) Twenty-five.

> (COLIN *turns away in despair, trying to dissociate himself
> from the proceedings*)

EDWARDS They'd been there a couple of hours, apparently. Boy
friend goes off. She's sitting there. Closing time. Attendant
Cooney tells me this. He couldn't get her off the premises. Rings
his bell. Calls the warning. (*He calls in his own professional
voice*) "Closing—five minutes please!" She wouldn't move. He
goes up to her and she's sitting there sobbing "I love him, I love
him, I love him."

> (*Over the above* COLIN *has turned round slowly and he now
> addresses* HILARY *accusingly*)

COLIN What was wrong with her?

HILARY (*Avoiding his eyes*) P'raps she'd had a disappointment.

COLIN   She was all right when he left.

EDWARDS   Shaking and sobbing.

HILARY   P'raps she'd been expecting too much of somebody. He might have made a promise and then let her down.

COLIN   He thought he'd explained what went wrong that day. Somebody let him down. He thought she understood.

HILARY   (*Sharply*)   He thought wrong!

(EDWARDS *has shown only the mildest interest during the above*)

EDWARDS   It's a shame though, in this day and age. Couples having to hang around in Sponge Rooms and coal mines. Artillery Museums—

HILARY   (*Impetuously*)   They ought to have rooms.

(HILARY, *aghast at what she has said, looks at* COLIN *in dismay.* COLIN *gives her a hasty look and quickly addresses* EDWARDS)

COLIN   (*Pointedly*)   Oughtn't you to be getting back to your birds?

EDWARDS   (*Agreeably*)   No, they won't fly away. Not them. No. (EDWARDS *crosses leisurely towards the entrance to the Bird Gallery and stands looking into it. Still looking, he repeats his previous movement: two side-steps to the left, back again, and then two side-steps to the right.* HILARY *and* COLIN *watch him curiously; he is taking his time over this operation. Eventually, without looking round, he beckons* COLIN *to join him*) Just come here, sir. Come here a minute. (COLIN *peevishly glances at his watch and crosses and stands at* EDWARD'S *side.* EDWARDS, *his eyes still fixed on the Bird Gallery, places his hands on* COLIN'S *shoulders and guides him into position*) I'm just going to show you an optical illusion now. You see the large bird there, in the central case? The Golden Eagle?

COLIN   Well?

(EDWARDS, *without speaking, proceeds to move* COLIN *in the same way as he moved himself—two side-steps to the left, back again, two side-steps to the right*)

EDWARDS   Do you notice anything?

COLIN   How do you mean?

(HILARY *has wandered over to join them out of curiosity.* EDWARDS, *to keep* COLIN *on tenterhooks, now turns to* HILARY)

EDWARDS   Come here, miss.

(*He repeats the procedure with* HILARY—*two side-steps to*

the left, etc. COLIN, *behind them, is reluctantly intrigued and he, too, repeats the side-stepping movement behind them, but slightly out of step*)

HILARY   It's eyes moved!

(EDWARDS, *pleased, rubs his hands and turns back into the room*)

EDWARDS   Correction. Appeared to move. Can't move! Glass eyes! No swivels, no mechanism. It's an optical illusion. Same with all of them. They're all the same. (*Demonstrating with a slow swivel of the head*) You walk past the owl-case. Fifty-three of them in there (*Correcting himself*)—fifty-two. Have you ever had the feeling you're being watched?

COLIN (*Fervently*)   All the time.

EDWARDS   Not altogether an unpleasant sensation. It's ironical. Here am I, Senior Attendant Edwards, Leslie, in charge of eight hundred stuffed birds. Sometimes I feel that they are in charge of me.

HILARY   My mother's got goldfish. They stare, too.

EDWARDS   It's not a stare, miss, it's a look. Trust and faith and sympathy. Reproach perhaps, you can't blame them cooped up. When I walk out of here in the evenings and that Great West Door slams behind me I always have a vague feeling that I've forgotten something. I make my way over to the Victoria and Albert. It's not generally known, but we have our own club there, down in the basement. (*Self-deprecatingly*) Just a bar and a snooker table. But I am a committee member and one is expected to put in an appearance. Well, I get down there, I have a frame, I have a chat. (*Shaking his head*) Something missing. (*Nodding toward the Bird Gallery*) My little guardian angels. I miss 'em.

HILARY   Haven't you got any friends?

EDWARDS   Oh, it's not as if I reject human contact! Far from it. No, no, no, no, no! I have my own small circle of friends. My own little world. My own little room to go home to. Nothing much. But it's cozy. (*As he continues* HILARY *and* COLIN *exchange and hold each other's glance*) I like to think that it's stamped with my own personality. A few migration charts on the wall, a deep armchair. I can reach out to the sideboard that belonged to my mother and pick out any one of a number of well-thumbed books: my *Father Brown Omnibus,* my *Handbook of British Birds*. I can sit there for hours in front of that popping gas fire. Very well contented, I assure you.

HILARY   It sounds wonderful.

EDWARDS (*Raising a finger*)   But! Something missing. (*Miming with his eyes*) The beady darting glance of the sparrow; the haughty stare of the falcon; the tranquil gaze of the London pigeon; the warm and placid doglike devotion of the owl. It's all I lack.

HILARY   We all lack something.

COLIN   In one way or another.

HILARY (*Shyly*)   Shall we tell him?

COLIN   He knows already.

EDWARDS   You need a room.

HILARY   Nothing much.

COLIN   Somewhere discreet.

EDWARDS   Private entrance.

HILARY   Somewhere warm.

COLIN   Simply furnished.

EDWARDS   Standard lamp, gate-leg table.

COLIN   Sideboard.

HILARY   Armchair.

EDWARDS (*Softly and casually*)   Bed.

> (*And there is an immediate silence.* COLIN *and* HILARY *look at each other.* EDWARDS, *overcasually, strolls over to one of the glass cases and, taking out his handkerchief, wipes away an imaginary speck*)

COLIN   What do you want us to do?

> (EDWARDS *turns at his leisure and, for a moment, he is the official again, rocking gently on his heels. He speaks at his leisure*)

EDWARDS   How do you mean, sir?

COLIN   You're offering us your room, aren't you?

> (EDWARDS *appears to think about this for a moment, his head on one side*)

EDWARDS (*As though conceding a point*)   Yes—yes—Yes, that's right, sir. I am.

HILARY (*Unable to believe her ears*)   But why?

EDWARDS (*Keeping them guessing*)   Flat B. Number seventeen, Mauncey Hospital Road. That's in the Turnham Green area. There are frequent buses and it is also well served by the tube. District Line. It has its own entrance. Second floor. And there's an Ascot heater.

COLIN   What about the landlady?

EDWARDS   Luckily, she is at this moment in Mauncey Hospital.

Yes, she was attacked by thugs in Hammersmith Broadway. Sustaining multiple contusions.

HILARY (*Helpfully*) We could send her flowers.

COLIN (*Practically*) What do we have to do?

> (EDWARDS *gives them both a last appraising glance. He crosses to each arch and looks out to see that no one is coming. He then crosses to the cupboard, unlocks it and takes out the cardboard shoebox that we saw earlier. He carries it across and places it on the central showcase*)

EDWARDS (*Ponderously*) I have been on the establishment of the London Museums for fourteen years. I've been a Probationer, an Attendant, and am now a Senior Attendant. When Chief Attendant Balmforth retires in four and a half years the mantle of office will fall on me. Always providing I keep my nose clean. Right?

> (COLIN *and* HILARY *nod. Ceremoniously* EDWARDS *picks up the box, takes off the lid and removes from the box a stuffed owl and sets it carefully upon the central glass case.* EDWARDS, COLIN *and* HILARY *arrange themselves in a group to look at it. There is a respectful pause before* HILARY *speaks in awed surprise*)

HILARY It's an owl!

EDWARDS Yes, it's a Tawny Owl! Well, it's a rich chestnut in this instance. They go through various shades. You see, it has a much shorter wing span than the Barn Owl.

> (HILARY *steps back to appraise it and repeats the side-stepping motion that they carried out with the offstage eagle*)

HILARY (*Delighted*) He is watching me!

EDWARDS She. Actually.

COLIN Is that important?

EDWARDS (*ignoring this*) As a museum attendant, naturally my life is governed by regulations. I'll only quote one to you: No employee may take into or out of museum premises any parcel or package whatsoever. (*An afterthought*) That includes annexes.

HILARY You can't take an umbrella into the National Gallery.

EDWARDS (*Disparagingly*) Oh, the National Gallery! You can here—you can come and go as you please.

HILARY (*Agreeing*) You can take a suitcase into the Science Museum.

EDWARDS As a member of the general public, yes. But as an attendant, no. (*Indignantly*) I can't even get my billiard cue in! Although you can see their point. As Chief Attendant Balmforth said, that billiard cue case would be ideal for smuggling out a rolled-up map. Or chart. (*He holds up his impressive bunch of keys*) Still. He's on leave at the present moment. Isn't he? (COLIN *as a man sizing up a job of work, surveys the owl. He picks up the cardboard shoebox which* EDWARDS *has placed on the bench and places it experimentally under his arm. Encouragingly*) They won't stop you.

COLIN (*Rubbing his chin*)   Is it just the one owl?

HILARY   Won't they miss it?

EDWARDS (*Counting on his fingers and replying to* COLIN)   Today's Tuesday. (*Half under his breath*) Tuesday, Wednesday, Thursday, Friday—I can get thirteen out before he comes back.

HILARY   We only have Tuesdays and Fridays.

EDWARDS (*Philosophically*)   All right then. Tuesday, Friday, Tuesday, Friday. I'll settle for four.

COLIN (*Thoughtfully*)   Mauncey Hospital Road?

HILARY (*Confirming*)   Turnham Green!

EDWARDS (*Persuasively*)   It's an ideal room. (*He takes the shoebox from* COLIN, *puts it on the glass case and picks up the owl, which he balances in his hand*) A room with character. I've tried to stamp it with my own personality. The charts, the books, I like to think if anyone walked in they'd say, "This is Mr. Edwards' room." "Yes," they'd say. "There's only one thing missing—" (*And he lovingly balances the owl up and down on his outstretched hand. He then holds it closer to his face*) Fourteen years I've known this little beggar. (*Briskly, breaking his mood, he puts the owl back in the shoebox and crosses to put it back in the cupboard*) Anyway, I'm not asking for a snap decision. Think it over. (*He locks the cupboard door and moves back towards the Bird Gallery. Looking into the Bird Gallery, he once again does his sidestepping ritual, and then speaks abstractedly*) I'm just next door.

>   (EDWARDS *goes out and there is a silence between* HILARY *and* COLIN. *They are rather shy with each other*)

HILARY   Turnham Green. That's near Hammersmith, isn't it?

COLIN   That's right. District Line.

HILARY   Isn't it on the Piccadilly Line as well?

COLIN (*in his slow ponderous voice*)   I'm—not—sure. Hammersmith is. I'm not sure about Turnham Green.

>   (*They both give the matter some thought*)

HILARY   Anyway, it's certainly on the District Line.

COLIN   Oh, yes. Certainly. (*They both ponder on the question of whether they can possibly add anything to this subject. Finally* COLIN *speaks ruminatively*) Mauncey—Hospital—Road.

HILARY   Yes. (*Pause*) I always thought it was a children's hospital.

COLIN   No. Great Ormond Street, that's a children's hospital.

HILARY   That's not at Turnham Green?

COLIN   No, no. (*Considering the matter*) Great Ormond Street.

HILARY   What sort of a hospital is it?

COLIN   (*Patiently*)   A children's hospital.

HILARY   (*Uncertainly*)   Which?

COLIN   The one in Great Ormond Street.

HILARY   I see (*Pause*) Actually I meant the one at Turnham Green.

COLIN   I see.

HILARY   Is it Mauncey Hospital or Mauncey Road Hospital?

COLIN   (*Ponderous again*)   I'm—not—quite—sure. (*Considering*) It's Mauncey Hospital Road, so I imagine it must be Mauncey Hospital. (*Considering again*) Otherwise it would be Mauncey Road Hospital Road. Wouldn't it?

HILARY   Yes. I imagine so. (*Again they both think*) Isn't there another hospital out there?

COLIN   Oh, yes. There's the Masonic Hospital.

HILARY   Oh, yes.

COLIN   There's Queen Charlotte's Hospital.

HILARY   It's quite a hospital district, really.

COLIN   Mm. Mm. I suppose it is.

HILARY   That's the children's hospital—Queen Charlotte's.

COLIN   No, darling, it's a maternity hospital.

HILARY   (*Firmly*)   No, it isn't, it's a children's hospital.

COLIN   (*Smiling*)   I'm sorry, Hilary. Maternity.

HILARY   Children's, darling!

COLIN   Well, darling, I don't want to quarrel, but I do happen to know, because Beryl happened to be confined there.

HILARY   Oh.

COLIN   Anyway, that's neither here nor there.

HILARY   No. (*Pause*) What do you mean, she happened to be confined?

COLIN   Well—

   (*With a wave of the hand*)

HILARY   (*Piqued*)   Women don't happen to be confined. You make it sound as if she was just passing and thought she'd call in.

COLIN (*Pleasantly*)   Actually, it was rather like that. It's rather funny really, because we're never in the neighborhood of Turnham Green—

HILARY (*Coldly*)   So I'd gathered.

COLIN (*Continuing his family anecdote*)   But on this occasion we'd trotted round to look at a Pedigree Pram. (HILARY *puts on an expression of deliberate boredom which* COLIN *does not notice*) We were waiting for the bus when Beryl said, "Do you know, Colin, I don't think I'd better go home," do you see. She said, "I think Little Colin's on his way"—well, she didn't say that, obviously, because we didn't know whether it was going to be a—(COLIN *realizing that he has been treading the dangerous, taboo ground of the family man's reminiscence, breaks off, floundering, his arm thrashing the air. He gabbles*) Anyway, you don't want to hear about that.

> (COLIN *steps away and walks around the room for a moment in long raking strides as if to shake his anecdote off.* HILARY *coldly watches him, turning when necessary so that he cannot evade her sight. Finally* COLIN *stops walking and peers intently into a glass case*)

HILARY (*With bitter sarcasm*)   At least it's not a children's hospital, we've established that.

COLIN   No. (*Pause*) It's not really at Turnham Green. (*Another pause*) It's nearer Chiswick.

HILARY (*In a gust of anger*)   I don't care if it's Kentish Town!

COLIN (*Heavily*)   Very well. I will never mention Beryl or the children again. Ever. It still doesn't make the slightest iota of difference to the fact that I am a family man.

> (*Again they go into their catechism, but this time it drives them away from, rather than into, their private world. They speak in bored resigned tones*)

HILARY   Family responsibilities.

COLIN   Wife never done anything to harm me.

HILARY   Kill her if she ever found out.

COLIN   Scandal of divorce would harm us all.

HILARY (*Sarcastically*)   Oh yes! We mustn't forget the man in the trenchcoat!

COLIN   I'm not forgetting the man in the trenchcoat, believe you me.

HILARY   That's the question isn't it?

COLIN   How do you mean?

HILARY   Whether I do believe you.

COLIN   (*Taking umbrage*)   Oh well, that's all I need. Thank you. Thank you very much indeed for your loyal support. (*With sudden indignation*) Do you know what I have to do in order to meet you? Every time? I don't just hop on the bus and roll up, you know. (*Recitatively*) I walk down the steps of the Air Ministry with my colleagues. Assuming the role of one family man among many. We move in a phalanx to the tube station chatting about gardening and education. I usually succeed in giving them the slip by the paper stand. I double back on my tracks. My pace quickens as I throw off the shackles of endowment policies, mortgages and long-term plans to insulate the loft with fibre glass. (*Pulling himself up*) I am a man hurrying to meet his mistress and I am a man.

(HILARY, *catching the mood, also draws herself up proudly*)

HILARY   I am in the eighth-floor cloakroom at United Fats. Twenty or thirty girls milling about in front of the long mirror, their mouths set in grotesque attitudes, as they apply twenty or thirty shades of lipstick. They pat their hair, change their shoes, smooth their skirts and I am one of them. We run, not walk, along the corridors, our high heels clacking on the composition tiles. The seven plate-glass doors burst open and they flutter off in all directions, towards the cafés and the cinemas and to meet their boy friends under clocks. I walk, not run, towards my assignation. I am a girl walking to meet her lover and I am a woman.

COLIN   (*Continuing recitatively*)   Taking care that I am not observed I catch a bus in an easterly direction. Two seats behind me a man sits motionless apparently reading a newspaper. (*Cunningly*) Loudly I ask for Liverpool Street Station. But! I alight at St. Paul's Cathedral, stroll across the road and then streak like a fugitive between tall warehouse walls towards the embankment. I can do no more. Already I have eaten into my two hours. I catch a bus for the museum knowing that soon I shall have to go home.

HILARY   (*Conversationally*)   I shall have to go home soon. (*A pause and then back in the recitative style*) A maisonette with a milk bottle on the second step. In the living room is someone I do not know, forever feeding goldfish. It is my mother. There's no conversation, only questions and answers. She shakes paper packets into glass tanks and wears rimless spectacles. She still believes in sound radio and library books. As long as I can remember the house has been filled with perpetual adaptations of *Barchester Towers*, and vases stuffed with borrowers' tickets.

(HILARY *looks across at* COLIN *out of her world of sadness, which he shares. There is a very long silence. Finally* COLIN *speaks in flat, sad tones*)

COLIN   You're lying.

(HILARY *does not look surprised; her expression does not change. There is another silence, and then she, too, speaks sadly*)

HILARY   Yes.

COLIN   There's no maisonette.

HILARY   No.

COLIN   No mother.

HILARY   No. (*Pause*) No man in a trenchcoat.

COLIN (*Sadly*)   My world is full of men in trenchcoats.

HILARY   It always will be. There's one waiting already at the corner of Turnham Green and Mauncey Hospital Road.

COLIN   Standing discreetly in the shadow of a tree.

HILARY   His eyes fixed on the second floor window of Flat B, number seventeen.

COLIN   Yes.

(*There is another pause between them during which* COLIN *surreptitiously looks at his watch. He crosses over to his coat*)

HILARY   How did you know that I didn't live with my mother?

(COLIN *does not reply, but shrugs on his raincoat, with his back to* HILARY *and the audience. It is a trenchcoat. He is a man in a trenchcoat. Still with his back to the audience he stands motionless, his arms held slightly away from his body*)

COLIN (*In a low voice*)   I followed you. (*He swings round accusingly*) I followed you home.

HILARY (*Falteringly*)   To the hostel?

COLIN   The United Fats Trust Hostel for Girls.

HILARY   The United Fats Trust Hostel for Business Girls.

COLIN   At any time during our relationship you could have taken a flat of your own.

HILARY (*Sadly*)   Yes. A room.

COLIN (*Reflectively*)   On the other hand, I shall miss your maisonette. (*Reminiscently*) You were very good at describing log fires. Often when I've been sitting at home in front of the slow-burning Cokemaster stove, sharing the dry stifling heat with a row of steaming woollies, I've imagined us together.

HILARY In our uncut moquette cocoon. Side by side on the sofa, and mother opposite in her easy chair, reading snippets from the Christmas numbers. And the goldfish popping in the background.

COLIN And that roaring fire.

HILARY Yes. It was always very warm.

COLIN (*Gently*) Why didn't you tell me, Hilary?

HILARY Tell you what?

COLIN That you were afraid.

HILARY (*Considering*) I was afraid to tell you.

(COLIN *gives a slow, understanding nod. He looks at her, but she is looking down, not caring to meet his eyes*)

COLIN (*Softly*) It's almost time.

HILARY (*Also softly*) I know.

(COLIN *suddenly breaks the mood by slapping his hands together and speaking in a brisk, buoyant voice*)

COLIN Well, time for my little alibis. Mark up my card. (*He chatters on as he takes a bridge score card and a pencil from his pocket*) I nearly forgot it today—I had to go back. What shall we do this week—lose again?

HILARY (*Detached*) Isn't it time we won for a change?

COLIN (*Cheerfully*) Rightyho! See what we can do. (*Beginning to write and talking to himself*) Now. We'll give north-south two hearts to begin with, that's sixty. Give them an overtrick, fifty—

HILARY Why does it always have to be bridge?

COLIN (*Absent-mindedly, still writing*) Well, I don't play chess, she doesn't approve of darts—The Air Ministry Bridge Club has got a good honest ring to it, I always think. Now, where are we?

HILARY (*Joining in*) We'll call six hearts.

COLIN Good, good. And be down three. (*Writing*) Five hundred for them above the line. (*Excitedly*) It's a good rubber!

HILARY Colin?

COLIN (*Still writing, he ignores this*) We call four spades. (*Examining his card, he announces in triumph*) I can lay it down! We've won!

HILARY When did you follow me?

(COLIN *pointedly goes on writing for a moment and then tucks the bridge card away in his pocket. He speaks with assumed casualness*)

COLIN   Couple of weeks ago, in point of fact. I had some time to spare. (*Pause*) Actually, Beryl was away.

HILARY   Is she still away?

COLIN   (*Conversationally*)   No, no, she just slipped off for the week, you know. Just up to Derbyshire. Just to see her mother.

HILARY   (*Flatly*)   I see. (COLIN, *still with his assumed casualness, buttons up his trenchcoat.* EDWARDS *enters from the Bird Gallery and stands framed in the archway.* COLIN *and* HILARY *do not look at him*) I don't think we should meet here any more.

COLIN   Perhaps not. (EDWARDS, *with a slight, resigned shrug, turns and presses his thumb on a bell-push on the wall, and we hear the closing bell which rings out through the museum*) You'll give me the usual minute, won't you?

HILARY   Of course.

COLIN   (*After a moment*)   What about Friday?

HILARY   I thought the Geological.

COLIN   (*Judiciously*)   Possible. Meteorite Room?

HILARY   Or the Crystal Room.

    (EDWARDS *is still standing in the Bird Gallery arch in a reverie.* COLIN *paces thoughtfully towards the exit arch, where he turns and calls to* EDWARDS)

COLIN   Good night!

    (EDWARDS, *coming out of his reverie, speaks overcheerfully*)

EDWARDS   Good night, sir!

    (*He slouches back into his reverie.* COLIN *stands thinking for a moment and then speaks to* HILARY)

COLIN   I—er—may be having a drink with my contact tomorrow.

HILARY   Good. (*Pause—she speaks enthusiastically*) I think I'll invite mine out for coffee.

COLIN   Good. The Crystal Room, then.

HILARY   The Crystal Room.

    (COLIN *goes out.* HILARY, *to kill time, wanders around the glass cases looking at exhibits.* EDWARDS, *after a moment, saunters over to the arch leading to Marine Biology. He calls out to the museum at large in his professional voice*)

EDWARDS   Closing five minutes, please!

    (HILARY *moves to the exit arch, where she turns*)

HILARY   Good night, Mr. Edwards.

EDWARDS   (*Warmly*)   Good night, miss. God bless. (HILARY *walks out briskly.* EDWARDS *crosses to the cupboard, opens it and takes out his cardboard shoebox. He lets the lid fall on the floor, takes out the stuffed owl, and lets the box fall on the floor also. He*

holds the owl in his hand, stroking it, and speaking to it softly)
Come on, then. (*He lifts the owl tenderly to his shoulder, where
he holds it with one hand, looking at it*) Up you come. Come on.
  (EDWARDS *limps slowly towards the Bird Gallery, holding
the owl on his shoulder. He makes soft, mournful noises to
it, imitating the call of an owl, "Hooooo! Hooooo!"*)
  Curtain

The Diary of Adam and Eve

from *The Apple Tree*

BY

Sheldon Harnick
and
Jerry Bock

Based on *The Diary of Adam and Eve*
by Mark Twain
Music by JERRY BOCK and Lyrics by SHELDON HARNICK
Book by SHELDON HARNICK and JERRY BOCK
Additional book material by JEROME COOPERSMITH

Sheldon Harnick
and
Jerry Bock

One of the most successful pairs of collaborators in the modern musical theatre, Jerry Bock and Sheldon Harnick first came into view in 1958 with the presentation of *The Body Beautiful*. Although that musical hardly can be classified as a hit, it was important as a personal success for the songwriting duo, for it so impressed producer Harold Prince, his late partner, Robert Griffith, and the doyen director George Abbott that they commissioned the collaborators to take on the assignment of creating the songs and musical numbers for *Fiorello!* This presentation ran for 795 performances, garnered a New York Drama Critics Award and the Pulitzer Prize, and propelled the team of Bock and Harnick into the front rank of the American musical theatre. It also was the harbinger of their most celebrated success, *Fiddler on the Roof* (1964; with book by Joseph Stein).

With *The Apple Tree* (three short musicals based on stories by Mark Twain, Frank R. Stockton and Jules Feiffer) the highly successful collaborators entered a new phase, for in addition to creating the words and music they also functioned as coauthors of the book.

Jerry Bock (composer) was born in New Haven, Connecticut, in 1928; raised in Flushing, New York; and attended Flushing High School (where he began his composing career) and the University of Wisconsin. He received his baptism as a "professional" composer at Camp Tamiment in the Poconos, later wrote much of the music for the Max Liebman television productions entitled *Your Show of Shows*, starring Sid Caesar and Imogene Coca. He also contributed songs (with Larry Holofcener as lyricist) to the revue *Catch a Star* and an edition of *The Ziegfeld Follies*. His first full

Broadway score was written for *Mr. Wonderful* (1956). It starred Sammy Davis, Jr., and ran for a year.

In 1958 Mr. Bock teamed up with Sheldon Harnick (lyricist). Born in Chicago in 1924, Mr. Harnick was inspired by his mother's passion for commemorating all occasions in verse, and while still at grammar school he picked up the thread and commenced to write poems himself—"mostly doggerel and mostly nonsense." In 1943 he entered the Army and it was while in service that he first started seriously to write songs which he performed at various USO shows, sandwiching them in between his violin solos.

In 1946 he returned to Chicago and enrolled at Northwestern University where he contributed songs to the annual student musicals and doubled as a fiddle player with the show's orchestra. After graduation from Northwestern, he worked for a while as a violinist with Xavier Cugat's orchestra, then after being fired for "swaying to the left instead of the right," headed for New York and a career as a songwriter.

In Manhattan, Mr. Harnick first contributed his talents to *New Faces of 1952* (notably, with the number "The Boston Beguine"). During this period (the 1950's), some other revues that included his work were *Two's Company; The Littlest Revue; Take Five; Kaleidoscope* and *John Murray Anderson's Almanac.*

The Messrs. Bock and Harnick collaborated on *Tenderloin,* in 1960, and *She Loves Me,* in 1963.

Jerome Coopersmith, who supplied additional book material for *The Apple Tree,* was born in New York City, studied at New York University, and following Army service began an active career as a television writer.

Mr. Coopersmith wrote the book for the 1965 Broadway musical, *Baker Street,* based on the adventures of Sherlock Holmes.

The Apple Tree was first presented on October 18, 1966, by Stuart Ostrow at the Sam S. Shubert Theatre, New York City. The cast of *The Diary of Adam and Eve* was as follows:

ADAM	Alan Alda
EVE	Barbara Harris
SNAKE	Larry Blyden

Directed by MIKE NICHOLS
Additional Musical Staging by HERBERT ROSS
Choreography by LEE THEODORE
Production and Costume Design by TONY WALTON
Lighting by JEAN ROSENTHAL
Musical Direction and Vocal Arrangements by ELLIOT LAWRENCE
Orchestrations by EDDIE SAUTER

The Diary of Adam and Eve
MUSICAL NUMBERS

"Here in Eden"	EVE
"Feelings"	EVE
"Eve"	ADAM
"Friends"	EVE
"The Apple Tree" ("Forbidden Fruit")	
	SNAKE
"Beautiful, Beautiful World"	ADAM
"It's a Fish"	ADAM
"Go to Sleep Whatever You Are"	EVE
"What Makes Me Love Him"	EVE

THE DIARY OF ADAM AND EVE

The scene is Eden on Saturday, June first.

As the curtain rises, the lights come up gradually to reveal ADAM *asleep on the ground. The garden is symbolized quite sparingly with a tree, a mound of flowers, and a scrim behind which we can faintly see an apple tree in the distance.*

A voice is heard as the music slowly fades.

VOICE   Adam—Adam, wake up. You are the first man. It shall be your task to name all the creatures in the Garden of Eden. You may eat the fruit of the trees and the fields, but stay away from the apple tree on the other side of the hill. Adam, wake up.

ADAM (*Stirring slowly*)   Just give me five more minutes.

VOICE (*Booming now*)   Adam! Wake up!

ADAM (*He wakes up and rises to his haunches*)   —name the creatures—(*Yawning and mumbling*)—well, I might as well get it over with. (*Rises*) I, Adam, by virtue of the authority vested in me, do hereby name all you creatures flying around in the sky —flyers. (*A musical chord sounds*) And you things crawling on the ground I name—crawlers. (*Chord*) And you things swimming around down there are swimmers, and you're growlers, and you're hoppers. Oh, my, there are thousands. I better start taking notes or I'll get everything all mixed up. (*To the audience*) This is the first day, Adamtime. Note: (*Chord*) Today I named the flyers, crawlers, swimmers, growlers, and hoppers. Further note: There are creatures here of every conceivable kind, but I, Adam, am the sole and single man. (*He smiles with pride, savoring the word*) Single. That word has a fine, open ring to it. (*He grabs his rib and winces in pain*) Ahh. Now what? (*A mound rolls onstage with* EVE *asleep on it.* ADAM *turns and goes to it. He circles it in curiosity*) I'll name it later.

(ADAM *exits and the music swells. The lights slowly change and* EVE *wakes, instinctively reaching out for a companion. She sits up and is struck with bewilderment and wonder*)

EVE (*Staring out front and sitting up*)   Sunlight? Hummingbirds?

Lions? Where am I? I? What am I? (*The music fades as she looks down and is startled by the sight of herself*) Oh!! (*She studies herself carefully, running her fingers over her face and hair*) Whatever I am, I'm certainly a beautiful one. (*She laughs suddenly*) It's very peculiar—but I feel like—an experiment. (*Laughing again*) In fact, it would be impossible to feel more like an experiment than I do. Then am I the whole experiment? (*She carefully surveys herself again*) I don't think so. I better start making notes right now. Some instinct tells me these details are going to be important to the historian some day. (*She gets up on her haunches and moves off the mound*) Saturday, June first. Note: (*The music to "Here in Eden" begins*) I arrived, feeling exactly like an experiment. Around me there is an incredible profusion of the most delightful objects.

   (*Singing*)
So many creatures,
So many things,
Each wondrous object is beautiful and striking,
And I see nothing that isn't to my liking
Here in Eden.

There's plums and peaches
And pears and grapes
So ripe and juicy and utterly inviting.
I find the apples especially exciting
Here in Eden.

As for me,
I can see
I was meant to rejoice
In the round,
Vibrant sound
Of my own voice.

It's all so perfect
And so ideal,
And yet I do have one tiny reservation:
There's nothing handy for making conversation
Here in Eden.

How'd I come?
Where'm I from?

THE DIARY OF ADAM AND EVE

Friedman-Abeles

What's my ultimate aim?
I don't know.
Even so,
I'm glad I came.

It's all so lovely
I may just weep.
I love this garden and ev'rything that's in it,
And something tells me to treasure ev'ry minute,
Blossom and bud,
Mountain and mud,
I know I'll be happy,
Perfectly happy,
Here in Eden.

> (*She hugs herself in delight and gazes about as* ADAM *enters with a fish, which he is mumbling at. They both stop and stare at each other*)

EVE   Drop that pickerel, you monster! (*He dives for his tree*) Put it back. (*She reaches down for a rock lying about.* ADAM *is up the tree by now*) Did you hear me?

ADAM (*From the tree*)   What do you think you're doing?

EVE (*Startled by his voice*)   You can talk!

ADAM   Get away from here!

EVE (*Her compassion for the pickerel makes her brave and she crosses to the tree*)   Throw that pickerel back!

ADAM   What pickerel?

EVE   That pickerel in your hand.

ADAM   That's a swimmer.

EVE   A pickerel!

ADAM   Swimmer!

EVE   Pickerel.

ADAM   Swimmer.

EVE (*She holds up the rock in her hand*)   What's this?

ADAM   A clod.

EVE   Well, if you don't throw that pickerel back, I'm going to clod you right out of that tree.

> (*She throws the rock and picks up some more to throw*)

ADAM   Wait!

> (*He throws the fish over her head. She puts the rocks down, crosses, and picks up the fish*)

EVE (*Hugging the fish soothingly*)   And don't you ever do that again, you bully. (*She crosses to the mound, picks up the rope tail, and pulls the mound offstage.* ADAM *leaps off the tree and picks up three rocks. He is about to throw them after her when she instantly appears*) I'm warning you!

    (*He pretends to juggle the rocks as she exits again. He puts the rocks on the tree mound and starts talking to the audience*)

ADAM   Second day, Adamtime. Note: I'm worried. Yesterday that new long-haired creature kept hanging around and following me. However, I believe I've hidden myself so cleverly, it probably thinks I've left the garden.

    (*He climbs the tree, gets a towel off a branch, and covers himself.* EVE *enters with a brisk, businesslike walk*)

EVE (*Suddenly turning to him*)   I must talk to you!

ADAM (*Throwing down the towel*)   About what?

EVE (*At a loss*)   Oh, I just like to talk. Don't you like to talk?

ADAM   Not particularly. (*Hitting at her with the towel*) Go away. Go away.

EVE (*Standing her ground*)   Please come down. There *is* something, and I think it's immensely important.

ADAM   What?

EVE   Will you come down?

ADAM (*Thinks for a moment*)   All right. I think I'm stronger than you.

EVE   Oh, I'm sure you are.

ADAM (*Jumping out of the tree*)   Now, what did you want to talk about?

EVE (*Moving to him*)   About us.

ADAM   You stay over there! (*She moves back*) What's us?

EVE   That's a name I thought of. It means you and me.

ADAM   What's so important about us?

EVE   I think we've both been put here for a great and noble experiment!

    (*She moves to him again*)

ADAM   I told you to stay over there!

EVE   Sorry.

    (*She moves back*)

ADAM   Go on.

EVE (*Turning to him*)   What?

ADAM   I said go on!

EVE (*Edging over to him*)   As I was saying—I think I'm the main part of this experiment, but you have a share in it, too.

ADAM Oh, that's very generous of you. What makes you think you and I have anything in common?

EVE (*Moving all the way to him*) Well, for one thing, you're the only other animal that can talk!

ADAM (*Backing away*) That's how much you know! So can—so can—(*Looking around for the illustration*) so can that flyer up there.

    (*He is pointing out front*)

EVE (*Looking out front*) Where?

ADAM In that tree.

EVE (*Staring hard*) You mean that parrot? I didn't know parrots could talk!

ADAM Well, they can. Why do you call it a parrot?

EVE Because it looks like a parrot.

ADAM Well, not to me it doesn't. It looks like a loud-mouthed fat-beak.

EVE (*Laughing condescendingly*) Nevertheless, it's a parrot.

ADAM What makes you so positive?

EVE I just happen to have this talent. The minute I set eyes on an animal, I know what it is. I don't have to think. The right name comes out by inspiration. So far, you're the only exception.

ADAM (*He thinks for a moment, then fires the following questions at her as fast as he can. She answers with equal, and casual, rapidity*) What's that?

EVE A horse.

ADAM That?

EVE Bull.

ADAM That?

EVE Goat.

ADAM That?

EVE Elk.

ADAM That?

EVE Wolf.

ADAM That?

EVE Duck.

ADAM (*Exasperated*) You're just guessing!

EVE I'm not guessing. Those are their names, because—

BOTH —that's what they look like.

EVE Yes.

ADAM How old are you?

EVE (*Figuring it out*) Two days.

ADAM   You'll never make it to four.

EVE (*Moving to him*)   Oh, dear, I've hurt your feelings.

ADAM   Ridiculous.

EVE (*Moving to him at the tree*)   Yes, I have. I can tell. I'm so sorry.

ADAM (*Turning his back to her*)   Well, don't be, because you're wrong. Anyway, I can't waste any more time here. I have to go empty the four-pronged white-squirter.

EVE   You mean the cow?

ADAM   Thank you very much!
   (*He exits*)

EVE   Somehow we got off on the wrong foot. I seem to aggravate it. I think it's a reptile. But I do wonder what it's for. I never see it do anything. Nothing seems to interest it—except resting. It's a man! If it *is* a man, then, it isn't an *it*, is it? No. It should be: Nominative: He. Dative: Him. Possessive: His'n. (*The music to "Feelings" begins*) I think that's right. It gets harder and harder to concentrate ever since I met the reptile. Just thinking about him gives me the most distracting sensations.
   (*Singing*)
   Feelings are tumbling over feelings,
   Feelings I do not understand,
   And I am more than slightly worried
   That they are getting out of hand.

   Sometimes they happen in my stomach,
   Sometimes they happen on my skin.
   What is the name of this condition
   That I am in?

   If I'm objective and observant,
   If I can keep an even keel,
   I'll be the first to pin a name to
   What I'm the very first to feel.
   (*The lights reveal a glowing bed of coals.* EVE, *coughing, kneels by them, fanning the flames*)
   Tuesday, June fourth. Special Note: I believe I've finally discovered something that will interest him. It happened while I was trying to bore a hole in one stick with another stick.
   (*As she gazes raptly at the fire,* ADAM *enters. He stops, sniffs the air, and traces the curious odor to its source, the fire*)

ADAM   What's that?

EVE (*Not at all snidely*)   What does it look like to you?

ADAM   Pink dust.

EVE   Its name is fire.

ADAM   How did it come?

EVE   I made it.

ADAM   What are those?

EVE '   Fire-coals.

> (ADAM *reaches down to pick one up.* EVE *watches. He drops it quickly, glares at* EVE, *and hurries off-stage, trying not to reveal the fact that his fingers are killing him*)

EVE (*Sadly*)   Nothing interests him.

> (*The music to "Feelings" begins again.* EVE *sings*)

I am the first to face this problem.
I am the first to have this dream.
How can I harness his attention?
How can I harvest his esteem?
Am I sufficiently attractive?
Should I do something with my hair?

> (*She holds a strand out*)

Is there some tidbit that will please him?
What should I wear?
What is the source of this congestion
That I must learn to rise above?
Is there a name for this condition?
Yes, there's a name. . . .
And it is hell!

> (*Blackout. The lights restore on* ADAM, *who is carrying a plank to construct some primitive shelter. The tree is gone, and there are other planks on-stage*)

ADAM   Sixth day, Adamtime. (*He drops the plank*) The naming goes recklessly on. I get no chance to name anything myself. The new creature names everything that comes along before I can get in a protest. And always on the same pretext—says it looks like the thing. For instance, take the great waterfall—the finest thing in the garden, I think. The new creature calls it "Niagara Falls." Why? Says it *looks* like Niagara Falls. Now that's not a reason. That's pure waywardness and imbecility. (*He begins to cross, but stops and returns with an afterthought*) And another thing. I'm not used to anything coming so close up to me. It makes me feel hampered and, uh, somewhat—anxious. (*He is covering over his confusion with a casual air. He tests the wind direction with a wet finger*) Uh, cloudy today. Wind in the east.

I think we'll have rain. (*He crosses and gets a wooden tub and bowl*) We? Where did I get that word? Oh. Well, I don't care about "we"—I'm going to build *me* a dry-top.

    (*He sets up the planks tripod style and is busily at work as* EVE *enters in a gay and cheerful mood*)

EVE Good morning. What are you doing? (*He hears her through all this but continues work*) Can I help? Are you hungry?

    (*She has an apple that she tosses in the air. He ignores her until the crunch from the bite she takes makes him turn. He grabs her, forces her down, and pulls the apple away*)

ADAM (*In a panic*) Give me that—spit it out—come on. Where'd you get that?

EVE (*Fighting back*) Help! Help! (*After he has taken the apple*) From that tree.

ADAM Are you sure it's not from over the hill?

EVE Positive. (*He whistles in relief, rises, and crosses to the tub*) I don't understand.

ADAM (*Pointing upstage*) Those apples are forbidden.

EVE Why?

ADAM Because they're dangerous. If we eat those apples—something terrible will happen.

EVE What?

ADAM I don't know.

EVE (*Rises*) Maybe we should just go find out.

ADAM (*Leaping to bar her way*) Stay away from that tree, numskull!

EVE (*Stiffly*) My name happens to be Eve.

ADAM (*Crossing to the hut*) I have no objections.

EVE (*Following him*) In the future, kindly use my name when you wish to speak to me, or when you wish to call me. That's what it's for.

ADAM Then it's superfluous.

    (*Puts a peg into the planks*)

EVE (*Despite her pique*) Superfluous! What a beautiful word! And it's so large! I'm proud of you . . . really I am. (*To the audience*) Superfluous! I don't think I've ever used it. (*To him*) Where did it come from?

ADAM (*Who has been watching her*) I don't know. I just kind of made it up. I was standing here looking at you, and I said to myself, "It looks superfluous."

    (*He picks up his bowl and his stone*)

EVE (*Moving in closer*)   I'm not an "it." (*Not angrily; she enjoys explaining*) I'm a "she."

ADAM (*Turning to her*)   Ah, well, I wish *she* would go play with the other animals, and I wish *she* would stop talking so much, because *me* have work to do.
>   (*He turns upstage*)

EVE   Can't I help?

ADAM (*Not even looking at her*)   No. She'd only be superfluous.
>   (*He sits in the hut and begins to carve the bowl. The lights change to a stormy blue and the "rain music" begins*)

EVE (*Reaching and putting a hand out*)   I think I felt a drop.

ADAM (*Sticking a hand out of the hut*)   It's starting to rain.

EVE   May I come in?

ADAM   It's crowded.

EVE   I don't mind.

ADAM   I mind.

EVE   Why do you hate me so much? I just can't understand it! I'm a very interesting person. And if you'd only talk to me nicely, I could be twice as interesting.
>   (*She begins to cry.* ADAM *looks at her with great curiosity and interest*)

ADAM   What are you doing?

EVE   Nothing.

ADAM   Yes, you are. You're raining, too!

EVE   I'm crying. But don't let it disturb you.
>   (*She turns away from him*)

ADAM   It doesn't, but . . . well . . . I don't like to see it. So . . .

EVE (*Eagerly turning to him*)   Yes?

ADAM   So either stop it, or go rain somewhere else. (*Now* EVE *truly wails, walks away, and sits on the ground.* ADAM *puts the bowl down and goes to her. With great exasperation*)   All right. All right. Come on in.

EVE   I don't want to.

ADAM   Why not?

EVE   It'll be too crowded.

ADAM   I'll make room.

EVE   Are you sure?

ADAM   I'm sure.
>   (*She goes into the hut; he follows. When they are both seated in the hut she leans on his shoulder*)

EVE   What's your name?

ADAM   What do I look like? Wait. My name is Adam.

EVE   Adam . . . Adam . . . that sound is pleasanter in my ears than any I have heard so far. (*She looks at the walls of the hut*) Adam?

ADAM   What?

EVE   What made you pick brown?

ADAM   Because wood is brown.

EVE   (*She rises. The end of this speech will be drowned out by a rising swell of musical "rain"*)   But berries are red. We could squeeze some berries against the wood, and make it nice and colorful . . . not all over, just from here to there. We'll have a border on top and bottom . . . and on that wall, some shells, I think. Have you thought of hanging grass in the doorway?

> (*The lights fade out as* ADAM *holds his head at her torrent of words. After a pause, the lights restore and we see a completely redecorated hut, just as* EVE *had envisioned it.* ADAM *is standing in front of the hut, a basket of melons in his hand. He turns to the audience and pantomimes "See—see what I mean?" He sits on the tub at the left of the hut and thumps a melon, listening for its hollowness. He keeps looking back at the hut and finally talks to the audience. The music has vamped throughout*)

ADAM   Sunday, June ninth. (*Singing*)

She keeps filling up the hut with rubbish,
Like flowers
And plants.
And not only is it overcrowded—
It's loaded
With ants.
She is definitely too intrusive,
A nuisance,
And yet . . .
She's an interesting creature—
This Eve.

She's developing a strange new habit
Which doesn't
Make sense.
She's forever reaching out to touch me,
Which makes me
Feel tense.
She is definitely quite eccentric,

A numskull,
And yet . . .
She's an interesting creature—
This Eve.

Colors drive her absolutely crazy
The gold of the sun,
The purple of the hills,
Crimson-colored clouds in the skies.
When I say this is sentimental hogwash,
Foolishness,
She simply sighs.
When I'd rather be alone and resting,
Then she comes
Around,
And invariably starts describing
Some wonder
She's found.
She invariably gets my back up,
Yet invariably I perceive
She's an interesting creature—
This Eve.

Once I saw her standing on a hilltop
Her head tilted back,
The sunlight on her face
Gazing at the flight of a bird;
And suddenly I saw that she was—
Beautiful—
Beautiful, yes, that's the word.

There are animals around this garden
More soothing.
Than she,
But there's nothing in the whole of Eden
More pleasant
To see.
If she'd only learn to keep her mouth shut
One minute at a time,
Why, I believe
I could possibly enjoy
Just watching

This curiously interesting creature—
Called Eve.

> (*On the last word of the song he slowly moves back to the tub and sits deep in thought and confusion.* EVE *enters, wearing a mad hat made of flowers. He quickly picks up a melon and goes back to his thumping*)

EVE   Adam, I just had a wonderful idea.

ADAM   (*Indicating her hat with distaste*)   Is that it?

EVE   (*Puts her basket in hut*)   No. What I thought . . . (*Turns to him*) Do you like it?

ADAM   I think it's unbecoming and ridiculous. And I want you to take it off this instant.

EVE   (*She does*)   I thought it would please you.

ADAM   How could it please me to see you walking around covered with rubbish?

EVE   Rubbish? Flowers, rubbish? These beautiful creatures that catch the smile of God out of the sky and preserve it? Rubbish? Does everything have to be useful? Isn't there anything you care about except thumping those melons? We've been given a world full of wonderful secrets and mysteries. There's so much to learn! Oh, Adam, to see everything and to know everything . . . why, that might take us weeks! How can you be so narrow?

ADAM   I have a lot of interests. It may surprise you to learn that only yesterday I invented something brand new.

EVE   Oh, Adam, what?

ADAM   (*Rises*)   Humor.

EVE   Humor?

ADAM   Does that word puzzle you? I thought it might. I'll be happy to explain. Yesterday, I was sitting beside the path that leads to the cornfield and I happened to notice this yellow clucker . . .

EVE   Chicken.

ADAM   All right!

EVE   It looks like . . .

ADAM   All right! Have it your way! I happened to notice this chicken. For a long time it walked slowly back and forth, hesitating, and then suddenly it zipped across the path. And I thought to myself, "Why did that chicken cross that path?" And then I thought, "To get to the other side!" (*He is hysterical and falls about, finally reaching up to her*) That's the world's first joke. And I made it up. Don't you see the humor of it? (EVE *has been growing increasingly puzzled by this whole thing. She obliges* ADAM *with a smile but shrugs apologetically*) I guess you had to be there . . . and I'm going there.

> (*He turns and starts to leave*)

EVE   Adam, don't you want to hear my wonderful idea?

ADAM   No.

EVE   Oh, Adam . . .

ADAM   (*He goes back to her*)   Well, what is it?

EVE   I've been thinking . . . we're different from anything else on earth. And our home should be different.

ADAM   I thought it was.

EVE   And today I had the feeling that the grass around our hut should be different from all other grass.

ADAM   Different how?

EVE   Shorter.

ADAM   How could it be shorter—unless it was cut? (*As* ADAM *and* EVE *stare at one another, the lights fade. When they come up again,* EVE *is gone and* ADAM *is alone. He sits on the wooden tub*) Monday, June tenth. Note: I finally discovered the purpose of the week. To rest up from Sunday. This relentless pursuit of improvements is making me feel more hampered than ever. What's truly puzzling is that the more time we spend together, the closer we get; and the closer we get, the more anxious it makes me. Anyway, there's one bright spot. She's taken up with a snake now. I'm glad, because the snake talks and this allows me a little time to rest. Eve has also taken to spending a great deal of time at the pond. I don't know why.

> (*The lights fade on* ADAM, *who exits, and come up on* EVE, *looking at herself in the pond and making up her face with petals*)

EVE   (*Singing*)
> Look at you,
> Look at me,
> How much more alike could
> Two girls be?
> Here we stand,
> Sisters and
> Friends.
>
> When I speak
> You speak too,
> And when I am silent

So are you.
That's the test
Of two best
Friends.

When my life is hard to bear,
Then I run to see you there,
And
My heart blooms,
Your face beams,
Nothing is as awful
As it seems.
We're such dear . . .
More than mere . . .
Friends.

> (*The lights fade on* EVE *and come up on* ADAM. *He's sitting on a tub*)

ADAM (*Laughing*)   Eve fell in the pond yesterday. She damn near strangled. She said it was so cold and uncomfortable in there that she felt sorry for the fish. So last night she got a lot of them out and brought them inside. And she put them in my bed to keep warm.

EVE (*Rises and crosses to* ADAM)   Hello, Adam.

ADAM   Eve, tonight those fish go back to the pond.

EVE   But it's so uncomfortable there!

ADAM   Eve, I've been watching those fish off and on all morning, and I don't see that they're any happier than they were before. They're just . . . quieter.

EVE   But . . .

ADAM   I don't want 'em in my bed. They're clammy!

EVE   But, Adam . . .

ADAM (*Rises*)   I want you to put 'em back! Do you understand me?

EVE   Yes, Adam.

ADAM   All right then.

> (*He picks up his tub and starts to leave*)

EVE   Where are you going?

ADAM (*Stopping*)   Somewhere I can be by myself.

EVE   Where?

ADAM   Over the falls.

EVE   Not in that leaky tub? Oh, Adam, I wish you wouldn't!

ADAM   Eve, this has nothing to do with you!

EVE   It makes me shudder! It's not safe.

ADAM   Well, I like it. It's cool. And I like the plunge.

EVE   Please, don't. Not in the tub. You can't imagine how it frightens me. I can't bear it.

   (*She tries to grab the tub. He pulls it away from her*)

ADAM   You can't? Well, I can't bear this everlasting complaining. First, you complained about my going over the falls in a barrel. So I made a tub. Did that satisfy you? No, sir. Now you complain about the tub! And if it isn't the tub it'll be something else. Eve, I won't have it. I don't want to be complained at, I don't want to be clucked over, I don't want to be clung to. I'm going to the falls, and after that I'm not sure where I'm going. So don't wait for me.

   (*He storms off. She yells after him*)

EVE   Adam, would you bring back some of those hollyhocks that grow by the falls?

ADAM   (*Offstage*)   I hate flowers!

   (EVE *goes back to the pond; her mood is a mixture of heartache, petulance, and pride*)

EVE (*Singing*)

And on days when he withdraws,

I'm less lonely now because

If

I should need sympathy,

You would never turn your

Back on me.

I have you.

Who needs two

Friends?

   (*The* SNAKE, *in tuxedo, smoking a pipe, enters behind* EVE. *He throws a pipe cleaner into the pond, making the reflection shatter*)

Wait! Don't go away!

SNAKE   There's no one there, Eve.

   (EVE *whirls, startled*)

EVE   What? Oh, hello, Snake.

SNAKE   I said, there's no one there.

EVE   There is so! My friend's there. And she'll be back.

SNAKE   No, Eve. That's what's called a reflection. (*He kneels down*) You see, when waves of one kind traveling in one me-

dium arrive at another in which their velocity is different, part
of their energy is turned back into the first medium. In this case,
the waves are light rays which appear to come from a literally
inverted replica of the luminous source, and it is this image
which is then focused on the retina.

EVE   I don't believe you.

SNAKE   Well, it's so. Look . . . (*He leans over* EVE *and wiggles his
arms and legs.* EVE *compares the reflection with the* SNAKE) See.
that's not my brother. That's me.

EVE   Then I have no one! No friend! Nothing!

SNAKE (*Leaning back*)   What about Adam?

EVE (*Turning, lying across his lap*)   He doesn't even like me! He
thinks I'm a numskull. And I am . . . so how could he like me!
Oh, I wish I was educated—like you.

SNAKE   Would you really like that?

EVE   Oh, yes!

SNAKE   Nothing could be simpler.

EVE   How? How?

SNAKE   You know that apple tree on the other side of the hill?

EVE   Forbidden fruit?

SNAKE   Who says?

EVE   Adam.

SNAKE   My dear girl, the forbidden fruit in this garden is hardly
apples. It's chestnuts.

EVE   Chestnuts?

SNAKE   Well, not literally. When I say "chestnuts," that's a figura-
tive term meaning old and moldy jokes.

EVE   The thing Adam calls humor.

SNAKE   Exactly. There's your forbidden fruit.

EVE (*Rising*)   Chestnuts! I didn't know that. See how ignorant I
am.

> (*The music starts. The* SNAKE *holds up his hand, freezing*
> EVE *in her tracks*)

SNAKE (*Singing*)
> Listen closely. Let me fill you in
> About the rich, ripe, round, red,
> Rosy apples they call forbidden fruit.
> What I'm about to say is
> Confidential, so promise you'll be mute.
> Because if every creature in the garden knows,
> They'll come 'round like hungry buffalos,

And in no time there'll be none of those
Precious apples left for you and me.

Now, in the average apple
You're accustomed to skin, seeds, flesh, and core.
But you will find that these are
Special apples that give you something more.
Why, every seed contains some information you
Need to speed your education; the
Seeds, indeed, of all creation are here.
Why, be foolish, my dear,
Come with me
To that tree.

EVE I don't think Adam would approve. Maybe they're not forbidden, but I still have qualms.

SNAKE (*Singing*)
With every sweet and juicy
Luscious bite of this not forbidden fruit,
You'll see your mind expand and
Your perceptions grow more and more acute.

And you can teach him plumbing and philosophy,
New techniques for glazing pottery,
Wood-craft, first-aid, home economy,
Madam, Adam will be overjoyed!

When he becomes aware of
Your attainments he'll beam with loving pride
And he will say,
    (*Holding her in his arms*)
"O, Eve, you're
Indispensable! Please, don't leave my side!"
And with your nifty, new-found education, he'll
Relish every conversation; why
    (*Moving around her*)
You'll be Adam's inspiration this way!
Just an apple a day.
Wait and see.
Come with me
To that tree!
Now!

(*He takes her arm and pulls her offstage. The lights fade;
when they come up again,* ADAM *is seated tranquilly on his
tub, drying himself with a towel. He is singing as if he is in
the shower*)

ADAM (*Singing*)

I see animals and birds and flowers,
Every color, every shape and size.
Moss and pebbles and a host of wonders
Gleaming everywhere I aim my eyes.
So if ever I'm attacked by boredom,
I'll just open up my eyes and see
This diversified, curious, fascinating, bountiful,
Beautiful, beautiful world,
I love.

(*He laughs and suddenly freezes. He calls out in alarm*)
Hey—hey—you there, growler—I mean, lion. Leave that lamb
alone. Don't do that, you'll hurt him. I said stop that! What do
you think you're doing? Stop it! Stop it! (*He steps back in
horror*) Oh, my God! Oh, my God! (*He looks about in anguish
as the stage darkens*) Oh, my God!

(*Thunder is heard rolling down ominously*)

EVE (*Entering, she throws her arms around* ADAM *in fear. She is
carrying an apple, though we don't see it as yet. She wears a
robe of flowers*)   There you are—Oh, Adam!

ADAM   You did it! You did it! I warned you. You ate the apples,
didn't you? The forbidden fruit! Do you know what you did? I
told you. I said don't touch that fruit—something terrible would
happen. And now death has come into the garden. (*He has
pushed her away and now throws his towel to the ground*) How
could you do it? How could you do such a damnable thing?

EVE   I didn't do it! I mean, it wasn't the apples—they're not forbidden.

ADAM   No? Then what is?

EVE   Chestnuts.

ADAM   Chestnuts? Where the hell did you pick that up?

EVE   The snake told me. And he knows everything. In fact, this
whole thing is probably your fault.

ADAM   My fault? I didn't eat any chestnuts.

EVE   Not that kind. This kind of chestnut is a joke. Have you been
making up jokes, Adam? Tell the truth.

ADAM   I did think of one . . . (*She reacts audibly and turns away*) but I didn't say it out loud! Oh, my . . . I was standing here—just before it all happened—and I was thinking about the falls. And I thought, "How wonderful it is to see that vast body of water tumble down there." And then I thought, "Yes, but it would be a lot more wonderful to see it tumble up!"

EVE   That's it. That's what did it.

ADAM   Oh, my. Oh my, oh my. . . . (*To heaven*) Why was I born so witty?

EVE   We have to leave the garden, don't we?

ADAM   We broke the rule . . . *I* broke the rule. I'm sorry, Eve.

EVE   Oh . . . you didn't know.

> (*They embrace.* ADAM *suddenly notices* EVE's *costume*)

ADAM   Eve, you know I can't stand to see you wearing that rubbish. Please take it off.

> (*He makes a gesture to help her off with her robe. To his surprise she resists, with some embarrassment*)

EVE   No, don't do that. You mustn't. Please, Adam. No, don't please!

ADAM   You're behaving like an idiot. If you want to make a silly spectacle of yourself, go right ahead. I know what I'm going to do. I haven't eaten all day.

EVE (*Showing it to him*)   Would you like an apple?

ADAM   Oh, it's one of those.

EVE   They're not forbidden.

ADAM   I know, but somehow it still goes against my principles. (*Takes the apple*) It's certainly a fine looking specimen, isn't it? Considering the lateness of the season and all. I guess principles have no real force unless you're well fed. (*He takes a bite and chews it for a moment. He reaches down and picks up his towel*) Turn your back. Don't you have any modesty at all?

> (*He wraps himself in the towel*)

EVE   Sorry. (*She turns her back*) Adam?

ADAM   What?

EVE (*Starting to cry*)   It looks like rain.

ADAM   I know. Come on. We'll have to build a new shelter somewhere.

> (*They exit, as Eden flys out. A platform rolls out with a rail on one end and a bench in the middle of it. It is night*)

ADAM (*Enters onto the porch, corn-cob pipe in hand, contentedly puffing as he sits on the bench. He picks up a piece of hickory twig and a knife and slowly whittles*)   Eve calls this place

Tonawanda. You know, it *looks* like Tonawanda. I find she's a good deal of a companion. I can see I'd be lonesome and depressed without her, now that I've lost my property.

EVE (*Entering onto the porch with a rough wool sweater which she throws over* ADAM's *shoulders. Giving him a quick hug, she talks from behind him*)   Did you like the baked apples?

(*She picks up a watering can and gardens*)

ADAM   Very tasty.

EVE   I like to try new things.

ADAM   I remember when you invented fire. I never thought it would be practical.

EVE   That reminds me—how's the multiplication table coming?

ADAM   I don't know. I get as far as five times nine is twenty-seven and the whole thing goes to pieces.

EVE   You'll get it, dear.

ADAM (*With a cough*)   Well, I'm tired.

(*He stands and gazes down at her. She puts the can down, stops weeding, and joins him on the porch*)

EVE   It's late.

ADAM (*His arm about her waist*)   Eve, is it my imagination or have you been putting on weight?

(*The lights fade out as they exit. The music to "It's a Fish" begins and the lights restore*)

ADAM (*Entering hurriedly from the house onto the porch. He paces back and forth*)   I just got back from a hunting trip up North and found that Eve had caught some new kind of animal. (*Singing*)

Now I could swear
That it's a fish,
Tho' it resembles us in every way but size.

She gives it milk,
And every night
She picks it up and pats and pets it when it cries

I always knew
She pitied fish,
But it's ridiculous to make them household pets.

She says it's not a fish.
I say it is a fish
'Cause it surrounds itself with water

Almost every chance it gets.

(EVE *enters from the cabin onto the porch carrying a bundle wrapped in a rough wool blanket, and acting very wary of* ADAM)

ADAM   Why won't you let me put it in the pond?

EVE   I told you it's not a fish!

ADAM   How will we ever find out what it is, if we don't experiment?

EVE   I don't *care* what it is! (*Her voice rises to a frenzied scream*) You keep away from it!

ADAM   You're standing in the way of science. (*She takes the bundle into the cabin. He follows her into the cabin; a beat later he backs out. He sings*)

It's not a fish.
Fish never scream,
And this one does, tho' on occasion it says "Goo."

Its legs are long,
Its arms are short,
So I suspect that it's a kind of kangaroo.

And since it came
I pity Eve,
She's gotten madder by the minute, and it shows.

Just now I said to her
That I would much prefer
To have it stuffed for my collection,
And she punched me in the nose!

(*The music to* "Go to Sleep Whatever You Are" *begins.* EVE *comes on carrying the bundle and looks around to see if she is alone. She sits on the porch rail*)

EVE (*Singing*)

Go to sleep, whatever you are,
Lay your head on my breast.

Close your eyes and open your paws,
You need plenty of rest

Doesn't faze me
If you grow up to be
Pony or poodle or sheep.

You're my own, whatever you are.

Sleep . . . sleep . . . sleep.

(EVE *goes in the house.* ADAM *re-enters*)

ADAM (*Singing*)

It's growing teeth,

And it can bite,

And I'm convinced that what we have here is a bear.

I'm worried sick,

But Eve is not.

She burned the muzzle that I made for it to wear.

I've searched the woods,

I've baited traps,

And yet I couldn't find its sister or its brother.

And tho' I've hunted far and wide

While Eve has hardly stepped outside,

I'll be damned if she didn't catch another!

(*Blackout. The lights focus on* EVE *on the porch bench. She is snapping beans in a wooden bowl*)

EVE   They are boys. We found that out long ago. It was their coming in that small, immature shape that puzzled us. (*Yells offstage*) Cain! Abel! Keep out of my garden! You'll ruin the flowers! The old garden. That seems like a dream to me. It was beautiful. Surpassingly beautiful. But still a dream. Making supper for three hungry males is not a dream.

(*The lights fade on* EVE *and come up on* ADAM, *who has a stylized plow and a rake*)

ADAM   They're nearly as big as I am now. Abel is a good boy. But if Cain had stayed a bear it would have improved him. I never know what's coming next. A fire started for spite; a creature killed without sense or reason. I have come to depend on Eve more than I would have believed possible. I used to think she talked too much. But now I'd be sorry to have that voice fall silent and pass out of my life.

(*The lights fade on* ADAM; *they come up on* EVE, *who is sewing a sweater*)

EVE   Some time back, my boys were fighting. And Cain struck Abel and ran away. Now Cain is gone, and Abel's dead. There is too much stillness in the house.

ADAM (*Enters, carrying the rake*)   Are you all right?

EVE (*Still sewing*)   Yes. Adam, I've been thinking. I hope that
when we die, we die together.

ADAM (*He puts his hand on her shoulder*)   That's a subject, I'd—

EVE   Wait. If one of us must go first, my prayer is that I'm the
one.

ADAM   I don't want to—

EVE   You're strong, and I'm weak. You're more necessary to me
than I am to you.

ADAM   That's not true.

EVE   Yes, it's true. It's always been true.

ADAM (*Changing the subject*)   Listen, listen—I've got a good one
for you. Why do I always wear brown suspenders?

EVE (*Laughing heartily*)   That's my favorite.
(*Still laughing*)

ADAM (*Beginning to laugh*)   Oh, I forgot . . .
(*He laughs, coughs a bit and exits, the rake over his shoulder*)

EVE (*Gazing after him and chuckling*)   Life without him would
not be life—I don't think I could endure it. And yet, if I ask myself why I love him, I find I don't know. It's not on account of
his gracious and considerate ways—he's a bit flawed in those
respects. I love certain birds because of their song, but that
hardly applies to Adam. (*Music begins and she sings*)

What makes me love him?
It's not his singing.
I've heard his singing:
It sours the milk.
And yet, it's gotten to the point
Where I prefer that kind of milk.

What makes me love him?
It's not his learning.
He's learned so slowly
His whole life long.
And tho' he really knows
A multitude of things, they're mostly wrong.
He is a good man,
Yet I would love him
If he abused me
Or used me ill.

. . .

And tho' he's handsome,
I know inside me
Were he a plain man,
I'd love him still.

What makes me love him?
It's quite beyond me.
It must be something
I can't define;
Unless it's merely that he's masculine,
And that he's mine.

(EVE *slowly gathers up the sweater and the bowl of beans. Feeling the chill of the night, she rises and exits into the house*)

ADAM (*Entering and bearing a great sadness*) Eve died today. I knew she would, of course. Well, at least her prayer was answered—she went first. Now that she's gone, I realize something I didn't realize before. I used to think it was a terrible tragedy when Eve and I had to leave the garden. Now I know it really didn't matter. Because, wheresoever she was, there was Eden. (*The lights pick up the flowerbed area*) And now, I have to go water her flowers. She loved them, you know.

(*The strains of "Here in Eden" are heard as* ADAM *picks up the watering can and tends the flowers. After a bit, he wipes his brow and bends down and weeds*)

Curtain

George's Room

BY

Alun Owen

Alun Owen

Alun Owen was born in 1926 in Menai, North Wales, and was educated at Cardigan and Liverpool. He began his stage career at fifteen when he joined the Perth Repertory as a bit-part actor and assistant stage manager. During World War II, he was a "Bevin Boy" (one who worked in the mines as a public service, as an alternative to conscription during the war) in the pits in South Wales before a mining accident led to his discharge. An assortment of jobs followed. He worked as a waiter, a lorry driver's mate, a warehouse hand, a seaman in the Merchant Navy, for two trips; and then as an actor in repertory, pantomime, and on the West End stage and television. He had meanwhile published poems in the United States and Wales, and had gradually become interested in dramatic writing.

After five radio scripts had been accepted by the British Broadcasting Corporation, his first stage play, *Progress to the Park,* was presented as a Sunday night production at the Royal Court Theatre in 1959, was then produced for a run at the Theatre Royal, Stratford East, and subsequently transferred to the Saville on the West End. His other plays include *The Rough and Ready Lot,* produced at the Lyric in Hammersmith, and *A Little Winter Love* which premiered at the Gaiety Theatre, Dublin.

In 1964 Mr. Owen's musical *Maggie May* (with music and lyrics by Lionel Bart, and starring Rachel Roberts) was an overnight success at the Adelphi Theatre, London, where it enjoyed a run of sixteen months.

A prolific author who transfers his allegiance from stage to television to films with equal facility, Mr. Owen received the 1960 award as Best Scriptwriter of the Year from the Guild of Television Producers and Directors, and was the recipient of the Television and Screenwriters' Guild award for the Best Original Television Play of 1961 in England—*The Rose Affair*. Additional honors subsequently came to him when he was nominated for a Hollywood Academy Award for his screenplay *A Hard Day's Night* (which starred The Beatles) and acquired the 1967 Gold Star Award from Britain's Associated Television for his play *George's Room*, published for the first time in the United States in this anthology.

In 1969 the author scored a resounding success on American television with his three-part drama, *Male of the Species*. The production was introduced by Sir Laurence Olivier and starred Sean Connery, Michael Caine, Paul Scofield and Anna Calder Marshall.

At present he is completing a screenplay, *Caribbean Idyll*, with filming on location scheduled to begin in November, 1969.

Mr. Owen is married, has two sons, and lives "mostly" in a large Victorian house in Cardigan, West Wales, on the banks of the River Teify.

GEORGE'S ROOM *was first presented on August 30, 1967, by the Associated Rediffusion Television Network, Great Britain, with the following cast:*

(*In order of appearance*)

WOMAN	Geraldine Moffatt
MAN	John Neville

Directed by Alan Clarke
Produced by Stella Richman

GEORGE'S ROOM

The action takes place in the living room of a very ordinary sub-urban house. The time is the present; it is afternoon.

The room could be duplicated a million times. There is a door in the center, leading to the hall. (When this door is open, the front door is visible.) On the left of the door is a glass cabinet; on the right is a sideboard. There are standard lamps, an armchair, a settee, a coffee table and a television set. The window is in the left wall, and on the right there is a door to another room.

When the curtain rises, the WOMAN *is sitting on the settee eating a chocolate. She is no more than thirty and very pretty, but not overly bright. She is very sensual. She speaks with a not unpleasant, refined North Country accent. She is well-made without being fat, and she is a slow mover. After a moment the doorbell rings. The* WOMAN *rises and goes to the hall leaving the door to the room wide open. She opens the front door. A* MAN *is standing on the doorstep. He is tall and good-looking, well dressed and well spoken. He is polite in the face of her fluster and has a great deal of patient charm. He raises his hat before speaking.*

MAN   I was sent by Elgin.

WOMAN   Oh, yes, Mr. Elgin.

MAN   He thought I'd catch you.

WOMAN (*Smiling vaguely*)   Well, he was right, wasn't he?
       (*She makes no attempt to invite him inside*)

MAN   He said you have a room to rent.

WOMAN   Oh, did he?

MAN   That he did.

WOMAN   Well, I do, but . . .

MAN   Yes?

WOMAN   I've never let a room before.

MAN   I don't know that previous experience is an absolute ne-
       cessity.

WOMAN   Oh, no, I'm sure . . . (*She trails off*) What I meant was . . .

MAN (*Politely*)   Have you a room to rent or not?

WOMAN   It's a very ordinary room.

MAN   Good.

WOMAN   I mean, it's nothing special.

MAN   But it does run to the usual walls and ceiling?

WOMAN   Oh, yes, it's got those.

MAN   That's reassuring. (*The* WOMAN *realizes he is joking, and giggles attractively. Patiently*) Well, now we've established it's a pretty run-of-the-mill room, would you think it too pushing of me to inquire as to its availability?

WOMAN   Oh, it's not very grand, I'm afraid.

MAN   Quite, but is it free?

WOMAN   Well, what I mean is you may not think it's suitable.

MAN   Ah, as to that, one will only be able to say when one has had the opportunity to examine it.

WOMAN (*Fascinated*)   What?

MAN   The room—when one has seen it for oneself.

WOMAN   Would you like to see it?

MAN   Dear lady, that is the sole purpose of my visit.

WOMAN   Oh, dear, you must think I'm silly.

MAN   I try not to be hasty.

WOMAN   No, I'm silly. Please come in.

MAN   Thank you.

(*She leads the way through the hall and into the living-room*)

WOMAN (*Moving near the settee*)   Have you known Mr. Elgin for long?

MAN (*Following her*)   No, not really, and never intimately, but I have had occasion to use his firm's amenities from time to time.

WOMAN   Amenities?

MAN   They have an excellent after-service and whenever I'm in the district I look them up.

WOMAN   It was Mary I knew—his sister. We were at the Secretarial College together. Of course, she went to Canada, but we've kept in touch, and Mr. Elgin was very nice about it when my husband passed away.

MAN   Yes, he mentioned you were a widow. I'm sorry.

WOMAN   That was nice of him. Of course, he didn't know George. Yes, that was very nice of him. He was always much older than me.

MAN Mr. Elgin?

WOMAN (*Moving around the settee; laughing*) No, my husband
—he was older than *me*, but even so, he was only middle-aged.
Mr. Elgin said if there was anything he could do . . .

MAN A reliable chap, Elgin, I'd say.

WOMAN Mind, he's a lot older than me, too, but he looks after
himself. His tummy's as flat as a board.

MAN He has a cycling machine in his office.

WOMAN Has he?

MAN Oh, yes, and a complete set of athlete's clothing, towel, track
suit, gym shoes. He does five miles before starting work, five
miles before lunch and rounds off the day with a final five miles,
making fifteen miles in all. You must admire his stamina.

WOMAN I often think I could do with a lot more exercise.

MAN What on earth for?

WOMAN (*Shyly*) Well, there's enough of me.

MAN I wonder if you would regard it as impertinent if I said
there was exactly the right amount of you.

WOMAN Oh.

MAN Anyway, that's what I think.

WOMAN (*Laughing*) Well, we're all entitled to our opinions.
Would you like some coffee?

MAN That's kind of you, but I came to see the room and if . . .

WOMAN (*Hurt*) Oh, I see.

MAN But, of course, I should be delighted . . .

WOMAN If you're in a hurry . . .

MAN It's very kind . . .

WOMAN I wouldn't want you to . . .

MAN (*Fiercely*) I should like it black with no sugar.

WOMAN (*Delighted*) Shan't be a mo'. (*The* WOMAN *exits to the
kitchen through the center door. The* MAN *sighs and looks around
the room. Offstage*) Sit down and make yourself at home.

   (*The* MAN *sighs and sits in the armchair*)

MAN Have you lived here long?

   (*The* WOMAN *returns with a tray and two cups of coffee.
She puts the tray on the coffee table and sits on the settee*)

WOMAN It was only a matter of putting some hot water on it.
Oh, it takes no time at all. Were you asking me something?

MAN It wasn't important. I just wondered if you'd lived here
long?

WOMAN (*Handing him his coffee*) Ten years ago he carried me

across that threshold. He'd been married before. He was a widow
—widower.

MAN   Was he?

WOMAN   Oh, yes, I worked in his office.

MAN   A businessman, eh?

WOMAN   He was the manager. You did say no sugar, didn't you?

MAN   Yes.

WOMAN   Good. I was his secretary.

MAN   Ah.

WOMAN   Oh, nothing like that.

MAN   Like what?

WOMAN   Like that.

MAN   I beg your pardon?

WOMAN   I was a good girl.

MAN   I never said otherwise.

WOMAN   You said "ah."

MAN   I didn't. I said "ah."

WOMAN   Oh, I'm sorry.

MAN   Not at all.

WOMAN   Do forgive me.

MAN   Of course.

WOMAN   Are you sure?

MAN   Please forget it.

WOMAN   No, it's just I'd always liked older men.

MAN   Your father died when you were quite young, I take it?

WOMAN   No.

MAN   No?

   (*The light starts to fade*)

WOMAN   No, not really. He's still alive and kicking, is my old
Daddy. Why did you ask?

MAN   I read a lot. It can make you altogether too flip in your
assessments, I'm afraid.

WOMAN   Oh, I'm sure that isn't true—well—I'm sure you're not
really like that.

MAN (*Amused*)   How odd, considering I've just told you I was.

WOMAN (*Laughing*)   Oh, men! You're always saying things.

MAN   Yes, I suppose we are.

   (*There is a pause while they look at each other*)

WOMAN   And you want a room?

MAN   Yes. In fact, I need one.

WOMAN   You're going to live round here, then?

MAN I think you could say that.

WOMAN My husband wasn't a local man.

MAN No?

WOMAN Oh, no, he was a Scot—from Scotland.

MAN Ah.

WOMAN You did it again.

MAN Did I?

WOMAN Yes, you said "ah."

MAN I'm afraid I did.

WOMAN You know, I think you always say that when you're pushed.

MAN Pushed?

WOMAN Yes, pushed for something to say.

MAN (*Ironically*) And I think you're being very astute. Indeed, I do have an unfortunate habit when I'm in a situation that demands a positive answer and I can't find one—I will fall back on a good old noncommittal "ah."

WOMAN (*Satisfied*) I thought so—my husband was like that.

MAN But he was an older man.

WOMAN Oh, I grew out of that. I mean, there are certain disadvantages to older men.

MAN Yes, they keep on getting older, and as they had a head start on you in the first place, they're liable to wind up too old.

WOMAN Mind, he was very considerate.

MAN To a fault, I'm sure.

WOMAN Well, he tired easily.

MAN And living is pretty strenuous nowadays.

WOMAN You don't look as if you'd tire easily.

MAN (*Firmly*) Looks can be deceptive.

(*The* WOMAN *draws in her skirts, and when she speaks she is slightly haughty*)

WOMAN Oh, well, you're probably right. I mean, lots of people are whited sepulchres underneath it all, aren't they? So you want a room?

MAN I'll be in the district three days a week.

WOMAN Which days?

MAN Tuesday, Wednesday, Thursday and Friday.

WOMAN That's four.

MAN I shall be going home on Friday through till Tuesday. What I need is a *pied-à-terre*, but of course I shall expect to pay for a full week.

WOMAN Are you married?

MAN   Oh, no, I'm on the loose, a freebooter, one might say.

WOMAN   I'm surprised.

MAN (*Amused*)   I'm rather surprised myself.

WOMAN   I bet you've had a few narrow shaves, though?

MAN   Oh, I don't know.

WOMAN   I bet you have. (*The* MAN *shrugs*) My George was a bit like that.

MAN   Like what?

WOMAN   Looked as if he'd had a past.

MAN   Is that how I strike you—as though I'd had a past?

WOMAN   Yes, but with him it was a false impression. He was just liverish. It made him look devil-may-care when all the time it was a vitamin deficiency.

MAN   I hope I don't give you that impression. I'm chock-a-block full of vitamins, though I say it myself.

WOMAN   Yes, I thought you might be. I mean, you look very—very —you know.

MAN   Thank you, and if I may so, you're looking prime yourself.

WOMAN   Yes, I'm pretty fit. Of course, it's different for a woman.

MAN   I'm sure it is, but why?

WOMAN (*Refined*)   Well, ladies are more passive, really, aren't they?

MAN   I could make out a pretty good case for them not being. A woman bursting with vigorous health is most attractive.

WOMAN   Oh, I'm active all right.

MAN   I said attractive.

WOMAN   I know you did. I was changing the subject.

MAN   I wish you wouldn't.

WOMAN   It's getting dark in here, isn't it?

MAN   I should light one lamp, the one to your left.

WOMAN   Why that one?

MAN   Its light will reflect on the glass of the china cabinet, and also outline your profile. It'll soften all the edges and make you look quite special, one might almost say unique. Some people are night people, some people are made for high noon. I know your time.

WOMAN (*Softly*)   And when is that, an it please you?

MAN   Dusk and autumn. Outside, light drizzle—and inside, just the one lamp, a nineteen-thirties lamp with a fringed shade. Do switch it on.

WOMAN   No, I'll have to get up and I'm comfy.

MAN   So am I.

WOMAN   If we sit here much longer, it'll be dark.

MAN (*Mildly*)   You have the answer.

WOMAN (*Playfully*)   And you call yourself a gentleman.

MAN   I never did.

WOMAN   But you would.

MAN   A gentleman, a real gentleman, leaves that to others.

WOMAN   Well, I'd have called you a gentleman—a real gentle-man.

MAN   Was your husband a real gentleman?

WOMAN   In his way, yes.

MAN   Would he have got up and switched on the light?

WOMAN   Oh—he'd have switched the light on.

MAN   In that case . . .

(*The* MAN *starts to rise, but the* WOMAN *anticipates him*)

WOMAN   No, I'll do it.

MAN   Are you sure?

WOMAN   Oh, once I've made up my mind there's no stopping me. (*She rises and moves to the door. She presses the switch and the two lamps come on together. She moves to the lamp on the right and turns it off*) Well, we don't need them both on, do we?

MAN   Hardly.

WOMAN (*Slightly embarrassed*)   Is something showing?

MAN   I beg your pardon?

WOMAN (*Smiling*)   The way you look at me, I feel something's loose or hanging down.

MAN   I was admiring your dress. It shimmers a bit.

WOMAN (*Moving around the settee*)   It's a man-made fabric.

MAN   Ah.

WOMAN   There, you said it again.

MAN (*Smiling*)   When are you going to come back and sit down?

WOMAN   I'm thinking about it.

MAN   It is a nice room?

WOMAN   What?

MAN   The room to rent.

WOMAN   It was my husband's room. There's a divan bed instead of a couch. It was the guest room as well.

MAN   I wish you'd come and sit down.

WOMAN   What difference does it make?

MAN   You seem so far away.

WOMAN   I'm looking at *you* now.

MAN   I see.

WOMAN   He always sat in that chair.

    (*The* MAN *moves uncomfortably in his seat*)

MAN   You were fond of him, weren't you?

WOMAN   He was very kind, and that counts for a lot these days. As soon as we became engaged, he moved me to another branch to prevent talk, and he insisted on going halves over the wedding expenses—that made a lot of difference to my old Daddy. I should have to charge you four guineas a week for the room. I couldn't let it go for less, and I think that'd be a fair price—not that I need the money. He looked after me very well. (*She indicates the door on the right*) If you want to see the room, it's through there.

    (*The* MAN *rises and moves to the door. The* WOMAN *remains where she is. At the door, the* MAN *hesitates*)

MAN   Aren't you coming in with me?

WOMAN   Oh, no.

MAN   Why not?

WOMAN (*Simply*)   I never go in there.

MAN   Never?

WOMAN   Mrs. Branton cleans it. I don't go in there. You go in and tell me what you think of it. I'll wait here.

    (*The* MAN *goes into the room, closing the door after him. The* WOMAN *crosses to the door, but turns away and sits in the chair the* MAN *has just vacated. She shudders slightly as if cold, but there is a look of pleasure on her face as she waits for the* MAN *to return. She lies back, relaxed, her eyes closed, her limbs slack. After a moment the* MAN *comes out of the room, closes the door behind him and leans on it. He looks across at the* WOMAN, *who could be asleep*)

MAN   Yes. (*There is no response*) Well, it's a nice room.

WOMAN (*Without opening her eyes*)   I thought you'd like it.

MAN   I do.

WOMAN   I knew you would. It's a man's room.

    (*She sighs*)

MAN   Monastic.

WOMAN (*Opening her eyes*)   What?

MAN   Well, it's more like a cell than a room, but it's restful.

WOMAN   He did a lot of thinking in that room.

MAN   There's just that one-bar electric fire, is there?

WOMAN   It heats the room very quickly, he always said.

    (*The* MAN *looks at her, then speaks deliberately*)

MAN   I like the pictures.

WOMAN (*Sitting up*)   What pictures?

MAN   I thought you said you never went in there?

WOMAN   I don't—but I've seen in there. There are no pictures.

MAN   I was just testing you.

WOMAN   Oh, I've got an inventory of all that's there. It's just that I don't go in there any more.

MAN   Since he passed away?

WOMAN   That's right. It's his room, or maybe a guest could have it—but *I* wouldn't go in there, would I?

MAN   But you did.

WOMAN   Oh, yes, but only by invitation. It was an arrangement we had.

MAN (*Sitting on the settee*)   Tell me about it.

WOMAN   No, it's silly.

MAN   I'd like to hear about it.

WOMAN   It was private, between George and me.

MAN   I'm sorry. I didn't mean to intrude.

WOMAN (*Anxiously*)   Have I been rude?

MAN   Of course not.

WOMAN   I have, haven't I?

MAN   I'm sure it's nothing to do with me.

WOMAN   I'll tell you, if you really want to know.

MAN   It's quite unnecessary.

WOMAN   I feel I owe it to you.

MAN   You owe me nothing.

WOMAN (*Urgently*)   Oh, don't be cold. I'm sorry. I want to talk to you—tell you—but I'm not used to talking to men. We didn't go about much.

MAN   What a great pity, because you should be seen in all the right places.

WOMAN   I'd like that, if I wasn't afraid.

MAN   You're only afraid because you lack certain graces that come with confidence. You'd pick them up in no time at all.

WOMAN   No, I'm afraid it's too late now.

MAN   Surely not.

WOMAN   Oh, yes, it's too late now.

MAN (*Casually*)   Yes, you're probably right.

WOMAN (*Falling into his trap*)   I am not!

MAN   Well, you're the one who said it, not me. I was only agreeing with you.

WOMAN   Well, don't. There are some things better left unsaid. You like the room, then, do you?

MAN   I'd have to move that divan.

WOMAN   Oh, I couldn't allow that.

MAN   I'd have to, I'm afraid.

WOMAN   Oh, no, he was very particular about his things; a place for everything and everything in its place.

MAN   Well, it'd have to be different for me.

WOMAN   No, it's got to be just so.

MAN   But then I'm alive.

WOMAN   What?

MAN   (*Rising*)   I'm alive, not like your husband—dead. It won't make any difference to him now, will it?

WOMAN   There's no call to be crude.

MAN   I really must refute that. Facts are facts. You've got to accept them. I'm alive, he's dead.

WOMAN   Stop saying that!

MAN   Why, it's true, isn't it?

WOMAN   In a way, maybe, but . . .

MAN   All right, tell me the way it isn't true.

WOMAN   I'll do nothing of the sort, and the room stays as it is.

MAN   All right. I'll take it.

WOMAN   (*Surprised*)   Oh.

MAN   If I move in on Tuesday, all right?

WOMAN   Well . . .

MAN   Oh, please I must have a decision one way or the other. (*She looks at him. She is very appealing, she is beyond making a decision*) Let me make it easier for you. I can see you have a sensitivity in this particular area. To me, that room is merely a room, but to you it is obviously much more. Well, in spite of that disadvantage, I'll take it.

WOMAN   Disadvantage?

MAN   Oh, yes, it's not everyone who would want to take up residence in a departed husband's room.

WOMAN   Departed?

MAN   It's my variation on your "passed away."
(*He smiles at her*)

WOMAN   I see.
(*In spite of herself, she is amused*)

MAN   Oh, yes, many a man would be put off, and I can also see a very good case for you preferring a lady lodger.

WOMAN   A what?

MAN   Certainly. A lady lodger in preference to a Gentleman Paying Guest. Very desirable, you could do your mending together and lend each other head scarves.

WOMAN   Oh, no, I couldn't. I wouldn't have that. I couldn't have stockings and things in that room.

MAN (*Amused*)   And things?

WOMAN   Oh, no, I'm afraid that wouldn't do at all. George would hate it. He didn't really approve of women being the way they are anyway. Of course, he accepted it, but he didn't like it. It upsets him.

MAN   At the risk of again being crude, isn't he now beyond being upset?

WOMAN (*Sniffily*)   I have my memories.

MAN (*Returning to the settee and sitting*)   Yes, a man who didn't approve of femininity but, when pressed, reluctantly accepted it. A man who kept a room to himself, and occasionally—when you were a good girl—let you, on formal invitation, enter his holy of holies.

WOMAN   I don't like your tone.

MAN   I'm only telling you what you've told me. You are my sole source of information.

WOMAN   Well, it doesn't sound right the way you tell it.

MAN   That's unfortunate, but that was the impression you gave me.

WOMAN   Well, you've got it wrong, all wrong.

MAN   All? Oh, surely not.

WOMAN   Well, some of it's right, but only the facts.

MAN (*With a grin*)   Oh, only the facts. I see.

WOMAN (*Defiantly*)   Yes, only the facts. There's a lot more to it than facts. It all depends on what you're looking for in a marriage.

MAN   I suppose it does.

WOMAN   I respected George and I must say he respected me. He had his little ways—well, I'm not saying I didn't have mine. We all do—but sometimes respect is more important than lust.

MAN (*Astonished*)   What did you say?

WOMAN (*Completely unaware of what she has said*)   I said, sometimes respect is more important than love.

MAN   You didn't say that, you know.

WOMAN   Of course I did.

MAN   Do you believe you did?

WOMAN   George was always saying it.

MAN   I bet he was.

WOMAN   It was one of his favorites.

MAN   Lust, you said lust.

WOMAN   Don't be silly, I've never said lust in my life. I wouldn't dream of saying it. Lust is common, love is nice.

(*The* MAN *shakes his head sadly*)

MAN   How long has your husband actually been dead?

WOMAN   Nearly a year.

MAN   And you've been alone here in this house ever since?

WOMAN   Of course.

MAN   Don't you have any friends?

WOMAN   My father moved to Worthing.

MAN   I mean friends—girl friends, men friends of your own age.

WOMAN   Oh, I don't have any of those—well, with George being older, we didn't know many married couples and all my old girl friends have got young families and that.

MAN   A dog?

WOMAN   What?

MAN   Maybe a dog or a budgie?

WOMAN   George didn't believe in pets.

MAN   So you just stay here all the time. Why don't you go away on a holiday?

WOMAN   Where to?

MAN   Anywhere. You could go anywhere.

WOMAN   Oh, I don't think I could.

MAN   Of course you could.

WOMAN   I don't think I'd care for that.

MAN   How do you know until you've tried?

WOMAN   I wouldn't like to leave the house alone.

MAN (*Rising*)   Look, I don't know you. This is the first time we've met, but I'm going to tell you something. You are a fine looking woman. (*She looks away from him. Sitting on the arm of the settee*) No, listen, it's imporant. I told you, you're attractive, you're good to look at, and it seems to me you should be out enjoying yourself. It's your time, you're free, you've got enough to live on, and there's a lot of fun to be had. What I don't understand is how you can just sit and waste yourself.

WOMAN   You shouldn't talk to me like that.

MAN   Oh, I'm beyond that sort of consideration. I'm going to take a chance on you and tell you a few things because you stand in need of telling.

WOMAN (*Rising*) Why are you talking to me like this?

MAN Probably because *I* like women. I approve of them and whenever I see a pretty woman walking down a street, all jiggle and sway, I feel like giving her a twenty-gun salute. I'm all for the way they are. I don't just accept them, I'm in there encouraging them. I'm on their side. I'm delighted to be Adam's heir. Women may upset me, but the feeling's delicious.

WOMAN Oh.

MAN And another thing, I find being in the same room as you just great. I'd never make any special arrangements about any room I had, you could come and go as you pleased. You see, I don't tire easily, and I'm not afraid of women. Oh, I admit you've got prettier hands and prettier legs than me and you wear softer clothes on your softer bodies. Well, oddly enough, I'm all for it.

WOMAN I don't think you've any call to talk to me like that.

MAN Time somebody did.

WOMAN (*Moving away*) Oh, it's all very well where you come from, but up here—well—really!

MAN (*Rising*) I can't be persuaded that people are that different in any particular region, and any honest man would feel the same as I do, after being exposed to your presence for the same amount of time.

WOMAN Well, I don't know about men.

MAN It's a pity, because you were made for men, and I mean that as a compliment. You disturb.

WOMAN George said that.

MAN I know he did.

WOMAN How do you know?

MAN Masculine intuition—and while we're on the subject of George, you were going to tell me about your arrangements— how you got to go into George's room.

WOMAN Stop calling him George. You've no right.

MAN I'm sorry, but that's how I've come to think of him.

WOMAN (*Moving round the armchair*) Oh, he wouldn't like that.

MAN (*Turning to her*) I'll take it up with him at a later date, but right now, are you going to tell me about "the arrangements," or not?

WOMAN Well, I did say I would.

MAN That you did.

WOMAN And I ought to keep my word.

MAN It's imperative.

WOMAN   Well, how can I put it—don't look at me—don't look at me while I'm talking.

MAN (*Turning his face away*)   Is that better?

WOMAN   Yes, that's better. (*She sits in the armchair*) Well, in the beginning, when we were first married—I was only nineteen then—we kissed and messed about all the time.

MAN   Messed about?

WOMAN   You know, kissed and cuddled a lot, but gradually George explained to me he needed his energies for more important things. (*The* MAN *sits on the settee, turned away from her. The* WOMAN *speaks as if repeating a lesson, hard learned*) He had a lot of responsibilities, and all the rest was foolishness, and I was being silly. You see, it was my fault. I was the one who wanted it, so he moved into that room and I used to go in there on Fridays to collect my housekeeping money. I'd wait outside until he called me. I wasn't to move or fidget, just wait until he called. Mind, I had to behave myself when I got in, none of my nonsense or I'd be sent packing until I'd come to my senses. Then I'd go in and sign for it.

MAN   Sign for it?

WOMAN   Oh, yes, George was very methodical. He kept records. Well, he may have been right, but I hated that room.

MAN   Is that why you want to rent the room?

WOMAN (*Appealing to him for help*)   I do and I don't.

MAN (*Turning to her*)   You want to, but you're still afraid of the room?

WOMAN   Yes.

MAN (*Rising*)   Well, I'm taking that room and I'm moving in on Tuesday. It might work out but then again it mightn't, but one thing I am sure about, I'm going to move that divan and all the rest of the furniture. I'm going to make it my room, and when you feel like coming in there you can come and fidget till you're blue in the face. (*The* WOMAN *giggles*) I mean it. Come in there with me now.

   (*The* WOMAN *is frightened now*)

WOMAN   No.

MAN   I want you to.

WOMAN (*Rising*)   I couldn't.

MAN   I'll be with you.

WOMAN   But I don't know you, not really.

MAN   Yes, you do, you know me. I'm all right. I'm on your side and I want you to come into that room and teach it a lesson. (*The* WOMAN *smiles in spite of herself*) You see, it's a joke, it's funny, and you can't be afraid of a joke, can you?

WOMAN I suppose not.

MAN Come on. (*He offers her his hand. The* WOMAN *takes his hand reluctanly. He starts gently to pull her toward the door of the room. He opens the door; she pulls back*) It's a joke, only a joke.

> (*The* MAN *laughs, and the* WOMAN *also laughs, nervously. He puts his free arm around her waist and together they go into the room*)

Curtain

Noon

from *Morning, Noon and Night*

B Y

Terrence McNally

Terrence McNally

Few of his colleagues would contest the fact that Terrence McNally was one of the most reviewed (and acclaimed) young dramatists of the 1968–69 New York theatre season. Six of his short plays were produced on Manhattan stages during the period, including *Next* (paired with Elaine May's *Adaptation*), a leading off-Broadway success at the Greenwich Mews Theatre; the double bill, *Sweet Eros* and *Witness,* at the Gramercy Arts; *Cuba Si!* with Viveca Lindfors, at the Theatre de Lys; *Tour,* a highlight of *Collision Course,* at the Café au Go Go; and *Noon,* included in the tripartite *Morning, Noon and Night,* at Henry Miller's Theatre. As if this were not quite enough, the author also enjoyed wide praise for his 1968 television production, *Apple Pie.*

The opening of *Noon* summoned up a good deal of praise for Mr. McNally. Clive Barnes of the *New York Times* termed him "A superb comic writer," while Richard Watts, Jr., of the New York *Post* wrote: "The triumph of the evening belongs to Terrence McNally . . . with his *Noon* episode he comes through with a brilliant interlude that is fresh, imaginative, genuinely hilarious and quite astonishingly charming, of all things."

The author was raised in Corpus Christi, Texas, and came to New York to attend Columbia University. A full-scholarship student, he graduated in 1950 with honors and a Henry Evans Traveling Fellowship for creative writing. In 1962 he won the Stanley Award for the best original play at the New York City Writer's Convention, Wagner College, Staten Island.

On March 20, 1963, Mr. McNally made his Broadway debut as playwright with a new adaptation of *The Lady of the Camellias,* designed and directed by Franco Zeffirelli. Two years later, the author again was represented on Broadway, this time with an original work that had had its premiere (1964) at the Tyrone Guthrie Theatre, Minneapolis—*And Things That Go Bump in the Night.* The New York presentation (1965) was directed by Michael Cacoyannis and starred Eileen Heckart.

Sweet Eros, Next, and Other Plays, a collection of Terrence Mc-Nally's short plays, was published earlier this year. His *Bringing It All Back Home* (included in this editor's volume of *The Best Short Plays 1969*) is scheduled for production in 1969 at the Café La Mama, Manhattan's renowned coffeehouse-theatre club.

Morning, Noon and Night was first presented on November 28, 1968, by Circle in the Square on Broadway: Theodore Mann, Paul Libin and Gillian Walker; at Henry Miller's Theatre, New York City. The cast of *Noon* was as follows:

(In order of appearance)

KERRY	John Heffernan
ASHER	Robert Klein
ALLEGRA	Jane Marla Robbins
BERYL	Charlotte Rae
CECIL	Sorrell Booke

Directed by THEODORE MANN
Scenery and Costumes by MICHAEL ANNALS
Lighting by MARTIN ARONSTEIN

NOON

While the house lights are still up, we hear a phone ringing—ringing and ringing and ringing. Endlessly. Just when the play is about to begin, the person on the other end gives up and the ringing stops.

We are in a large room, maybe a loft, no furniture, perhaps a few crates to sit on if necessary.

KERRY, *in his early thirties, medium build, pleasantly outgoing, enters. He carries a flight bag. He's out of breath from climbing stairs.*

KERRY   Christ! oyve! and mamma mia! (*Catches his breath*) Somebody ought to report this place to the Red Cross. *Whoof!* I thought there were laws about this sort of thing. I mean this beats Mexico City. Dear God! My heart! (*Calls*) Hello! I'm here. You said after twelve and . . . (*Looks at his watch*) well, you know what the early bird catches! (*Pause*) Hey? Anybody home? Dale? (*BONG. BONG. Enormously loud tolling sounds as a clock somewhere nearby begins to tell the hour. BONG. BONG. BONG.*) *Ow!* (*Covers his ears. The clock continues to toll.* ASHER, *in his early twenties, tall, thin and nervous, will come up the stairs and into the room during the following. He is carrying several books. It is impossible to talk over the tolling, but* KERRY *tries to get a word in whenever he can*) I thought Big Ben was in London! (*BONG. BONG*) I'll be with you in a minute! (*BONG. BONG*) The door was open! (*BONG*) I took the liberty! (*BONG*) I hope you don't mind! (*BONG*) I SAID THE DOOR WAS OPEN, AND I TOOK THE LIBERTY OF JUST WALKING IN! (*The clock has stopped tolling*) Hey, friend, you got the time?
    (*He laughs*)

ASHER (*He looks at his wrist watch*)   It's just noon.

KERRY   No kidding! (*Shaking hands*) Hi. I'm Kerry.

ASHER   Hello.

KERRY   Nice place you got. All you need is a ski lift and earplugs. Did you check for nose bleed?

ASHER   This isn't my place.

KERRY   You don't live here?

ASHER   No.

KERRY   Good! I can stop feeling sorry for you. And if I didn't have to worry about getting my tail back down, I could even stop feeling sorry for me.

ASHER   Oh. The stairs. Yes. They're really something.

KERRY   I don't have to ask if you do this often. You'd be up on manslaughter charges. (*Reading from an imaginary headline*) "Large numbers have heart attacks climbing stairs. Dale is charged."

    (*He laughs*)

ASHER   It's quite a climb, all right.

KERRY   Just out of curiosity, what was wrong with your place?

ASHER   Hunh?

KERRY   Your place. What's wrong with there?

ASHER   Nothing.

KERRY   Got a roommate, hunh? Me too. She's a bitch about things like this. Come to think of it, she's a bitch, period.

ASHER   I don't have a roommate.

KERRY   No?

ASHER   I mean a lover.

KERRY   Oh.

ASHER   Mistress is what I'm trying to say!

KERRY   Then you're married?

ASHER   Me?

KERRY   You keep a very large dog then?

ASHER   What dog?

KERRY   Yon can't be *that* ashamed of your place . . .

ASHER   I'm not.

KERRY   You *do* have a place, don't you?

ASHER   Well, sure.

KERRY   'Cause I'd sure as hell love to know what was wrong with it. If it's any worse than this, you ought to write your congressman. How are you fixed for time?

ASHER   Fine.

KERRY   I'm supposed to be on a business lunch. (*Sits on a crate*) Dale what?

ASHER   Hunh?

KERRY   Not that it really matters, but anyway, Dale what?

ASHER   Dale what?

KERRY   You. Your last name.

ASHER   I'm not Dale.

KERRY   I thought you said Dale.

ASHER   No, it's Asher.

KERRY   On the phone it sounded like Dale.

ASHER   What phone?

KERRY   My phone. Your phone. Last night.

ASHER   I think you're confusing me with someone else. My name's
Asher.

KERRY   (*Shaking hands*)   Hi, Asher. I'm still Kerry.

ASHER   Hello.

KERRY   Do we start all over again?

ASHER   This isn't my place.

KERRY   I think we've pretty well established that.

ASHER   I'm supposed to be meeting someone here.

KERRY   No kidding?

ASHER   Hunh?

KERRY   After all those stairs, it figures you're meeting *someone* up
here. Unless you're some kind of calf-nut.

ASHER   What?

KERRY   (*Slapping at his leg*)   Calf-nut. Here! Leg muscles.

ASHER   No. Not especially.

KERRY   Me either. I'm a chest-and-biceps man. You work out?

ASHER   In a gym? No.

KERRY   At home? You know, those Royal Canadian Air Force exercises really work. I took an inch off here with isometrics.

ASHER   I don't work out anywhere.

KERRY   How come?

ASHER   I . . . just . . . don't.

KERRY   You should.

ASHER   I know.

KERRY   You look like you work out.

ASHER   Thank you.

KERRY   You look like you work out a lot.

ASHER   (*Beet red by now*)   They said right after twelve.

KERRY   You're right on time. (*Loosening a few buttons*) It's hot up
here.

ASHER   I know.

KERRY   Take your jacket off.

ASHER   I know I'm right on time!

NOON

KERRY   We both are.

ASHER   It's my problem. I'm never late for anything. Everybody else always is and I'm always waiting. Sometimes I think I'm the only person in the world who thinks right after twelve means right after twelve. God knows, girls never do. They're always late. I have a theory why.

KERRY   I like your trousers.

ASHER   Hunh?

KERRY   Your pants. They're nice.

ASHER   Oh.

KERRY   They're a good fit. Nice and snug on you.

ASHER   They're just off the rack.

KERRY   It's a nice fabric, too.

ASHER   I guess.

KERRY   Lightweight.

ASHER   They're just summer pants.

KERRY   Clinging, though.

ASHER   What?

KERRY   Clinging. It's a good clinging fabric.

ASHER   They shrunk a little.

KERRY   (*Shaking his head*)   Then they'd just be tight. No, yours cling.

ASHER   They're just pants.

KERRY   Well, I'd sure as hell love to get my hands on a pair like yours.

ASHER   Ordinary summer pants. They sell them anywhere.

KERRY   Not with that clinging quality.

ASHER   Sears and Roebuck.

KERRY   (*Still shaking his head*)   Your usual lightweight summer trousers don't give you support like that. Not anymore.

ASHER   What?

KERRY   Support. Here. Keep the whang from waggling. It's a problem.

ASHER   (*Taking off the jacket*)   You're right.

KERRY   You hang out all over the place, too?

ASHER   It's hot up here! (*Suddenly*) Can I ask you something?

KERRY   Sure.

ASHER   Are you—

KERRY   (*At once*)   Unh-hunh!

ASHER   . . . Are you meeting someone named Dale too?

KERRY   (*Momentarily deflated*)   Oh, I *thought* I was meeting someone named Dale. Why?

ASHER   I think we both are.

KERRY   Dale gets around.

ASHER   Do you know Dale?

KERRY   No. Do you?

ASHER   No.

KERRY   Does it matter?

ASHER   I guess not.

KERRY   'Cause any friend of Dale's is a friend of mine.

ASHER   You just said you didn't know Dale.

KERRY   All right, screw Dale!

ASHER   That's what I had in mind.

KERRY   Ditto! (*Pause.* ASHER *paces*) I guess you don't even need shorts with trousers like that.

ASHER   Shorts?

KERRY   Underwear. B.V.D.'s. Skivvies.

ASHER   Sure you do.

KERRY   Well, whatever you've got on under there, they're doing a fantastic job.

ASHER   What?

KERRY   Of keeping you in place.

ASHER   Oh.

KERRY   Are they boxers?

ASHER   What?

KERRY   Are you wearing boxer-type shorts or jockeys?

ASHER   Jockey. Boxer. The baggy-type ones!

KERRY   (*Solemn agreement*) Yeah, they give you more mobility. Now your jockeys are more for support. It's a real choice. I switch back and forth myself.

ASHER   (*Trying to change the subject*) Do you know Dale the way I know Dale?

KERRY   (*Not really letting him*) I thought we'd just agreed that neither of us had had the pleasure. Yours, of course, are as fantastic as your trousers.

ASHER   My what are fantastic!

KERRY   Your shorts. It doesn't look like you're wearing any and that's the whole secret, of course.

ASHER   I mean, did you put one of those ads in one of those papers and someone named Dale answered?

KERRY   What do you think?

ASHER   Maybe one of us ought to leave.

KERRY   I don't follow.

ASHER   Well, you were here first. I mean, it might be awkward, three of us.

KERRY   That depends on Dale, wouldn't you think?

ASHER   You see, I hadn't planned on an . . . (*Almost swallowing the word*) an orgy.

KERRY   Do you mind if I ask what make they are?

ASHER   Make?

KERRY   Your fabulous undershorts. What brand are they?

ASHER   I couldn't tell you, I'm sure.

KERRY   Where'd you pick them up, then?

ASHER   I don't remember.

KERRY   A men's specialty store?

ASHER   I wouldn't think so.

KERRY   Because if they're from a men's specialty store, they're probably a French or German import. The French are fantastic with men's underwear. The work with nylon has been extraordinary.

ASHER   I'm sure these are just Fruit of the Loom.

KERRY   Oh.

ASHER   Or something like that!

KERRY   I bet not, though.

ASHER   I don't think I've ever been in a men's specialty store.

KERRY   You probably have and didn't know it. They're popping up all over the place lately.

ASHER   I don't even know what a men's specialty store is!

KERRY   Do you always pace in little circles?

ASHER   Only when I'm nervous.

KERRY   I'm not making you nervous, am I?

ASHER   No, this does! Even my palms are sweating.

KERRY   What?

ASHER   This. Up here. I've never done it before.

KERRY   Now you're really putting me on.

ASHER   Why? Have you?

KERRY   You couldn't tell?

ASHER   I don't mean sex. Sex doesn't make me nervous. I love sex.

KERRY   Only your palms sweat.

ASHER   Taking an ad to have sex and then some girl answering it makes my palms sweat! I may never do this again. I'm a wreck already!

KERRY   Oh! I thought you were trying to tell me you were a virgin.

ASHER   A virgin! Hah! That's a good one. A virgin! Hah!

KERRY I wouldn't have minded.

ASHER Well I would! A virgin! Jeez! I can't think of anything I'm more definitely not. A virgin. Ha!

KERRY Some people have all the luck.

ASHER Luck?

KERRY Fruit of the Loom and a fit like that!

ASHER I wasn't thinking about that!

KERRY Of course you weren't. Why should you? If I could find summer pants and shorts like that, I wouldn't think about it either. I guess I'll just have to stick with these until something better comes along. Talk about hot! I don't think it's possible to have hotter pants than I do. They've actually steamed up on me! My knees are roasting. And they're tight, too! I mean, here's your real difference between lightweight summer-clinging and plain goddamn tight. I feel like I'm going to burst out of these half the time. Look at the thighs alone. Tight as two sausages in these. And support! I don't even want to go into that. Hell, it's like flying buttresses in here. I'm so supported I could split.

   (*He's standing right in front of* ASHER)

ASHER Why don't you buy bigger pants?

KERRY They're no answer. It's all in the fabric and the kind of shorts.

ASHER Oh.

KERRY No, I'll just bide my time with these until the right fabric and pair of shorts come winging my way.

   (*During the following he will take an air mattress out of his flight bag and begin to inflate it with a pump.* ASHER *will try not to notice*)

ASHER What made you think I was a virgin anyway? Jeez! I kissed my cherry good-bye way back in the eighth grade. Whatever men call it, I lost it. After a hayride around White Rock Lake. It's in Dallas. That's where I grew up. Her name was Mary Beth Page. She was a little tubby, but still she was pretty. And she wasn't any town pump, either. It was her first time, too.

KERRY (*Still pumping*) Are you sure those are Fruit of the Looms?

ASHER I told you I thought so.

KERRY But you're not sure? The only reason I ask is I'd hate to go out and invest in a pair and then get home and find out I wasn't getting the same kind of support.

ASHER I'm pretty sure that's what they are.

KERRY I wish you could be more definite.

ASHER Well, when I get home I suppose I could look and call you, if you want.

KERRY I won't be in.

ASHER Tomorrow then.

KERRY I'm leaving town. I don't know how long I'll be away.

ASHER I'm sorry.

> (KERRY *has finished pumping. The mattress is just lying there now*)

KERRY I don't suppose you'd . . . I know it's an imposition, but I'd really appreciate getting this thing settled for once and for all.

ASHER There's no place to . . . !

KERRY We're just two men.

ASHER What if Dale walked in? I'd look ridiculous.

KERRY (*Explosive*) Got it!

> (*He leaps toward* ASHER)

ASHER Hunh?

KERRY Turn around.

ASHER Turn? . . .

KERRY I can just pull the waistband up and read the label right off.

ASHER (*Pulling his shirt out of his pants*) Well, if it's really that important to you! . . .

KERRY Hey, your shirt's nice, too! What is that? Cotton percale?

ASHER Really, I don't know! Please, hurry up.

KERRY You try reading upside down.

ASHER Fruit of the Loom uses an insignia. A cornucopia, I think.

KERRY A.R.S.? Arse?

ASHER That's my laundry mark!

KERRY You know something? You've got your shorts on backwards. Either that or the brand name's up front.

ASHER Backwards?

KERRY Backwards! I can feel the fly crotch opening.

ASHER My underwear's on backwards?

KERRY (*Laughing*) All these years of looking for the one underwear with the perfect support, and his trick is to wear them backwards! It's incredible!

ASHER I've never put my underwear on backwards in my life!

KERRY You did this morning, God bless you! And I think we've found something. This is it, baby, this is it!

> (*He's turning* ASHER *around*)

ASHER   What are you doing?

KERRY   Front or backwards, I still want to know what make they are.

ASHER   I can do it!

KERRY   Stand still.

ASHER   Really I can!

KERRY   J.C. Penney!

ASHER   That's *like* Fruit of the Loom.

KERRY   J.C. Penny cotton boxers worn backwards! A rank amateur gets his drawers on cockeyed and successfully and single-handedly dynamites every theory of male genital support going. Like I said, it's incredible! (*He's undone* ASHER's *belt, unzipped his fly.* ASHER's *pants drop to his knees*) Shoes.

ASHER   Hey!

KERRY   You can't get your pants off with your shoes on. Dummy!

ASHER   I don't want my pants off!

KERRY   What are you? Some kind of faggot?

ASHER   Faggot?

KERRY   Or are you trying to call me one? For Christ's sake, I just want to see you in your shorts.

ASHER   I know, but ...

KERRY   Guys are guys.

ASHER   Hunh?

KERRY   You're a guy, aren't you?

ASHER   Well of course I am.

KERRY   Be proud of it!

ASHER   I am!

KERRY   You'd never know it.

ASHER (*Half trips, half stumbles out of his pants*)   All right?

KERRY   How can I tell?

ASHER   Hunh?

KERRY   Your shirt.

ASHER   My shirt?

KERRY   It's in the way. I can't see you or your shorts.

ASHER (*Pulls his shirt up*)   Okay?

KERRY   Just take it all the way off, hunh?

ASHER   I ...

KERRY   You're sure acting like a faggot. And a faggot virgin at that.

ASHER   Well, I'm not. Either one!

KERRY   I said you were *acting* like ...

ASHER All right! (*Takes off his shirt*) There. Okay?

KERRY Turn around. Slowly! (*While* ASHER's *back is turned,* KERRY *gathers his clothes and hides them*) Again.

ASHER I feel like a . . . a . . .

KERRY What do you do?

ASHER A model!

KERRY You're a model?

ASHER I feel like a model. I'm a writer.

KERRY Figures.

ASHER Hunh?

KERRY What else do you do?

ASHER What else? . . .

KERRY God, you're exasperating. In bed. What do you do in bed?

ASHER Everything.

(*He's scratching his head, puzzled, looking around for his clothes.* KERRY *is putting a 45 rpm record on his portable phonograph. The music is a Jackie Gleason "Music for Lovers Only"-type selection*)

KERRY Everything?

ASHER You know . . . everything. I'm not inhibited, if that's what you're asking. My ad said it. "Culmination of your most sensuous desires."

KERRY (*Sniffing an amylnitrate capsule*) Keep talking!

ASHER Say, have you seen my? . . . (*Sees* KERRY *sniffing*) What's that?

KERRY "Have poppers." That's what my ad said. (*Long ecstatic moan*) Oooooooooooh!

(*He offers a sniff to* ASHER)

ASHER No, thank you.

KERRY I thought you did everything.

ASHER In bed.

KERRY That's what this is for.

ASHER You mean? . . .

KERRY Gets those colored lights going.

ASHER *Streetcar.*

KERRY Hunh? Now you've got me doing it.

ASHER *A Streetcar Named Desire.* Colored lights going. Tennessee Williams.

KERRY Tennessee Williams uses poppers?

ASHER I wouldn't be surprised at anything Tennessee Williams uses. Did you ever read his plays?

KERRY (*Offering a "popper" again*)   Here. Relax. Fly with me.

ASHER   I guess they're a lot like marijuana and opium and stuff like that?

KERRY   You'll see! You'll see!

ASHER   I don't really approve of drugs . . . *any* artificial stimulus, for that matter . . . but I think a writer has to leave himself open to any new experience. Don't you?

KERRY (*Putting the "popper" in* ASHER's *hand*)   Wide open.

ASHER   Look at George Plimpton! (*Sniffs*) Wow! (*Sniffs again, laughs*) You know something? I don't see my pants. (*Sniffs again*) You know something else? I don't care. (*Sniffs again*) I'm getting a headache. (*Sniffs again*) Hey, it's gone already! (*Reeling happily*) Hoo! Do I feel wild and randy! Randy and wild!

KERRY (*Getting* ASHER *onto the air mattress. It's a job*)   Just lie back. It's going to be beautiful.

ASHER (*Lying down now, eyes closed*)   Where's Dale?

KERRY (*Quickly stripping to flowered bikini shorts*)   "Young gay man, mid-twenties"—that's me, baby—"digs groovy sex with hung horny bisexual guys over eighteen." (*A snore from* ASHER; KERRY *bends over him*) Asher? (ALLEGRA's *voice offstage is heard calling brightly:* "Bonjour!") Shit!

(*He hides quickly as* ALLEGRA, *early twenties, with a nice face and body, taut-nerved, bounds into the room. She seems unaffected by the stairs*)

ALLEGRA   Bonjour! Bonjour! (*Her accent is execrable*) *Je regrette d'être en retard* . . . (sorry to be late!) . . . *le trafic, ça c'est formidable* . . . (the traffic was terrible) . . . but *me voici tout de même* . . . (I'm here all the same!) *Bonjour! Bonjour!* (ASHER *mumbles something in his daze*) *Ne parle pas anglais, mauvais garçon* . . . (bad boy) *Il faut parler français tous les temps* . . . (all the time) . . . *si vous vraiment voulez parler comme un native* . . . (really want to speak like a native). (ASHER *mumbles again*) *Non, non, non et non!* (ASHER *regards her with a glassy stare*) *Je m'appelle Allegra. Allegra* . . . (that's Italian for full of pep!) *J'ai lu votre avertissement* . . . (read your ad) . . . *et je suis allée dehors de ma tête* . . . (went out of my head!) You want French lessons? You're going to get French lessons! *Fou du sexe!* . . . (sex maniac!) (*Moves away from him. His dazed eyes are never off her*) *Première leçon français. Les articles des habits!* . . . (articles of clothing!) I'm double-parked, so we'd better get right to it, *mon élève* . . . (you student, you!) (*Pointing out each article of clothing*) *Voici la blouse. Voici les boutons de la blouse. J'ai un . . .* (*Unbuttoning as she counts them*) *. . . deux . . . trois . . . quatre boutons.* (*Her blouse is open*) *J'enlève ma blouse.* (*Takes off her blouse*) *Voici la jupe. Voici le zipper de la jupe.* (*Unzips her skirt*) *Adieu à la jupe.* (*Steps out of her skirt*) *Voici les nylons.* (*Takes off her stockings, sings the* "*Marseillaise*" *while she does so*) *Patriotique chanson français!* (*Stands in front of* ASHER) *Maintenant je suis presque nue . . .* (*nearly naked*) *. . . mais pas encore . . .* (not yet, brown-eyes). *Je reste dans brassière et panties pour le temps . . .* (I'm keeping these on for a while). *Il faut savoir d'abord . . .* (first) *. . . les parts du corps . . .* (parts of the body . . . yours and mine, long lashes!) (*Comes right next to him*) *La bouche.* (*She kisses him*) *Les cuisses.* (*Hand on his thighs*) *La poitrine.* (*Other hand on his chest*) *Le coq.* (*Points this time*) *Le chat.* (*Points at herself, then laughs wildly*) *Je ne suis pas vraiment nymphomanique . . .* (I'm not really a nympho) *. . . mais . . .* can we drop the French lesson a minute? There's something I really want to tell you. I've never done anything like this in my life. Honest. I've wanted to, but I come from a pretty conservative background. Dull, you'd call it. *Séducteur!* (*Gives him a playful nudge*) But when I read your ad in that paper, it like turned me on. Turned me on? I'm a girl on fire! (*Moving around the room now*) You see, I'm stuck out in Flushing with this creep-liberal-intellectual-lawyer husband, who likes to talk about it all the time, and I'm going out of my mind out there with him and all his damn books. It's his fault I'm here. His and Grove Press. He's a big liberal about all sorts of things, but especially Grove Press. Those books can warp a girl. But try telling him that. "The only obscene word in the English language is the word obscene." Him, Carlton Schapiro, and he's the Oscar Wilde of Greater Flushing! I didn't even want to read them at first. But he was always nagging at me. "They're not dirty," he'd say, "they're not dirty." Fuck him, they're not dirty! I practically had a nervous breakdown over the last one he gave me. *Moist,* it's called. Just *Moist.* It's about an American girl tourist in Spain who ends up on a breeding ranch . . . out there on the pampas, with the bulls she's doing it! . . . but Carlton says it's an allegory. I could just kill him. I mean, he's down at the Civil Liberties Union or the NAACP half the time, and I'm stuck in Flushing reading Grove Press stuff and climbing the walls. I've tried branching out with him. You know, wilder stuff, like I've been reading about. And he says, "What's the matter with you,

Allegra? My mother said you dancers were all sick in the head
and sex maniacs." (I'm a dancer, I guess you noticed.) I said,
"Dancing has nothing to with it, Carlton. It's what I'm reading
in those books." I wish you could have heard him. "That's only in
books. Real people don't do things like that. You're a sensitive,
intelligent girl." I could have slugged him for that crack. I'm so
sick of being a sensitive, intelligent girl after reading Grove
Press, I could spit. I mean, I'm still a nice girl deep down inside,
but I can't be a nice girl twenty-four hours a day. Not after what
I went through last weekend with *Moist.* Your ad saved my life.
You see, Carlton got me started reading those kinds of newspapers, too. I think he subscribes to every one of them. It took
a lot of nerve to call you . . . thank God, you're a stranger, that
makes it okay at least . . . but when I finally got my nerve up and
dialed and then you sounded so . . . well, sexy, just like your ad
. . . I mean like I flipped. (*Pause*) You don't waste much time
chatting a girl up, do you, Dale? It's better you don't talk. I
came here to degrade myself. Treat me bad, Dale, treat me
really bad. (ASHER *is starting to come out of it*) I know. Keep it
in French. "Beginner in French needs female with firm, clean,
shapely body to practice on. No charge for this service. Special
attention given to handicapped girls." That last part is so Grove
Press! I hope these'll do for handicaps.

    (*She starts to remove her bra*)

ASHER (*Fully awake, in horror at what he sees approaching him*)
    Aaaaaaaaaaaaaaaaaaaa!

    (*He runs screaming from the room*)

ALLEGRA Dale? *Merde!*

    (BERYL, *fortyish, handsome, large-boned, has come into the*
    room)

BERYL Thanks for telling us about the stairs!

ALLEGRA The . . . ?

BERYL My husband's having a stroke on one of the goddamn
  landings!

ALLEGRA Your . . . ?

BERYL I told you we'd be bringing equipment!

ALLEGRA Equip—?

BERYL Now get your pink little tuch down there and help him!

ALLEGRA I . . .

BERYL Look, you little chippy, no lip!

ALLEGRA (*Beside herself*) Yes!

    (*She runs out of the room*)

BERYL (*Scowling at the room*) A two-hundred-thousand dollar home in Westchester County with special rooms for this sort of thing and we have to come here! I swear I'm going to divorce that man one day . . . divorce him so fast he won't know what hit him! (*She's seen the phone, dials a number*) Hello, Mrs. Firth? It's me again. I forgot to tell you. Caroline has a dance class at one-thirty. Someone will be by for her, but see that she's got her leotard on this time. (ASHER *has edged back into the room. She sees him*) What are you doing, you little nit? They're on the stairs. Give them a hand!

ASHER Who? . . .

BERYL You heard me! (ASHER *hurries off*) And Mrs. Firth, if the man calls about the pony for Johnny's birthday tomorrow, tell him to have the little beast there at two . . .

(KERRY *has come back into the room. She sees him*)

KERRY Hello.

BERYL Well don't just stand there, newt! They need you.

KERRY Who?

BERYL Them. On the stairs. Now go to it!

KERRY Yes, ma'am.

(*He hurries out*)

BERYL Is the baby sleeping? . . . Well, tell the nanny she *can't* go on strike! I swear, Mrs. Firth, I swear, being a suburban mother is even harder than being a city one . . . I appreciate your solicitude. It's what we're paying you for! (*Hangs up*) God, God, God. What's to become of us all? (ALLEGRA *has returned. She is struggling with a large trunk*) How is he?

ALLEGRA Fine, I guess.

BERYL You guess, you little tramp?

ALLEGRA I offered to help him and he beat me off with his cane.

BERYL And you loved it! He's a forceful man, my husband. Over there! (ALLEGRA *drops the trunk; crashing metallic sounds*) You'll pay for that, my pet.

ALLEGRA I'll? . . .

BERYL Not so fast! You'll have to wait for it. Beg.

ALLEGRA Hunh?

BERYL I'll have my martini. Eight-to-one. With a twist.

ALLEGRA Your martini?

BERYL You thought that was a purse, didn't you, you silly bitch?

ALLEGRA It looks like a purse.

BERYL Of course it looks like a purse! It's a portable bar. They're

the rage in Westchester. Now hop to it. (*While* ALLEGRA *mixes*)
Pretty deplorable diggings, if you ask me.

ALLEGRA   You know something?

BERYL   I don't remember addressing you, whore.

ALLEGRA   You're pretty forceful yourself.

BERYL   Thank you.

ALLEGRA   I mean, I don't even know you and you've got me waiting on you hand and foot. That plus the insults.

BERYL   The fault, my dear Dale, is in your nature. Yours is a submissive one.

ALLEGRA   I'm not Dale. My name is Allegra.

BERYL   But you're willing to serve. Submission and discipline,
that's the ticket! (*Toasting with her martini*) Discipline and
submission! (*Spits it out*) I said eight-to-one, you jelly-slimed
harlot! You left baggage, you painted tart! You bloated lymph
node, you raven-trussed hussy!

ALLEGRA   Tressed. You mean raven-tressed.

BERYL   Silence, bitch, when I'm reviling you!

ALLEGRA   Oh, now really, Beryl!

BERYL   Beryl?

ALLEGRA   It's what they call you, isn't it?

BERYL   You dare use my name?

ALLEGRA   It's stenciled right on the bag. Beryl and Cecil.

BERYL   I'll blind you first! With white-hot tongs. Pluck those eyes
from your head with pincers.

ALLEGRA   If you're not careful, you're going to hit someone with
that riding crop.

BERYL   You! You!

ALLEGRA   I wouldn't recommend that. I know karate.

BERYL   Bravo! I love a slave with spunk.

ALLEGRA   I'm very good at it, in fact.

BERYL   Cecil should be here for this.

ALLEGRA   I'm a black belt!

BERYL   He adores black belts!

ALLEGRA   I'm warning you!

> (*They struggle, but it's more like shadowboxing. No real
> contact is made.* BERYL *flailing at the air with her riding
> crop;* ALLEGRA *warding her off with a few karate chops*)

BERYL (*Huffing*)   Don't *try* so hard! I'm not a teeny-bopper!

ALLEGRA   You started it!

BERYL   I'm just trying to turn you on.

ALLEGRA   With a riding crop?

BERYL   Our ad *specified.*

ALLEGRA   What ad?

BERYL   The one you answered!

ALLEGRA   I'm here for French lessons!

> (CECIL *has entered the room in a sedan chair borne by* KERRY *and* ASHER. *He's just in time to see* BERYL *lunge at* ALLEGRA, *only to trip and fall instead*)

CECIL   Seize that woman! (ASHER *lets his end of the chair drop, spilling* CECIL *onto the floor*) Unh!

> (ASHER *has taken* BERYL*'s arm and is helping her up*)

BERYL   Not me, you idiot! Not the queen. Her!

ALLEGRA   (*To* ASHER)   Where have you been? I told you I was double-parked!

ASHER   Hunh?

BERYL   (*Deflated, to* ALLEGRA)   You didn't have to take *all* the fun out of it!

KERRY   (*Attending to* CECIL)   Mister! Hey, mister! (*To* BERYL) Hey, lady, is this your husband?

BERYL   Well, he's not my *lover!*

KERRY   He's blacked out.

BERYL   Of course he has! He does this to me all the time. Can't wait till he gets there, and then I'm the one with egg on her face.

> (*She joins* KERRY *and* CECIL)

ALLEGRA   (*To* ASHER)   I wish you'd told me how many people would be here.

ASHER   I wish you had.

ALLEGRA   Hunh?

ASHER   Is your name Dale?

ALLEGRA   Isn't yours?

ASHER   I'm Asher.

ALLEGRA   I'm Allegra.

ASHER   Who's Dale?

ALLEGRA   That's Beryl and he's Cecil.

ASHER   And he's Kerry.

ALLEGRA   Oh, dear.

> (*They are both suddenly aware of their lack of clothes, but there's not much they can do about it gracefully*)

BERYL   Cecil, wake up, Cecil! You're causing a scene.

KERRY   He's out like a light.

BERYL   You're making a fool of yourself, Cecil, in front of *them!*

KERRY   Wait! I think he's . . .

BERYL   Nobody obeys *fainting nellies,* Cecil!

KERRY   Yes! He's coming around!

CECIL (*Opens eyes, looks around, gets to his feet, everyone in the room is watching him. He speaks with a German accent*)　All stripped down, are we?

BERYL　That's my Cecil!

ASHER　Well, you see, I—

CECIL　All stripped down and ready to have a go at it, were we? (*He's methodically tearing his clothes off. Underneath he's wearing black leather underwear and high leather boots*)

BERYL　They were, Cecil, they were! I caught them at it!

ALLEGRA　I only—

CECIL　All stripped down and ready to have a go at it without waiting for Cecil and Beryl, were we? Were we?

BERYL　Punish them, Cecil, punish them!

CECIL　Swine! Pigs! Dogs!
(*He blacks out again*)

ALLEGRA　What was that all about?

ASHER　Is he mad at someone?

BERYL　I'm terribly sorry. What can I say? You said right after twelve . . . we show up half an hour late . . . the traffic was unbelievable, it gets worse all the time . . . and now this. I'm sorry and that's the long and the short of it. Shall we get started? He'll wake up. (*She has started to undress*) I'm delighted there's more than one of you. Of course it was naughty of you not to mention it. One of you will pay for that. By the way, I'm Beryl. Which one of you is Dale?

ALLEGRA　What unusual lingerie!

BERYL　It's lizard, you tacky trollop!

ASHER　Hey, now just a minute!

BERYL　Shut up, slime!

KERRY　Who the hell do you think you are?

BERYL　You, too, you little blob! Now which one of you is Dale?

ALLEGRA　None of us is.

BERYL (*Thrown*)　You're joking. You must be joking.

ALLEGRA　I'm Allegra.

ASHER　I'm Asher.

KERRY　I'm Kerry.

BERYL　Oh, God.

ALLEGRA　I think you owe us all an apology.

BERYL (*In great and sudden panic*)　Cecil! Wake up, Cecil! We're in the wrong place!

CECIL (*Responding*)　Our subject for today is leather.

BERYL (*Mortified*)　Cecil, please, they can hear you!

CECIL (*Starting to rave*) What is leather? What are its origins? Its uses?

ASHER I know!

BERYL Must you humor him? Can't you see he's a sick man? (*Urgent, to* CECIL) It's the wrong place, Cecil!

CECIL (*Shaking her off, moving about the room*) Why is leather the symbol of intellectual genius?

ASHER I never heard that before.

BERYL I could just die, I'm so embarrassed. Cecil, sshh!

ASHER (*To* ALLEGRA *and* KERRY) I'm a writer. It seems to me I would have heard about leather being a symbol of genius.

CECIL (*Railing at them*) All the great geniuses have belonged to the leather cult!

ASHER I can't think of one.

CECIL Goethe, Schiller, Beethoven, Thomas Mann!

ASHER All Germans.

CECIL And all leatherists! What do you think Goethe was wearing when he wrote his *Faust?* Cotton? Was Schiller in silk when he created his masterpieces? Would the world have Beethoven's nine symphonies had he been wearing satin? Can you mention Thomas Mann and wool in the same breath? You cannot!

ASHER What about Mozart?

CECIL (*Apoplectic*) Mozart! Mozart was Austrian, you *Dumm-kopf!* All great art is German, and German art is leather!

KERRY Leather?

CECIL Leather! Leather, I tell you!

ALLEGRA (*To* ASHER) I like Mozart, too.

CECIL Beryl, Beryl, who are these people? Must they be disciplined like all the others? *Ach, Mein Herz* is heavy!
     (*He's getting a whip out of the trunk*)

BERYL If you'd just listen to me!

CECIL Speak, *Liebchen*, speak.

BERYL I've been trying to! We're in the wrong place.

CECIL (*Stunned*) What do you mean? . . . the wrong place? . . .

BERYL They're not our kind of people.

CECIL Not our kind? . . .

BERYL Just look at them.

CECIL (*As if transformed; all trace of German accent vanishing*) Well . . . hello there . . . I guess I got a little carried away just then . . . hah, hah, hah! . . . Cecil's the name . . . you're right, it's warm up here. Kind of makes you delirious . . . well, I guess the missus and I better shove off now . . . the kids'll be wanting their

supper . . . hah, hah, hah! . . . Whew! Sure is warm! . . . Hell of
a day for a ballgame!

BERYL   Cecil has these little attacks, you see.

CECIL   Never know when they're gonna hit me.

BERYL   It could be anywhere.

CECIL   Let's face it, I'm a dying man.

BERYL   We certainly hope we haven't inconvenienced you . . .
interrupted anything . . . barging in like this.

CECIL   I told Beryl it didn't look like the place. Hah, hah, hah!
(*Awkward silence*)

KERRY   May I say something?

BERYL   I wish somebody would.

KERRY   I think we should all put our cards on the table.

BERYL   Stop pussyfooting?

KERRY   Exactly. Now we all came here expecting to meet someone
named Dale. Right? (*Embarrassed assents, much head-hanging*)
Right after twelve, he said.

ASHER   *She*. It was a she.

KERRY   I don't think that matters much at this point.

ASHER   To me it does.

KERRY   The fact is, this Dale person called all of us, conveniently
forgetting to mention he-or-she had spoken to the others.

CECIL   When we saw the three of you, naturally we thought . . .
hah, hah, hah!

BERYL   Cecil, please!

KERRY   And now Dale doesn't show.

ASHER   (*Looking at his watch*)   It's still only . . . I mean, maybe
he . . . *she's* still on her way.

KERRY   Not very likely.

CECIL   Do you suppose? . . . No, it couldn't possibly.

BERYL   What?

CECIL   Right after twelve meant right after midnight?

BERYL   Don't be ridiculous.

ASHER   It is the more usual time for it.

ALLEGRA   It?

ASHER   (*Gulping*)   You know!

KERRY   I think it's a pretty safe assumption someone's played a
trick on us.

BERYL   No!

KERRY   I'm afraid so.

BERYL   What kind of sick mind would do a thing like that?

ASHER   It takes all kinds of people to make up a world!

BERYL   But what kind of perverted, twisted, warped, maimed, mutilated mind would play a joke like that?

CECIL (*Shaking his head*)   I don't know, I don't know what people are coming to any more.

ALLEGRA   What a spooky weirdo this Dale must be!

ASHER   And noon's such an inconvenient time for . . . I mean, people are busy at noon! I had a deadline with my publisher. I write textbooks.

ALLEGRA   What about me, all the way in from Flushing?

BERYL   We drove in from Westchester in this heat and traffic!

KERRY   Listen, I don't know if I still have a job when I get back.

CECIL   Morning, noon or night, wild horses couldn't drag me up here again.

KERRY   All right then, let's put the *rest* of our cards on the table. Since we're all here . . . and at no little inconvenience . . . I suggest we try working something out.

CECIL (*Brightening at the prospect*)   You mean? . . .

KERRY   I mean!

CECIL   What do you think, honey?

BERYL (*Weighing it*)   Well . . .

KERRY (*Persuasive*)   After all, we did all come here for the same thing. Hell, we even advertised, we wanted it so bad.

ALLEGRA   I beg your pardon! I answered an ad. I never took one. There's a big difference!

KERRY   Really? What?

ASHER   Are you people talking about an . . . (*Gulping on the word again*) orgy?

BERYL (*Becoming convinced*)   I hate to see an afternoon wasted.

CECIL (*Agreeing*)   I had work, too. I mean I'm not exactly unemployed, you know.

KERRY   Asher?

ASHER (*Bluff bravado*)   Sure, sure! Why the hell not?

KERRY   You, Allegra?

ALLEGRA   It's certainly worth a try. Even if you're not Dale, you're both kind of sexy. I mean we could . . . wow!

ASHER   Don't talk like that.

ALLEGRA   What's wrong with you?

ASHER   Nice girls don't say things like that.

ALLEGRA   Wait a minute! Are you that "sensitive writer, Harvard Ph.D., who's seeking a grownup girl to share wonderful conversation and Bach," who's been advertising like mad lately?

ASHER   It's a Columbia Ph.D., actually.

ALLEGRA That's the creep!

ASHER What's wrong with that?

ALLEGRA Give Carlton a toot on the phone next time. You two were made for each other. (*To* KERRY) I guess that makes it us. What do you say? *Qu'est ce que vous dites?*

KERRY (*Nodding toward* ASHER) I want him, actually.

ALLEGRA Him?

KERRY He turns me on, what can I tell you?

ALLEGRA *Ecch!*

BERYL Tolerance, dear, a little tolerance for God's creatures.

ASHER *You* were the queer!

KERRY Elementary, my dear Watson.

ASHER You could have fooled me!

KERRY Well? What do you say?

ASHER You mean? . . . Of course not!

KERRY It doesn't exactly hurt, you know.

ASHER I said no!

KERRY Come to think of it, you're not masculine enough.

ASHER (*Aghast*) Not . . . masculine enough!

KERRY (*Appraising* CECIL *now*) I like a man with balls in his voice, hair on his chest . . .

ASHER (*To* ALLEGRA) I've got hair on my chest.

ALLEGRA Drop dead!

KERRY A guy with nice musky male smells.

CECIL (*So affably*) You see this fist, fruit?

KERRY (*Smiling at him*) It was worth a try, wasn't it?
(*They laugh and shake hands*)

BERYL Cecil?

CECIL (*For both of them*) "Extremely attractive Westchester couple—

BERYL (*He's left a word out*) White!

CECIL ". . . both of dominant nature, seek couples and singles who would enjoy serving as our slave—"

BERYL Any combination of you would do.

CECIL "Must be of submissive nature and be willing to serve."
(*A pause*)

BERYL (*Still hopeful*) Discretion assured!

ALLEGRA I've read *The Story of O*, thank you.

BERYL And didn't you like it?

ALLEGRA I thought it was funny.

BERYL Funny? Funny!

KERRY You don't go my route, I don't go yours.

CECIL   I think we've . . . as the saying has it . . . bombed out, Beryl.

KERRY   (*His turn to be affable*)   I'm sorry, but I specifically stated no disciplinarians.

ASHER   (*Dawning on him*)   I know what that means. Oh, gosh. Oh, gosh!

BERYL   (*Trying to figure something out*)   Maybe if we . . . you and she could . . . no! Cecil and him . . . and then . . . *no.*

CECIL   (*Eagerly*)   What, Beryl?

BERYL   Nothing. Just a wild thought.

ASHER   (*To no one in particular*)   All I want is a sensitive girl I can relate to. What's so unusual about that?

ALLEGRA   (*A voice in the wilderness*)   Fucking, anyone?

KERRY   (*After a beat*)   Well, *that* . . . as the other saying has it , . . would seem to be *that.*

BERYL   And I'm getting dressed.

ALLEGRA   I think we'd all better.

ASHER   I've had it with advertising. I'm going back to hanging around the Village. NYU's down there.

KERRY   The next time I meet anyone, it's going to be at my place.

ALLEGRA   I'm so mad I could spit.

CECIL   Can we give anyone a lift?

ASHER   Do you go up the West Side?

BERYL   My dear, we stay as far away from the West Side as we possibly can.

(*Ring. The telephone. Everybody freezes*)

ASHER   Hey, the phone's ringing.

(*Ring*)

CECIL   Did you tell Mrs. Firth where we'd be?

(*Ring*)

KERRY   It's not for me.

(*Ring*)

BERYL   Don't move anybody. Just stay put.

(*Ring. Ring. Ring*)

ALLEGRA   Maybe it's Dale.

BERYL   Oh, my God! Quick! (*They race for the phone.* BERYL *gets it*) Hello . . . who is *this?* (*To the others*) It's Dale! It's Dale! (*They gather around her*) Yes, this is Beryl . . . my husband? He's right beside me . . . (*To* CECIL) he said hello, Cecil.

CECIL   Well, you tell that practical joker he can just—

BERYL   Yes, Allegra's here, too. . . . (*To* ALLEGRA) He said "*bonjour.*"

ALLEGRA Tell him *va aux enfers!* Go to hell!

BERYL Yes, they're both here, too . . . of course they didn't hit it off!

ASHER (*Recoiling at the thought*) You can say that again!

KERRY (*Trying to get the phone*) I'll tell that bitch a thing or two!

BERYL Let me handle it.

CECIL She's terrific at this.

BERYL (*Into the phone*) Listen, you, wherever you are . . . Paramus! . . . I *know* where Paramus is; now you just listen to me. You have some nerve, getting us all here and then not showing up. I suppose you think that's pretty funny. Well, let me tell you something—

CECIL (*So proudly to the others*) What'd I tell you?

BERYL (*Sudden delight*) You couldn't make it because you're all tied up? (*Sotto voce*) Cecil! (*Back into the phone; cooing*) What do you mean, you're all tied up? (*Angry again*) Oh, you're just busy you mean! (*Resuming her tirade*) Well, let me tell you—(*She listens, then to the others*) Do we want to go to Paramus?

CECIL Out of the question.

ASHER Paramus, that's in New Jersey.

KERRY I'd rather cruise Hackensack.

BERYL (*Back into the phone, with great dignity*) We're afraid not. Nothing could get us out there. Not after this.
      (*She listens*)

CECIL I guess that's telling him.

BERYL (*Hushing* CECIL, *then into the phone*) What? You're disciplining someone? . . . Where? . . . a bowling alley? At this time of day? What kind of bowling alley is *that?* . . . *OH!*

CECIL (*On the alert*) What? What?

BERYL Sshh! (*Back into the phone*) Who? . . . a young man . . . yes . . .

KERRY (*Eagerly*) Keep talking!

BERYL And he wants a young girl to practice German lessons with? (*Looking at* ALLEGRA) Will French do?

ALLEGRA Don't split hairs! I'm very lingual.

BERYL And he's got his sensitive sister with him? (*She's looking at* ASHER) A poetess?

ASHER A poetess? Oh, wow!

BERYL (*Businesslike now, getting the facts*) Now let me get this straight. You're in Paramus, at a bowling alley, disciplining a young man who wants a young girl to practice German lessons with, and he's got his sensitive poetess sister with him? (*To* CECIL) How soon can we get there?

CECIL   Fifteen minutes.

BERYL   We can make it in ten! (*Into the phone*) What's the address?

ALLEGRA   Ten minutes? In this traffic?

CECIL   Just watch us.

BERYL   (*Writing it down*)   143. Got it. Now hold everything and just sit tight . . . (*Harsh*) Ten minutes, half an hour, just wait for us! (*Listens*) You'll answer for that, pig (*Sweetly*) Yes, of course we'll hurry. (*Listens, looks at* KERRY) What? . . . Don't bring the fag. You hate fags. He wouldn't fit in. Of course I understand. (*Looks away, rambling on*) Tell me something, are they being very naughty? (*She relishes the answer*) We're on our way! (*She hangs up*) Don't just stand there, CECIL. *Pack!*
    (*There is a great flurry of activity now as they make ready to leave*)

ASHER   Are you people talking about another orgy?

BERYL   (*Making haste*)   The branding irons, Cecil. Don't mix them with the tongs!

ALLEGRA   I'll be right behind you. It's a blue Plymouth.

BERYL   Cecil drives like a bat out of hell.

ALLEGRA   I'll keep up.

ASHER   (*Watching them get ready*)   Hey! Hey! Everybody! What about me? I'm willing to try it, at least. I've never been to an orgy, orgy! ORGY! before. See? I'm losing my inhibitions. To be frank, I could use the experience!

BERYL   Take the trunk.

ASHER   Wow! Thanks a lot! A poetess. Oh, wow!
    (*He goes down the stairs*)

ALLEGRA   (*Following*)   Paramus, *ici je viens!* Paramus, here I come!
    (*They are both gone*)

BERYL   Paramus! Whoever dreamed I'd end up in Paramus!

CECIL   (*On the stairs*)   Say, isn't that where Dot and Hugh live?

BERYL   I wouldn't put it past them. (CECIL *is gone. She sees* KERRY) Come on, anyway.

KERRY   (*Mustering up all the dignity he can*)   I've been on my goose chase for the day, thank you.

BERYL   But a bowling alley! I'm sure we can whip *something* up for you.

KERRY   No, thank you.

BERYL   Well, just don't get too depressed. Promise? Something will turn up. It always does. Hope! We can't live with it and we can't live without it!

> (*She runs down the stairs. We hear them all laughing as their voices die away*)

KERRY   (*Shouting down the stairs*)   Sure, go ahead, laugh! You'll get *there* and nothing'll happen either! I bet there's no such thing as Dale! (*Paces, yells down again*) And thanks a lot. I was here first, just remember. Hell, I wasn't going to hurt anybody. (*Pauses, paces, yells again. He's been hurt, you see*) I hope you get stuck in the tunnel. (*Realizes they're gone*) I hope it caves in on you!

> (*He is alone in the room. Slowly, sadly, he begins to gather his things, and make ready to leave. And then—at a great distance—we hear a* VOICE *on the stairs*)

VOICE   (*From afar*)   Dale? (KERRY *freezes*) Dale? . . . (KERRY *goes to the stairwell, looks down*) Dale? (KERRY *runs his fingers through his hair, generally spruces himself up. The* VOICE *is getting closer*) Dale? (KERRY *has started to smile. The future is his*) Dale?

> (*Slow fade*)

Curtain

Bea, Frank, Richie & Joan

from *Lovers and Other Strangers*

BY

Renée Taylor
and
Joseph Bologna

Renée Taylor
and
Joseph Bologna

With their first Broadway play, *Lovers and Other Strangers*, Renée Taylor and Joseph Bologna, husband and wife as well as coauthors, not only drew press encomiums (Clive Barnes wrote in the *New York Times:* ". . . a happy, light-hearted opening of the new Broadway season. Yet there is such warmth and humor here, not least when the authors are showing us at our most hysterical and neurotic, that we get a lot of gentle smiles as well as a few genuine, belly-laugh guffaws."), but also a sizeable preproduction film sale, just a few hours before the premiere.

Although it was this four-in-hand view of love and sex in disparate New York apartments that brought the team immediate recognition for their writing, they had collaborated previously—notably on a motion picture short, entitled *2*, which won an award at the San Francisco Film Festival and is enjoying world-wide distribution, and the screenplay of a feature film, *Made for Each Other*, scheduled for production in 1969.

Both Mr. and Mrs. Bologna, who have been married for three years, are in their early thirties. Before they assumed the mantle of Broadway playwrights, he was a busy director of assorted television commercials and she was—and still is—an actress and television personality. (In 1960 she auditioned as a singer for Jack Paar, didn't quite make it, and to cushion the turndown reminisced about her past jobs. Her account of her experiences engendered much hilarity and she was engaged to appear on the Paar show as a "talker" and appeared frequently until the TV master of the revels made his tearful departure from the popular late-night show.)

The Bolognas have a Manhattan penthouse and a country place in Woodstock, New York, both of which they happily share with two dogs and a cat.

Lovers and Other Strangers was first presented on September 18, 1968, by Stephanie Sills, in association with Gordon Crowe, at the Brooks Atkinson Theatre, New York City. The cast of *Bea, Frank, Richie & Joan* was as follows:

(*In order of appearance*)

FRANK	Richard Castellano
BEA	Helen Verbit
RICHIE	Bobby Alto
JOAN	Candy Azzara

Directed by CHARLES GRODIN
Scenery by ROBIN WAGNER
Costumes by DOMINGO A. RODRIGUEZ
Lighting by JOHN GLEASON

BEA, FRANK, RICHIE & JOAN

Characters

FRANK: *A man of 45 to 55, strong, stubborn, old-fashioned, not much formal education; a second-generation American father.*
BEA: *Female counterpart of Frank.*
RICHIE: *Mid-twenties, average looking, introspective.*
JOAN: *Mid-twenties, pretty, overly romantic and not too bright.*

The scene is an apartment in New York City. It is a Saturday night in spring.

BEA, FRANK *and* RICHIE *are eating dinner at a kitchen table.*

BEA   Have some more soup, Richie.
RICHIE   No, thanks.
BEA   Go ahead, it's vegetable soup.
RICHIE   I don't want any more soup.
BEA   How about you, Frank? You want any more soup?
FRANK   No, I don't want any more.
BEA   Go ahead, it's good soup.
FRANK   All right, let me have some more soup.
BEA   Don't you want some more soup, Richie?
RICHIE   No, thanks.
BEA   You sure?
RICHIE   Yes.
       (*There's a pause*)
BEA   You want some more veal, Richie?
RICHIE   No, Ma, I'm full.
BEA   You want some more veal, Frank?
FRANK   Maybe later.
BEA   The butcher gave you good veal, Frank.
FRANK   Yeah, he's a good butcher.
BEA   It's not veiny.
       (FRANK *thinks for a minute*)
FRANK   I hate veiny veal.

BEA   So do I, Frank. (*There's another pause*) Frank?
    (FRANK *takes another spoonful of soup*)

FRANK   So, ah . . . what's the story, Richie?

RICHIE   There's no story.

FRANK   We're your parents . . . you should tell us the story.

BEA   Tell us the story, Richie.

RICHIE   There's nothing to tell. We're breaking up. That's all.

FRANK   If you're breaking up, there has to be a story.

BEA   How can you break up? You're a married couple.

FRANK   You had a fight, is that it?

RICHIE   No, that's not it.

FRANK   How can they break up if they didn't have a fight?

BEA (*Screams*)   They're getting a divorce, Frank! Do something!!

FRANK   Shut up, Beatrice!

BEA   I'm sorry, Richie.

FRANK   So, ah . . . what's the story, Richie?

RICHIE   We're just not compatible.

FRANK   Did you hear that, Beatrice? They're not compatible.

BEA   I heard, Frank, but I'm not listening.

FRANK   They're married six years and all of a sudden they're looking to be compatible.

BEA   It's a phase they're going through, Frank.

FRANK   Stupid kids today. They don't know what to do with themselves, so they get a divorce—for kicks.

BEA   That's what it is Frank, kicks.

RICHIE   Look, it's 1968. It happens to a lot of couples. There's nothing you can do about it.

FRANK   It's never happened in our family.

BEA   We don't believe in it.

FRANK   It happens to people who don't give a damn.

BEA   You think the King and Queen of England would get a divorce?

FRANK   Of course not.

BEA   They don't believe in it.

FRANK   That's why they're together all these years.

BEA   They know what would happen to England if they broke up.

FRANK   But our son believes in it.

BEA   He wouldn't care what happened to England. He wouldn't
care what happens to anybody. It's 1968, so he's getting a divorce. He was such a handsome groom. Everybody said it was
made in heaven. His grandmother was so happy she lived to see

him marry. Jackie next door has three kids and he never even
went to college.

FRANK   So, what's the story, Richie?

BEA   My sister Pauline's going to be so upset. How could you get
a divorce?!

FRANK   Shut up, Beatrice.

BEA   I'm sorry, Richie.

RICHIE   Look, this is not a spur-of-the-moment decision. Joan and
I talked it out and believe me, it's better this way.

FRANK   Better?

BEA   Better?

FRANK   For who? For your mother?

BEA   For your father?

FRANK   I'll tell you who it's better for—for *you.*

BEA   Always *you.*

FRANK   What do you know what's better for you?

BEA   You don't know what's better.

FRANK   Did you listen to me when I told you not to marry her in
the first place?

BEA   Listen to your father.

RICHIE   Don't you understand? Joan and I are just not happy together.

FRANK   Did you hear that, Beatrice? They're not happy.

BEA   I heard, Frank.

FRANK   Who's happy?

BEA   Who's happy?

FRANK   Do you see me running around dancing in the streets? Or
your brother?

BEA   Or your Uncle Mike?

FRANK   Or your cousin Jerry?

BEA   Or your cousin Nicky?

FRANK   Do you think your sister's happy with that bum she's married to?

BEA   Or Jackie next door? I say, "When you make your bed, you
suffer in it."

FRANK   You think your mother and I are happy?

BEA   Huh?

FRANK   Huh?

RICHIE   You mean you and Dad aren't happy?

BEA and FRANK   No.

RICHIE   Then why did you stay together?

FRANK   We're content.

BEA   We're content.

FRANK   These kids today, all they're looking for is happiness.

BEA   Don't look for happiness, Richie. It'll only make you miserable.

RICHIE   If I'm going to be unhappy, I don't want to be married.

FRANK   What do you think only married people are unhappy? What about Eddie Shrie?

BEA   Or Tommy Pizzo?

FRANK   Or your Aunt Pauline?

BEA   Or Father Burke?

FRANK   You want to end up like them?

BEA   Unhappy?

FRANK   Unhappy! Why do you think we all keep our marriages together—for happiness? Don't be stupid. For the family.

BEA   For the kids!

RICHIE   We don't have any kids.

FRANK   I told you not to have any kids? (*To* BEA) I told him not to have any kids?

BEA   You didn't tell him not to have kids, Frank.

FRANK   If you listened to me you'd have had a lot of kids right away.

BEA   Then you wouldn't be able to get divorced.

FRANK   You'd have the kids to think about.

BEA   Children are a blessing in disguise.

RICHIE   Well, we don't have kids to think about, so we're lucky.

BEA and FRANK   Lucky.

BEA   What about your nephew—Mark? You and Joan are his godparents.

FRANK   You have a responsibility.

BEA   Who's going to take care of him if, God forbid, we all die in a fire?

FRANK   We could all get killed crossing the street by a truck.

BEA   Or die of a heart attack in the living room.

FRANK   Or get electrocuted in the bathtub.

BEA   Dying is no picnic.

RICHIE   Look, if you don't talk intelligently, I'm not going to discuss it with you.

BEA   Oh, God, Frank, do something. Do something!

FRANK   Don't tell me you're not going to discuss it with us. I'll take off my strap and give you a good beating. I don't care how old you are.

BEA, FRANK, RICHIE & JOAN   *Bert Andrews*

BEA   Don't you touch him, Frank! That's all you know is the strap! Where were you when he was young and he really needed you to give him a beating? It's all your fault!

FRANK   Don't give me that. It's your fault. You spoiled him. Every morning you made him bacon and eggs, toast and milk! And me, I was lucky to get a cruller. It's your fault!

BEA   No, it's your fault, Frank.

RICHIE   Will you stop it! It's nobody's fault!

FRANK   Don't give me that! It has to be somebody's fault. I want to know *whose* fault. I want to know whose fault it is! (*The doorbell rings*) Who the hell can that be?

BEA   It's Joan.

RICHIE   Joan? What's Joan doing here?

BEA   I asked her to come over.

RICHIE   What did you do that for? You're only going to make it worse.

FRANK   Worse.

BEA   Worse.

FRANK   I want to hear Joan's story.

BEA (*To* RICHIE)   It's not nice to play favorites.

FRANK   There's more here than meets the eye.

BEA   Believe me, Frank.

RICHIE   This is stupid. You shouldn't have done it.

BEA   Richie, I asked Joan to come over because in a time of stress a family has to come together and open their hearts to each other and try to overcome whatever it is that's making people act crazy. That's all I ever wanted for any of my children. (*The doorbell rings again but* BEA *is getting carried away*) I did the best I could to bring you up to be a good boy and now this. Oh, God, why did this happen! I always did my best. All right, sometimes I was a bad mother, but . . .

FRANK   For Christ sakes, Beatrice, will you open the door!

BEA   I'm sorry, Richie. (*She opens the door and lets* JOAN *in*) Hello, Joan.

JOAN   Hello, Mom.

FRANK   Hello, Joan.

JOAN   Hello, Dad . . . Hello, Richie.

RICHIE   Hello, Joan. I'm sorry about this.

JOAN   That's all right.

BEA   Sit down. Oh, what a pretty dress. Is it new?

JOAN   Yes.

BEA   The color is very becoming. What is that, a pale peach, or a shrimp pink?

JOAN   I think it's peach.

BEA   Well, you look very pretty. Don't you think so, Richie?

RICHIE   Yes.

BEA   Don't you think so, Frank?

FRANK (*Mumbles*)   Mmm . . .

BEA   It's pale peach, Frank. You want something to eat, Joan?

JOAN   No, I ate already.

BEA   How about a glass of milk and some crumb cake?

JOAN   No, thank you.

FRANK   You got crumb cake?

BEA   Yes, from Cakemasters.

FRANK (*Thinks*)   Save me a piece for later.

BEA   You sure you don't want any crumb cake, Joan?

JOAN   No, thank you.

BEA   How about you, Richie?

RICHIE   I don't want any.

> (*There is a long pause.* BEA *looks at* FRANK, *but he doesn't want to get involved*)

BEA   Frank?

FRANK   So—uh—uh—understand from Richie that—uh . . . you two are having some compatible difficulties. Listen, there's nothing to be ashamed of. Believe me, it happens to the best of people. Even Bea and I have had our little differences. We're married—what—nineteen—uh—thirty-five—uh . . .

BEA   Thirty-three years, Frank.

FRANK   Thirty-three years, and anyone who looks at us will tell you we're the perfect couple, but just between you and me, it's only natural that once in a while you can't help but hate each other's guts. Am I right, Bea? But—uh—that's—uh—what marriage is. I always say, "Where there's a will, there's a way." "Rome wasn't built in a day." And "It takes two to tango." Am I right, Joan? I was telling Richie here of all my daughter-in-laws you've always been my favorite. You're not a loudmouth like that William's wife, or a flashy dresser like Robert's wife, but you're a nice quiet girl with a good head on your shoulders, and —you know how to save money when you shop. Am I right, Richie? . . . So, what I mean to say is. So, what's the story, Joan?

JOAN   Well, it's a combination of a lot of things. Like . . . uh . . . well, like my birthday, for instance.

RICHIE   Do we have to go through that again?

JOAN   Richie, let me tell it my way.

RICHIE   Oh, come on . . .

BEA   Children, please, be nice. Life is too short for fights, especially in times of stress.

JOAN   I asked Richie to get me a book for my birthday.

FRANK   What kind of book?

JOAN   It was a book about Spain. You know, with colored photographs. I've always had a big thing about Spain because I love Spanish music and Spanish people.

BEA   I love Spanish music too, especially the tango. Even on our honeymoon in Atlantic City, they had a band on the boardwalk. Remember, Frank? And he wouldn't do the tango. He said if I wanted to tango, I should have married Rudolph Valentino.

FRANK   A hundred people standing around looking at us and she wants me to get up and do a tango. They would've thought I was a fairy, or something. Am I right, Richie? Go on, Joan.

JOAN   Well, uh . . .

BEA   Rudolph Valentino was no fairy, Frank.

FRANK   Go on, Joan.

JOAN   Well, I was just telling you that I saw this book on Spain and a book to me means love because when you give a book about a romantic place you give something with pages in it and each page could be a day in your life and the cover to me is like happiness and it's like saying that all the days in your life should be as romantic as Spain and surrounded by a cover of happiness. So I mentioned to Richie that I wanted it.

RICHIE   She didn't mention it. That's *all* she talked about day and night for a month.

JOAN   Well, he always forgot my birthdays. I reminded him, that's all.

RICHIE   I didn't get it for her because I don't like to be told what to get someone. Maybe I wanted to get her something better than a book. For instance, I saw this little stuffed spotted rabbit in a window made out of real monkey fur. It was like a music box. You wind it up and it plays "Happy Birthday" while it hops across the floor.

JOAN   All he ever got me for my birthday was stuffed animals.

RICHIE   You used to love stuffed animals. You were always asking me to get you a lion or a duck . . .

JOAN   But this time I wanted a book.

FRANK   So, what did you get her?

RICHIE   What?

FRANK   For her birthday.

RICHIE   Nothing. I forgot what day it was.

(*The following conversations go on simultaneously. Throughout it all,* FRANK *keeps trying to follow* RICHIE *and* JOAN's *story*)

JOAN   You always forget. Anything that's important to me, you forget.

RICHIE   Maybe you make such a big thing out of it that I want to forget.

JOAN   Well, I can't see the logic in that.

RICHIE   Well, I got you the book anyway, didn't I? I got her the book anyway.

JOAN   Sure, after we had a fight and I went to my mother's house and was up all night crying and the next night he comes over and says, "Here," and he throws it at me.

RICHIE   I didn't throw it at you. I handed it to you and said, "Happy Birthday," and she takes the book and rips the pages out and flushes them down the toilet.

JOAN   I didn't rip it up. You ripped it when I threw it back at you.

RICHIE   Look, if you're not going to tell the story the way it happened, there's no sense talking about it. So, let's just forget the whole thing.

JOAN   O.K., we'll just forget the whole thing.

BEA   Frank, you're the same way. Remember I sent you out for a can opener last Friday, and don't you know, he came home without it . . . I said, "Frank, don't forget to pick up a good can opener that doesn't rust" . . . and he walks in the house and I said, "Where's the can opener?" And he says, "What can opener?"

FRANK   (*To* RICHIE)   She flushed the book down the toilet? (*To* BEA)   Why'd she flush the book down the toilet?

BEA   I don't know. I missed that part, Frank.

FRANK   Why'd you rip up the book, Joan? Why'd she rip up the book?

BEA   Joan ripped up the book Richie gave her? Why'd she do that, Frank? Why, Frank?

FRANK   For Christ's sakes, that's what I'm trying to find out! . . . What's the story, Richie?

FRANK   (*Taking over*)   All right! All right! (*He bangs his fist on the table and everyone becomes quiet*)   I don't want any-

body to talk until I ask them to talk and then I don't want anybody to interrupt who's talking. Then, maybe we can discuss
this like civilized people and get to the bottom of it . . . All
right? (*They all nod "yes"*) All right now, I'm going to talk first
and when I'm finished we can discuss all the implications of
everything I have to say.

(*There's a long pause*)

BEA (*Screams*) Frank, they're getting a divorce, Frank. Do
something!

FRANK What the hell do you think I'm trying to do, for Christ
sakes! . . . Now listen to me, Joan. Maybe you don't think so,
but I've been through these things and speaking from my own
experience, whenever there's difficulties in a marriage, it's
usually caused by one of the parties involved causing—uh—
friction. You know what I mean, Joan? I mean one party is causing it and the other party—uh—you know what I mean, Richie?
I mean, whenever there's difficulties in a marriage, the two people have . . . you know what I mean, Beatrice? (*He looks back
to* JOAN) I mean—uh—Beatrice, take Joan in the other room,
I'll talk to Richie alone.

(BEA *and* JOAN *start to leave*)

BEA Come, Joan. You want a sweater, Frank? It's getting a little
chilly.

FRANK All right, let me have a sweater.

BEA You want your pullover, or your cardigan, Frank?

FRANK My pullover—er—my cardigan.

BEA Oh, your cardigan's in the cleaner's, Frank.

FRANK (*Thinks*) Then let me have my pullover.

BEA It's very heavy, Frank.

FRANK (*Thinks again*) Uh . . . never mind. (BEA *and* JOAN *leave*)
So, what happened? You had something on the side and she
found out about it?

RICHIE That's not the reason.

FRANK Come on, you can tell me. I never told you this before, but
you're grown up now. I strayed too, when I was young. Don't
get me wrong. I never went looking for it but, you know, sometimes you're walking along and it falls in your lap.

RICHIE You don't have to tell me this.

FRANK Look, it happens to everybody. I love your mother, but,
you know, sometimes you need a little more stimulation. You
know? . . . All right, thank God she never felt that way. (*He
makes the sign of the cross*) But—uh—there was this one time

when—uh—your mother found out about it. Her stupid sister
Pauline opened her big mouth and told her. She walked out on
me for four days, but then she came back. Where's she gonna go?
All right, she was mad and she felt very hurt and I never heard
the end of it, and—uh—that *stupid Pauline!* I could've broken
her head. (*He begins to have a recall*) Just before that happened, I slipped on Pauline's porch and hurt my back. I was
out of work for two weeks and I had to pay for the doctor, the
X-rays and a week in the hospital. It cost me, uh—two hundred
and fifty—uh—eighty-five—uh—twenty-five—uh—about three
hundred and ten dollars. I had an open-and-shut negligence
case, but she got mad because they raised her insurance a
lousy seven dollars a year. So, to get even with me, she runs
over here and tells your mother about the time she saw me in
Big Joe's with a female companion. Stupid Pauline! So, your
mother and I had a lot of—uh—difficulties there for a while,
and like I was telling Joan, when there's difficulties in a marriage, it's usually caused as a result of one of the parties involved
causing friction. In our case, it was . . . *Pauline.* That stupid
jerk! . . . But—she got over it, just like Joan will get over it.
Women know how to take things.

RICHIE   I told you, that's not the reason.

FRANK   You mean to tell me, in six years, you never strayed once?

RICHIE   Yeah, a few times, but it was just physical.

FRANK   Then why do you want a divorce?

RICHIE   I don't know. I was just too young when I got married. I
didn't know who I was, or what I wanted.

FRANK   Who you are? What you want? Where'd you get these
thoughts? Not from me. I sent you to college to get an education,
not to get these thoughts. You know what you need? A psychiatrist.

RICHIE   I've been thinking of going to one.

FRANK   What, are you crazy? There's nothing wrong with you.

RICHIE   Look, pop. I may not know what I want, but I do know
what I don't want.

FRANK   And why don't you want Joan?

RICHIE   When Joan and I first got married we had a perfect relationship. She was working days and I was working nights. And
then, the more we saw of each other, the more I realized we
were strangers.

FRANK   We're all strangers. But after a while, you get used to it.
You become deeper strangers. That's a sort of love.

RICHIE   No, that's habit and I want more than that.

FRANK   More. Everyone wants more.

RICHIE   Then why don't they go get it?

FRANK   Because there is no more.

RICHIE   There's got to be more.

FRANK   More.

RICHIE   What's the sense of talking. We don't seem to be getting anywhere.

FRANK   More. More. You think I don't understand, don't you? I understand. There were times with your mother when I thought maybe I didn't do justice to myself. You know what I mean, Richie? I love your mother, but I never thought she was as intelligent as I am and that used to bother me a lot. Everyone wants to be married to someone on his own level. A couple of years before I married your mother, I met this schoolteacher. Her name was Mary Rose. A real society girl. She was Bulgarian. We had everything in common—same interests, same mentality—and I used to think if I had married Mary Rose, I wouldn't have yelled and screamed so much around the house. I figured I would have been a different person if I had married her, but—uh—she wouldn't go out with me. So, I married your mother. I'm going back to 19—uh—36. That's —uh—1968—'58 —uh—I'm talking—uh—'36—thirty-one, thirty-two years ago. That's a long time ago. The best thing about the past is you forget what it was that could have made you happy. And for the past fifteen to twenty years your mother and I have been —uh—like I said—content. You're forced to find things in common. For instance, your mother and I are very interested in various types of food—a good roast beef, leg of lamb smothered in onions, Yankee Pot Roast with lots of little baby baked potatoes and gravy, and there's always something to talk about— Who's getting married? Who died? Who just had a baby? How much we should give? Marriage is a wonderful thing if you can enjoy your wife for whatever she is.

   (*The lights fade and we come up on* BEA *and* JOAN *looking at a wedding album*)

BEA   And Joan, of all the pictures in your wedding album, my favorite is this one. The whole family together. Everyone happy and smiling. You and Richie, me and Frank, your mother and father, and Richie's cousins—Freddie and Rita, cheek to cheek; David and Loretta, kissing; Carmel and Vinnie, hugging— Freddie and Rita, cheek to cheek. Did you know that Freddie

has not said one word to Rita for two years . . . but they're still
together. David and Loretta, kissing—Well, you know what people in the family say about David, that he's a little funny? You
know what I mean? Peculiar. I don't think he really is. It's just
his way to lock himself in his room all day Sunday and play
with his cars. Look, it takes all kinds to make a world. Who's to
say the man is a degenerate, or worse . . . but they're still together! Carmel and Vinnie, hugging—when Carmel and Vinnie
first got married, they lived with Vinnie's parents because he
was out of work a lot and Vinnie's mother was always picking
on Carmel. She kept blaming Carmel for Vinnie's laziness. Well,
one night Carmel told Vinnie if his mother made one more remark to her, she was going to smack her in the face and Vinnie
started yelling, "Don't you dare lay a hand on my mother!" and
Carmel said, "Oh, go to hell, the both of you!" and she stomped
out of the house and Vinnie chased her down the block and
dragged her back by the hair and Carmel spit right in his face
and he started choking her by the throat over the open window
and the super had to come and pull Vinnie off Carmel . . . and
they're still together.

       (BEA *sits back obviously pleased with herself*)

JOAN   Mother, maybe they're right to stay together. I don't know.
All I know is that my problem with Richie is much more basic.

BEA   More basic than Carmel and Vinnie!

JOAN   I'm sorry. I don't want to hurt you. You've always been
closer to me than my own mother, but . . .

BEA   And I love you like my own flesh and blood. That's why we
can talk to each other. What, Joan? Tell me.

JOAN   Well . . .

BEA   Yes?

JOAN   Mother, ever since I was fifteen, I loved Richie from afar.

BEA   Uh-huh.

JOAN   And the whole time we went together I was just floating on
air and we had so much fun together because we both loved the
beach.

BEA   Uh-huh.

JOAN   We were always kissing and hugging and everyone said
how great we looked on the dance floor. So I really thought we'd
get married and live happily ever after, but I guess we just
weren't that lucky. I mean, I knew it was the real thing because I
loved everything about him. I loved the way he moved. Some-

times, I'd just spend hours and hours and just watch him move around.

BEA   Uh-huh.

JOAN   And his hair. Well, you're going to think I'm crazy, but I loved the way his hair smelled, like raisins. And when he'd kiss me, I never told him this, but the best part of being in his arms was that I could get a good whiff of his hair. Oh, and his arms were so big and smooth. Right here, they went around and then down. (*She sighs*) Well, now I don't know if it's me, or Richie that's changed, but it's just no big deal any more to feel him or smell him.

BEA   Joan darling. You don't even know what basic is. I'm going to tell you something that's so basic, you won't even believe it. I've never told anyone this. It's very private. Promise me you won't discuss it with anyone. Okay, Joan?

JOAN   Okay.

BEA   You promise?

JOAN   I promise you.

BEA   Well, here it is . . . you see, Joan . . . I've had a very hard life. (*She sighs deeply*) When I met Frank, he was very handsome and so clean. So clean. Did you see *Seventh Heaven* on the late show the other night? (JOAN *nods* "yes") Well, Frank was clean like Charlie Farrell was in *Seventh Heaven* when he met Janet Gaynor who was very innocent like I was. So, it was a big shock to me on my honeymoon when I found out what a physical person he was. You know what I'm talking about, Joan?

JOAN   Sex?

BEA   *You* said it, not me. It's very hard for me to talk about these things. That's why I wasn't ready to get raped on my wedding night. Oh, God, if I live to be a thousand, I'll never forget my rape, with you-know-who! I was so nauseous but I didn't say a word, I just ran in the bathroom and locked the door, because I don't like to make a scene.

JOAN   You mean you never enjoyed sex?

BEA   What's to enjoy? Love is not physical. Love is spiritual. Like the great love Ingrid Bergman had for Bing Crosby in *The Bells of St. Mary's* when she was a nun and he was a priest and they loved each other from afar. But Frank didn't want to know from that. You see, it's very hard for a man to understand how a woman feels inside, although I tried to understand Frank. Not that there was that much there to understand. But no matter how I felt about that business, Frank was my *husband* and my body was his sacred erotic right. That's why I couldn't understand it when Frank strayed. That's right. Frank. Look, it's a sin, but it happens. I left him for a few days, but I came back. Where was I gonna go? And you know me, I always try to look at the bright side. I said to myself, at least she's the one who'll be nauseous now. I was very hurt, Joan. Very. But I stuck it out and so did Frank because we believe in the highest form of love—obligations. And as impossible as it seemed to be at the time, somehow Frank and I together still built—uh—a life. Do you know what I mean, Joan? Frank and I have a . . . life . . . together . . . me and Frank . . . together . . .

       (*There's a pause as they both think*)

JOAN   I don't know what to say, except, I love you and I hope you'll forgive me.

BEA   You mean after all I said, you're still going to leave Richie?

JOAN   I'm sorry, Mother. I'm sorry. I have to go now.

       (She *goes back into the kitchen.* BEA *goes after her.* FRANK *and* RICHIE *are sitting there looking off into space*)

BEA   Frank, Joan's leaving. Say something.

FRANK   She's leaving? (*To* BEA) Did you straighten it out? How can she leave if you didn't straighten it out?

JOAN   It's very late.

BEA (*Screams*)   Frank, do something!

RICHIE   I'll go with you.

FRANK (*To* BEA)   Why is she going? Did you upset her? I'm sorry if Bea upset you, Joan.

BEA   I didn't upset you, did I, Joan?

JOAN   No.

RICHIE   Come on, let's go.

FRANK   Where are you going?

RICHIE   Home.

FRANK   I'm not through talking to him. Where's he going?

BEA   Leave them alone, Frank. They're going together.

FRANK   Is that true? You're going together? It's good you're going together.

RICHIE   Good night, Pop.

BEA (*To* JOAN)   Joan, you let Richie bring you flowers and take you to a show.

       (FRANK *tries to give* RICHIE *five dollars.* RICHIE *tries not to accept the money, but he does*)

FRANK   Buy her a new book.

(JOAN *and* RICHIE *leave.* BEA *and* FRANK *sit down at the kitchen table*)

FRANK So . . . uh . . . what was Joan's story?

BEA She said she loves me even more than she loves her own mother and she doesn't want to hurt me because I've always been good to her and honest with her and she can talk to me.

FRANK (*Pause*) Did she say anything about me?

BEA She was shocked that you strayed, Frank.

FRANK For Christ sakes, Beatrice, what did you have to tell her that for?

BEA It came out in passing.

FRANK Why the hell does she have to know our business?

BEA I was making a point about friction, Frank.

FRANK All right!

BEA To err is human. To forgive is divine.

FRANK All right!

BEA What are we going to do, Frank?

FRANK What can you do?

BEA You live and learn.

FRANK You have to take the good with the bad.

BEA What can you do?

FRANK You live and learn.

BEA What will people say?

FRANK People don't have to know.

BEA You raise a boy. You teach him values.

FRANK That stupid Pauline.

BEA You teach him a family.

FRANK You have to take the good with the bad.

BEA Life is for the living.

FRANK I could have broken her head.

BEA I can understand her wanting to leave.

FRANK That's how life is.

BEA But I can't understand her leaving.

FRANK That's how life is.

BEA You have to take the good with the bad.

FRANK I think I'll have my crumb cake now.

Curtain

Madly in Love

(A sky-blue comedy)

from *Blue Comedy*

BY

Paul Ableman

Paul Ableman

Paul Ableman, novelist and dramatist, was born in Leeds, Yorkshire, England, and brought up in London and New York.

Green Julia, his best-known play to date, was staged in Edinburgh and London in 1965 and since has been performed in Australia, New Zealand, Argentina, Holland and the United States. Among his published works are three popular novels: *I Hear Voices; As Near As I Can Get;* and *Vac,* which was published in 1968.

One of Britain's busiest young television writers, Mr. Ableman also has created some fifty abstract and surrealist playlets which have been performed at Peter Brook's Theatre of Cruelty experimental series at the Lamba Theatre, London, at the Edinburgh Festival, and on the British Broadcasting Corporation's Third Programme. A group of the playlets was published in Britain in 1966 under the title *Tests.*

Most recently the author scored a success in London with his *Blue Comedy,* a double bill consisting of two farcical comedies, *Madly in Love* (published here for the first time in the United States) and *Hank's Night.* Both plays offer complementary variations on a single theme. When *Blue Comedy* premiered at the Open Space Theatre in Tottenham Court Road, it brought cheerful notices and swelling box-office receipts to the comparatively new experimental playhouse, jointly operated by Charles Marowitz and Thelma Holt.

Early in 1969 *Blue Comedy* was scheduled to be transferred to the West End, under the management of Bernard Delfont and Donald Albery and, at this writing, a New York production is planned for later in the year.

Blue Comedy was first presented on October 21, 1968, at the Open Space Theatre, London. The cast of *Madly in Love* was as follows:

(*In order of appearance*)

MRS. ELSIE TODD	Janet McIntire
ANGUS MACFEE	Jonathan Lynn
MR. REGINALD TODD	Gordon Whiting
DR. GORDON MACNAIR	Jonathan Burn
MARY TODD	Sarah Atkinson

Directed by CHARLES MAROWITZ
Designed by JOHN NAPIER
Lighting by PETER BEVIS

MADLY IN LOVE

The place: The living room of the Todd home. The time: The present for as long as it lasts.

Enter MRS. TODD, *who looks younger than her forty-one years, with a bearded, rather seedy-looking man of about twenty-eight who is carrying a small suitcase. His name is* ANGUS MACFEE. *He is at present calling himself Dr. Macfee. He is really a poet.*

MRS. TODD I had no idea Dr. Macnair had a partner.

MACFEE No, he keeps it very dark.

MRS. TODD Why?

MACFEE He's a very secretive sort of person. You must have noticed.

MRS. TODD I've always found him most outgoing.

MACFEE Aye, he's a good mimic. All psychopaths are.

MRS. TODD Dr. Macnair? A psychopath?

MACFEE Aye. It takes a nut to catch a nut.

MRS. TODD May I ask, how long have you and Dr. Macnair been partners?

MACFEE A hell of a long time. We graduated together from the psychiatry faculty of Dundee University and came down here to combat the spreading psychosis in the Thames valley. It's uphill work. There's a bug per square yard, but we're slowly getting on top of it. (*Pause*) Well, you're not as young as I thought you'd be, but we'd best get cracking.

MRS. TODD I'm not the patient. It's my daughter.

MACFEE That's more promising. Wheel the dolly in please and then leave us alone. I have to administer some electric shocks.

MRS. TODD My daughter is not quite ready. You're earlier than you said you'd be. Just why couldn't Dr. Macnair make it this morning?

MACFEE ˙ Grave case. Patient with depressive hallucinations went into a catatonic trance. The only hope is continuous hypnosis for twenty-four hours. It might be fatal if Dr. Macnair stirred from the cage.

MRS.TODD   Cage?

MACFEE   Shrinker's slang for therapy room. Listen, I wouldn't say "no" to a brimming tumbler of whisky and water. If you've nothing more stirring than Guinness in the house, I could make do with that.

MRS. TODD   Dr. Macnair never takes a drink while he's on duty.

MACFEE   (*Irritably*)   My dear woman, kink-straighteners are human like everyone else and humans differ. Dr. Macnair doesn't take drink because he detests the stuff. I, on the other hand, am practically an alcoholic. Gives me insight into their dismal condition.

MRS. TODD   Well, I'll ask my husband, who should be down in a moment. And while we're on the subject of my husband, his tic's getting worse.

MACFEE   Tic? Ah yes, tic. You mean he does this?
    (*He demonstrates a tic*)

MRS. TODD   Well, not exactly. It's more like this.

MACFEE   (*Interestedly*)   Aye, I recognize it. In the trade, we call that one the Rangoon tic.

MRS. TODD   Why?

MACFEE   (*Darkly*)   Have you ever *been* to Rangoon?

MRS. TODD   (*After swallowing*)   My husband has recently received a major promotion. He is now in charge of distributing the three hundred and twenty-one products his company manufactures throughout England, Scotland and Wales.

MACFEE   You mean he drives a frantic van?

MRS. TODD   No. No. He is the executive in charge of sales and promotion. He is one of the youngest ever to have achieved such a position. Now what I am wondering is: do you think it can be the enormously increased burden of responsibility that has caused the deterioration in his tic?

MACFEE   It's possible. You never know with tics. Sometimes it's the weather. Sometimes it's the news. It might just be a flaming allergy. I suggest he consult a good tic man—there are many listed in the Greater London telephone directory. But for the moment I must insist that we forget your husband's jittery pan and concentrate on your daughter. We're wasting good shrinking time.

MRS. TODD   Very well, I'll see if Mary's ready.
    (*Enter Mr. Todd*)

MR. TODD   Elsie, it's worse! It makes me look like a leering yeti! How can I address the sales managers? Oh! Who's this?
　　(*He tics*)

MRS. TODD (*Shuddering faintly*)   This is Dr. Macnair's partner, Dr. Macfee.

MACFEE   Now that I've had a squint at it, I can see that your wife's imitation was unprofessionally vague. That's not the Rangoon tic at all. It's a much more sinister variant known as the Jolly Roger tic.

MR. TODD   Is there no (*Tic*) cure?

MACFEE (*Shuddering*)   For a tic like that, surgery. All other treatments are merely palliative.

MR. TODD   Then it can be (*Tic*) improved?

MACFEE   Och aye. Five or six really swinging sessions on the couch and we'd have that horror down to a little twitch as subtle as a street tart's wink.

MR. TODD   But I have to make a speech to the sales managers (*Tic*)—twenty-eight of them—this afternoon. What am I to do?

MACFEE   Wear a mask. Now if you'll kindly fetch me a brimming bumper of your best malt I'll just prepare to shock your daughter.
　　(*He starts to take an electrical apparatus from his case*)

MR. TODD   But—
　　(*He tics*)

MRS. TODD   Dr. Macfee apparently relies heavily on liquid support. Would you get him a drink, dear? (MR. TODD *tics*) Quickly, dear!

MR. TODD   Very well.
　　(*He goes off*)

MRS. TODD   I'll go and call Mary. (*The doorbell rings*) There's the doorbell.
　　(*She goes off.* MACFEE *continues arranging a piece of equipment that includes a press button.* MRS. TODD *returns with another man about the same age as* MACFEE, *but not raffish looking. Indeed the new arrival is smartly dressed and thoroughly professional in manner. He, too, carries a case*)

MRS. TODD   But I understood from Dr. Macfee that you were unavoidably detained with an urgent case, Dr. Macnair?

DR. MACNAIR   You understood from *whom*?
　　(MACFEE *displays signs of acute discomfort*)

MRS. TODD   Your partner, Dr. Macfee. Here he is.

DR. MACNAIR (*Contemplating his "partner"*)   Oh yes, here he is.

MACFEE   Ah Gordon, I didn't expect to see you. He snapped out of it, then?

DR. MACNAIR   Who snapped out of what?

MACFEE   Whist, man, you needn't be so canny. I've mentioned no names. (*To* MRS. TODD) Gordon's a demon for professional ethics. The patient I mentioned, the one with galloping psychosis, is a very eminent man. It wouldn't do if his colleagues in the cabinet suspected he was cracked as yesterday's egg. Now would you mind leaving us for a moment, Mrs. Todd, while we sketch out some supersonic therapy for your wee lass?

DR. MACNAIR   Just what the hell are you—

MACFEE   (*Hastily*)   Gordon's had a bad night, haunting this loony's bedside. I know he'd be glad if we had a spot of hush for consultation.

MRS. TODD   It's quite all right. Naturally you must have privacy. I'll go and see how Mary's getting along.

(*She goes off, closing the door behind her*)

DR. MACNAIR (*Grimly*)   You neglected to mention that you were going to assist me on this case, *Doctor* Macfee.

MACFEE (*Sullenly*)   It was just an impulse.

DR. MACNAIR   Which sprang up, no doubt, after I informed you I wouldn't be able to keep this appointment?

MACFEE (*Reproachfully*)   You told me you'd forgotten you had an appointment with your dentist.

DR. MACNAIR   Aye, so I did. And I asked you to phone Mrs. Todd and change the time of the session. But then my dentist phoned to say he'd forgotten an appointment with his chiropodist. Thank God he did!

MACFEE   Why?

DR. MACNAIR   Because I'm damned sure if I hadn't providentially arrived, this house would have been the witness of scenes beside which the horrors of war would shine like beacons of hope. You scoundrel!

MACFEE   Och, you're leaping to conclusions.

DR. MACNAIR   Then what the hell *are* you doing here?

MACFEE   I'm tired of being your bum-boy, that's all.

DR. MACNAIR (*Astounded*)   Bum-boy!

MACFEE   Aye, bum-boy! I'm a genius and I'm sick of crawling round you like a lackey.

DR. MACNAIR   Lackey! You ungrateful Fifeshire jackal, didn't you come to me, broke and discouraged, a year ago and, on the strength of our alleged childhood friendship, which as I recall amounted to no more than a particularly vicious stone-throwing duel, ask me for help?

MADLY IN LOVE   *John Haynes*

MACFEE Och, rubbish! We were close friends at Dundee University.

DR. MACNAIR I barely set eyes on you there and never sober. I do recall once warning you: do something practical. But no, you had to write a thesis on the influence of Icelandic meters on the proto-Celtic saga. Numbskull! I told you you'd have to earn a living one day!

MACFEE I'm a poet.

DR. MACNAIR You're a dreadful poet. I showed your verses to a psychotic critic and he thought they were nearly as risible as McGonagall's.

MACFEE Real critics, at least sane ones, praise me highly.

DR. MACNAIR But no one'll publish you, will they? But to resume, did you or did you not apply to me for help a year ago?

MACFEE I happened to be passing.

DR. MACNAIR Well I wish you'd just passed, since you seem bent on getting yourself locked up and me struck off the Freudian register. I took you in. I gave you a decent room in my flat. I gave you all your meals and ten clear pounds a week with which to encourage the distilling trade and instead of pitching gratefully into the few light tasks I envisaged for you, you devoted yourself exclusively to attempting to seduce my wife.

MACFEE I've been slaving away as your combined receptionist, charlady, secretary and cook for long enough.

DR. MACNAIR Then I'm surprised you should voluntarily add the arduous role of partner.

MACFEE You've been exploiting me. I quit.

DR. MACNAIR You don't quit. You're sacked!

(*They glare balefully at each other.* MR. TODD *enters with whisky and a glass. Throughout the rest of the action* MACFEE *periodically replenishes his glass. He does not, however, become visibly intoxicated*)

MR. TODD Dr. Macfee, I've brought you a drink.

MACFEE Give it here. I'm ripe for one.

MR. TODD (*Handing him the drink*) Don't forget, I must discuss the matter of my tic with you.

MACFEE You can discuss it till your aunt's made Pope, it'll still flash over you like an advertisement for hell. (*He shudders at the tic*) Tow the horrid thing out of here, will you? I've got troubles enough.

DR. MACNAIR (*Indignantly*) Mr. Todd, you must forgive—er— Macfee. He's not himself today.

MR. TODD   Dr. Macnair, are you here too? I'm really so distracted—
this dreadful tic—it's deteriorated (*Tic*) and I have to address
hordes of sales managers this afternoon.

DR. MACNAIR   I'll look into it in just a moment. If you could leave
us now, please.

MR. TODD   I couldn't sell flour to a baker with this tic.
   (*He tics*)

MACFEE (*Shuddering*)   Och, get out!
   (MR. TODD *goes off*)

DR. MACNAIR   How dare you be rude to my patients?

MACFEE   You've upset me. I don't want to be rude to your patients.

DR. MACNAIR   No, you want to rape them!

MACFEE (*Sighing*)   Jock, for the love of St. Andrew and in the
name of Robert Burns, let me go through with it.

DR. MACNAIR (*Narrowly*)   A man can stand on a nugget and
search vainly for gold. I've been too close to you, monster, to
spot the madness. I'm going to have you certified before you
write a new chapter in the history of perverse crime.

MACFEE   Och, scrap the melodrama, Jock. What harm would it
do the lass?

DR. MACNAIR   You're seriously proposing that I should hand over
to a totally unqualified lecher a girl suffering from one of the
most fully developed obedience compulsions I've ever encountered?

MACFEE (*Eagerly*)   Is it really true? Like it says in the file? Will
she really do anything you tell her and then forget it afterwards?

DR. MACNAIR   Why do you think this is the only case I visit at
home? Simply because arranging expeditions for poor Miss Todd
involves such acute problems of chaperonage that humanity
compels it. Aye, it's perfectly true. If you give her any command in a sharp, firm voice—

MACFEE (*Beside himself*)   Like, take off your—

DR. MACNAIR (*Sternly*)   Any command in a sharp, firm voice, Miss
Todd, in obedience to some complex crossed circuitry of the
super-ego-ego complex, will obey it. The phenomenon is accompanied by total amnesia for the duration of the act of obedience.

MACFEE (*Reverently*)   It's the promised land. Jock, give me a
chance.

DR. MACNAIR (*Heavily ironic*)   Och aye, it's a small thing you ask.
Shall we fetch Miss Todd and you can get to work? I presume
you'll want to start with a little lascivious entertainment? You

can order the lass to do a strip-tease while you whistle "Comin'
Through the Rye." After that—

MACFEE   Jock, I shall give her one command and one only. I shall
say, in a sharp, firm voice: lassy, make love to me!

DR. MACNAIR (*Thoughtfully*)   It might be very interesting, from
a purely clinical point of view, to see how she responded.

MACFEE   That's it! I'd thought of that one! You can't do it yourself
because of your silly scruples. Jock, I'll give you a full report. I'll
feel her pulse and note the contraction of her pupils, and anything else you require. Man, it might give you the clue you
require for curing her. I don't see how you can ethically refuse
the experiment.

DR. MACNAIR (*Narrowly*)   You haven't set eyes on Miss Todd yet.
How do you know you'd fancy her?

MACFEE   She's twenty-two, isn't she? I read that in the file. She's
female, isn't she?

DR. MACNAIR (*Gently*)   Angus, I understand. I know you've had a
difficult time. But, naturally, what you propose is totally and
categorically unacceptable.

MACFEE (*In despair*)   I shall kill myself. I shall obliterate the
incurable case that is my life.

DR. MACNAIR   Och, you have lots to live for. I was being unfair to
your poetry in the heat of the moment. You're a very promising
poet, Angus.

MACFEE   I'm a rotten poet. And I'm a rotten human being. And
everything bad about me—everything bad and thwarted and
envious about me—comes from the same incredible reason, that
fact that at twenty-eight, healthy and probably as presentable
as most of the mammals you see in the public streets, at twenty-
eight, I, Angus Macfee, am still a virgin.

DR. MACNAIR   You need psychoanalysis.

MACFEE   *I need a woman!*

DR. MACNAIR   Well it can be managed. Don't spend all your money
on whisky.

MACFEE   I will not pay for it, not the first time. The shame would
kill me.

DR. MACNAIR (*Firmly*)   Well I can't have you tampering with my
patients.

MACFEE   Then I'm done for. It was my last hope.

DR. MACNAIR   Och, you've got a tongue in your head and two
strong arms. You can win a lass like another man.

MACFEE (*Passionately*) I can't! It doesn't work, not with me. Look at your wife—I courted her for six months, as you mentioned. I took her tea in bed. I carried her shopping. I read her my poems. I told her I revered her body more than Moslems revere Mecca. A kiss on the cheek and one glorious half-hour holding hands—while you were shrinking that kleptomaniac judge—that was the total of my reward.

DR. MACNAIR (*Wryly*) Aye, I noticed you weren't making much speed with Peggy which I'll admit is a pretty elementary test! If a man can't bed my wife he'd best tool up for lifelong celibacy.

MACFEE (*Almost moaning*) The terrible ordeals I've endured! I've courted at least a hundred girls and not one of them have I made. I've had them spend nights at my pad and somehow it always winds up with them dossing in the bed and me yearning in the armchair.

DR. MACNAIR But what's the reason?

MACFEE (*Dismally*) Something about me they sense! A quality combining naivety and corruption. At first I was an idealist. I dreamed of romantic love. I didn't fit in with the swinging kids around me. Girls respected me for my nobility but rejected me for my unworldliness. Then, as I realized time was passing, I became desperate. Then they feared me for my importunity and repulsed me for my coarseness. The result was that over the years I declined from innocence into decadence without ever losing my virginity.

DR. MACNAIR Listen, Angus, I'll have a word with Peggy. She's an obliging lass and—

MACFEE (*Gloomily*) She won't. She told me positively that she'd go to bed with the Marquis de Sade or with a choir boy—but not with both at once.

DR. MACNAIR (*Sighing*) Well, I can't have you interfering with Mary Todd.

MACFEE (*Sarcastically*) Och no, it would be immoral wouldn't it?

DR. MACNAIR Aye, it would.

MACFEE And what about the immorality of condemning me to suicide?

DR. MACNAIR (*Positively*) You won't commit suicide. You'll just write poems about it.

MACFEE Bad poems. And I could be writing good ones. Don't you see? The spirit of Rabby Burns is leaping in my veins. But he's leaping with frustration! Burns had only to wink at a lass and she was flat on her back in a rye field, making him a bairn—

DR. MACNAIR You'd be doing the same for Mary Todd.

MACFEE I would not! I've got a packet of wee rubber shields I bought in the chemist's shop.

DR. MACNAIR Have you paused to consider she may be a virgin?

MACFEE Then she wears it lightly, according to the results of your physical examination. I read the file, Jock, remember? (*Wheedling*) Where would be the harm, Jock? A simple, hygienically performed act that she'd have no memory of?

DR. MACNAIR But how could it help you? You can't tell me it would satisfy you for the rest of your days?

MACFEE Och, you dolt! It would be the catalyst. It would change everything. I would be reborn. I guarantee, within a week I'd have a lass of my own to hug all the night through.

DR. MACNAIR (*Weakening*) Och, Angus, it's ethically unthinkable.

MACFEE (*Pressing his advantage*) But my mangled corpse under a tube train—that's ethically delightful, is it?

DR. MACNAIR I'd be disgraced. I'd be struck off the Freudian register.

MACFEE Be unconventional for once, Jock.

DR. MACNAIR (*Wretchedly*) Aye, handing one's patients over to be ravished by sex-starved poets might be described as that.

MACFEE (*Very persuasively*) I'll bring you a full report. It might be the salvation of two human beings, me and Miss Todd. Now, Jock, all the great discoveries of science were made by those who defied convention.

DR. MACNAIR And the discoverers were usually burned at the stake.

MACFEE That was in the Middle Ages. The very worst that could happen to you would be that you were struck off the register and slowly declined into a pathetic wreck of a meths drinker.

DR. MACNAIR Well that's not so seductive either!

MACFEE But it won't happen! No-one will ever know. It'll be our little secret. (*Briskly*) Now Jock, it's really quite a small thing, magnified in your mind by deep-rooted bourgeois prejudices.

DR. MACNAIR (*Irritably*) I haven't got any deep-rooted bourgeois prejudices. I'm a man of science.

MACFEE I was hoping you'd remember that. Now look, Jock, slip quietly away through these French windows. Hasten back to your consulting room and have a chew of your fingernails. In less than two hours I'll be with you and we'll be roaring with delight about the whole thing.

DR. MACNAIR (*Looking sick*) We'll be roaring with delight, eh?

MACFEE We will. And whether or not you'll have the essential clue for curing poor, stricken Miss Todd, you'll have the inestimable satisfaction of meeting a new and useful citizen: Angus Macfee, poet and man!

DR. MACNAIR (*Miserably*) If the lass should protest—

MACFEE (*Impatiently*) Naturally if there's the smallest hitch, I'll scrub the whole project. I'd never do anything irregular, Jock.

DR. MACNAIR No but—eh?

MACFEE Now, look lively, Jock. The lass'll be dithering about, eager for therapy.

DR. MACNAIR (*Reluctantly allowing himself to be propelled to the door*) Well—well—och, I never thought I'd be a consenting party to the most sensational breach of professional ethics since the Emperor Nero—

MACFEE Off you go, Jock. That's the way—

> (MACFEE *pushes* DR. MACNAIR *out.* MACFEE *stands back and rubs his hands. He glances cautiously about and does a small, gleeful jig. Then he goes back to setting up his electrical apparatus. Enter* MR. TODD)

MR. TODD Dr. Macnair—eh? Where's Dr. Macnair?

MACFEE He had to skip off and tell jokes to a depressive.

MR. TODD But what about my tic?

> (*He tics*)

MACFEE (*Shuddering*) I'd forgotten that grim item. (*Sighing*) Well, we can try one or two simple techniques—

> (*Enter* MRS. TODD)

MRS. TODD Mary's ready now.

MACFEE Excellent. Now I can't handle two cases at once so I'd like you to assist me, Mrs. Todd.

MRS. TODD Very well, doctor.

MACFEE (*To* MR. TODD) Just—(MR. TODD *tics*)—ugh!—slink next door, my dear fellow. I wish to give your wife some instructions.

MR. TODD But I need qualified attention!

MACFEE What you need is a hand-bell. People should be warned of your approach. Let me remind you that my job here is to make—er—treat your daughter. Nevertheless I propose, from a deep sense of social responsibility, to concern myself briefly with your writhing physiognomy. I will instruct your wife in what measures to take. (MR. TODD *tics*) Now off with you at a furtive lope before we both turn into stone.

MR. TODD   Well I—

(*He tics*)

MACFEE   Avaunt!

(MR. TODD *departs*)

MRS. TODD (*Nodding thoughtfully*)   I think I see the idea, doctor. You're trying to shock him out of the tic, aren't you?

MACFEE   Aye. Though so far he's getting the better of it. Now what is the origin, cause or etiology of his dreadful affliction? Are you frigid?

MRS. TODD (*Uncertainly*)   No—o—a little chilly perhaps but at this season—

MACFEE (*Disgustedly*)   Och no, are you not conversant with elementary psychological concepts? I mean do you and your old man really swing in the sack?

MRS. TODD (*Puzzled*)   I'm afraid I don't—

MACFEE   Well, never mind for now. We'll have to leave deep analysis for another day. Now here's what I want you to do: sneak up behind him and say "boo!" If that doesn't work, get him to hold his breath and count up to twenty.

MRS. TODD   But those are hiccup cures.

MACFEE   Certainly they are. Time-tested remedies. All sound medicine is based on the conservation of proven traditional methods.

MRS. TODD   But Reginald doesn't have hiccups.

MACFEE   Just what do you imagine a tic is? It's only a displaced hiccup. We can't get at the psychological roots in the time available so we have to rely on empiric methods. If the techniques I've outlined don't work: get him to drink a glass of water while standing on his head. As a very last resort, bind up his face with sticking plaster. This will at least mask the horrid thing. Now be patient and thorough. Give each method a fair trial and I'll pop out later and see how you're getting on.

MRS. TODD (*Dubiously*)   Well, if you think—

MACFEE   Don't argue, Mrs. Todd. Delay will prejudice the chances of a successful cure. Send your daughter in and then go and minister to your afflicted husband.

MRS. TODD   Very well, doctor.

(*She goes off.* MACFEE *resumes work on the electric machine. A moment later a most fetching girl enters. She is, of course, the over-obedient* MARY TODD)

MARY   Good morning.

MACFEE (*Briskly, without glancing round*)   Good morning. (*He makes a last adjustment to the electric machine, connecting it to the mains, and turns. He does a double-take at sight of the glorious* MARY, *gulps several times, recovers some semblance of composure, adopts what he takes to be a severely professional manner*) So—so, you're the patient?

MARY   Yes, doctor.

MACFEE   You're beautiful.

MARY   What?

MACFEE (*Hastily*)   You're a beautiful case. Dr. Macnair says you're one of the most remarkable examples of an obedience compulsion he's ever encountered. (*Reverently*) I see you have dark blue eyes.

MARY   Is that relevant, doctor?

MACFEE (*Severely*)   Every physical particularity of the patient is significant. Who knows—(*Reverently*) the way your hair falls in shining waves—(*Severely*)—may prove a vital clue. (*Reverently*) Your slender form—(*Severely*)—may conceal diagnostic data. (*Reverently*) Your lovely white hand—(*He takes this in his own*)—may hold the secret of your dismal disorder. (*Recollecting himself, he abruptly releases her hand*) Now then, I should like to introduce myself. I am Dr. Angus Macfee, Dr. Macnair's partner.

MARY   How do you do, Dr. Macfee?

MACFEE   I do better than for many a long day, Miss Todd. Now would you be so good as to sit down here at this table.
> (*He seats her in front of the electric machine. He is behind her. He gulps visibly*)

MARY   Are we going to do the electric shocks again?

MACFEE   Aye. We'll start off with them anyway, and then perhaps we'll go on to something a little more ambitious.

MARY   But they don't do any good.

MACFEE (*Sternly*)   Miss Todd, who is the nutcracker here, you or me?

MARY (*Unhappily*)   But I've been doing the electric shocks for weeks with Dr. Macnair and I'm sure I'm no better.

MACFEE   Well, he uses a battery model. I've got this one wired up to the mains. Now, young lady, you are suffering from a compulsion to obey commands, is that not true?

MARY (*Sighing*)   Yes, Dr. Macfee.

MACFEE (*Trying to keep the gloating out of his voice*)   You find it impossible not to obey any order, no matter how repugnant to you?

MARY (*Sadly*) I'd jump out of the window if I was ordered to. Oh doctor, it's awful. It's worse than being in prison. I can't go out alone. I can't meet strangers. It's not even safe for me to listen to the wireless in case a voice says: "Get out, and never come back!"

MACFEE (*Nodding judiciously*) I wish to get a complete picture of the condition. Is it true that you remember absolutely nothing afterwards?

MARY It's quite true, doctor. It's as if it had never happened at all.

MACFEE You're completely at the mercy of the person giving you orders?

MARY Completely, doctor.
    (MACFEE *sways slightly at this intoxicating prospect, then masters himself*)

MACFEE Very well. We'll just test those statements with the buzz machine here. I take it you know the rules of this game, Miss Todd?

MARY Only too well.

MACFEE I order you to press the button. You do so. You then get a sharp jolt of voltage and the theory has it that you're discouraged from obeying orders henceforth.

MARY (*Miserably*) But since I can't remember the shock, I don't see how it can possibly work.

MACFEE Are you presuming to question our professional competence, young woman? Do you realize that whole lifetimes of dedicated research have gone into perfecting these sophisticated techniques?

MARY But—

MACFEE Be still and prepare yourself. Now, are you ready?
    (MACFEE *moves round in front of her*)

MARY (*Sighing*) Yes, doctor.

MACFEE Right. Press the button! (MARY *presses the button. She gets a tremendous shock and is transfixed, shuddering.* MACFEE *gazes at her in alarm*) That's enough! Release the button! (*But the girl is paralyzed*) Stop! (MACFEE *grabs her hand to tear it off the button. He instantly succumbs to the current and is also paralyzed. They are both locked, quivering. After an appreciable time,* MACFEE *collapses onto her lap. Her chair rolls over backwards and they both wind up in a heap on the floor. For a while*

they are both too dazed to move. Then MACFEE *slowly sits up*)
The mains model seems a bit fierce.

    (MARY *slowly pulls herself together*)

MARY   What happened?

    (MACFEE *gets up*)

MACFEE   Miss Todd, are you all right?

MARY   I'm not sure. I feel—very strange.

MACFEE (*Alarmed*)   My God, you're not cured are you?

MARY (*Dazed*)   Cured?

MACFEE   I mean, it might be severely traumatic if you were to recover all at once. Come, stand up. (*He helps her to her feet*)
How do you feel?

MARY   The last thing I remember, you ordered me to press the
button—

MACFEE   Aye, well there'll be no more button-pressing this afternoon. I think I'll offer that little item to military intelligence.
Now, I'd better just give you a few trial orders, to make sure the
compulsion is intact. Ready? Whistle "God Save the Queen"!
(MARY *attempts to obey but, like most girls, she cannot whistle
and so no sound emerges*) Well, you may not be musical but you
seem loyal. Right, stop whistling. (*She stops*) Now, turn round
three times. (*She does so*) Looks like we've nothing to fear.

MARY   Am I obeying?

MACFEE   Perfectly.

MARY   But that's bad, isn't it?

MACFEE   It's monstrous. But one can't help admiring the perfec-
tion of the syndrome. Now, the crunch—that is the conclusive
test. Ready?

MARY   Yes.

MACFEE (*Extending his hands towards her and speaking somewhat
unnaturally*)   Hold my hands.

    (MARY *obediently takes them.* MACFEE *inclines his head and
gazes adoringly down at her. Enter* MRS. TODD)

MRS. TODD   Oh Dr. Macfee—

    (*She observes their positions with some surprise. Macfee
instantly disengages himself and adopts a lofty professional
manner*)

MACFEE   Ah, Mrs. Todd. Just performing some elementary co-
ordination tests on Miss Todd. Now, how goes it with your old
man's condition?

MRS. TODD   Doctor, it's worse!

MACFEE   Describe to me exactly what has occurred?

MRS. TODD   Well, I sneaked up behind him and said "boo," as you suggested, but it didn't have any effect. Then I got him to hold his breath and count up to twenty. He's a little asthmatic, so we had to do it thirty-four times before he managed to reach twenty. By that time his tic had deteriorated.

MACFEE   In what way?

MRS. TODD   Well, you know it was like this?
(*She demonstrates*)

MACFEE   If you're to be of any value as an assistant, you must be more precise. In fact, it was like this.
(*He demonstrates*)

MRS. TODD (*Shuddering*)   You're quite right. Anyway, now it's like this. (*Demonstrates*) You see, it's affecting the other side of his face as well.

MACFEE (*Enthusiastically*)   You've modified it!

MRS. TODD   Yes, but—

MACFEE   Splendid! The treatment is taking effect.

MRS. TODD (*Dubiously*)   Well, perhaps it is but I'm afraid if it takes much more effect his head will fall off.

MACFEE   The tic is now in an unstable state and ready for final cure. Apply the water-drinking therapy.

MRS. TODD   Well—all right. But Reginald is getting very distressed.

MACFEE   Distressed! He'll be lucky if we can keep him from being lynched! Back to the attack, Mrs. Todd. (MRS. TODD *sighs and goes off.* MACFEE *turns back to* MARY) It's asking a lot of a man, treating two loonies at once. Did you know the incidence of mental disorder is growing? Now what happens, Miss Todd, when you crackpots outnumber we sane people? Oh, all the world's a bin—

MARY (*Puzzled*)   I'm sorry?

MACFEE (*Recollecting himself*)   Ah—yes. Now then I have reached a specific conclusion in your case. It is my considered and authoritative opinion that for reason or reasons at present unknown you are malingering.

MARY (*Indignantly*)   What do you mean?

MACFEE (*Sternly*)   I mean you're no nuttier than I am. You can perfectly well resist the commands if you wish to. Confess.

MARY   It's not true! I—

MACFEE (*Sharply*)   Touch your toes! (MARY *promptly does so*) Ah, nearly caught you there, didn't I? You've had a lot of practice. Your reaction time is swift. But you won't deceive Angus

Macfee, the Freud of Dundee, for long. Why don't you come clean, Miss Todd? Admit you're a fraud. Come along, come along, get it off your conscience. Is it not a fact that—clap your hands! (*She does so*) Just made it, eh? I saw that split-second hesitation, that quick calculating look in your eyes. Why this deception, Miss Todd? What do you hope to gain from it? Perhaps you just can't face life, is that it? Perhaps you're hatching some fraudulent confidence trick? Well, if you imagine I could either countenance or abet any such—kiss me! (*She obeys. He takes her in his arms*) Och, Mary, my darling, I'm convinced. (*Enter* MRS. TODD *who gapes in amazed horror.* MACFEE *instantly releases* MARY *and turns on her mother*) What the hell do you keep bobbing in and out for like a demented housemaid? How am I to straighten your daughter's twisted seams in the face of these incessant intrusions?

MRS. TODD (*In horrified tones*)   You were kissing her!

MACFEE   Precisely.

MRS. TODD   You were kissing my daughter!

MACFEE   I was. And, if you wish, you can stay for a repetition of the experiment. Miss Todd, kiss me!

    (MARY *moves to obey*)

MRS. TODD   Stop!

    (MARY *stops*)

MACFEE   Kiss me!

    (MARY *moves to obey*)

MRS. TODD   Stop!

    (MARY *stops*)

MACFEE   Kiss me.

    (MARY *moves to obey*)

MRS. TODD   Stop! (MARY *stops. To* MACFEE) I believe you're a fraud!

MACFEE (*Elaborately ironic*)   May I ask, Madame Todd, you perhaps studied in Vienna under Fischbein? No? Doubtless then you acquired your impressive grasp of psychology from the great Kramer, now I believe active at Harvard? Not there either? Then, may I courteously ask, mustering as much patience as can reasonably be expected of me, where the hell do you get the right to question my methods?

MRS. TODD   Your methods are those of a shady dancehall!

MACFEE   Then doubtless you can acquaint me with other and superior techniques of eliciting data as to the degree of moral control exercised by patients such as your daughter? (*Shaking his head sadly*) I begin to discern, Mrs. Todd, that you're the really unbalanced one in this household. I won't dignify your morbid condition with the language of psychoanalysis. You've simply got a mind like a cesspool.

MRS. TODD (*Somewhat on the defensive*) Dr. Macnair never found it necessary to kiss Mary.

MACFEE Is that a fact?

MRS. TODD Mary, did Dr. Macnair ever kiss you?

MARY I don't know.

MACFEE Amnesia is part of her condition, as you should know if you took the least interest in your poor girl, Mrs. Suspicious Todd. If I know Macnair, a most thorough diagnostician, he's kissed your daughter innumerable times. How else is one to acquire data as to innate and ulterior fixation of inhibition? Miss Todd, kiss me!

(MARY *does so*)

MRS. TODD Stop!

(MARY *does so*)

MACFEE Kiss me!

(MARY *does so*)

MRS. TODD Stop!

(MARY *does so*)

MACFEE Kiss me!

(MARY *does so*)

MRS. TODD Stop!

(MARY *does so*)

MACFEE I warn you. If you interfere once more I shall leave you and your daughter to the quacks.

MRS. TODD But—it's immoral!

MACFEE Och, now I understand! You don't want her cured. You want her uplifted. Then I suggest you contact the nearest Sunday School.

MRS. TODD But surely there's some other way of—of—

MACFEE Is there? I'd be very grateful to know it. If you think clinical osculation, as the technique is known amongst us binmen, has any charms, you're greatly mistaken. Catch cold every other day!

MRS. TODD (*Indignantly*) Well, all right—but you can hardly wonder at my being suspicious.

MACFEE (*Wearily*) Madame, we who mend the mad wonder at nothing. All I wish to convey is that if I'm to be interrupted every two minutes by your manic intrusions then Miss Todd has no more chance of renewed health than a fish finger.

MRS. TODD (*Contrite*) I'm sorry. Please continue, doctor. I'll go back to—(*She suddenly recalls why she came in the first place*) —oh yes, Reginald can't stand on his head.

MACFEE Well, divorce him and marry an acrobat. (*Muttering*) What kind of kinky complaint is this?

MRS. TODD You prescribed a glass of water while standing on his head.

MACFEE Did I? Ah yes, deep tic therapy. And he can't stand on his head? Well, here's a trick that's nearly as good. Get him to lie flat on his back and trickle the water into his mouth from a jug. You'll need to use at least three jugsful to test the efficacy of the cure. If that doesn't work, you'll have to glue his clock together with sticking plaster, as previously agreed.

MRS. TODD I still think he's getting worse.

MACFEE Tics are always darkest before the dawn. Back into battle, Mrs. Todd! (*She starts to depart*) And don't come in here again until I summon you. (MRS. TODD *goes off.* MACFEE *gives a sigh of relief. He turns and contemplates the delicious* MARY. *He gulps at the prospect before him. He clears his throat*) Now then, Miss Todd, I am glad to say that I am at last convinced as to the reality of your lamentable condition. I am here to help you. Lock the door! (MARY *does so*) The question is, how are we best to approach your disorder? Switch on that lamp! (MARY *does so*) We have already discredited aversion therapy so we must seek something a little more—potent. Draw the curtains! (MARY *does so*) I propose to try a new approach! Go over to the settee! (MARY *does so.* MACFEE *closes his eyes for an instant in rapture and then steals over to her*) Miss Todd, Mary—the moment is here, the moment of healing! Now do what I tell you. M—m—m—m—(*He is too wrought up to get the words out. He clears his throat.* MARY *stirs uneasily*) Bards and muses, don't desert me now! Miss Todd, my command is, m—m—make—

(*There is a sharp knock at the door, and* MRS. TODD's *voice*)

MRS. TODD Dr. Macfee, I must speak to you.

MACFEE (*With a grimace of fury*) Gibbering psychotics, she's back again!

MRS. TODD (*Trying the door*) Why is the door locked? (*Loud banging*) Open the door at once!

MACFEE (*In a rage*) Get back to your kennel, you old bitch!

MRS. TODD If you don't open the door instantly, I shall send for the police!

MACFEE (*Muttering*)   Inspector, I resign from the case.
> (*He goes, with a surly air, to the door and opens it.* MRS.
> TODD *bursts in*)

MRS. TODD   Mary, are you all right?

MARY   Yes of course, Mother.

MRS. TODD (*To* MACFEE)   Why did you lock the door?

MACFEE   To keep *you* at bay for five minutes. I'd sooner shrink a neurotic ape than try to cure anyone in *this* monkey-house. What do you want now?

MRS. TODD   Reginald! It's spread!

MACFEE   What's spread?

MRS. TODD   The tic. It's now affecting the upper part of his body and particularly his limbs.

MACFEE (*To* MRS. TODD)   Well, we'll have to try occupational therapy.

MRS. TODD   What's that?

MACFEE   Just what it sounds like—treatment by occupation. We'll get him to make his stupid speech. Here's how we'll do it. I'll turn off the lights. We three will be the expectant audience. Mrs. Todd, you wheel him in and seat him at that desk. I will then switch on the footlights and he launches into his spiel. We'll see if that has any effect on his grim ailment. All right, prod the wreck in, Mrs. Todd. (MRS. TODD *goes to fetch* MR. TODD) Miss Todd, come and sit here beside me. (MARY *does so.* MACFEE *dims the lights.* MRS. TODD *returns, ushering a spastic shape emitting glottal sounds and installs it behind the desk. She then joins the other two*) Ready? Let her rip, Mr. Todd! (*He turns up the light. Poor* MR. TODD *is seen to be in a melancholy state. He is drenched with water from the water cure. Ribbons of sticking plaster, torn loose by the convulsive efforts of his countenance, dangle from his cheeks. His face is red and working. His limbs shoot out in the gestures of a mad politician. The following speech thus becomes a ghastly parody of a business address*)

MR. TODD   Colleagues, (*Tic*) the three hundred and twenty-one products our great company manufactures constitute a unique consumer service. Think! (*Tic*) Rack your brains! (*Horrible tic*) Have we a serious competitor? Where else can the wise housewife (*Tic*) purchase both potted shrimps (*Evil gesture*) and Madras curry powder (*Several tics*) in the same familiar package? A patriotic package! (*Horrible tic*) Red, white and blue, surmounted by the shrewd yet benign face (*Ghastly tic*) of our founder, Sir Guthrie Bennington Carew! (*Obscene gesture*)

Three hundred and twenty-one products! (*Slight tic*) Ranging from dried mushrooms to wet cider, ha ha (*The rhetorical laugh founders in a particularly hideous tic and shudder*) We in this room (*Tic*) are proud to serve the consumer! (*Horrible tic*) A village grocer in the Outer Hebrides (*Various twitches*) or the manager of a huge London supermarket (*Gestures vaguely reminiscent of itching palms accompanied by a leer*) receive the same prompt and courteous service! (*Veritable barrage of tics and gestures*) Colleagues! (*Faint sniff*) Profits are up by nearly twenty-seven per cent over last year! (*Series of horrible smiles and gestures*) Maintain this progress! Go out and—(*The series of exhortations becomes a race with the onset of something approaching convulsions*) Sell! Sell! Sell! Sell! SELL!

   (*With a final mighty shudder* MR. TODD *collapses forward onto the desk, and, unfortunately, onto the electric machine. He instantly starts vibrating*)

MRS. TODD (*Horrified*)   Reginald!

   (*She grabs him and is, of course, trapped*)

MARY   Mother!

   (*She reaches for her mother*)

MACFEE   Stop!

   (*He grabs* MISS TODD *to stop her but she has already touched her mother. All four are locked, vibrating, with the shrill buzz of the machine supplying the only sound. After an appreciable time they topple gravely over onto the floor in a heap. The two men recover first. They pick themselves up*)

MR. TODD (*Dazed*)   Eh? What? Where?

MACFEE (*Springing into action*)   Quick, we must join the ladies. This calls for the kiss of life. I'll handle your daughter. You resuscitate your old Dutch. Quickly, man!

   (MACFEE *seizes* MARY TODD *and kisses her ardently.* MR. TODD *attempts to do likewise to* MRS. TODD *but the latter sits up and glances around. She sees* MACFEE *and* MARY)

MRS. TODD (*Horrified*)   Eee! He's kissing her again!

MR. TODD   It's all right, my dear. It's a medical technique.

MRS. TODD   But it's the only one he ever uses! (MARY *stirs and revives*) Reginald, are you going to tolerate this? I don't believe this monster is a doctor at all. When he's not passionately embracing Mary, he's trying to electrocute us all. Order him out of the house!

MR. TODD (*Bravely*)   Dr. Macfee, have you any answer to these charges?

MACFEE I have.

MR. TODD What is it?

MACFEE That the healer's art is mysterious to the layman.

MRS. TODD Reginald, throw him out!

(MR. TODD *looks rather uncomfortable but moves to do so*)

MACFEE (*Theatrically*) Aye stone me, mob me, sue me—t'was ever the fate of mankind's benefactors. The unknown genius who discovered that the skin of a toad is an infallible specific for dandruff was doubtless hounded from his native parish. But we, the healers, our shoulders are broad. Our backs are strong. We will never cease from our unremitting efforts to liberate mankind from its sickening burden of sickness. That will be one hundred guineas, please.

MR. TODD (*Surprised*) What will be one hundred guineas, *Doctor* Macfee?

MACFEE The cure.

MR. TODD (*Sarcastically*) What cure are you referring to, *Doctor* Macfee?

MACFEE The rigidification of your dial, Mr. Todd. (*Seizing a mirror and holding it up for the others to see*) Look! Your countenance no longer resembles an earthquake! You're cured!

MR. TODD (*Wonderingly*) What? (*He raises his hands to his face and tremblingly palpates it*) It's true! The tic's gone! My face is quiescent! Elsie! Look, I'm cured! (*To* MACFEE) You're a genius! I'll reward you! You'll get your fee! And more too. What would you say to a free monthly case of corn crisplets for the rest of your life? We can discuss it later. We have a delicious new line: prawn brawn. Give it some thought. But now—Elsie! Quick! I'll be in time to make my speech! You'll have to help me. Come along. I shall need a close shirt, that is a clean shave! Come along!

(*He grabs his wife and tugs her out of the room.* MACFEE *gives a sigh of relief. He takes a long, approving look at* MARY. *He whistles a highland air. He strolls to the door and locks it again*)

MACFEE Alone at last! Och, you're a bonny lass, Mary Todd. Have you any idea where we are, my wee pet?

MARY (*Surprised*) In our living room.

MACFEE (*Chuckling tolerantly*) Wrong! Wrong! You must not be deceived by dreary appearances. Can't you see how the glen is brawling? Can't you feel the warm sun shining down on the meadow? Can't you smell the grass and the heather?

MARY Is all this part of the treatment?

MACFEE You might say it was the very heart of it. (*He sighs*) Aye, we have reached the final stage. (*He goes to the sofa*) Come here, lass! (MARY *does so*) Strange, this time I am full of confidence and calm. All hesitation has left me. Mary?

MARY (*Trustingly*) Yes, doctor.

MACFEE (*Holding out his arms to her with a blissful smile*) Make love to me! (*She instantly slaps him hard on the cheek. Amazement and dismay cause him to shrink back as from a snake. He gazes at her long with the shocked incredulity of a man who finds a large cockroach in an expensive soufflé. For some time he says nothing. Then, cowering, he edges cautiously around her as if afraid she might explode at any moment. Finally he manages to speak*) Why did you do that?

MARY (*Innocently*) What?

MACFEE Why did you—you know what you did! You know damn well, admit it!

MARY (*Unhappily*) What, doctor? What do you mean?

MACFEE That command, that command I gave you. Why didn't you obey it?

MARY What command was it? I don't understand.

MACFEE You know what you did just now.

MARY I don't! I don't! What did I do?

MACFEE (*Muttering*) Who's conning who around here? (*Briskly*) Young woman, I have to—touch your toes! (MARY *promptly does so*) And furthermore I should like—clap your hands! (*She does so*) Hmm, was it just a fluke? Mary, are you listening?

MARY Of course, doctor.

MACFEE Then—(*Cautiously*) Make love to me! (*In spite of his alertness, her quick slap connects. He skips back with a strangled oath. He stares at her long and bitterly*) It's the Gods! They've singled me out from all men to endure these hideous disappointments. No, I will not yield! I will not bow to my fate! Mary! Touch your toes! (*She does so*) Clap your hands! (*She does so*) Make love to me! (*She slaps him and he stoically bears the blow*) Touch your toes! (*She does so*) Clap your hands! (*She does so*) Make love to me! (*She slaps him*) Touch your toes! (*She starts to, then stops and gazes at him, blinking in a puzzled way*) I said, touch your toes!

MARY (*Vaguely, rubbing her forehead*) What?

MACFEE Touch your toes at once!

MARY (*After a faint shake of her head*) Why?

MACFEE Because I ordered you to. Now touch your toes!

MARY No.

MACFEE (*In anguish*) Freud and Jung! She's cured! (*Sharply*) Clap your hands!

MARY No!

MACFEE Whistle "God Save the Queen"!

MARY I can't whistle. Anyway, I don't want to!

MACFEE (*Anguished soliloquy*) The end—its the end! Eden has gone out of business! No more visas to the promised land! Oh Macfee, your destiny is clear. You've cured the lass. You've helped her. It's your fate to do good deeds against your will. Aye, you will take to the roads—a dusty wanderer, brooding on the felicity of your fellow men. Macfee, the orchard is not for you, the luscious fruit, the soft grass, but only the rutted trail that crosses the harsh plain. Resign yourself, lad, to your austere fate. The oracle of events has spoken and—

MARY (*Who has been sitting with a frown of wonder on her face now stands up abruptly*) I'm cured, aren't I?

MACFEE Aye.

MARY I don't have to obey orders any more. My mind is my own again! I can live like other people, make my own decisions, decide for myself what I should or shouldn't do!

MACFEE Aye.

MARY (*Ecstatically*) Oh it's wonderful, marvelous, heavenly, delightful!

MACFEE (*Smiling ruefully*) Aye, rejoice lassy! Savour your new-found health. For you, the world begins. For Macfee the curtain is coming down, the lights are going out and the sweepers are trailing up the aisles. The performance—

MARY (*Impulsively throwing her arms round him*) Oh, I'm so grateful! Oh, you marvelous man! Oh, I'll do anything for you!

MACFEE (*With a sad smile*) Aye, you're a good-hearted lassy, but—(*He starts and gazes at her intently*) Anything?

MARY Oh, anything! Anything you want! Just tell me!
(MACFEE *gazes at her with a strange light on his face. He looks not unlike a mystic who has lost and then recaptured the beatific vision*)

MACFEE Anything—well now—I see—indeed—aye, well there might be a little—that is—Mary, my pretty hummingbird, are you fond of poetry?

MARY   I haven't read much. Why?

MACFEE   It just occurs to me—perhaps you'd care to hear one of my poems?

MARY   Oh, do you write poetry?

MACFEE   Aye. In fact I'm really more of a poet than anything else. The shrinking is something of a sideline. But come—come over here to the sofa. (*He leads her to the sofa and sits her down*) So you've not read a great deal of poetry, Mary?

MARY   No, I haven't.

MACFEE   I think you may like this one. It's a romantic little thing I composed just recently, a love poem really, intended for a dolly, a fair maid, as it might have been, your very self.

MARY   I'd love to hear it.

MACFEE   And so you shall. (*He puts his arm round her and draws her towards him*) I have an idea, Mary, the cure is about complete. Are you listening?

MARY   (*Nestling against him*)   I'm listening.

MACFEE   Not a masterpiece, perhaps, and yet I'm not ashamed of it. And it expresses just what I'm feeling, my lovely Mary. Ready?

MARY   (*Nodding happily*)   Ready.

MACFEE   (*In a sonorous voice, as the lights start dimming, he declaims, hugging her ever closer*)

> O my Luve's like a red, red rose
> That's newly sprung in June:
> O my Luve's like the melodie
> That's sweetly play'd in tune.
> As fair art thou, my bonnie lass,
> So deep in love am I . . .

(Darkness and curtain)

ABOUT THE EDITOR

STANLEY RICHARDS is a man of wide experience in the world of the theatre. He has written twenty-five plays, among them *Through A Glass, Darkly; Tunnel of Love; August Heat;* and *O Distant Land.* He is the editor of the recently published *Best Short Plays of the World Theatre: 1958-1967, The Best Short Plays 1968* and *The Best Short Plays 1969.* Twelve of his own plays have appeared in the prize annuals *The Best One-Act Plays* and *The Best Short Plays.* His television play *Mr. Bell's Creation* holds a record: it has had more live network productions (both here and abroad) than any other play.

Mr. Richards' latest play, *Journey to Bahia,* adapted from a prize-winning Brazilian play and film, premiered at the Berkshire Playhouse and was produced in Washington under the auspices of the Brazilian American Cultural Institute. (It has been recently published in book form.)

His plays have been translated for production and publication abroad into Portuguese, Afrikaans, Dutch, Tagalog, French, German, Spanish and Italian.

In addition, he has been the New York theatre critic for *Players Magazine,* and a frequent contributor to *Theatre Arts, Playbill, Writer's Digest, Writer's Yearbook, The Theatre, Actors' Equity Magazine,* and *The Dramatists Guild Quarterly.* He is now the editor of the annual *The Best Short Plays.*

As an American Theatre Specialist, Mr. Richards has been awarded three successive grants by the United States Department of State's International Cultural Exchange Program to teach playwriting and directing in Chile and Brazil. He taught playwriting in Canada for over ten years and in 1966 was appointed Visiting Professor of Drama at the University of Guelph, Ontario. He has produced and directed plays and has lectured extensively on theatre at universities in the United States, Canada and South America. Mr. Richards, a New York City resident, is now at work on a collection of *Best Plays of the Sixties.*